Jean Benedetti was born in 1930 and educated in England and France. He trained as an actor and teacher at the Rose Bruford College of Speech and Drama. After graduating in 1959 he worked as an actor and director before turning to writing and translating. In 1970 he returned to Rose Bruford as Principal of the College, leaving in 1987 to resume full-time writing.

He is author of a number of semi-documentary television plays. His published translations include Brecht's Edward II and A Respectable Wedding, Georges Michel's A Sunday Walk and two plays by Arrabal, The Grand Ceremonial and The Architect and The Emperor of Assyria, the latter translated at Kenneth Tynan's request in 1965 but not produced until 1971 owing to censorship difficulties.

His first book was a biography of Gilles de Rais. In 1982 he published Stanislavski: An Introduction, which has been repeatedly reprinted. He is working on a book on the history of the Moscow Art Theatre.

Since 1979 he has been connected with the International Theatre Institute (UNESCO), being first President of the Study Committee and later of the Theatre Education Committee which he helped create. He is a frequent visitor to the Soviet Union where he has seen and discussed the latest developments of the Stanislavski System.

STANISLAVSKI

By the same author

Stanislavski: An Introduction

STANISLAVSKI

BY

JEAN BENEDETTI

ROUTLEDGE

First published in Great Britain in 1988
by Methuen Drama,
Michelin House, 81 Fulham Road, London SW3 6RB
and in the United States of America by
Routledge, 29 West 35th Street,
New York NY 10001, USA

Printed and bound in Great Britain by
Richard Clay Ltd, Bungay, Suffolk

CONTENTS

ILLUSTRATIONS . . . .

Front cover
Stanislavski, 1888

Between pp. 116–117
Stanislavski's mother, Elisaveta Alekseieva and father, Sergei Alekseiev.
The Alekseiev house at Red Gates where Stanislavski lived from the age of a few months (1863) to 1903.
The Alekseiev children in 1875.
The theatre at the country estate in Liubimovka built when Stanislavski was 14 in 1877.
The Mikado 1887. Yum-Yum – Alekseieva. Nanki Pu – Stanislavski.
Stanislavski as the Knight in Pushkin's *The Miserly Knight*, 1888.
Stanislavski as Ferdinand in the play *Kabale und Lieber* (Schiller). His wife, Lilina, as Louise.
The Fruits of Enlightenment (Tolstoi). Stanislavski, 1891.
Foma (Dostoievski/Stanislavski) Lilina, Stanislavski.
Much Ado About Nothing Stanislavski as Benedick, 1897.
The Last Sacrifice (Ostrovski) Stanislavski, 1893.
Uriel Acosta, 1895.
Chekhov with the Art Theatre Company.
Uncle Vania Stanislavski as Astrov, 1899.
Uncle Vania (Chekhov) Act III. Stanislavski as Astrov, Olga Knipper-Chekhova as Elena.
Stanislavski as Vershinin in Chekhov's *The Three Sisters*.

Between pp. 224–225
The Cherry Orchard (Chekhov) Stanislavski as Gaev, 1904.
Ivanov (Chekhov) Stanislavski as Shabielski, 1904.
Stanislavski as Satin in *The Lower Depths* (Gorki), 1902.
Stanislavski, Gorki, Lilina. Yalta, 1900.
Woe from Wit Stanislavski as Famusov, 1906.
Woe from Wit Stanislavski as Famusov, 1914.
The house at Carriage Row where Stanislavski lived from 1903 to 1921.
Le Malade Imaginaire Stanislavski as Argan, 1913.
Stanislavski as Cavaliere Rippafratta in *La Locandiera* (Goldoni).
Enough Stupidity in Every Wise Man (Ostrovski). Stanislavski as Krutitski, 1910.
Stanislavski and Sokolova at work, 1924.
Lunacharski, Stanislavski and George Bernard Shaw.
Stanislavski.

AUTHOR'S NOTE

The agreed international system for the transliteration of Russian words, used by scholars, is not familiar to most readers. Names have therefore been transliterated as directly as possible. The arbitrary usage of /y/ and /i/ which does not correspond in any consistent way with the two /i/ sounds in Russian, has been avoided.

It has not, however, been possible to be entirely consistent. Certain names, particularly of musicians, are so familiar that they have been left in the form readers will know best. Thus, while Chekhov is current, so is Tchaikovski, although both names in Russian begin with the same letter.

All dates up to February 1, 1918 are given according to the Old Style Julian Calendar. Dates thereafter are given in the New Style Gregorian Calendar. By a decree of the Bolshevik government of January 22, 1918, February 1 became February 14. The dates given, therefore, correspond to those which appear on the documents quoted.

INTRODUCTION

1988 marks the 125th anniversary of Stanislavski's birth and the 50th anniversary of his death. The moment seems opportune for a reappraisal of his life.

The Stanislavski System is known and used in one form or other throughout the world. It remains the only fully worked-out method of acting available. Though aspects of it are much disputed, no one has come forward with an equally well-organized alternative. As Lee Strasberg commented in his autobiography:

'The teachings of Constantin Stanislavski and his disciples changed not only my life, but that of the entire twentieth-century theatre. Just as our understanding of human behavior and modern physics is still turning on the revelations of Freud and Einstein, so our contemporary knowledge of the actor's craft is still heavily indebted to Stanislavski's 100-year-old discoveries.'

The System is taught in the form codified by Stanislavski's pupils in the Soviet Union, Eastern Europe, China and parts of the Third World. Its modified form, the Method, has been instrumental in shaping some of the finest American actors. In England its history has been slightly more chequered, for although Stanislavski's methods and practice were familiar to the likes of Harley Granville Barker, the theatrical profession at large did not have an opportunity to see the Art Theatre until 1958, long after Germany, Austria, Czechoslovakia and France. Much information was gleaned second-hand from émigrés like Fidor Komissarzhevski, whose version of the System by no means met with Stanislavski's approval, or Michael Chekhov, who developed his own, related but independent method. Perhaps the only major English actor of the twentieth century to have applied the System consistently was Michael Redgrave.

The production methods which Stanislavski and the Art Theatre pioneered have been absorbed into theatre practice world-wide and are now accepted as the norm. Yet Stanislavski himself remains for the most part a shadowy figure. For that he is, to some extent, responsible. One of the greatest obstacles to a proper understanding of the complexity of his character is his own book, *My Life in Art*. Written in haste at a time when his ideas and practice were under attack in Russia it is less autobiography than an *apologia*. It is a justification of the System and a demonstration of his path through failure to it. Many of his early achievements are played down. The reader can get no idea of his immense fame and reputation even before the creation of the Moscow Art Theatre. A further problem is that it does not deal with his last highly-productive years. The first American edition stops in 1922 and the Russian edition does not go beyond 1924 – that leaves the years up to 1938 to evaluate. English-speaking readers are at a double disadvantage because of the poor quality of the translation by J. J. Robbins, who had to cope against the clock with Stanislavski's prevarications and delays. The result seems at times to be written in an English of Robbins' invention. Its worse fault is to betray the tone of Stanislavski's voice. Purple passages apart – and Stanislavski was prone to them even when speaking in public – the Russian text is much more easy going, more directly conversational than the unidiomatic English text would suggest. Generations have grown up thinking of Stanislavski as alternately naïve and po-faced.

The 1926 and 1928 Moscow editions differ substantially from the American edition. Much material was added, in particular the critical penultimate chapter in which Stanislavski described his response to developments in Russian theatre during his two-year foreign tour. The revised Russian version, not currently available in English, still contains errors of memory, telescoping of events, misdating of performances. For that reason I have tried to avoid too heavy a reliance on *My Life in Art* and to approach Stanislavski's life through other documentary sources. In the last 40 years a considerable amount of published material has become available, notably the 8-volume Complete Works, soon to be replaced by a 12-volume edition, 4 volumes of Production Plans, 2 volumes of extracts from the *Notebooks*, exhaustive studies by scholars of Stanislavski's career as actor and director, and innumerable Memoirs by individual actors or critics.

Studying these works, it becomes still more apparent how incomplete a picture *My Life in Art* gives. Stanislavski appears to be living in a void without contact with the artistic, social and intellectual movements of his time. One of the tasks of this book is to describe the development of a creative mind in its artistic and historical context and specifically in its Russian context. There are aspects of Russian thinking or art, politics and society which are essential for a full understanding of Stanislavski and the aesthetic position he adopted. In *My Life in Art*, Stanislavski was able to assume a common culture and a common frame of reference with his Russian readers. Much was therefore left implicit. As a non-Russian, writing for non-Russian readers, I have tried to make what was implicit, explicit.

Given that much of the material I have used is not easily available and has not been previously translated I have tried, within the limitations of space, to quote the texts rather than summarize them, in the hope that the original voice will be heard. All source references and dates are included in the body of the text so that the reader may immediately see the origin of the information.

Some published works deserve particular mention. Any contemporary biographer of Stanislavski must be indebted to Vinogradskaia's monumental 4-volume documentary biography, *Zhizn i Tvorchestvo K. S. Stanislavskovo*, which took some 15 years to compile. It provides invaluable archive material and press reviews. It also directs attention to many original sources. Other important studies to which I am indebted are M. M. Stroeva's detailed 2-volume study of Stanislavski's productions at the Art Theatre and Elena Poliakova's study of his career as an actor, *Stanislavski Aktior*. Poliakova is also the author of a well-researched and eminently readable recent biography, published in Moscow in 1977, and available in an English translation. For the discussion of individual productions I must acknowledge my debt first, to Laurence Senelick for his indispensable account of the Craig-Stanislavski *Hamlet*, and, second, to A. Smelianski for his authoritative account of the much disputed production of Bulgakov's *Molière*.

I would like to thank Professor Brian Jarman of St Mary's Hospital, Paddington, for his advice on medical terminology and on the possible interpretation of such medical evidence as is available. Finally I would like to express my deep and continuing gratitude to Aleksei Bartoshevich, Professor at the State Institute for Theatre Arts (GITIS) and the State Institute for Research and a member of the executive committee of the Theatre Workers' Union of the USSR, for his help in directing my attention to certain essential reading, and his patient elucidation of questions of cultural context. Any errors of judgement are, of course, entirely my own.

PART ONE

AN OPEN THEATRE

CHAPTER ONE

ALEKSEIEV

Stanislavski was born on January 5, 1863 into what Lady Bracknell described as the purple of commerce. Baptised Konstantin Sergeievich Alekseiev, he was the son of a wealthy textile manufacturer Vladimir Vladimirovich Alekseiev and Elizaveta Vasilievna Alekseieva. The imposing family mansion at 29, Great Alekseievskaia Street, with its giant portico and classical façade, was visible proof of the advance the Alekseievs had made since the beginning of the eighteenth century when they had been no more than starving, if ambitious, peasants.

Most of what we know of the Alekseiev family and of Stanislavski's early life comes from accounts left by his brother, Vladimir, two of his sisters, Zinaïda and Anna, and Anna's son, Georgi, who wrote a history of the family business.

Where their fortune originally came from no one knew for certain. Family legend had it that Stanislavski's great-great-grandfather, known as Petrov the Younger, had made money as a street vendor, selling peas; it was suggested that he might have been a money-lender but no proof of this story exists. All that is clear is that Petrov made an extremely rapid rise up the social ladder. Born a serf in Yaroslavl, in 1724 he made enough money to buy his freedom and go some 150 miles south west to Moscow. In 1746, at a mere 22 years old, he was legally registered by the magistrates as belonging to the merchant class. In 1785, Semeon, his son, went into the textile business, a growth industry in the Moscow area. He decided to specialize in gold and silver thread. It was an astute choice. The product was at the top end of the market and demand constant. It was needed for church vestments, court dress and uniforms both civil and military. He prospered and by 1812 was able, in common with other leading citizens, to make a contribution of 50,000 roubles towards the war effort against Napoleon.

His associates were by this time seriously worried that so respectable and solid a citizen did not possess a real surname. Alekseiev was no more than a patronymic – son of Aleksei. A proper and more respectable name was therefore manufactured for him. Since he dealt in silver goods – *serebriani* – he would be known as Serebrenikov. The name, however, never caught on and he and his descendants continued to be known as Alekseiev without loss of prestige.

Stanislavski's grandfather, Vladimir Semeonovich, married a woman of superior culture and refinement, Elizaveta Alexandrovna, and the family's life-style underwent a change. The virtues of application and hard work remained – as they were always to remain, no matter how much money the family made – but time could now be found for the arts of living. Grandfather Vladimir lived like a gentleman, though without ostentation, and it was he who built the house in which Stanislavski was born. It was situated, for all its grandeur, in an industrial suburb, next to the family's factory. For the Alekseievs, industry and art went together.

Stanislavski's father, Sergei Vladimirovich, came up the hard way. He was born in 1836 in the new family mansion. Like his father before him he learned every aspect of the business before finally becoming Chairman of the Board. As a boy he cleaned the office and ran errands. As in the rest of Europe, however, the rising bourgeoisie was beginning to adopt the manners and customs of the aristocracy. Thus Sergei, apart from acquiring the necessary competence in mathematics and bookkeeping, learned to speak reasonable French and German, indispensable accomplishments for anyone with social pretensions. He also had a good knowledge of Russian literature, Gogol being his particular favourite. Like most educated people he subscribed to the major literary journals of the time, the so-called 'thick' magazines which were so important in shaping progressive opinion. Not that he sympathized with the radical tendencies that lay behind much of the writing; Sergei Vladimirovich's sense of social responsibility expressed itself in terms of paternalism and philanthropy. He was a good employer and a skilled fund-raiser. Hospitals and orphanages benefited from his efforts.

The choice this mild-mannered, conventional man made for a wife sent shock-waves of disapproval through the family. They wanted him to marry someone with a good solid background in Moscow society. Instead he fell in love with an eighteen-year-old girl from Petersburg, who had no position, was half-French, illegitimate and, to complete the catalogue of social disasters, the daughter of an actress. Elizaveta Vasilievna Yakovlieva and her sister, Marie, were the result of a liaison between a wealthy Petersburg merchant, Vasili Abramovich Yakovliev, and a French actress of small talent and less brain, Marie Varley. Yakovliev was famous for erecting the memorial to Aleksandr I in front of the Winter Palace. Elizaveta's godfather was Sosnitiski, a leading player at the imperial Alexandrinski Theatre. She was christened Adèle and brought up as a catholic.

Marie Varley very soon found her children an encumbrance and, when Elizaveta was eleven, abandoned them. Yakovliev acknowledged them legally as his own, which he need not have done, and took them into his home. He then married a rich wife, Aleksandra Bostanzhoglo, but unfortunately omitted to warn her that she was to be presented with two ready-made daughters. One of the step-mother's first acts was to have them baptized into the Orthodox church. Adèle thus became Elizaveta.

Relations between the two girls and their step-mother were, understandably perhaps, never good. When her sister married and went to Moscow, Elizaveta followed her by overnight train, properly chaperoned by her governess. She was by no means destitute in Moscow. She was taken in by her step-mother's family, the Bostanzhoglos, who played a leading role in social life. It was in their house that Sergei Vladimirovich met her. It is easy to understand the attraction. Elizaveta was bi-lingual in Russian and French and widely read in the literature of both languages, although her preference was for French. She was also an exceptionally good pianist. The great virtuoso, Nikolai Rubinstein, often expressed regret that she would not allow him to teach her. As to Marie Varley, she invented her own romanticised version of events, claiming that her daughters had been abducted. She later tried to reestablish contact but she was never admitted to the Alekseiev home. None of her grandchildren ever met her.

This was uncharacteristically harsh of Elizaveta Vasilievna as she was essentially generous and warm-hearted by nature. Much as she wanted, however, to exclude her mother from her present life she nonetheless shared the same volatile temperament. If Marie Varley created drama in the theatre, her daughter created drama in the home, shouting at the servants one minute and begging their pardon the next. She never changed and was as tempestuous at sixty as she had been at twenty.

Despite the family's initial misgivings and the differences of temperament between the partners the match proved ideal. No one in later years could recall a single quarrel, they complemented each other so perfectly. They had ten children in all; nine survived. Vladimir, Konstantin, Zinaïda, Anna and Georgi were born in the 1860s. Boris, Liubov, Pavel and Maria followed in the 1870s. Stanislavski, the second child of the marriage was born on January 5, 1863.

Grandfather Vladimir had died in 1862. This marked the end of an era and a further stage in the upward progress of the family. A few months after Stanislavski was born, the family decided to leave the house near the factory and the industrial slums that surrounded it and move to central Moscow. They bought a mansion at Red Gates, on Sadovaia Street, a fashionable district some half-an-hour's walk north-east of Red Square. The new house was large enough to accommodate three generations of Alekseievs with their attendant staff and it was here that Stanislavski lived until he was forty. The old house, on Great Alekseievskaia Street, was donated in the late 60s as a home for the widows and orphans of the merchant class.

Sergei Vladimirovich had no intention of imposing the stern regime he had known on his own children. Elizaveta Vasilievna, for her part, having been handed on from a mother who gave her little affection to a step-mother whose main concern was to play the society hostess, made her family her life. Neither parent was willing to abandon their children in order to participate in the frantic social life around them. In the season Sadovaia Street witnessed an endless succession of carriages, of glittering jewels and dresses; armies of flunkeys attended the people who arrived for the nightly round of balls and receptions given by their neighbours. Sergei and Elizaveta preferred to enjoy the company of their children. When the Alekseievs went out it was as a family; when they received, it was as a family.

What was important to them was their proximity to the artistic life of the city. The mid-nineteenth century was a period of unprecedented cultural richness. Russia was in the process of discovering a new artistic identity in almost every domain – music, opera, ballet, literature, theatre, painting. Educated and affluent families like the Alekseievs lived within the ambit of the artistic world. Savva Ivanovich Mamontov, a railway magnate, a near neighbour and Stanislavski's cousin by marriage, spent a considerable amount of his fortune indulging his passion for the theatre, mounting performances, particularly of opera, which set new standards of production and design. In time the Alekseiev home became noted for its literary and musical soirées and concerts. Actors from the Mali, dancers from the Bolshoi, musicians and writers were regular visitors to the house and became family friends.

The children grew up in this materially and artistically privileged environment. They were, of course, spoiled, although it does not seem to have done any of them ultimately very much harm. Each child was individually considered. Each had its own special kind of sweets and its own kind of bread at breakfast. There was no early rising. Nine o'clock was quite soon enough. Elizaveta Vasilievna took an active part in their upbringing, her insistence on supervising almost every aspect of their lives leading to regular and spectacular quarrels with Nanny Fiolka. A heated exchange would invariably end in Nanny packing her meagre belongings and storming out of the house while the children set up a collective wail. Ten minutes later she would be back and order would be restored – until the next time.

Much less beneficial to the children's welfare was their mother's fanatical obsession with health. In the country she would sleep over the stables on the pretext that the fumes of horse manure were beneficial. The children were not allowed to walk past hospitals for fear of infection; before they were allowed out in bad weather they were wrapped up to the point of suffocation lest they catch cold. These precautions produced the opposite effect to the one desired. Bathed in perspiration before they got beyond the front door they immediately caught chills. From his early childhood Stanislavski retained two things – a disposition towards colds and flu and an indisposition to get up in the morning.

Sergei and Elizaveta Alekseiev had the gift of drawing others in to their magic circle. Loyalty and affection extended beyond the immediate family. Nanny Fiolka and Elizaveta Vasilievna's elderly governess had their own rooms and their place at table. It was a house of nicknames. Normal diminutives in which Russian abounds were abandoned in favour of a family version. Thus Vladimir, instead of being known as Volodia, became Vovosia; Konstantin was not Kostia but Kokosia. The coachman was known as Pirozhok (Meat-pie) and the children's governess, Evdokia Snopova, as Papusha.

True to their determination not to relinquish their children's company but to watch and help them grow, Stanislavski's parents insisted they be educated at home. A fully equipped gymnasium was installed to ensure adequate physical development. As each child grew up he or she was handed on from Nanny Fiolka to Papusha, or her successor, and thence to a series of tutors – a Swiss tutor for gymnastics, a Swedish tutor for music and a certain Mademoiselle Adeline Schmitt for French. French was spoken regularly in the home but the formal study of grammar began at the age of five. Mathematics were taught by a young man named Lvov, who was rumoured to be something of a revolutionary. There were, in addition, dancing lessons from members of the Bolshoi company and in particular from Ermolov, uncle of Stanislavski's favourite actress, Ermolova. There was also, for a period, a young, rather eccentrically-dressed musician, a pupil of Nikolai Rubinstein, who came to play the piano, which he appeared to do day and night, throwing off a cascade of scales, studies and exercises. All these diverse personalities were welded into a small private community. When the family made a trip to Kiev in 1877, two complete railway carriages were taken; the first, a ministerial coach, including a sitting-room, for the family and their doctor, the second for the servants, the nursemaids and the tutors.

Stanislavski was by no means the 'star' of the family. On the contrary. Nanny Fiolka remembered him as 'nothing much'. His early years were dogged by almost continuous ill-health. As a baby he had difficulty in holding his head up; it would loll forward. This caused a minor accident when he was nine months old. The family doctor was attempting to inoculate him against smallpox when his head suddenly fell forward onto the lancet, cutting his lower eye lid. The scar remained with him for the rest of his life. He also suffered from scrofula which meant various forms of medicated baths. When he learned to speak he had problems with the sounds 'l' and 'r'.

Zinaïda recalled that she and her brother were the 'Cinderellas' of the family. It was a condition of Elizaveta Vasilievna's self-esteem as a mother that her children should be 'showable'. This meant that though she loved them all dearly, her special favour was reserved for those among them who, like Vladimir and Anna, would most readily perform their party pieces, playing the piano or reciting poems. Stanislavski felt intimidated by Elizaveta and her demands for, though he was lively enough in the nursery, in the presence of adults he withdrew into himself. Much as he adored his governess, Papusha, he resisted all her attempts to make him learn little verses to speak for guests. The sudden improvement in his general health at the age of seven made little difference. There was now colour in his cheeks and he began to gain in strength. The physical education sessions in the family gymnasium, the dancing and fencing lessons developed his body and at the same time laid the foundations of his technique as an actor. When, in 1869, his father bought an estate in Liubimovka, a short distance from Moscow, he was able to pass the hot summer months in outdoor pursuits such as boating and riding which helped him grow in strength. He soon became an excellent horseman. But he still did not shine. His mother's unreserved approval was only forthcoming when he achieved a reputation as an amateur actor but by then it was too late. The older he grew the more constrained he felt in her presence, although in middle age he was able to write to Chekhov about her with a degree of amused detachment. It was his father who provided the background of security and his brothers and sisters who gave him the affection and support he needed.

Outside the family he only ever had one close friend, Fedia Kashkadam-ov, known as Fif, the son of his tutor in Russian. Fif was the model companion, someone who could enter Stanislavski's world on equal terms. He was highly intelligent, musical, playing both the piano and the violin; he wrote good poetry. Later, he took the lead with Stanislavski in organizing amateur theatricals. Stanislavski loved and respected him but Fif suffered from a weak heart and died at the age of twenty-four. Stanislavski never again had a friend who was his contemporary.

A reserved boy, Stanislavski could, however, turn into an obstinate demon. Just as he refused to learn even simple poems, he resisted his piano lessons, although he was extremely musical. He refused to play duets with his teacher and would time his lesson to the second, declining absolutely to go one instant over the allotted time. He even managed to drive his tolerant and mild-mannered father into a quite exceptional rage one day by endlessly repeating 'I will not let you go to Aunt Vera's'. He was at first requested and then ordered to stop but would not or, rather, could not. Something had taken possession of him. His outraged father eventually stormed out of the room. Only then did the young Konstantin relent. Stanislavski regarded this incident as the first manifestation of his will to succeed. It was this obstinancy that enabled him to get things done.

Play, make-believe and fantasy played a large part in the Alekseiev children's early education. For this Papusha was responsible. She was barely nineteen when she was engaged. She was well educated with an instinctive understanding of children's needs ahead of the conventional wisdom of her time. She used creative play as part of the learning process. She used fantasy to explain away fears and anxieties and encouraged the children to act out situations or characters from history. At other times they would improvise small scenes to entertain the family on special occasions. It was thanks to her that Stanislavski made his stage 'debut'.

In great secrecy she rehearsed the children in a series of tableaux vivants. *The Four Seasons*, a conventional subject for the period, which were intended as a surprise offering in honour of Elizaveta Vasilievna's name-day, September 5. The performance took place in a dilapidated out-building at Liubimovka. A small stage had been constructed and a curtain improvised out of tartan rugs. Stanislavski played Winter, or Grandfather Frost.

He found it, if we are to believe *My Life in Art*, a puzzling experience. His account, however, is homiletic rather than historically accurate. In the first American edition he states that he was two or three at the time; in the Russian edition he changes this to three or four, but neither is possible. Liubimovka was not purchased until 1869 and the earliest date a performance could have taken place there was 1870, when he was seven. He claims that this was the first occasion on which he experienced the embarrassment of being on stage with no motivation for what he was doing. It was an omission he quickly remedied.

His little scene was so successful that it was considered he merited an encore:

'They put a lighted candle in front of me, hidden in brushwood, to represent a bonfire and gave me a stick which I was to pretend to put into it.

"You understand? Pretend. Don't really do it," they explained to me. And so I was strictly forbidden to put the stick into the fire. All this seemed quite senseless to me. "Why pretend if I really can put the wood in the fire?"

As soon as the curtains opened for the encore I stretched out my hand with the stick towards the fire with considerable interest and curiosity. It seemed to me that this was a completely natural and logical action, one with thought behind it.' (SS, I, p. 9.)

The stick went up in flames, setting light to the cotton wool that covered the set. Stanislavski was grabbed from the stage and taken straight up to bed in tears.

This sixty-year-old man's account of the reasoning processes of a child of seven is far too sophisticated but, placed as it is in *My Life in Art* side by side with the Aunt Vera incident, it indicates his determination to see his later life and personality in terms of his earliest experiences. This performance marked for him the beginning of his preoccupation with the problem of illusion and reality on stage.

Theatre was the Alekseiev family passion, be it the Punch and Judy men and clowns who roamed the streets and came knocking at the door, the circus, the Mali or the Bolshoi. The children were taken to the theatre and concerts almost as soon as they could walk. On the whole they were resistant to the weightier dramatic and musical works. They made it clear to their parents that if their treats were to be limited in number, the 'heavy stuff' was not to count.

Stanislavski's favourite was the circus – 'the best place in the world', he declared aged nine. He liked to sit where he could see the artists preparing to come on. The physicality, the speed, the colour of the spectacle carried him away. His parents were amazed when, one day, this boy, normally so reserved in public, seeing his particular favourite, Elvira, an equestrienne, jumped out of the family box, ran to her and kissed the hem of her skirt. When he ran back to his seat his parents registered a mild protest – 'Kostia, qu'as-tu fait?' – but he just sat, all unheeding, staring into space.

Other great occasions included visits to the ballet. Ermolov's dance classes had awakened Stanislavski to the expressive possibilities of his own body. He went to the Bolshoi, therefore, with active interest. The glory of the Tchaikovski ballets and the full development of a choreographic style were yet to come. The children's favourites were works like *The Corsair*.

The Alekseiev family descended on the theatre *en bloc*. Picnic refreshments were provided and they took with them a board that could be placed across the seats so that the children could have a proper view. The parents preferred No 14, next to the Imperial Box, so as 'to be seen'. The children preferred boxes 1 or 2, at the side, so that, as at the circus, they could see the artists preparing in the wings. All had their own favourite ballerina; Kostia's was Stanislavskaia. During the intervals the children were allowed to run and play in the theatre's hallowed corridors. Their noisy antics were smiled upon both by the theatre's venerable and bewhiskered officials and by the lackeys whose magnificent blue livery was decorated with silver braid which had doubtless come from the Alekseiev mills. After the performance the children were gathered up by the nursemaids, lifted into the carriage by the servants and taken home.

For a time Zinaïda and Anna could think of nothing else but being sent away to ballet school. Their father, indulgent as ever, preferred not to confront them with a direct refusal but dutifully wrote a letter of application which he assured them he had sent. His closing sentence was, however, sufficiently tongue-in-cheek to indicate his request would be granted over his dead body. No answer was ever received.

Theatre visits provided material for play. Scenes from the ballet – usually those involving death and destruction – were performed. With Fif, Stanislavski created the Konstantin Alekseiev Circus. The children were by turns jugglers, clowns, acrobats. Since they could not always reproduce the more spectacular acts they resorted to puppets. They persuaded the family carpenter to construct a special table complete with trap-doors, footlights and overhead lighting. Notebooks and pencils were taken along to theatre visits and sets and costumes were duly noted to be reproduced at home. Everyone in the household was drawn in to help. Performances were given for sympathetic friends and a sell-out was not unusual. Sometimes Vladimir, who confined himself to accompanying the performance on the piano, would sabotage the occasion by shouting, 'The idiots! They imagine it's a real circus'. Stanislavski would be momentarily angry but nothing could destroy for long his belief in the world of illusion he had created.

Papusha left the family service in 1874, when Stanislavski was eleven. She had been with him for seven formative years. He was always grateful to her. Dedicating a photograph in 1928 he described her as his 'second mother'. Her departure presaged more radical changes.

The following year, Sergei and Elizaveta, much against their will, were obliged to send the two older boys to school; compulsory military service had been introduced and to qualify for exemption young men needed to demonstrate an approved level of education. This meant taking public examinations. Vladimir and Konstantin took the entrance examination for the grammar school at 4 Pokrovka Street and passed. Vladimir entered the Third Form and Konstantin, the Second. The school was considered one of the best although Stanislavski's comments are distinctly unflattering.

The young Kostia cut a strange figure. Although only twelve he was exceptionally tall. According to Vladimir, he stood among his contemporaries like Gulliver among the Lilliputians. As an adult he was well over six-feet tall and in group photographs can be seen towering a good head above the people around him. This caused problems of coordination which took many years of effort to resolve.

He showed the same reserve at school as he showed with adults. He made no friends in his own form. Such companions as he had were drawn from his brother's year. He was always, as his headmaster recalled, unfailingly courteous to masters and pupils alike, but no more. He remained polite but distant.

Learning at school had none of the excitement and stimulation of lessons at home. Instead of Papusha and lively-minded tutors he had a pompous master who peppered his remarks to his pupils with endless deferential 'Excellencies'. He was, as Stanislavski put it, 'a bit dotty'. School meant boredom and frustration. The authorities had decided to emphasize the importance of classical languages. Try as he would the young Kostia could not master irregular Latin verbs. He copied them out, page after page, in his attempt to get them by heart but to no avail. He failed Latin regularly.

Stanislavski never had any capacity for parrot-learning or the mechanical acquisition of facts nor, conversely, did he have any gift for abstract or conceptual thought. He learned when confronted with concrete problems or when his imagination or, as he later put it, his will to create, was aroused. Motivation was everything and it was the theatre that provided the stimulus.

Theatre could unblock his obstinate memory. This is illustrated by two incidents which occurred in his mid-teens. The boy who could not learn Latin verbs surprised his parents during a public dress rehearsal of Molière's *Le Mariage Forcé* at the Mali by reciting one of Pancrace's long speeches from memory. On another occasion he took advantage of the master's absence from the classroom to act a whole scene, playing all the parts, from Groboiedov's *Woe from Wit*. Unfortunately he was so absorbed in his performance that he did not notice the master's return. He was punished for indiscipline. Playacting would not enhance his examination prospects or his career.

CHAPTER TWO

STANISLAVSKI

1877 marked a turning-point in Stanislavski's life. His father was elected head of the merchant class in Moscow, one of the most important and influential positions in the city. He could rise no higher, for while the aristocracy might be mortgaged to the state for two-thirds of its wealth, all important posts in central government, the army and the church were still reserved, by law, for its members. One of his first acts was to raise 1,000,000 roubles for the families of casualties in the latest Russo-Turkish war.

He had always been fond of his estate at Liubimovka. Soon after buying it he had created a medical-centre in the village and named it after his wife. Now he decided to convert the out-building which had been used for the tableaux vivants into a proper theatre for the enjoyment of family and friends. Amateur theatricals were a popular pastime among the summerfolk at their dachas and estates. Few, however, apart from Mamontov, could aspire to a fully-equipped theatre. The finished building was handsome with a dressing-room each for the gentlemen and ladies, a wardrobe and a prop-store. The footlights could be covered by lowering a board over them when a blackout was required. Guests could either spend the intervals on the verandah or in a specially provided sitting-room when the weather was bad.

Elizaveta Vasilievna's name-day, September 5, was selected for the gala opening. Guests were asked to present themselves at Yaroslavl station from where they were to be taken by special train to Liubimovka to arrive in time for dinner before the performance. The entertainment was to consist of four short pieces, directed by the mathematics tutor, Lvov. Stanislavski appeared in two of them, *A Cup of Tea* and *The Old Mathematician*.

He was in such a state of tension and excitement that he could scarcely contain himself and almost fell out of the carriage. It was to be his great day. In the event it proved more problematic than he could have anticipated. He was confronted for the first time with the contradiction between what an actor and an audience feel about a performance. In *A Cup of Tea* he had felt comparatively at ease but the audience had not responded. In *The Old Mathematician*, however, where he had felt less secure, he was declared by director and audience alike to have played much better. He was thoroughly confused.

An immediate consequence of the grand opening was the creation of the Alekseiev Circle which consisted of the immediate family, Fif Kashkadamov and his brother, and various cousins. A further, and, in the long-term, more significant consequence was Stanislavski's decision to note down and analyse his performance. He had kept a series of notebooks from his earliest childhood on subjects that interested him. He now began the first of a series of notebooks in which he described and analysed his work from role to role and performance to performance. He continued this practice for the next sixty years. The last of the books was at his bed-side on the day he died. The notes he so carefully and assiduously made provided the basis for much of his published work.

The first entry, written on the evening of the performance runs:

'In the role of the Mathematician I played coldly, lifelessly, without talent, although I was no worse than the others but I in no way showed talent. The audience said the part did not suit me. . . .

In *A Cup of Tea* I was successful, the audience laughed – not at me, however, but at Muzil whom I copied, even down to the voice.' (SS, V, p. 85.)

He noted, too, that he gabbled his lines and waved his arms about like a windmill.

This entry, like later examples, must be read with caution. In common with many talented actors who are only concerned with improvement, Stanislavski tended to see only the negative side of his work. His sister, Zinaïda, rejected his account of the gala evening:

'In his Notes Kostia writes, "I was not successful in *The Old Mathematician*". That is not quite true, rather he himself was dissatisfied but at the same time even in that first production he distinguished himself from the rest by the naturalness of his playing and it was not at all evident that he was nervous or shy.' (Z. Sokolova in *K. S. Stanislavski*, p. 382, Moscow 1955.)

Whatever the actual quality of his performance may have been, the fact that at the age of fourteen, he was able to analyse the technique of a leading character actor, Muzil, and consciously copy it is evidence of an insight and understanding beyond his years.

The standards by which Stanislavski judged his own work were drawn principally from the performances he saw at the Mali Theatre, his 'university', as he put it. The Mali was the home of psychological realism. At the time it was founded, in 1823, Pushkin was struggling with the problem of verisimilitude. What is believable in the theatre? How does the spectator enter the world of the play? The reader can lose himself in a book, to the exclusion of the world around him but how can a member of a theatre audience, sitting with 2000 other people, in a space which is divided in two parts, one for those watching, the other for those performing, believe in the reality of what is going on? Since, at this period, the auditorium remained fully-lit during performances there was no surrounding darkness in which he could lose himself.

For Pushkin it was not historical authenticity that made a play credible since classic authors like Shakespeare, Racine, Corneille and Calderón were manifestly anachronistic. Does not a clock strike in *Julius Caesar*? What then is verisimilitude? Wherein does it lie? Pushkin came to the conclusion that the only truth which interested classic authors was truth of character and situation: credible behaviour in believable circumstances. In an unfinished article on the history of drama, drafted in 1830 but not published until after his death, he summarized his findings in what came to be known as his Aphorism:

'The truth concerning the passions, verisimilitude in the feelings experienced in the given circumstances, that is what our intelligence demands of a dramatist.' (Pushkin, *Sobranie Sochinenii*, VI, p. 265.)

Gogol developed the notion of psychological probability further. In his *Notes on how to Act the Inspector General*, he enjoined the actor to go first to the core, the kernel of the character, before concerning himself with externals:

'The intelligent actor, before seizing on the minor quirks and superficial oddities of his role, must endeavour to capture those features which are *common to all mankind*. He must reflect on the purpose of his role, the principal, the primary concerns of the character, what it is that rules his life and continually occupies his thoughts, the immovable nail planted in his head. Having grasped this the actor must assimilate it so thoroughly that the thoughts and strivings of his character seem to become his own and never leave his mind for the length of the performance. . . . One should first grasp the soul of a part, not its trappings.' (Gogol, *Izbrannie Stati*, p. 324, Moscow 1980.)

Caricature, pointing up, demonstrating were to be avoided. The actor, as he wrote in another context, 'must not *present* but *transmit*'.

The insistence on the primacy of inner psychological truth radically distinguishes the concept of realism from subsequent notions of naturalism if naturalism is defined, as Stanislavski came to define it, as the undiscriminating replication of the surface of life. Shakespeare and Molière are realist writers. Griboiedov's comedy *Woe From Wit*, written in an elaborate stanza form, is a realist play. Tchaikovski could describe himself as a realist composer. The task of the actor is to create a characterization which is both individual and typical not merely idiosyncratic and contingent.

Pushkin and Gogol found their ideal actor in Mikhaïl Shchepkin. He insisted that an actor get into the skin of a character, that he should identify with his thoughts and feelings. The actor had two sources of material: knowledge of his own nature and observation of life. Writing to the actress Aleksandra Shubert on March 27, 1848 he said:

'It is so much easier to play mechanically – for that you only need your reason. Reason will approximate to joy and sorrow just as an imitation approximates to nature. But an actor of feeling – that's quite different. . . . He just begins by wiping out his own self . . . and becomes the character the author intended him to be. He must walk, talk, think, feel, cry, laugh as the author wants him to. You see how how the actor's task becomes more meaningful. In the first case you need only pretend to live – in the second you really have to live. . . .' (Shchepkin, *Zhizn i Tvorchestvo*, I, pp. 199-200, Moscow 1984.)

By this attack on the theory of the consciously calculating, objectively cool performer advanced by Diderot in his *Paradoxe sur le Comédien* Shchepkin drew up the battle-lines for later conflicts concerning the nature of the actor's art.

In a short time the Mali came to be known as the House of Shchepkin, just as the Comédie Française was known as La Maison de Molière. He passed on his methods, training young artists, as was the practice at the time, by taking them into his home. His influence would have been confined to his immediate circle had not Pushkin bullied him, much against his will, into writing his biography. Pushkin drafted the first sentence himself daring the actor to refuse to continue. The resulting *Memoirs of a Serf-Actor* became the bible of all actors whose ambition it was to achieve a naturalness of style. It charts Shchepkin's battle with himself. Trained in his early days in the prevailing school of rant and rhetoric it was many years before he could behave like a recognizable human being on stage. Stanislavski's own heavily-annotated copy survives in the archives and the story it contains forms the prototype for his own struggle to master truth and banish theatrical cliché.

By the time Stanislavski began attending performances the Mali was already in decline. Shchepkin died in August 1863, eight months after Stanislavski was born. There was no school to teach his methods and all attempts to establish. a systematic approach to the education of the young actor failed. Ostrovski's well-thought-out training programmes were shelved. The company drifted and standards fell. Nonetheless there were still some members of the company, who had been trained by Shchepkin and continued his tradition. Some, like Medvedeva, were friends of the family with whom Stanislavski could spend an evening and ask advice.

The company was revitalized from time to time by actors of outstanding talent and none more gifted than Aleksandr Pavlovich Lenski who arrived from Odessa in 1876. At 29 with his good looks, elegance of movement and well-modulated voice, he was not only the perfect example of the romantic lead but, as a painter, sculptor and writer, a model of the literate, cultivated artist Stanislavski wanted all actors to become.

Lenski dealt in subtlety and nuance. He used as little make-up as possible transforming himself from within. He looked for the inner logic of the character's psychology. Not until he had created a mental image of the character did he learn the lines or concern himself with external appearance. His silences were proverbial, filled with thought and inner action. His great gift was his ability to show the slow, organic growth of an emotion. When playing Benedick in *Much Ado About Nothing* he took a long pause before the soliloquy, 'Ha! Against my will I am come to bid you in to dinner; there's a double meaning in that.' A twitch was seen at the corner of the mouth which developed slowly into a radiant smile enveloping the whole face. The audience burst into a delighted round of applause before he had uttered a word. For the external appearance of his characters he went to paintings, turning for Victor Hugo's Hernani to Velasquez.

Apart from the leading artists of the Mali, Stanislavski drew his notions of acting from the foreign artists tour in Moscow, mostly during Lent, when Russian actors were forbidden, for religious reasons, to appear. In March and April 1877 the great Italian actor, Ernesto Rossi appeared as Hamlet, Othello, Romeo, Macbeth and Lear. For Stanislavski it was a revelation. He was presented with a virtuoso display of natural talent: physical and vocal freedom, free-flowing emotion, clarity of expression, all apparently achieved without effort. It was with these performances in mind that he made his appearance at Liubimovka and began his notebook.

He prepared for his theatre visits carefully. The texts were read in advance – in the case of French classics, Racine, Corneille and Molière, in the original language. At the same time he was building up a scrapbook in which he collected pictures and sketches of possible models for characterizations.

No such energy and enthusiasm, however, went into his school work which remained a problem. In 1878 both he and Vladimir had been transferred to the Lazarev Institute for Oriental Languages. The grammar school had deteriorated to such an extent under a headmaster known as 'the human beast' that many parents were taking their children away. Besides, Stanislavski's father calculated that given the family business's connections with the east a knowledge of oriental languages would be useful. Konstantin's Latin, however, remained a stumbling block. If he did not pass he could not go on to higher study. Even though his father promised him an English horse if he passed he failed again in 1879, but got the horse anyway. In 1881 he took the easy way out. He scribbled as much as he could on his shirt cuffs, prepared a number of cribs and cheated his way through. The notion of going on to Moscow University, like Vladimir, held no attraction for him. He decided that his formal education must come to an end and persuaded his father to let him join the business. His academic failure shadowed him all his life.

Any disappointment he felt was more than compensated by his sense of freedom. Liberated from his school books, he could do what he liked. He enjoyed the new role of the active young business executive and acted it out to the full. Once he had fulfilled his duties at the office he was his own man. He could devote himself to the theatre. His father converted two rooms in the house at Red Gates into a second family theatre. It was lavishly decorated in red plush and gilt and could seat 300 people. The house more than ever became a focus of artistic and cultural life with musical soirées and literary evenings. Stanislavski could now make theatre all year round. He was now also a complete balletomane and suffered the inevitable infatuation with one of the Bolshoi dancers, Pomialova. This adolescent passion worried his parents particularly when on February 19, 1881, while yet at school, he did not come home all night.

In the following year Stanislavski was provided with another demonstration of theatrical mastery. The great Italian tragedian, Tommaso Salvini, gave an Othello which combined minimum effort with maximum emotional impact. Stanislavski was shaken and stunned. Salvini's talent obsessed him. He followed his idol around for days, striking up a conversation with anyone who knew him, trying to discover the basis of his technique. All he learnt was that Salvini arrived at the theatre two hours before curtain-up to think himself into the role.

Living a part was now Stanislavski's major concern. It seem to him that the test of the truth of a characterization was the ability to maintain it in real life. While at Liubimovka the members of the Alekseiev Circle disguised themselves as tramps and drunks in the evenings and went down to make a nuisance of themselves at the railway station. The startled reaction of the passengers on the platform gave them great satisfaction and when the porters chased them away they knew they had succeeded. On another occasion they dressed up as fortune-telling gypsies and played an elaborate hoax on a visiting cousin who was completely taken in.

In the summer of 1883 Stanislavski decided to apply the principle of living the role to a production of Diachenko's comedy, *The Practical Man*. He insisted that the cast should sustain their characterization outside rehearsals in their daily life and maintain the relationships laid down in the script. The young actors found the task of improvising their own dialogue difficult at first but gradually acquired greater facility. Stanislavski undermined the value of his own experiment, for while he was improvising he was also busy aping Sadovski's performance as Meliusov in Ostrovski's *Artists and Admirers*. His characterization, which was much praised, owed less to his own creative imagination than to his skill in absorbing another actor's technique and mannerisms.

Stanislavski found he could not build up a sound and independent technique by imitation or by trying to develop scraps of information about other actors' work habits. He needed a teacher. He had failed to make contact with Salvini, but when the German actor Ernst Possart came to Moscow on tour in 1884 Stanislavski called on him and asked for lessons. Possart possessed a fine voice and a graceful body. His somewhat bizarre method of teaching, however, consisted in making his pupils recite to piano accompaniment, using note values to denote the rhythm of the words. As Stanislavski's German was poor, the whole exercise was reduced to a farce.

Opera now claimed Stanislavski's attention. Thanks to the Bolshoi and touring Italian companies he acquired a knowledge of the standard repertoire – *La Traviata*, *Aida* (Verdi), *I Puritani* (Bellini), *L'Africaine*, *Les Huguenots* (Meyerbeer), *Le Roi de Lahore* (Massenet), *La Gioconda* (Ponchielli), *Carmen* (Bizet), *Lucia di Lammermoor* (Donizetti), *Faust* (Gounod) and *Evgeni Onegin* (Tchaikovski). For a wider knowledge of the Russian repertoire he had to turn to Mamontov's Private Opera, launched in 1885 which premiered Rimski-Korsakov's operas, *The Tsar's Bride* and *The Golden Cockerel*, both of which Stanislavski later directed. Mamontov also championed the much-criticized Moussorgski and rescued Chaliapin from provincial obscurity.

In January, 1884, Stanislavski decided that he should develop his vocal technique. It was typical of him that he should turn to the best teacher in Moscow, Fiodor Komissarzhevski, a leading member of the Bolshoi company and professor at the Conservatoire. Stanislavski, who had a pleasant, light bass-baritone voice and natural sense of phrasing, made a great impression on Komissarzhevski who saw a combination of dramatic ability and musical talent worth developing. The lessons went well, so well that Stanislavski toyed with the idea of an operatic career. On April 8, 1886, he appeared as Ramfis in extracts from Verdi's *Aida* given as part of a concert by pupils from the Conservatoire and presented at Red Gates. Plans were made to stage extracts from Gounod's *Faust* and Dargomizhski's *Rusalka*.

Stanislavski had been fascinated by Gounod's opera ever since he first saw it in January 1881. The *Notebook* for 1885 contains an entry, *Dreams of How I Would Direct and Play the Role of Mephistopheles in Gounod's Faust*; it consists of a description of the opening scene in Faust's study. The emphasis is on the realism of the setting, on the creation not of a conventional stage-set constructed out of wings and flats but of a specific room. The furniture and props are exactly described. Illustrations of the characters, taken from books, are pasted in, with small pen sketches in the margins. This approach to the problem of design owed much to Mamontov. All Stanislavski needed to do was to take a short walk along Sadovaia Street and he could see leading artists, scene-painters and carpenters at work on sets considerably more realistic than the drops, flats and wings in current use. Mamontov selected his designers among those painters who, like the Itinerants, were concerned to give a more accurate picture of Russia past or present. What applied to Russia could be made to apply to medieval Germany.

Stanislavski came to the *Faust* project, therefore, with clear ideas but they were never to be realized. He began to experience serious vocal problems. His voice gave out under pressure. Komissarzhevski was convinced that the cause was not technical but physiological:

'I am more and more convinced that all the problems with the voice stem from pharyngeal catarrh. The purity of all sounds *piano* indicates that the laryngeal mechanism is more or less in good order but the catarrh impedes the proper exertion of the vocal cords. And that's a pity because you are a very gifted man with an excellent musical memory and an active theatrical understanding. . . . in every rehearsal I saw that you had great gifts and for that reason we must hope for an improvement in your throat.' (K. K. Alekseieva Archive.)

Komissarzhevski continued to give him lessons and even when he cut down drastically on his work offered private classes between 6.30 and 7.30 in the evening. Stanislavski continued his studies well into 1887. But the hoped-for improvement did not occur. Stanislavski's voice was always described as muted and later problems with vocally-taxing classical roles, such as Othello, may have had their roots in this basic medical condition. He did not help himself, it must be said, by smoking heavily.

Stanislavski's work with Komissarzhevski extended beyond pure questions of vocal technique. Together they explored the problem of coordinating voice and body. Stanislavski hired a pianist to improvise while they moved, sat, stood or were simply silent in time and rhythm to the music. Feeling that he had found a sympathetic collaborator, in August 1884, barely six months after they had started working together, Stanislavski suggested the creation of a musical-dramatic group, within the ambit of the Alekseiev Circle, where young people could develop their talents more 'scientifically'. Komissarzhevski agreed that a well-organized private group would probably be more effective than the sprawling and unwieldy Conservatoire. His own participation, however, would have to be discreet, given his post at the Conservatoire. The project had to wait three years before coming to fruition.

Stanislavski could not wait for proper training until he was able to start his own school. He was twenty-two and in a hurry. In September 1885 he auditioned for the Moscow Theatre School. He prepared conscientiously. While the rest of the family went to Liubimovka, he had spent the summer alone in Moscow working on voice, diction and movement, mainly in front of a mirror. He would start at seven in the evening and go on well into the night. For his audition he gave a stirring rendering of the poem, 'Napoleon', and was accepted.

His experience at the school was short-lived. He left within three weeks. Any illusions he might have had about receiving insights into the actor's creative process were quickly dispelled. He was asked to copy his masters' interpretations, their manner of playing a role, their tricks. This was not the logical, 'scientific' training he wanted but imitation of the worst kind. The only person who might have been of real help to him was Glikeria Fedotova, a pupil of Shchepkin, and the mother of one of his schoolfriends but she left the school a week before he did. The last thing he needed, in any case, after his experience of school, was another institution with formal structures. He was led by nature and upbringing to demand exclusive, individual attention.

Sergei Vladimirovich did not seem averse to his son's attending theatre school as he had been, earlier, to his daughters' going to ballet school. Doubtless he believed the whole idea was impractical. It would be impossible for his son to work full-time at the office and attend classes. Lack of time was, indeed, the reason Stanislavski gave for quitting.

It never for one moment occurred to Sergei Vladimirovich that his son harboured ambitions to become a professional actor. Such a notion was unthinkable. The status of the professional actor was even lower in Russia than in the rest of Europe. Actors, including the great Shchepkin, had been serfs within living memory, the property of the nobility, humiliated and beaten when they did not come up to standard. To be an actor was to be legally disqualified from any form of public office. The taboo against turning professional was absolute.

The future pattern of Stanislavski's life was, whether he liked it or not, being laid down for him. With his father head of the merchant class and his highly ambitious cousin, Nikolai, now Mayor of Moscow at the early age of thirty-one, the path he would be expected to take was obvious. He had proved himself more dynamic and able at the factory than his brother, Vladimir, who was altogether a softer personality. He must, therefore, take his proper place in society and assume power and responsibility.

He was soon caught up in the inevitable round of committees which, on the whole, he found tedious. Relief came in 1886, when his cousin invited him to take over as Chairman of the Russian Music Society and Conservatoire. He was duly elected on February 17 and immediately began working with leading composers such as Tchaikovski and his pupil Taneiev, and patrons of fine art like Tretiakov. Tchaikovski found him *très sympathique* and was sufficiently impressed with his singing voice to consider writing a one-act opera for him on the subject of Peter the Great.

The Society benefited considerably from Stanislavski's energy and business experience. While he acquired experience of the problems of programme-planning and the negotiation of artists' contracts. The Society's school also attracted his attention. He found its facilities inadequate and said so. In October 1887 he was invited to work out a scheme for improvement and cost it. The plan he put forward was accepted early the following year.

The Alekseiev Circle had, in the meantime, continued to offer its programmes of light pieces and vaudevilles. In 1882, Stanislavski made his directorial debut with something a little more serious, a production of Molière's *Le Mariage Forcé*, which he had seen at the Mali with Lenski. Stimulated by his studies with Komissarzhevski, he decided that the Circle should launch into operetta. Vladimir, who had always been diffident about appearing on stage, now came into his own both as a musician and a translator. The first work he adapted was Hervé's *Lili*, which the family had seen in November 1883 when the celebrated French actress, Anna Judic, was on tour. The rehearsal period was exceptionally long by contemporary standards. Mamontov could mount a full-scale opera in two weeks. Work on *Lili* began in the spring of 1885 and extended into the first two months of 1886. Mamontov, of course, did not care much about the standard of acting in his productions, Stanislavski did. The play finally opened at Red Gates on February 18 and was well received.

The Circle had now been in existence for ten years and had achieved a level of performance which set it well above other amateur groups. Stanislavski decided to stage the Russian première of *The Mikado* which Zinaïda and Anna had seen in Paris and Vienna. Once again Vladimir grappled with the problem of translating the libretto not, it must be assumed, from the English original. As with *Lili* the preparation period was long. Work began in the summer of 1886 and went on into the following April. Stanislavski's developing ideas of realism came into play. He sent to Paris for costume material which was cut in the authentic manner. By chance a group of Japanese acrobats were appearing at the Moscow Circus. They became regular visitors at Red Gates, instructing the cast in movement, gesture and deportment. Even the giant Stanislavski managed to make himself look small.

The opening night on April 18, 1887 was a huge success and earned Stanislavski his first professional review. The *Moskovski Listok* reported that a performance had taken place in the home of one of Moscow's most respected business men.

'. . . . the soloists . . . were so vital and witty that even the best of our artists could learn something from them. First honours must go to the beautiful voice and sensitive phrasing of K. A———v.' (Moskovski Listok, May 3, 1887.)

The absence of the full name and the use of 'K. A———v' was a necessary gesture, a clear indication of amateur status.

By the time he came to *Lili* and *The Mikado* Stanislavski had formalized an acting method based on a series of articles the actor Nikolai Struzhkin had published in the magazine, *Teatralnaia Biblioteka* in 1879 and 1880. In the *Notebook* for 1885, Stanislavski notes thirteen 'aspects' which need to be considered:

1. What is the temperament of the role.
2. To what nationality or period it belongs.
3. The physiological aspect of the role.
4. The psychic aspect of the role.
5. Relationship to other roles.
6. Age.
7. Maturity.
8. What type (*emploi*) of role.
9. The most recent presentation of the character.
10. The author's intention.
11. Opinions of other characters concerning this role.
12. The most outstanding passages in the roles.
13. The outward appearance of the role.

Stanislavski was still thinking in conventional categories, of temperament (sanguine, melancholic etc.,), role-types (romantic lead, heavy etc,); and still concerned with other actors' performances. The notion of individuated psychology, was, as yet, beyond him. Unfortunately he had little opportunity to put even this limited discovery into practice.

The life of the Alekseiev Circle was coming to a natural end. Fif had died in 1886, brothers and sisters were growing up, marrying, acquiring responsibilities for family and children. The Circle no longer enjoyed pride of place in their lives. Productions were fewer and farther between. Stanislavski's appetite for acting, however, was as insatiable as ever and wherever he could K. A———v appeared with respectable amateur groups, performing in plays of quality such as Gogol's *Marriage* and *The Gamblers*. At the same time a 'Mr Stanislavski' was appearing with various groups outside the family's circle of acquaintance. Many of the plays he appeared in were not only inferior but risqué by contemporary standards. They were thrown on, sometimes half improvised. Performances often took place in dirty and unkempt premises and with companions whom the Alekseiev family would have considered to be definitely *louche*. The company consisted of men whose only object was to get the actresses into bed and women whose virtue had long ceased to be a matter of concern to them.

Stanislavski had to keep this double life secret from his parents. The easiest solution was to take a stage name. He inherited 'Stanislavski' from another amateur, Dr Mako, a friend at Liubimovka, and an admirer, as he had been as a boy, of the ballerina Stanislavskaia. It was a safe name to adopt. Of Polish origin, it suggested humble status and was unlikely to be associated with one of Moscow's most eminent bourgeois families. Stanislavski used it for the first time on March 3, 1884 when he appeared in a comedy by the popular dramatist Ivan Krilov. His sister, Zinaïda, now married, was in on the secret as he sometimes used her flat to change costume when the theatre could not provide proper dressing-rooms.

The deception could not last for ever. One evening when appearing in a three-act French vaudeville, which included rather daring love scenes that would never be allowed at Red Gates, he made his first entrance only to be confronted by his father, mother and her elderly governess sitting in the large box centre. He froze. Any pretence at characterization disappeared. No longer a dashing dandy, he turned into a shy, respectable young man. He managed to avoid his family that night but had to confront his father in the morning. Sergei Vladimirovich greeted him with the brief sharp sentence, 'If you really want to act in your free time start a proper dramatic circle with a decent repertoire but stop appearing in muck with God knows who.'

It has not been possible to date this incident precisely, nor discover the title of the play in question but in late 1887 Stanislavski finally set about creating the Moscow Musical-Dramatic Amateur Circle which he had discussed with Komissarzhevski three years earlier. Its first production, Ostrovski's *The Forest*, was presented on December 6.

Early in the following year the Alekseiev Circle went out in style. On January 9, 1888 it staged a revival of *Lili*, which, like *The Mikado*, drew an appreciative notice in the press. Zinaïda was praised, as was Stanislavski.

> 'The gifted Mr K.S.A. was very good indeed, both as actor and singer, in the role of the soldier Antoine Planchard ... and ... especially in the third act when he really was a crusty old soldier.' (*Russki Kurier*, January 13, 1888.)

The season ended well. He felt he was making progress as an actor. On February 29 he appeared as Freze in a production of Krilov's *Spoiled Darling* and, for once, took his characterization from life. One evening, while at the Mali, he saw a foreigner who was just the type he needed. He managed to change seats so as to be next to his chosen model, engaged him in conversation and then invited him to return to the theatre on another occasion. A dash to the box office resulted in two adjacent seats for the next production. He thus had another evening in which to study his companion's voice, movements, intonations and facial expressions. The consequence was a highly successful performance in a role that was to remain one of his favourites.

Spoiled Darling was also important for more personal reasons. In the cast was his future wife, Maria Petrovna Perevostchikova. She came from a respectable professional background: her grandfather had founded the Moscow Astronomical Centre, while her father was a well-known lawyer. To avoid her family's blushes she acted under the stage-name, Lilina.

Stanislavski's last appearance before the summer break flattered his self-esteem. On April 3 he took part in an evening of excerpts which included scenes from the production of Ostrovski's *The Forest* which he had presented the previous December. Two stars from the Mali, Ermolova and Yuzhin were on the same bill. It was a sign of his growing reputation that he should have been invited to appear in such company. He was able to approach his next venture with confidence.

CHAPTER THREE

THE BROAD PATH TO TRUE
NATURE

Even as he launched the Moscow Amateur Music-Drama Circle Stanislavski knew it had been overtaken by events. In January 1887 he had been invited to take part in a semi-professional production of Gogol's *The Gamblers*, to be directed by Aleksandr Fedotov, the estranged husband of Glikeria Fedotova. Like his wife, Fedotov had been a member of the Mali theatre and trained in the realist school of Shchepkin. His youthful ambition had been to create a people's theatre, with seats at prices ordinary people could afford. In 1870 he had got together with a number of friends and drawn up a plan for a company, run more or less as a collective, based at a theatre that would include not only a stage and an auditorium but a reading-room, a school, a tea-room and a dining-room. He eventually found a venue in the new building created for the Technical Exhibition in Moscow. He had no intention of putting on the cheap farces supposed to be the staple diet of the lower orders and the proper repertoire for 'popular' theatres. He wanted to produce classic plays such as *The Inspector General* or *Georges Dandin* which experience had shown working-class audiences enjoyed. True to Gogol's precepts he demanded a simple truthful ensemble acting from his company, without false declamation or exaggerated 'business'.

A major obstacle in his path was the state monopoly of theatres, deliberately designed to keep a tight grip on what was performed and to obstruct projects such as this. Eventually, after long and tortuous negotiations, the theatre was launched on June 4, 1872 with a programme which included *The Inspector General*. The choice of play was as much political as artistic; Gogol had once described the theatre as a platform from which to give a living lesson to the masses, a point the authorities were not slow to understand.

On July 10 Tsar Alexander III, who was visiting the exhibition, attended part of the performance. He arrived in the middle of Act II and left in the middle of Act III so that he might be in time for Gluck's *Orfeo*. On July 15 *The Inspector General* was banned. A confidential telegram to the Governor of Moscow stated that the play was not conducive to the public good. It did not fulfil the 'wholesome objectives for which popular peformances had been started, namely to mollify and ennoble the people's temper'. The theatre did not reopen after the summer break.

Not wishing to return to the Mali, Fedotov had readily accepted an offer to stage foreign-language performances in Petersburg only to find that the performances in question were not of plays but operetta. Despairing of even modest change in Russia, like so many intellectuals of the period, he left for Paris where he made a successful career. Now 46, though looking much older, he felt the time had come to return home and reestablish himself. He had no job to come back to, no offers from the Mali or any other imperial theatre. He would have to make his mark through amateur or semi-professional companies. Hence his invitation to Stanislavski whose name may well have been suggested to him by his son, Aleksandr.

Stanislavski has left no account of the rehearsals or the performance of *The Gamblers* which opened on February 6, 1888 but the impact of Fedotov's disciplined, rigorously professional methods was decisive in determining his own future development. For the first time he encountered a director with an organic sense of the structure and purpose of the play. Fedotov understood the dramatic function of individual characters and their contribution to the plot-line. He forbade self-indulgence and eliminated gratuitous effects. The company was unanimous that some way must be found of staying together though no one could see how it could be done.

After working with Fedotov, Stanislavski realized there could be no going back to old ways, that he could never again be satisfied with amateur methods. The Moscow Amateur Music Dramatic Circle was now no more than a temporary group with which to work.

While, for the most part, Stanislavski displayed the characteristic Alekseiev caution when it came to money, he was capable of extravagant gestures when his enthusiasm was aroused. Then it was all or nothing. As chance would have it, 1887–1888 had been an exceptionally profitable period for the Alekseiev factory and he suddenly found himself with 25–30,000 roubles more than he expected. It was the first time he had ever possessed such a sum and it went to his head. In the spring of 1888 he decided to spent it all on an ambitious scheme, which would bring together artists of all kinds – writers, musicians, painters, actors, – into an organisation which would be known as The Society of Art and Literature. Not only would the Society become the focal point of the arts in Moscow, it would be suitably accommodated. He rented the Ginzburg House on Tverskaia Street and proceeded to convert it into a luxurious clubhouse with a large stage and several exhibition rooms. The problem of meeting year-by-year running costs once his money had run out did not enter his mind.

Friends and relations did their best to discourage him. Glikeria Fedotova spelled out the difficulties he was bound to encounter but he attributed her warnings to resentment of her ex-husband. His cousin Nikolai was distinctly put out when, in order to have more free time, he resigned as Chairman of the Russian Music Society. To abandon so prestigious a post in favour of some hare-brained scheme was nonsensical. Young Kostia 'had something wrong up top' and, moreover, he was spending much less time at the factory than he should.

Stanislavski, Komissarzhevski and Fedotov began drafting the statutes both of the Society and of the School which was to be attached to it. As the Society and the School came under separate Ministries two sets of negotiations had to be conducted simultaneously. All three men were determined that the training the school offered would be systematic. Fedotov began work on a manual, setting out a rigorous, logical programme of study.

Stanislavski at the same time addressed the question of repertoire. His first thought was to open with an adaptation of Dostoievski's novella, *The Village of Stepanchikovo*. He had learned from Dostoievski's widow that her husband had originally conceived the work as a play but had decided finally that the material was too complex to be staged. He wrote to Dostoievskaia asking permission to create his own version and on March 7 received a favourable response. It was a bold and unexpected choice for an opener but his showman's instinct convinced him of the importance of making an impact. A Dostoievski première would be an event nobody could ignore.

While waiting for the script to be completed work began on the second play of the season, Pushkin's *The Miserly Knight*. Stanislavski was still basking in the afterglow of his evening of glory when he had appeared side by side with the great Ermolova. He had developed an entirely false idea of himself as a romantic actor in the Lenski mould. Excellent as Lenski was as an example of technical accomplishment and inner truth, he was a different type of actor altogether. Handsome Stanislavski certainly was – 'an Adonis' Knipper later called him – and attractive to women, but he was not a personality actor and was never good at playing himself. His admiration for certain dashing, swashbuckling singers did nothing to help him towards a more balanced view. Before rehearsals even began he decided that the character of the Knight would be based on Saint-Bris in Meyerbeer's opera, *Les Huguenots*, which he had seen at the Bolshoi. His complacency was shattered when he learned that Fedotov and the designer, Sollogub, intended him to play the part as a decrepit old man. Neither was prepared to listen to his objections. Both poked merciless fun at his conventional, 'theatrical' notions. It was, on the face of it, a surprising decision to ask a handsome 25-year-old to play a crumbling wreck of a man, yet it may be that Fedotov, with his wide experience, realized Stanislavski's potential as a character actor long before he did himself.

Fedotov was not interested in the bundle of imitative tricks Stanislavski had acquired over the years and so began what Stanislavski later described as 'a surgical operation' to cut away his theatrical airs and posturings. Fedotov suggested that they spend a night in the same room together. There, in his nightshirt Fedotov, who was already crooked and bent, with thinning hair, demonstrated how an old man moves. He outlined his interpretation of the play and the role. Stanislavski noted, copied and allowed himself to be more or less choreographed into the role, trying to achieve, by trial and error, a facsimile of what Fedotov demonstrated. Yet, despite his earlier work with Komissarzhevski he could not coordinate his thoughts and actions. When concentrating on the physical aspects of the role, he was reduced to a mechanical delivery of Pushkin's lines. When rehearsals came to an end for the summer break in May he was no nearer to a satisfactory solution and the conflict between his own idea of the part and Fedotov's was still unresolved.

The summer was overshadowed by a family tragedy. In June Stanislavski was called to a small village near Samarik where his brother Pavel, who was suffering from tuberculosis of the bone-marrow, was seriously ill. On June 10 he died, aged 20. The emotional impact on the close-knit Alekseiev family was considerable. Stanislavski was deeply marked by the incident. Tuberculosis was in the family and, in later years, he himself had to cope with the illness of his own son, Igor, and finance his treatment one way or another.

Stanislavski's characteristic reaction to grief was to travel. On July 3, with his brothers Boris and Georgi, he left for Vichy, stopping over in Petersburg, where he saw a performance of *Carmen*, Berlin and Paris. In Vichy, on the 22nd, he saw *Mademoiselle Nitouche* with Anna Judic, one of the family's favourites, in the lead.

His battle with *The Miserly Knight* continued. In a desperate attempt to get inside the role he reverted to one of his earlier experiments: living the role in real circumstances. He persuaded the proprietors of a château not far from Vichy to allow him to spend two hours alone locked up in its vast dungeons. The intention was to get the feel of the conditions in which the knight lived, to absorb the atmosphere. All he got was a cold. He ran the lines in the dark, among the scurrying rats, but the exercise seemed pointless. Lived experience does not transfer to the stage unless mediated by a creative, or a re-creative, process.

On July 28 he moved to Biarritz keeping up a regular correspondence with Komissarzhevski and with D. N. Popov who had been appointed as the Society's assistant administrator. On July 24 Komissarzhevski wrote outlining his ideas for the school and asked Stanislavski to find out all he could first about the rehearsal methods at the Comédie Française and, second, the teaching methods at the Conservatoire. Which subjects were taught and how much time was allotted to each of them? Stanislavski moved on to Paris and spent most of August and September observing classes and attending performances at the Comédie Française where he was impressed, once again, by the restrained acting style, the economy of gesture and the use of pauses. He was equally and less usefully taken with the elaborate bows and flourishes which accompanied Molière's comedies.

Popov wrote on August 3 describing the progress of the conversion work on the Society's premises and again on August 8 with the news that the day before the Ministry of the Interior had given permission for the Society to be set up. Permission for the School was granted by the Ministry of Education on September 29. The Society's Board was formed at the beginning of October, with Komissarzhevski as chairman, Fedotov as Deputy Chairman and Stanislavski as administrator and treasurer. Departmental Heads were nominated for each of the other sections, music, literature and design.

By now Stanislavski had changed his mind about the opening play for the season. He wrote to Zinaïda that he had now thought it best to put *Stepanchikovo* second and start with *The Miserly Knight* and another classic. *Georges Dandin* seemed the obvious choice. Two reasons dictated this change of mind. In the first place the script of *Stepanchikovo* had still not been submitted to the censor and was not, in fact, sent until October 13. It was presented under the title, 'The Village of Stepanchikovo and Its Inhabitants. Scenes in Three Acts from the Story by Dostoievski. Adapted for the Stage by K.A.' Twelve days later it was banned. This was the first of Stanislavski's many battles with the Tsarist censorship, which had the distinction of banning or mutilating, either for political or religious reasons, every major work of Russian literature in the nineteenth century. Even Pushkin's *Boris Godunov* was not played complete until after the Revolution. A second, more practical reason, was that Fedotov knew *Dandin* well and it was better for him to start with that than tackle a new and untried script with an inexperienced company.

The Society of Art and Literature was ceremonially inaugurated on November 3. All the intelligentsia were invited. Chekhov and Lenski were present. Two days later, on the 5th, the hundredth anniversary of the Shchepkin's birth was celebrated with readings from his works and lectures on his place and importance in the development of acting. The next day the *Moskovski Listok* reported that almost the entire company of the Mali had attended.

The school was already in operation, having opened on October 8. The atmosphere there was described as 'serious' and 'hard-working'. From time to time Stanislavski would attend Fedotov's acting classes and pass on some of the work he had seen at the Paris Conservatoire. He was particularly excited by exercises which required actors to play characters who were at contradiction with themselves – a queen who is, in fact, a beggar-woman who sells matches, a devoted wife who is forced to send her beloved husband to the war.

Yet while he was happy to pass on the knowledge he had acquired, he still had his own problems to solve. Rehearsals for the opening presentation, began in October. It had been decided finally to present a triple-bill consisting of excerpts from one of Fedotov's own plays, *The Miserly Knight* and *Georges Dandin*. The role of Claudine in *Dandin* was offered to Lilina after Stanislavski learned that she had recently been sacked from her job as a schoolmistress at the Catherine Institute for offending against good taste by appearing in public as an amateur actress.

Fedotov was as ruthless with the Molière as he had been with the Pushkin. Stanislavski arrived at the first rehearsal with the whole battery of tricks he had picked up during the summer. 'My God,' Fedotov remarked, 'you've brought the whole orchestration with you.' Out went the bows, the swoops, the flourishes, the whole Molière 'style'. In its place Fedotov wanted something much more difficult, the simple, relaxed playing he had learned from Shchepkin. But Stanislavski, like the young Shchepkin himself, could only offer a loud, rapid delivery accompanied by a multitude of gestures. He was, in truth, producing neither the best in French acting or in Russian. The most he was able to achieve, as he ultimately recognized, was a passable imitation of the role which Fedotov step-by-step demonstrated to him. He did not act on the basis of his own experience or on the observation of real-life models but on the basis of a reality mediated by Fedotov's personality and skill. What there was of himself in the part came, as was so often the case at this time, by accident. Right up to the first dress rehearsal he was caught between Fedotov's demands and his own natural inclinations until, while making up, he suddenly realized that his face looked silly. Everything fell into place. His own personality was released and the part came alive.

The Society's opening performance on December 8 was a glittering occasion with an audience of actors, artists, professors and dukes. Stanislavski scored a great personal success, a success that would not have been possible had he been no more than Fedotov's puppet. *The Miserly Knight* attracted the most attention. The critic of the *Novosti Dnia* reported:

'Until *The Miserly Knight*. . . . I did not know who this Mr Stanislavski was. When the curtain fell it was obvious to me that Stanislavski is a splendid actor, thoughtful, hard-working, with a great gift for dramatic roles.' (*Novosti Dnia*, December 14, 1888.)

The correspondent of the St Petersburg *Novoe Vremia* of December 17 admired his sincerity, his capacity to capture the right tone, his ability to wear costume, his elegant gestures and his talent for creating a real, living character. He was, the article added, although an amateur, 'obviously experienced and gifted and superior to the average Moscow professional'.

In his notes, Stanislavski set down his own reactions: a slow start in scene one, with too many long pauses, picking up in scene two, the monologue, with more fire and energy. But there was still the paradox he had experienced at his début in Liubimovka:

'It's strange, when you feel you are right inside it, audience reaction is not so good; when you are in control of yourself and don't let the part take you over, it is better. I am beginning to understand how a role moves forward. I have tested out the technique of acting without gestures (in the last scene there were only two). I know how to wear costume, I really feel that. My powers of physical expression are developing, I am beginning to understand pauses. Facial expression progressing. They say I died well, good body and truthfully'. (SS, V, p. 90.)

He noted the comments of the professionals on both the Pushkin and the Molière. Most, including Fedotova, were favourable and were able to point to passages where he had been technically and emotionally right. The next day he was the talk of the Mali.

Three days later he appeared as Ananias in Pisemski's *Bitter Fate*. The play was more or less thrown on in three rehearsals. Stanislavski just did as he was told although, like the rest of the company, he was convinced the evening would be a disaster. When he made his entrance on the first night he had no idea how to play Act One. The evening was nonetheless a success and in his *Notebook* he was able to point to real progress in his understanding of his craft:

'I remember that while I was acting I consciously considered where I wanted to hold back, where I wanted to pick up the level if it dropped. I watched the others. When it came to a dramatic passage I let fly for a few moments and got carried away. Only during the performance itself did I understand how to play Act One and I carried it off so well that I got four curtain calls. . . .

The second act went well and without a single gesture. The audience was amazed at the calm and truthfulness of the acting. . . .

The moment after the murder must have gone well. At least suddenly I pulled out a gesture I had never made in rehearsal and I felt that the audience went along with me.' (Ibid., p. 91.)

He was showered with compliments both during the intervals and after the performance. One enthusiastic critic called him a future Salvini.

He slowly relaxed into the part and began introducing spontaneous changes. On February 5 he noted progress both in emotional depth and technical control. The following day, at the barber's, he met the actor, Yuzhin whose wife had been at the performance:

'He said to me. . . . "Tell me, why don't you come to the Mali? It it your family circumstances?" I answered that I had no wish to be an insignificant artist and that I dare not compete with Yuzhin and Lenski. "What do you mean. The more good artists there are, the better."' (Ibid., p. 101.)

Flattering as the offer was, for the Mali whatever its shortcomings was still the foremost theatre in Russia, Stanislavski was right in feeling that, quite apart from the social problem to which Yuzhin referred, he was not ready to take the leap into full-time professional work. It was one thing to come up with one or two good performances under the watchful eye of a demanding but helpful director, another to perform regularly and in competition with other highly-experienced actors.

His technique was not yet secure and the battle with his romantic self-image was by no means won as his next important role demonstrated. In January the Society presented Pushkin's *The Stone Guest*, in which he played the minor role of Don Carlos. Prince Kugushev, who was playing Don Juan was evidently not up to it. The production had somehow to be rescued and Stanislavski was asked to take over. He prepared the part carefully and felt before the first rehearsal that he understood the text and what was needed. He loved himself in the role, peacocking about in front of the mirror, with his sword and shiny boots, going through the entire part to see how he looked physically. Parading about at home did not, however, necessarily produce a convincing performance. He consoled himself with the thought that even if he was not very good at least he would please the ladies, a remark which he immediately realized said little for his integrity as an artist. The ladies did indeed love him and that, as he had anticipated, was good for his self-esteem even if it did nothing for his acting. He asked his brother Vladimir to make notes on his performance and also asked Fedotova for her frank opinion. As usual she gave it.

'She took me to task for being too emotional and too theatrical. She said that the last two scenes should be taken more lightly, that I should show fake, not real, emotion – in a word, I should adopt the same tone I had used in the scene when I was waiting for Dona Anna in the graveyard. That scene, to use her own words, I had played perfectly, just like the scene with the Commendatore.' (Ibid., pp. 87–98.)

Fedotova's remarks stuck in his mind and when he next played the part on February 16 he changed his interpretation completely. On his way to the theatre he decided that Juan was no longer the fiery passionate suitor he had been but a man fascinated by women and interested only in deceiving them. He presented this new reading without rehearsal and without telling the rest of the cast. Their reactions are not recorded.

A few weeks after his flashy first appearance as Don Juan, Stanislavski made his breakthrough as an actor in Fedotov's play, *The Rouble*. He drew his characterization, as Obnovlenski, from his knowledge of the behaviour of his own class, the merchants and entrepreneurs of Moscow. He still had to wait for the dress rehearsal and the make-up for everything to come together but once on stage he felt that he had lived the role. He presented not the usual theatrical stereotype but a genuine, natural villain who could have been seen in any drawing-room in Moscow. He was in control. The pauses came easily and naturally. Fedotov realized that his pupil had finally found his feet, he was dependent no longer:

> 'You gave me great pleasure because this character was your own; it was *your* creation. In other interpretations it was just me playing.' (Ibid., p. 102.)

This new-found independence was demonstrated in his first production for the Society. In March he directed a one-acter, *Burning Letters*. He intended to reproduce the sober style he had seen in Paris, a style, which he assured the company, would be new to Russian audiences. He insisted that everything should be 'simple, natural, elegant and, above all, artistic'. The actors were not to push their voices. Critical and audience response was divided between the intelligentsia who were delighted, and the solid bourgeois who wanted the old, familiar approach. Nikulina, an actress from the Mali, was particularly pleased when one of the characters turned his back to the audience, an innovation unheard of at a time when everyone played out front. Stanislavski had noted as far back as March 1885:

> 'It is very truthful and life-like on stage when two people are talking in the doorway with their profile to the audience. . . .' (Ibid., p. 77.)

Reaction to his own performance was equally mixed but his reply was uncompromising: the actor's task is to educate an audience, not pander to its tastes for the sake of cheap success. There is a new note of seriousness in the voice and a new sense of purpose. The search for theatrical truth had become a moral issue. In a diary entry for April he noted his fear of falling victim to theatrical cliché, to routine. Yet what was 'routine'? What is the genuine theatricality? What is the difference between theatre and 'Theatre'? Was routine a particular, a conventional way of speaking and moving? Should there not be a distinction between that kind of convention and the essential, inescapable demands that the theatre, the performing space, by its very nature imposes and which distinguish it from real life? The problem was to transpose life, truth onto the stage without falling victim to routine but at the same time remaining, in the true sense, theatrical. It was a problem he had to solve if he was to make progress. He felt he had acquired a basic technique, a basic 'grammar' as he put it. An actor must be able to feel at home on stage and in front of an audience. He needs to be able to control his nerves, to develop self-confidence. This, by and large, he had done. But it was only a beginning:

'It seems to me. . . . my work is only just beginning, work for the intelligence and spirit, only now the creative process is beginning to open up the broad path to true nature. This is the task, to find that true nature. Of course that path is the most proper which leads to truth and life. To achieve it one must know what truth and life are. This then is my task: to study both. In other words, one must educate oneself, one must think, one must develop in the moral sense, one must keep pulling at one's intelligence.' (Ibid., p. 116.)

Stanislavski's contact with Fedotov had done more that revolutionize his acting technique. It had forced him out of the confines of the Alekseiev family and their friends into a wider world. As prominent members of the establishment the Alekseievs worked within the constraints of the prevailing order. Their interest in the arts was, in the non-pejorative sense of the word, dilettante, for pleasure. But to go beyond personal pleasure, to take the arts seriously in nineteenth-century Russia meant coming to terms with the nexus aesthetics-politics-morality-ethics. In a country where the discussion of politics was not possible, where, indeed, the names of dissident philosophers could not even be printed, literary and dramatic criticism became the vehicles whereby fundamental social issues were treated. In evaluating a work of art the content took precedence over form, since discussion of content, for those who understood the code, meant discussion of the political realities with which the work of art dealt.

Fedotov was a member of the intelligentsia, that group of artistically, intellectually and socially-aware people who came together, irrespective of social class, to form an élite whose task it was to modernize and liberalize a stagnant and repressive society. The word 'intelligentsia' had been coined by the polemicist and critic Vissarion Belinski and it was from him that Stanislavski derived his concept of the artist. Belinski dominated the intellectual life of his period. Gogol declared that his name was known in every village in Russia. Herzen and Turgenev left affectionate portraits of this difficult and choleric man who by the time he died in 1848 at the age of 37 had set the agenda for all discussion on the relationship between art and society for a century or more.

Belinski had a vision of the artist as missionary whose task was to declare the poetic nature of the world itself. Contemporary literature, written in an age of science, had to abandon the realm of myth and legend and the subjective expression of emotion to address itself to the problem of describing the world of external reality as it impinged on human consciousness and experience. To describe the sun as a natural phenomenon, a star travelling through infinite space rather than as Phoebus' chariot driving across the sky was not to abandon poetry as such but to exchange one kind of poetry for another, more mature kind – the poetry of the real. The role of the contemporary artist was to present the world 'in all its truth and nakedness'. The drama, Belinski noted, was less able to provide those significant touches of detail and local colour which the novel and the short story could offer.

Belinski demanded that the artist see the general in the particular. He must find the truth beneath the surface but in imaginative not in political terms: for while science and art tend to the same end, the improvement of society, they use different means which must not be confused. An economist may, by the use of statistics, convince the intellect that the condition of a particular social class has deteriorated but a novelist like Dickens, by appealing to the imagination, makes the reader feel that it is so:

'[the artist's] mind must penetrate to the heart of things; he must apprehend the secret motives which led the characters to act the way they did, he must understand the critical moments in events which make them unique, whole, complete, self-sufficient. Only a poet can do that. . . .' (Belinski SS, VIII, p. 359, Moscow 1982.)

[He must not] be the instrument of this or that party or of that sect, which might be ephemeral and disappear without trace, but the instrument of the profound and secret thoughts of a whole society, the instrument of aspirations of which they may only as yet be dimly aware. In other words, the poet should express not the particular and the contingent but the general and the necessary which give the age in which he lives its flavour and meaning.' (Ibid., p. 362.)

The artist thinks and works in images, not in philosophical concepts:

'In the final analysis [the artist] will be guided mainly, perhaps exclusively, by his instinct . . . the poet is only effective . . . as long as he follows . . . instinctively, unconsciously, the promptings of his own talent. As soon as he starts to reason and embarks on philosophy he trips and falls, indeed he does . . .!' (Ibid.)

Charged by nature with a sacred mission to speak for his times and for people as a whole the artist must, above all else, himself conform to the highest moral and ethical standards. He must not delude himself that he could live a devil and write like an angel. The truthful artist must be a truthful man.

In Belinski's philosophy Stanislavski found a moral justification for his own passion to perform and ideas which were consonant with his family's sense of social responsibility and the ethical standards by which he had been brought up. The humanitarian and libertarian values to which he was now committed went beyond his father's notions of philanthropy but stopped well short of a revolutionary ideology.

By the spring of 1889 he had formed a view of the theatre and its function that was a combination of ideas drawn from Belinski and Gogol. So much is evident from a letter he wrote on April 23 to Lilina, three days after he had set out his need for moral education in his diary. The two were playing opposite each other in Schiller's *Kabale Und Liebe*. The production was a great success and Stanislavski's dashing, elegant Ferdinand widely praised, producing fresh invitations to join the Mali. On the other hand, Lilina's simple, unaffected interpretation of Luisa was coolly received by the audience. This made Stanislavski angry. In an attempt to comfort her, he wrote a long letter on the mission of the artist in terms that come directly from Belinski. 'The artist' he wrote, 'is a prophet who appears on earth to bear witness to purity and truth. . . . He must be an ideal man'. His strictures on audiences also demonstrate a clear knowledge of Gogol's *Petersburg Notes* of 1836. An undiscriminating public, Stanislavski wrote, looking only for amusement or a chance to wallow in the mire of everyday life, destroys artistic ideals and reduces the theatre to a plaything. But a serious, thinking public finds satisfaction in the natural, the real. A noisy, spectacular success under those circumstances is to be treated with suspicion. It is no good looking to audiences for help or guidance if progress is to be made. They even begrudge paying proper prices for their seats. The best course for the true artist is constant self-criticism and dedication.

Few people were privileged to share Stanislavski's innermost thoughts in this way. Normally they were confided to the privacy of his diary and *Notebooks*. What he had written, in his own special way, was a declaration of love. Only someone who shared his ideals could share his life. Everyone in the cast of *Kabale Und Liebe*, watching the way the two acted together, realized how deep their affections ran. No one was surprised, therefore, when they were married at Liubimovka on July 5, 1889.

CHAPTER FOUR

SAXE-MEININGEN IN MOSCOW

Stanislavski and Lilina spent their honeymoon in Biarritz, returning to Moscow at the end of September. Stanislavski was as fortunate as his parents in his marriage. Lilina was a remarkable woman, always supportive yet never offering blind adulation, offering criticism where needed and going her own way artistically if she had to. They occupied the ground floor of the house at Red Gates in an apartment that was comfortable but not lavish, a curious mixture of stage-set and home. The thick wooden door to Stanislavski's study with its great iron studs had been taken from Sollogub's set for *The Miserly Knight*. Throughout his married life there was a continuous to and fro of furniture and objects from flat to theatre and back again.

While away Stanislavski had been studying a new role, Imshin in Pisemski's *A Law unto Themselves*. The role of an ageing general, betrayed by a lecherous brother and deceived by a young wife, was perhaps a curious one for a good-looking young man on his honeymoon but it did allow him to continue his exploration of the movement of old men begun in *The Miserly Knight*. He studied the effect of the removal of dentures on the speech mechanism. He started to develop Imshin's imperious, autocratic manner. He had taken the precaution however of providing himself with a photograph of Samarin who had played the role at the Mali probably because he was to work for the first time with a new director and was uncertain how much help he would get.

It had taken less than a year for jealousies and rivalries to appear at the Society. Komissarzhevski and Fedotov did not get on, each suspecting the other of receiving more favourable treatment, each demanding more time and money. Stanislavski bore the expense. In October, Fedotov resigned. His limitations as a director were becoming plain. He was excellent at dealing with comedy, especially French comedy, but he had no real feeling for serious drama. Riabov of the Mali was invited to replace him.

Stanislavski found Riabov less talented than Fedotov but no less exacting. He was stopped on every line which he found highly frustrating. Riabov shaped and coloured the whole interpretation. The result of their combined efforts was a performance of almost unremitting grimness. When the play opened on November 26 the audience found the evening hard-going but appreciated the actors' skill. Stanislavski scored a critical success. Riabov called him a 'gold-mine' and was reported by his son to have declared 'if you took Possart, Salvini and Rossi and rolled them into one they would not amount to half a Stanislavski.'

Others were more critical. Fedotova, as was her wont, poked gentle but pointed fun at him:

'We adored you, my dear. You played beautifully, my dear fellow. Such wild animals, these autocrats. Such stupid people! You know, I have a watch-dog just like that, he gets angrier and angrier and then suddenly stops. . . . It's not easy to play tragedy. . . . I was so frightened! Thank you, my dear, dear boy, but watch your voice.' (SS, V, p. 566.)

Riabov had to agree finally that the performance had been all on one note.

How then, Stanislavski asked himself, is an actor to find light and shade within the broad lines of an interpretation? He found the answer to this problem, as it were, under his nose. In *My Life in Art* he relates that he attended rehearsals for one of the Society's other productions in which he was not involved. He found a certain monotony in his colleagues' work and he realized that if a role calls for a great deal of weeping you must do something other than weep. There must be a counterbalancing element. It was at this moment, he states, that he formulated his famous dictum: when you play a villain look for what is good in him, when you play a good man look for what is evil in him. Not for the last time his memory appears to have played him false. His notes suggest that he only arrived at this principle of opposites many years later when recalling comments Fedotova had made to him. The more Stanislavski worked on the role of Imshin, and the more he thought about the production, the more pedestrian it appeared. When the play was given again on December 6 he had redirected it completely.

Still determined to stage his adaptation of *Stepanchikovo*, he had reworked, changed the name to *Foma* and, on the advice of friends, altered the names of the central characters in an effort to disguise the work still further. The script was resubmitted to the censor on December 16, 1889 and passed the following January. Dostoievski's name, however, still worried the authorities, for although his early radicalism had long since changed to religious conformity he remained politically suspect right up to his death. They insisted that the work appear as Stanislavski's own. Stanislavski refused to lend himself to such a paltry deception and, when the play was performed, no author's name appeared on the posters. Everyone, in any case, knew who the real author was. At the end of February Stanislavski sent the revised script to Dostoievskaia and received her final approval on April 10. He was less fortunate with his own one-acter, *Monaco*, which he had submitted to the censor at the same time as *Foma*. It was banned.

Stanislavski's final role of the season, Paratov in Ostrovski's *The Girl Without a Dowry*, obliged him to recognize finally that he was a character actor. Paratov is a Don Juan type, an obvious temptation for him once more to indulge in superficial swaggering as in *The Stone Guest*. Only by creating a character other than himself could he avoid the obvious pit-falls. To be a personality actor one must have absolute confidence, on stage at least, in oneself. He had no such confidence. He was not entirely certain he liked himself. His struttings and posturings were a front. His deep-seated natural reserve prevented him from exploiting his own personality. He needed the protection of another individual's identity and the mask of make-up.

'Deprived of the typical characteristics of a role I felt completely naked on stage and it was pure embarrassment for me to stand in front of an audience as myself, so shamelessly exposed.' (SS, I, p. 125.)

The highly-charged condemnation of the personality actor which accompanies his account of this role in *My Life in Art* is a product of his later crusading zeal rather than his thinking at the time.

His resolution never again to indulge in egotistical display was reinforced when in April 1890 the company of the Duke of Saxe-Meiningen came on its second tour to Russia. Stanislavski had, unaccountably, not seen them on their first tour five years earlier. They brought a repertoire of Shakespeare and Schiller *Julius Caesar*, *The Merchant of Venice*, and *Twelfth Night*, *Die Verschwörung Des Fiesco*, *Wallensteins Tod*, and *Der Jungfrau Von Orleans*. Stanislavski prepared himself by rereading Shakespeare. He appears to have ignored Schiller.

The Meiningen company was a director's company. In March 1885 Ostrovski had recorded that he had attended a performance of *Julius Caesar* but he had seen neither *Caesar* nor Shakespeare but a well-drilled group of actors who were essentially nondescript and often cast merely because they resembled the characters they played. It was the crowd scenes which impressed. The extras were as strong as the leads. Here was an ensemble of clock-work precision. Much of the impact, however, came from the lighting and sound. Any well-equipped theatre, he remarked, could do the same. But the Imperial Theatres were not so equipped and much of the asperity of his remarks may be due, in part at least, to his inability to push through the reforms he wanted.

Stanislavski later denied that the acting was as mediocre as Ostrovski had claimed but there is no doubt that the interest for him lay less in the performances than in the production style. The Meininger, for all their limitations, offered a coherent approach. Everything hung together. The sets, costumes and props were historically accurate and, while Ostrovski and Lenski may have found this concern with authenticity excessive and not necessarily theatrical, it was a salutary corrective to prevailing Russian practice where the same stock sets and stereotyped costumes were brought out time and time again. What the Meininger demonstrated was the artistic level even a mediocre group of performers could achieve if properly drilled and presented in productions that were through-designed.

Stanislavski went to the theatre armed with notebooks and pencils. He made sketches and recorded his impressions. He was particularly struck by the use of off-stage sound, as in *Der Jungfrau Von Orleans* where the illusion of a battle was created by two or three actors with trumpets blaring in the background. In *Fiesco*, Act Four scene seven, he noted, the entry of each character was preceded by distant knocking, the bass voice of the sentry, a response, the officer's voice, stating 'Advance', the opening of the gates and chains being dragged over a stone floor. Once the character had made his entrance there was the noise of the gates being relocked. Dramatic tension was increased by the way in which the on-stage characters listened, in silence, to the off-stage action. The impression created was of real space, in a real world, in real time.

Of *The Merchant of Venice* Act Two scene four he noted:

'The gondolas run very smoothly on rails. One gondola sets off, is stopped by people standing on a bridge. It returns. Conversation between the people on the bridge and the people in the gondola. Characters appear, for the most part in gondolas. Finale – carnival. The people riding in the gondolas ask for money.' (K.S. Archive.)

Reminiscences of this moment occur, forty years later, in his production plan for *Othello*.

Stanislavski was fascinated by the personality of the Meininger's director, Chronegk. Autocratic, precise, he marshalled his company like a military commander. Rehearsals were orderly, beginning and ending precisely on time. Discipline was absolute. An actor who arrived late found that his part had been given to someone else, while he was assigned elsewhere. Chronegk drilled and timed everything to a split second. No variations were allowed. It was thus possible to cover up the deficiencies of the actors. They had merely to execute the set pattern. Seeing Chronegk look at his watch and begin work exactly on the hour Stanislavski was reminded of his childhood when he would do the same to his piano teacher.

Much has been made of the influence of the Meininger on Stanislavski, perhaps too much. He never denied his debt, or the fact that his own method as a young director, working with inexperienced casts, was modelled on Chronegk, but the impact was something less than a theatrical Road to Damascus. What Stanislavski found was a working tool that would help him along the path he was already travelling. The vague ideas he had, the sketchy notions, the 'dreams' of staging Gounod's *Faust* were crystallized with diamond-like precision by the Meininger. His ideas were not so much radically changed as pushed several steps further. The task that remained was to bring together the creative, imaginative actor as defined by Shchepkin and Gogol and the organically-conceived production as staged by the Meininger.

On May 1 his first child Xenia, who had been born in March, died of pneumonia. The effect was devastating. In June he and Lilina retreated to Liubimovka, spent three weeks in Finland in July and in October went down to the Caucasus. They did not return to Moscow until the beginning of November.

The Society of Art and Literature was now in serious financial difficulties. Subscriptions did not cover costs and Stanislavski could not go on endlessly subsidizing its activities out of his own pocket. All his 30,000 roubles had been spent. Some members, mainly the painters, had already left. They had objected to being pressed into painting sets for the Society's productions when all they wanted to do was play cards.

Stanislavski resisted the obvious temptation to wind up the whole enterprise and found a compromise solution. The house on Ginzburg Street was taken over by the Sporting Club. The Society's school and music section had to close but the theatre company survived and was allowed access to the stage on condition that it put on a play a week. This was a treadmill and far from ideal but Stanislavski was forced to admit that it gave the company much needed experience in tackling a variety of roles and increased their confidence on stage. The Society gave its last performance at Ginzburg Street on January 3, 1891. On the night of January 10 the building burned down.

Stanislavski decided the time had come to take full control both of repertoire and production. His first choice was Tolstoi's *The Fruits of Enlightenment* which the censor had just passed for performance. He approached the production methodically, casting with great care, preparing everything in advance, planning all the moves and drilling his cast in true Meininger fashion until they got it right. His account of the play dates from November 1891, ten months after the opening performance. In it he refers confidently to 'my usual production method' which included close work with individual actors who were having difficulty.

Stanislavski was now concerned with more than the quality of individual performances. He wanted the production to show the pattern of social relationships. He saw three distinct strata, like the storeys of a house – gentry, peasants and servants – whom he wanted played not according to established theatrical stereotypes but truthfully, as in life. He did not find his own characterization as Zvezdintsev easy. While adept at playing the very old, he discovered, as Fedotov had once told him, that it is more difficult, to play a middle-aged man than an old one. The physical difficulties of the aged are more obvious and easy to demonstrate. The production was awaited with considerable interest. On January 29 the *Novosti Dnia* reported:

'The amateur Society of Art and Literature is preparing the play very thoroughly. They have already had ten rehearsals and intend to have the same number more.'

In the event there were fourteen or fifteen rehearsals.

The opening night, February 8, was a triumph both for the production and Stanislavski's own performance. In his review in *Novosti Dnia* on the 10th, Nemirovich-Danchenko said it was the finest amateur performance he had seen. Indeed, had he not been told he was watching amateurs he would not have believed it. Here was ensemble acting, *intelligent* acting. The *Moskovski Listok* of February 16 reported:

'A brilliant future awaits [the Society] if in its future activities it follows the path it has taken in its presentation of this play of L. N. Tolstoi.'

As to Stanislavski's own performance:

'This talented artist carried through his difficult role so thoughtfully, so truthfully that his whole interpretation emerged as a great *chef d'oeuvre* of dramatic art.' (*Moskovskaia Illustranovannaia Gazeta*, February 12, 1891.)

Nemirovitch wrote:

'If I were the theatre editor I would devote a whole article to him as would many others. He put so many subtle details into the role. . . .'

In December of the same year the same play was staged by the Mali; writing to his friend Suvorin in March 1892, Chekhov noted, 'they say these amateurs played *Fruits* far better than it is currently being performed at the Mali.'

The Society's final performance for the season took place on February 18 and a fancy-dress ball was given on March 2. In April, Komissarzhevski, having no real function any longer, left the Society. Glikeria Fedotova agreed to become Chairman of the Board and quickly introduced stricter standards of professional discipline. During the Lent break Anna Judic returned to Moscow once more with a season of operetta at the Paradiz Theatre. In May, Duse was on tour with Dumas' *La Dame aux Camélias*, Shakespeare's *Anthony and Cleopatra* and Sardou's *Odette*. The summer was a period of private happiness following the birth on July 21 of a second daughter, Kira.

In the new season Stanislavski fulfilled his ambition to stage *Stepanchikovo* (*Foma*) which opened on November 14. He found the production rewarding from every point of view. He felt a natural affinity with the role of Rostanev (Uncle), a man hounded on one side by a mother whose approval he cannot win and duped on the other by the Tartuffe-like figure of

Foma who gradually takes control materially and morally of the entire household. In Dostoievski's grotesque satire it is gentle, mild-mannered, much-put-upon Uncle, who finally in an outburst of rage drives Foma from the house only to relent and readmit him to the fold.

The technical challenge of the role was to pull violent emotion 'out of the bag', with no build-up. The December number of *Artist* was particularly impressed by Stanislavski's skill in negotiating the double transition from a mild-mannered almost spineless character to a figure of towering animal-like fury and back again. The *Artist* also noted the accuracy of the sets and costumes which conveyed the Russia of the 1830s. It was better than the Mali.

Critics noted, though not with universal approval, Stanislavski's use of silences, or, as he called them, 'vibrant pauses'. At the end of Act Two he delayed the curtain:

'The stage remains empty for some time. A shaft of moonlight picks out the edge of a bench on which a forgotten scrap of paper is lying. Aleksandr snuffs out the candle and there is total silence, broken only by the distant sound of late-night merry-makers and occasional trills from a nightingale. Somewhere, far off, a night-watchman reminds us of his presence with his rattle, then once again silence falls after a particularly turbulent day, with the expectation of storms to come. . . .' (K. S. Stanislavski, p. 514, Moscow 1955.)

The influence of the Meininger is evident but there is a significant difference. The Meininger effects were grandiose. What Stanislavski introduces are the ordinary, mundane elements of life, common sights and sounds which, Belinski had noted, gave prose literature its distinctive quality but were absent from drama. Stanislavski uses the theatre and its technical possibilities as an instrument of expression, a language, in its own right. The dramatic meaning is in the staging itself.

The critic Nikonov, writing in the paper *Razvlechenie* on December 1, noted that it was a pity that Stanislavski's talent was denied to the imperial theatres. His was one of many voices now urging Stanislavski to turn professional, but he was again made aware of the limitations of acting technique when in March of the following year he participated for the first time in a full-length professional production at a benefit performance of Nemirovich-Danchenko's play *The Lucky Man* for the actor Levitski. It was to be given first in Riazan on the 23rd and then four days later at Red Gates. The only amateurs in the cast were Stanislavski and Fedotova's son, Aleksandr. The rest, including Fedotova herself and Sadovski, were almost all members of the Mali where the play was already in the repertoire. Although familiar with the play they set about rehearsal with a business-like professionalism, a commitment and a degree of energy which Stanislavski found difficult to match. He had never been required to work on a daily basis, maintaining a regular level of competence, controlling his imaginative and emotional resources at will. He tried to bluff his way through, pretending to understand when he was, in fact, completely bewildered. He confided his difficulties to Fedotova who told him kindly but firmly that he was a mess, albeit a talented and promising mess, but a mess all the same. He had to improve his working method by more regular contact with professionals. She passed on one or two key notions that she had learned from Shchepkin. He must not work in isolation. He must look into the eyes of the person he was speaking to. He must never lose vital touch with the other people on stage.

As the rehearsal period drew to a close he became a bundle of nerves. He travelled to Riazan on the 22nd. He spent a sleepless night and could not eat anything the next day. As he reached the theatre his legs were giving way beneath him. As usual he was critical of his own performance: Act One was under-energized, Act Two sagged in the middle and in Act Three he had another attack of nerves and lost control. He was, as he wrote in his *Notebook*, not at all happy with his début with actors of the Mali. Fedotova told him that the beginning and end of Act Two were good. Other colleagues and friends, who were not necessarily uncritical, thought highly of his performance. As one wrote to Lilina:

'Tell Konstantin Sergeievich not to be down-hearted or to imagine he was a failure. Everyone I know is in raptures over his performance.' (SS, V, p. 576.)

Wisely, he preferred to believe Fedotova.

On April 3 he and Lilina travelled to Lyon partly for pleasure but mainly to buy new machinery for the factory. They stopped over in Warsaw, Vienna and Mulhausen, reaching Lyon in May. Stanislavski surprised himself when he discovered a genuine interest in the machines he was shown and congratulated himself on having done a good job as a buyer. He stopped over in Paris on the return journey but saw little of interest outside the Comédie Française and the can-can which he saw for the first time. He arrived back in Moscow on May 14 to find Aleksandr Fedotov waiting on the station platform. There was a crisis. A performance of *The Happy Man* was scheduled to be given by the Mali at the Civic Theatre in Yaroslavl. Yuzhin, who was playing Bogucharov had fallen ill. Could Stanislavski take over? He travelled to Yaroslavl immediately and went on without a rehearsal.

The Society's new season could not offer comparable excitement. It consisted mainly of revivals performed for the most part in the Sporting Club's new premises. 1893, too, was a fallow period artistically. Family concerns predominated. On January 17 Stanislavski's father, Sergei Vladimirovich, died, and in March his cousin Nikolai was assassinated, gunned down outside the Town Hall, not for political reasons but as an act of personal revenge by a jealous fiancé. Stanislavski was now in charge of the family firm and realized that some reorganization was necessary. New plant was needed and this, given the poor state of Russian technology, had to be imported from abroad. In April he returned with Lilina to Lyon to look at the latest developments in textile machinery. On their return he negotiated a merger between the Alexeiev and another company, P. Vishniakov and A. Shamshin. This did not receive government approval until January of the following year.

This unwelcome period of exclusive attention to business was relieved by a meeting on October 29 with Lev Tolstoi. Stanislavski was so overawed that he was scarcely able to utter a word. He felt that he had appeared totally stupid. This was a characteristic response to great men of letters whom he regarded with almost religious awe. And, indeed, to come into Tolstoi's presence was to encounter a mixture of a saint and a demi-god. Tolstoi is the final great influence on Stanislavski's views on aesthetics. In 1898 he published his essay, *What Is Art?* in which he advanced the notion that a work of art must be immediately intelligible and of moral use to simple, unsophisticated minds, without the need for commentary or explanation. It must be 'transparent'. This led him to a number of extreme conclusions. Many classic writers, Shakespeare included, were found wanting and consigned to oblivion. Nonetheless the idea of 'transparent action' became central to Stanislavski's thinking and he consistently opposed theatre which revealed its truth to theatre which proclaimed its message.

The following February the Society mounted a production of Ostrovski's *The Last Sacrifice*. Reviewing the production on the 22nd, the *Moskovski Vedomosti* saw the Society as the one bright spot in an otherwise depressing theatrical landscape. The Mali appeared to be in terminal decline. Shortly afterwards Stanislavski was invited to make a guest appearance in Nizhni-Novgorod playing opposite Ermolova in a special performance of *The Girl Without a Dowry*. This was the most significant tribute so far to his talent and he collected excellent notices for a performance distinguished for its fire, precision and originality. No one now thought to mention the fact that he was an amateur. The word no longer had any meaning.

The Society, or what was left of it, still had no permanent home and during the summer Stanislavski began negotiations with the Sporting Club. Confident now in his reputation and his mission as artistic director, he was prepared to lay down a number of essential demands. In early August he wrote a long letter to the Sporting Club's directors pointing out that artistic results could only be achieved through efficient management and discipline. He required better working conditions than he had enjoyed so far and he required respect. A performance needed to be accompanied by a sense of occasion. If the theatre was to be more than a bear-garden and fulfil its civilizing mission, actors, technicians and audience had to approach a performance in the right frame of mind.

'. . . can you play any kind of serious part when not a yard away from an actor who is trying to get into the mood there is a door creaking and his voice is drowned by the shuffling feet of members of the audience still coming in? Can one surrender to the mood when a step away from the people acting on stage there are drunken technicians stamping about, whispering or openly swearing at each other? If an actor cannot believe in his feeling under such conditions what can you expect of the audience who can see nothing of what is happening on stage because of the stream of people going in and out and hear nothing because of the shuffling feet and creaking door?' (SS, VII, p. 86.)

He detailed the kind of equipment he wanted and the conditions under which rehearsals and performances were to be conducted. He insisted that once the curtain had gone up no one was to be admitted until the interval, an ambition he was only to achieve at the Moscow Art Theatre and even then not immediately. The letter is an advance warning of what he would require when he had the requisite power.

On September 14, his son, Igor, was born just as Stanislavski started work on his most ambitious production to date, *Uriel Acosta*, a now-forgotten play set in the Jewish quarter of Amsterdam in the seventeenth century. It is the story of an intellectual outsider, Acosta, and his battle with the rigid mentality of his community.

It was a bold choice. The play was immensely popular and had long been in the repertoire at the Mali, with Lenski and Ermolova in the lead roles. Stanislavski knew what he was taking on. The Society's productions had often been compared favourably with the Mali's but *Acosta* would be a trial of strength. Stanislavski was now inviting open comparison with the idol of his youth, Lenski.

Work began immediately after Igor's birth and went on into the new year. The company was drawn from the worlds of business and education. Rehearsals began in the evening after work and went on until midnight. One observer described them as sheer torture. Stanislavski was now the complete director-dictator. Every word, every gesture was criticized, repeated, discussed. Nothing, not the most minute detail, was allowed to deviate from the prepared production plan. Thus, the crowd scene in Act Two:

'As the curtain rises there is a noise of high spirits. Everyone on stage must laugh 3 times. Those entering bow to the ladies. The gentlemen offer their arms to the ladies who place their hands on them near the elbow. Those entering bow to Manasse. They offer both hands. They talk to him. The conversation lasts 10 seconds. Absolutely no gestures. *Cue for silence when N. D. Popov and A. S. Shteker quit the rostrum and go off. . . .* the crowd must be reminded not to stop talking all at once and to disperse on different sides. Music as soon as N. D. Popov and A. S. Shteker have gone. After 15, 20 seconds. . . . Simon and Manasse come right down stage. . . .' (*Uriel Acosta* Production Plan, K.S. Archive.)

In order to avoid the somewhat mechanical acting of the Meininger crowds Stanislavski gave every extra specific dialogue drawn either from the script itself or rhythmically consistent with it. There was to be no rhubarb, rhubarb. Conversations were established in couples or small groups followed by moments when the entire stage was gripped by silent emotion. All gestures were strictly choreographed.

The first dress rehearsal was not without its comic side. When the cast appeared in costume for the first time they were a sorry sight, 'a motley collection of ragamuffins' Stanislavski called them, as useless as a row of coat-hangers. By 4 a.m. he had transformed them, thanks to a painstaking series of individual demonstrations, into an authentic-looking group of seventeenth-century Dutch Jews.

Acosta, perhaps, established the myth that all the props in Stanislavski's productions were real. Certainly Stanislavski's insistence on accuracy, his excursions inside and outside Russia to buy materials, clothes and furniture could easily give rise to such a notion. But the fact was that much of what appeared on stage, if only for reasons of cost, was created in the props-room. The 'authentic' goblets which caused such excitement at the time, were made of gas-brackets and wood.

Acosta was the first of Stanislavski's productions to be analysed by the critic Nikolai Efros, who was to chronicle the artistic development of the Society and then the Moscow Art Theatre for 25 years. He was always very open in his criticisms and in the early years Stanislavski resented his comments deeply suspecting him, without just cause, of personal animosity. Writing years later, Efros noted that the historical authenticity of the production went beyond surface detail to the very psychology of a closed Jewish community:

'. . . you could feel the Hebrew way of life, dominating, swamping the personality, the binding force of centuries-old tradition of religious and national fanaticism.' (Nikolai Efros, *The Moscow Art Theatre*, pp. 68–9, Moscow 1923.)

In his review in January 1885 he noted the terrifying impact when Acosta is torn limb from limb by an angry mob:

'. . . the fiendish delight of the crowd which cannot endure 'exceptional intelligence' grew; passions flared, a single, wild emotion seized the crowd, thirst for revenge on this audacious madman. And when Acosta, unable to endure the shameful rite of recantation to the very end, ran back into the synagogue shouting that everything he had just been reading was a lie, the frenzy of the crowd reached its uttermost limit and toppled over into *delirium*, into some sort of collective madness. The crowd rushed at the man who had dared oppose it and tore him to pieces ... It was frightening to be sitting there in the theatre.' (N. Efros, *Artist* January 1895.)

The careful orchestration had not restricted the display of emotion.

Praise for the production was almost universal but Stanislavski's own performance was criticized. It ran counter to the accepted interpretation of the character established by Lenski. Lenski opted for the sublime, concentrating on the expression of poetic feeling. His Acosta was a dreamer, a man set apart, a transcendental being. Stanislavski, on the other hand, was more low key, concentrating on the human dilemma. Efros found this difficult to take and said so, laying the foundations of Stanislavski's dislike of him. This Acosta:

'... was neither a philosopher nor a thinker for whom the truth of ideas is above everything else and for whom the contemplation of truth is the highest pleasure ... on the contrary, before us stood a man who was oppressed by his own reputation as an outcast and did not bear it with pride, someone who even had doubts about the probity of his conduct – not his ideas but precisely his conduct. It was as though someone had loaded an impossible burden on his back, which he had to bear, whether he would or no, to the bitter end.... The finer qualities of the hero disappeared in such an interpretation; his halo was tarnished.' (Ibid.)

This 'tarnished halo' upset other people. Stanislavski was accused of creating a 'non-hero', of failing to exploit his own dramatic gifts. Other critics, however, responded positively:

'Most people were disappointed because for all the means he has at his disposal to make Acosta a hero, Stanislavski did not do so.... This condemnation of the non-heroic which Stanislavski offers springs from intellectually short-sighted attitudes, backward thinking where everything that is old and hackneyed seems great and everything that is rational, living, fresh is a failure and to be rejected....' (S. Dudishkin, *Russki Listok* January 13.)

Fedotova was overwhelmed. According to Stanislavski's mother she wept uncontrollably during the performance. Afterwards, she went up to the dressing-room, called Stanislavski out to her, and kissed him repeatedly.

Nothing Stanislavski had done before had provoked such controversy. Earlier criticism had been concerned with technical competence not with basic interpretation. Now, with his performance in this role Stanislavski nailed his colours to the mast and challenged received ideas.

The intellectual origins of this new challenge may well lie in Belinski. In an article on the Russian short story, written in the mid-1830s Belinski made a radical distinction between drama which is a lyrical outpouring of the poet's own personal feeling and drama which is dictated by the outer form and inner logic of the character's behaviour. He took as an example the long tirade which Karl Moor delivers, in Schiller's *Die Raüber*, over his father's body:

'Some people. . . . say that a man in Karl Moor's situation, when he speaks to the brigands about his father, would have found one or two words sufficient rather then a long speech. I think he would not have uttered a single word but simply shown his father in silence. . . . In actual fact it is not the character who is speaking but the writer: this work does not contain the truth of life but the truth of feeling; there is neither reality or drama but a deep well of poetry; attitudes are false, situations unnatural but the feeling is correct and the thought profound. . . . Karl Moor's speech cannot be considered as the ordinary, natural expression of a character in a real situation but as an ode, designed to express anger. . . .' (Belinski, SS, I, pp. 147–8 Moscow 1976.)

In making this radical distinction, Belinski set out one of the modern actor's greatest problems: how to resolve the contradiction between the stylistic demands of a rhetorical text and the obligation to present plausible, probable behaviour. Stanislavski attempted to achieve such a resolution with his still more controversial next role, Othello.

Othello had haunted him ever since he had seen Salvini play it. It was a hurdle he had to jump. The whole production was intended as a vehicle for himself. He wanted to shine, to demonstrate his virtuosity as director, actor and designer in a classic play.

He spent the summer as usual at Liubimovka, working on the production plan. A reading of Shlosser's *Universal History* convinced him that he should give the Cyprus scenes an oriental flavour as the island had been for so long under Turkish domination. When the plan was ready he invited a few friends down so that he could outline his ideas to them. Nikolai Popov registered it as an important event in Stanislavski's development as a director. He went through the whole play in a completely different way, not relying on the text as such, with quotes from important speeches, not providing a 'literary' explanation, but speaking in terms of the play's dynamic, its action, the thoughts and feelings of the protagonists, the world in which they lived. His account flowed uninterruptedly from moment to moment.

Stanislavski decided to create his own designs to ensure his concept of the play's dynamic was carried over into the action. He showed his colleagues a rough model representing the eastern quarter of the town. A number of narrow streets ran into a small square. Houses with flat roofs, two storeys high, were piled on top of each other. On the roofs were lines of ragged washing, tubs with trees in them, carpets and rush mats.

Just how this set was used is illustrated in the production plan for Act Two scene three:

'A shot, then a single cry, shouting grows, clash of sabres. All leap up, music stops, Noise and shouts. All run on stage. There the shouting grows stronger. Trumpets. Bells ringing. Soldiers run from the palace. Turks run on from the wings left and off up the street right. Noise fades.

The stage is empty. Rodrigo runs down the street right, no sword, crying help with all his might. Cassio runs after him, carrying a sword. Iago who has hidden himself at the street corner near the turning on the left, stops Cassio, Montano overtakes him and also restrains Cassio.

Another shot, trumpets, shouts off-stage grow louder. Soldiers run down the street right and hide at the angle of one of the houses. Left a group of Turks runs in and collides with them. A fight. At the climax Othello's powerful voice is heard and he rushes into the midst of the mêlée.' (Production Plan, K.S. Archive.)

Stanislavski went to Paris in August to buy books on costume and select material for Desdemona's outfits. There he had a chance encounter reminiscent of his meeting with the young foreigner at the Mali. Seated at a café terrace was a handsome Arab in full robes. Stanislavski engaged him in conversation and invited him to dinner. During the meal he was able to observe his guest's movements and gestures. He was even allowed to try on his robe. Back at his hotel half the night was spent in sheets and bath-towels reproducing the pattern of physical behaviour he had observed. Thus Othello the 'Moor' was born. In early October, after a stay in Biarritz, Stanislavski visited Venice where he bought rapiers, chain-mail, leg-padding and hats, and made copious notes and architectural sketches. He saw the interaction of canals and buildings which gives Venice its special character. The stage direction for Act One scene one reads:

'Curtain. Ten seconds. The distant chime of a bell or clock. A peal of bells, Five seconds. The distant splash of an approaching boat. Rodrigo and Iago enter right, in a gondola. . . .' (Ibid.)

The set, however, with its canal crossed by a bridge, owes as much to the Meininger set for *The Merchant of Venice* as to his own drawings.

Rehearsals began immediately after his return on October 16. The production plan was detailed and elaborate, with the text marked up in different colours in a code to which the key has been lost. Stanislavski was well aware that everything depended on the quality of the production and not on the modest talents of the cast. Busy as he was with other productions – notably a much-improved revival of *A Law Unto Themselves* – with his business and his family, he needed quick results. Those who could not deliver the goods had to be dragooned into doing what he wanted. He had not yet acquired the ability to draw out performances from his actors. When all else failed he followed the old dictum: when an actor is weak, create a diversion. His Iago, although a professional, was just such a case. During one of his more important soliloquies he found himself practically unlit while Stanislavski brought on a doorkeeper with a lantern to distract the audience's attention from a tedious moment.

The play opened on January 19 and was received with almost universal acclaim. Efros commented:

'I do not offend against truth if I say that Moscow has never witnessed such a production of this Shakespeare play. The décor, props, costumes were distinguished by great taste, originality, living truth and, so experts in these matters tell me, absolute historical accuracy.' (*Novosti Dnia*, February 2, 1896.)

The twenty-two-year-old Meierhold noted in his diary on January 29:

'The Society of Art and Literature's production of *Othello* made a great impression on me. Stanislavski has enormous talent. I have never seen such an Othello, not even Rossi. . . . The ensemble is splendid. Really, every minor role lives on stage.

Meierhold's positive assessment of Stanislavski's performance was shared by other critics, in contradiction to what Stanislavski writes in *My Life in Art*. He was dissatisfied with his voice which did not have the range, pitch and flexibility demanded by the text. The vocal mechanism gave way under pressure just as it had in opera and his obsession with this difficulty clouded his reaction to the whole performance. For his contemporaries, however, it was the deep psychological realism which mattered:

'It is a long time since I have experienced the aesthetic pleasure which Stanislavski provides at the beginning of Act Four, at the moment where he is listening to Iago's slanders yet still not believing them. As far as I can remember everyone who has played Othello, apart from Salvini, starts to shout at this point and plays the 'hero'. Stanislavski at this point was simply a man. He listened to Iago but his soul, the soul of a child, was still calm. He adores his Desdemona, he speaks tenderly about her clothes, her desire to please. . . . He is just a man. This is magnificent. What you see is not the way jealousy takes hold of his soul all at once but how passion, little by little, takes possession of his whole being.' (V. Marov, *Russki Listok*, January 22, 1896.)

The shadow of Salvini certainly hung over the performance, his legendary restraint and his barely audible *andiamo* which reduced audiences to jelly. But another influence is discernible here, Lenski. Stanislavski had mastered his capacity for conveying the slow, inward progress of an emotion which only gradually expresses itself in outward, physical terms.

The judgement that mattered to Stanislavski was that of Ernesto Rossi who saw the play on January 22 and applauded warmly. The next day he sent a congratulatory note 'to the amateurs who discharged their roles with the intelligence and love of real artists.' Encouraged by this, Stanislavski called on him a few days later, in the hope of receiving more detailed criticism. Rossi cut through the elaborate paraphernalia of the production; this was a useful device to conceal the weaknesses of the cast but an unwelcome distraction when it came to actors of talent, such as Stanislavski himself. Rossi was tactful and judicious, suggesting that Stanislavski was not perhaps quite ready for the great classic roles. He had considerable ability but 'there must be art. That will come of course.' Where, Stanislavski asked, was he to learn this art? Rossi answered, if there was no great teacher available – and there was none – he would have to teach himself.

Rossi had indicated the next crucial step in Stanislavski's development as an actor. In avoiding the pit-falls of personality acting, in opting for the 'mask' behind which he could hide, he had become nothing but the mask. He had developed a polished external technique and knew how to calculate his effects but what he offered on stage was a shell. Something deeper was required: the integration of the actor's personality into the role and the release of personal, creative energy so that actor and character became indistinguishable.

Stanislavski accepted Rossi's brief, elliptical comments without argument. He was much less accommodating with his friend, the distinguished French theatre critic, Lucien Besnard, who was spending two months in Moscow. On December 18, he had seen *A Law unto Themselves* and wrote a letter congratulating the company on a good performance of a bad play. He looked forward to *Othello* but the production proved a bitter disappointment to him. Writing on the same day that Rossi was offering his encouraging comments Besnard criticized Stanislavski's interpretation as being too edgy, too modern. It was not in the 'tradition'.

Stanislavski did not answer the letter for almost a year and a half. When he did so he provided what amounts to an artistic credo, a clear statement of his thinking on the eve of the creation of the Moscow Art Theatre. At the heart of his reply is a long discussion of Hamlet's speech to the Players. This he sets against the 'tradition', which is no more than a miscellany of the most impressive moments in past performances by great actors, cobbled together without regard to the way they corresponded to the actor's own personality. A creative discovery becomes a prescription. Tradition of this kind provides a safety net for the mediocre performer – if he follows the rules he cannot fail – but offers no opportunity for the real artist to create afresh. It produces a dead uniformity. He had seen two famous French actors, Coquelin Fils and Leloire, in Molière's *L'Avare*. Their 'traditional' performances were indistinguishable from one another, and dull. He had, in fact, seen livelier, funnier performances of Molière in Germany and in his own native Russia, particularly by Lenski, because the material was created afresh to suit contemporary taste. Nature and an apprehension of human conduct must be the guide:

> It was Ben Jonson – Shakespeare never – who loved pathos, affectation, the picturesque and pseudo-theatrical effects, in fact, heroics. He made fun of Shakespeare because his passion was for everyday characters. In every one of his plays Shakespeare was carried away by the specific traits of a role but thanks to his extraordinary gifts he not only portrayed his characters vividly but they acquired universal significance. If Ostrovski in our time has been called the writer of the ordinary then so was Shakespeare in his. I am not for a moment comparing their talents, I am merely saying that they are very close in their attitude to art. Not for nothing does Hamlet say in Act Two, in the scene with the Players: 'They are the abstracts and brief chronicles of the time.' (SS, VII, pp. 114–17.)

Critics and commentators also come under attack. They, too, are part of this false 'tradition'. They smother a text with notes and glosses until it disappears from view. In terms too reminiscent of Tolstoi to be accidental, he insists that art must be simple, direct and immediately accessible to audiences. Shakespeare can reach audiences. He needs no apparatus.

> 'Shakespeare is life itself, he is simple and therefore can be understood by everybody. If you pick away at every word and look for every kind of hidden meaning then Shakespeare loses all his brilliance, his passion, his beauty . . . and all that remains is a philosopher and talker, who is only of interest to scholars. . . .' (Ibid.)

If the French theatre, which he admires, would jettison its false tradition and take a lead he would gladly follow for, he concluded:

> '. . . it is the task of our generation to liberate art from outmoded tradition, from tired cliché and to give greater freedom to imagination and creative ability. That is the only way to save art.' (Ibid.)

He was by now convinced that if anyone was to save art it was himself.

CHAPTER FIVE

NEMIROVICH

Stanislavski was approaching a crisis. He had become a model employer; at the factory he provided not only ideal working conditions – clean buildings and a large sick-bay, but a reading-room and a theatre as well. He was respected and, thanks to the merger, richer than before, but it was all ashes in the mouth. What he wanted was theatre. He confided his ambitions to his diary as early as 1890. The entry for March 21, records the factory accountant's reaction to his indifference:

'The old man is astonished at the indifference with which I glance at the annual reports. "What's this," he says to himself, "I work the whole day and he can't spare so much as a glance. . . . What's it to me? I don't get anything out of it. His money comes easy! . . . If God takes his capital away then he'll sing another tune."

Maybe he doesn't know it but perhaps the old man is right. I put little value on the gifts God has given me and I would honestly not be afraid to lose my money. If there were no money I could go on to the stage. I would go hungry, it's true, but I would be able to act to my heart's content. Yes, my work at the factory is pointless and therefore of no interest.' (K. K. Alekseieva Archive.)

His ideas on the function of theatre had taken firmer shape. Building on Fedotov's example, in conversation with friends, he outlined a scheme whereby touring companies would be set up in selected towns and would bring plays of quality to the surrounding area. His intention was to create theatres which would be 'open', a term which the authorities would find less alarming than the subversive-sounding 'popular'. Early in 1896 he discussed his plans with Efros and engaged in active preparations for the launching of a professional company and a popular theatre.

Pressure was now mounting on all sides for him to take the initiative. Russian theatre had to move forward and reach new audiences. Young actors had to be trained. During the 90s a number of drama schools sprang up but no one could guarantee their quality. There was a movement in the making but it needed a leader. Stanislavski had created The Society of Art and Literature and had turned it into the most powerful and original theatre group in Moscow. The intelligentsia now considered that his talent, energy, and influence needed to be applied on a wider scale.

What was considered desirable by the artistic community, however, was not necessarily attractive to the family. Lilina's parents in particular were worried. Their daughter had married well in their terms but they were only too aware that the success of the Alekseiev factories also depended on Stanislavski's talent and energy. His brothers did not seem capable of taking real responsibility. If he were to devote himself exclusively to the theatre business might decline, income drop off. What would happen to the family then? For the first time, too, there were tensions within the marriage. Although an actress herself, Lilina felt her husband's continual absence acutely and became ill. The children saw little of him although it was always exciting when he did go to the nursery. He would tell them stories from Shakespeare on which they would then improvise.

An enforced separation brought matters to a head. In April 1896 the house at Red Gates was commandeered by the government to house the German delegation who were attending the coronation of Tsar Nicholas II. Lilina and the family were sent to stay with relatives in Kharkov while Stanislavski took another apartment.

The separation was painful but gave them both a little space for reflection. In his letters Stanislavski seems to be pleading with her to accept the inevitable. Trying to sort out his confusion, on May 1 he went to see his old friend, the actress Medvedeva:

'As yesterday was a public holiday I got up at about 12. The house was empty so where would I go? I thought about it and thought about it . . . then I went to see Medvedeva. I stayed from 2 till 8, had lunch, drank tea and talked for the whole six hours . . . about theatre, of course. She wanted to get to the bottom of everything. Why were you ill? Was it perhaps because you were jealous of my love for the theatre? I wondered how she could possibly know. It turned out she has gone through the same thing with her husband all her life. Forgive me but I did confess to her that part of the reason for your illness was due to the fact that you see so little of me. Medvedeva understands how I am torn between being an artist and being a husband and how difficult it is to reconcile both forces. She understands this duality in an artist. Love for one's wife is one thing; love for the theatre another. They are two completely different feelings. One does not exclude the other. . . . I think she talked very well. I decided that when you return we'll both have a talk with her. It seems to me that, as a woman, she will understand you and, as an actress, will understand me. All the time, no matter what the subject she came back to the idea that *I have a duty* to do something for the theatre, that *my name must go down in history*.' (SS, VII, p. 98.)

In other letters he describes himself as leading the life of the typical business man, dividing his time between the factory and evenings of boring conversation during which most of his companions got drunk. He would return home with a bad headache and a worse temper. Another letter describes a tedious evening spent discussing finance with a government minister. Behind all these accounts is the implicit question: is this the way you want me to live? By the early summer they appear to have reached some sort of compromise. On May 27 he wrote:

'I am terribly happy that you are beginning to understand that artists have to be a little different. That is their charm and their misfortune.' (K.S. Archive.)

Stanislavski's intention was to develop and expand the Society into a professional company and he planned the new season with that in mind, selecting plays which would give him an opportunity to display his skills as an actor and as a director. He scored great successes as Matthias in *The Polish Jew*, better known in English-speaking countries in Irving's adaptation as *The Bells*, and as Benedick in *Much Ado About Nothing*.

In *The Polish Jew* which opened on November 19 he gave free rein to his new-found love of lighting effects, and demonstrated his ability to play upon an audience's feelings:

'We must give credit to Stanislavski: he put all his directorial and artistic talent into making the audience experience "a night of horror". He kept the audience in darkness for half an hour – dark in the auditorium, dark on the stage. A beam of electric light picked out Matthias' face from the gloom as he stretched to his full height in the pillory. In the surrounding shadows and gloom a voice read the indictment. Stanislavski, with exceptional "realism" conveyed the agonising delirium of a man who is suffering a terrible nightmare.' (*Russki Listok*, November 22.)

In the first-night audience was the German actor Ludwig Barnay, a member of the Meiningen company. *The Polish Jew* and *Uriel Acosta* were both in his repertoire. On December 4 he sent a letter of warm congratulations for both performances.

The Polish Jew was followed in February 1897 by *Much Ado About Nothing*. Stanislavski's dismissive comment on his own Benedick – that it had been liked only by 'nice, uncritical schoolgirls' – is belied by the reviews:

'The soliloquy at the end of the second act when Benedick changes his mind about love and marriage was simply a masterpiece and could serve by itself alone as a clear model of Stanislavski's talent for economy.' (*Russki Listok*, February 13, 1897.)

On February 15 he met Anton Chekhov. He had been playing *The Miserly Knight* as part of a literary-musical evening. After the performance:

> 'A[nton] P[avlovich] came up to me and thanked me . . . not for *The Miserly Knight* but for my part . . . in his play *The Bear* which I had performed not long before. "Listen, they say you acted wonderfully in my play. I didn't see it, you understand. I'm just an author . . . someone to chuck out."' (SS, V, p. 615.)

The next day the two men participated in an open discussion on creating a popular theatre which was reported in the *Russkaia Misl*. In February and March, with a group of other artists, including Ermolova, Stanislavski set up yet another literary-artistic circle. At the same time he was heavily involved in organizing the first all-Russian conference on the theatre.

His future intentions were still vague when he and Lilina went abroad in the middle of April, and they would have remained so had he not been propelled into action by two letters which were waiting for him when he went to Red Gates on June 18. They were from a man he hardly knew but who had desperately been trying to contact him, Vladimir Nemirovich-Danchenko. The first, written on June 7 from his wife's estate in the country, was brief:

> 'Dear Konstantin Sergeievich,
> Are you in Moscow? I drafted a huge long letter to you but as I shall soon be in Moscow myself I shan't send it. . . .
> If this letter finds you away from Moscow I will send the longer one I wrote earlier. But where?
> I will be in Moscow between June 21 and 26.' (Iz Pis., I, p. 89.)

The second, dated June 17 when Nemirovich tried again, was written on the back of a visiting card:

> 'Did you get my letter?
> I hear you will be in Moscow tomorrow, Wednesday. I will be at the Slavianski Bazar at one o'clock – could we meet? Or let me know at the enclosed address when and where.' (Ibid., p. 90.)

Stanislavski replied by telegram, suggesting lunch at 2 o'clock on the 22nd.

Stanislavski knew of Nemirovich-Danchenko as a successful dramatist and critic whose plays were in the repertoire at the Mali and who had twice won the coveted Griboiedov Prize for Play of the Year, the second time in competition with Chekhov's *Seagull*, a judgement which Nemirovich described as senseless.

Nemirovich came from a military family and his brother Vasili had a considerable reputation as a war correspondent. He did not enjoy the benefit of private means, and earned his living mostly as a professional writer and critic. He was an elected member of the Russian Society of Authors and of the Russian Society of Psychology and had been appointed to the Repertoire Committee of the Imperial Theatres which brought him into close contact with the Mali. In 1891 he had taken over the drama department of the Moscow Conservatoire where he gave courses in actor training that were as rigorous and intelligent as anything Stanislavski could have wished. Among his pupils were Meierhold and Olga Knipper.

Nemirovich, too, was at a turning-point in his career. He had virtually ceased to write plays. He had seen enough at the Mali to make him realize that radical changes were necessary. Year after year he presented programmes of reform but always came up against the same bureaucratic inertia. He, too, was committed to the notion of popular theatre. In 1897, shortly before contacting Stanislavski, he had submitted two schemes to the government, the first for the creation of an 'open' theatre, the second for the total reorganization of the Mali. His hope was that one or the other would result in his being given an official appointment. He was in Moscow to press his case.

There was no harm, however, in killing two birds with one stone. If he could make no headway with the authorities it might be possible to create a privately-backed theatre. He already had a scheme to form a company from his ex-pupils and take it to the provinces. He was aware – as who was not? – from gossip and the press of Stanislavski's plans for a professional theatre. He was also aware that nothing had yet been decided. Might not the two of them work in collaboration?

Later correspondence, when the two men were no longer on good terms, reveals what Nemirovich meant by 'collaboration'. As a writer he believed in the absolute supremacy of the dramatist. Theatre consisted in the translation of the author's intentions into stage terms. Unfortunately he was, by his own admission, a conservative not to say pedestrian director. His productions were worthy rather than inspired. He did, on the other hand, possess an outstanding ability to analyse a play and reveal its hidden meanings. No one could rival him in this field and successive generations of young directors benefited from his teaching. Stanislavski, on his side, possessed the directorial flair Nemirovich lacked. He had demonstrated his skill in creating vivid theatrical images, in selecting significant detail. What Nemirovich was looking for was not only someone who would put up the money but someone who would give his literary insights theatrical life. Such was his hidden agenda for the meeting on June 22.

Nemirovich was not certain what sort of man he was lunching with. Would he be confronted by an egocentric 'star', a would-be *monstre sacré*, who would insist on playing every leading role, on directing everything, on hogging the limelight? Stanislavski had to pass a character test. Nemirovich's description, in his autobiography, of his approach to the meeting is unconsciously patronising in tone. He portrays himself as the practised professional giving the gifted amateur the once-over. At all events his fears proved groundless. The person he encountered was both modest and distinguished, no over-resonant actor's voice, no extravagant gestures, but an elegant, graceful, quiet-spoken man who made no attempt to mark himself off from the crowd.

Stanislavski had no agenda, hidden or otherwise but he, too, needed more solid support for his schemes. No one in his immediate circle, for all their goodwill, possessed the expertise to help him launch a professional company. There had been talk, a great deal of it, but nothing concrete had materialized. Stanislavski later acknowledged that without Nemirovich he would have had a far greater struggle, for, quite apart from his literary gifts, Nemirovich had a firm sense of theatrical management. He understood budgets, schedules and deadlines – some said he was obsessed by them. Stanislavski had never been obliged to apply his own industrial management disciplines to his artistic life. He had only been concerned to get the production right, whatever the time-scale, and had financed his indulgences out of his pocket. A commercial theatre would require tighter control.

The two men met, therefore, on the best possible basis: common need. They possessed complementary skills; they shared the common views and aspirations of the intelligentsia, yet these factors alone cannot explain the extraordinary chemistry of that meeting which, having almost failed to happen, became one of the great legends of theatrical history.

They lunched in a private room so as not to be disturbed. The vast cavern of the main dining-room of the Slavianski Bazar is not the ideal place for a serious conversation. Their talk began at 2 o'clock on June 22 ended at 8 o'clock on the morning of the 23rd over breakfast at Liubimovka. In those eighteen hours they agreed to found an Art Theatre with seats at popular prices; they agreed to create an ensemble which would place artistic aims above individual vanity. They went through the list of members of the Society and of Nemirovich's pupils at the Philharmonic School and selected those they considered capable of meeting the high ideals they had set. More importantly, they agreed a fundamental division of authority. Nemirovich was to have the last word in all matters concerning repertoire, Stanislavski was to have final control over all matters relating to actual staging. Each had a veto. This arrangement seemed to put each man's particular gifts to their best use. Before parting they agreed that it would take a year to set up the new company adequately. The euphoria of this first meeting left essential questions unresolved. Each man left Moscow for the summer – Nemirovich for Yalta, Stanislavski for Liubimovka – assuming that the new company would be set up on his terms but serious divergences of opinion on basic issues surfaced almost immediately and had to be resolved by letter across the length of Russia.

On July 12, Nemirovich sent a relaxed letter, written in pencil for speed and convenience, giving an account of meetings he had held, many of them encouraging, and of actors, seasoned professionals, he thought they could attract. Practical as ever, he gave an outline of possible takings and of the salaries they might have to offer. He wanted a provincial launch. His feeling was that a tour in the provinces would weld the new company together and bring it to a point where it could confront a Moscow audience by the 1899–1900 season. His assumption was that the theatre, in the initial stages at least, would be financed and owned by Stanislavski personally. It was important to Nemirovich that it should be kept private, with Stanislavski as the only shareholder. Stanislavski would control the company and, by implication, he would control Stanislavski. If extra finance was needed shareholders could be brought in at a later stage, say after three years, when policy was firmly fixed.

Stanislavski had his own ideas and, in his reply of the 19th, said no to both proposals. Success in the provinces, he assured Nemirovich, would cut no ice in Moscow. His plan was to expand the Society bringing in new blood. He had reached a tentative agreement with Vladimir Schulz, who arranged tours by foreign artists, to share the use of the Paradiz theatre, which had recently been renovated and modernized. Any productions he mounted would alternate with seasons by Réjane, Coquelin and the Lessing Theatre. It would thus be possible to demonstrate the potential quality of the projected new theatre to a sceptical Moscow public.

He could not and would not create a privately-owned theatre. He did not have the means. His capital was modest, some 300,000 roubles tied up in the factory and trust-funds. He had no right to speculate with his family's future. He was also aware of the kind of criticisms that would be levelled against him if he set up a private company; it would immediately be labelled a money-making exercise. A public company, on the other hand, would be seen as a philanthropic, educational undertaking. Stanislavski, in fact, never at any time put money into the Moscow Art Theatre. It may be, although it is impossible to prove, that the family, having seen the vast sums poured into the Society of Art and Literature, made it a condition of their agreement to his engaging in professional activity that none of the Alekseiev capital should be involved.

Nemirovich was not to be put off. Replying on August 2, he expressed the fear that a limited company could all too easily degenerate into a purely commercial affair; shares could change hands and shareholders with an eye only to profit could start dictating artistic policy; a company controlled by Stanislavski would remain faithful to its original, educational ideals. 'The more I think about it,' Nemirovich wrote, 'the more I incline to an open and not just simply an art theatre.'

Stanislavski, in his next letter, spelled out the facts of bourgeois life more clearly:

'. . . Moscow society will neither trust in a private undertaking nor take it seriously, or if it does, it will be too late, when our pockets are empty and the doors of the theatre are boarded up. Moscow will label my participation in a private scheme – look at the attitude to Mamontov – as petty commercial tyranny. But the creation of a limited company, and what is more a popular-price theatre, will endow me with the merit – that is what they'll call it – of being an educator, of serving an artistic and educational charity. I know the businessmen of Moscow. In the first instance they won't go to the theatre *on principle* and in the second, *on pure principle*, they will stump up a pile of money to support *something they have created*.

I learned recently that Mamontov has drawn up statutes for a popular-price opera–dramatic theatre and wants to submit them to the Ministry. Needless to say I lost no time in engineering an apparently chance meeting with him. He has promised to send the statutes to me in the next few days. It would seem that a public company is the latest thing.' (SS, VII, pp. 123–4.)

Stanislavski was wise to be cautious. Within a year Mamontov, who had excited both envy and enmity by his success, was jailed on trumped-up charges of fraudulent share dealing and lost his entire fortune. As to a provincial launch the answer was still negative. He had spend ten years creating a company and his intention was to build on it. It would, in any case be impossible for him to abandon his business for the whole of the winter; he might just manage it for a public company but certainly not for a private one, with all the financial risks that involved.

Stanislavski's polite but firm ultimatum settled the matter. Nemirovich knew that without Stanislavski the new theatre was doomed before it started. But his anxieties ran deep and were never really assuaged. He could never rid himself of the fear that Stanislavski would be won over to the commercial ideas and values of his class, and became inordinately suspicious of anyone, however good their motives, who appeared to be gaining too much financial control. Thus, while having to accept the company Stanislavski had created, his entire strategy, over 20 years or more, was based on the necessity to acquire management control to protect his ideas.

On their return to Moscow both men canvassed support from potential investors. Even Stanislavski had underestimated the hostility of the possible reaction from the business community. The Society was one thing – it was part of respectable Moscow life – a new professional theatre, quite another. Attitudes were either frigid, ironic or openly hostile. The alternative was to apply for government money. On December 31 Stanislavski went to see Prince Golitsin, Chairman of the City Council, with a request for an annual grant of 15,000 roubles. Nemirovich made a follow-up visit on January 5,

1898. Since the notion was to provide good theatre at popular prices people could afford, the matter was referred to the Welfare Committee.

If the mills of God grind slow the mills of the Moscow City Council ground still slower and by the time the inevitable refusal was received the 'Art Theatre' had been open for a year. Nemirovich used his connections in the Philharmonic Society to persuade a number of its directors to put up money, mainly small sums of 1000 or 2000 roubles. Similar sums were provided by members of the board of The Society of Art and Literature. The largest single investor was Savva Timofeievich Morozov who subscribed 10,000 roubles. The Morozov family, whose rags to riches story rivalled the Alekseievs', had interests in textiles, railways and banking. Savva Morozov had taken a degree in chemistry and followed this by a period of studies in England. Despite his thick-set, rough, Tartar appearance, he was a man of great sensitivity and understanding. Few, meeting him, would have guessed that he was a depressive. His one condition for investing such a large sum was that he should always be the principal shareholder. This aroused Nemirovich's hostility. It seemed to confirm his earlier fears of an eventual surrender to commercial values, but he had no choice but to accept since Morozov was offering one third of the total launch capital of 28,000 roubles, slightly less than Stanislavski had personally invested in the Society of Art and Literature.

On April 19, 1898 Stanislavski assumed his role as Principal Director of the Association for the Establishment of the Moscow Open Theatre. On April 23 the *Russkie Vedomosti* published the names of the eleven shareholders. Stanislavski also signed a lease for the Hermitage Theatre on Carriage Row. His intention was also to present plays at the Sporting Club, thus preserving the connection with the Society.

The repertoire had yet to be decided and here again there was a wide divergence of views. Stanislavski was, on the whole, drawn to the classical or traditional repertoire. His instinct was to hand on the legacy of the past to the broad mass of the people and he tended to select plays which he had either seen in Moscow or on his travels. The list he put forward consisted either of works in the Society's current repertoire – *The Fruits of Enlightenment, Foma, Uriel Acosta, Much Ado About Nothing, The Bells, The Inspector General* – or which had been considered for future presentation – Aleksei Tolstoi's *Tsar Fiodor Ioannovich*, Goldoni's *La Locandiera*, Pushkin's *Boris Godunov*, Gogol's *Marriage* and Shakespeare's *The Taming of the Shrew*. He was to put on Lev Tolstoi's *The Power of Darkness*. Nemirovich, on the other hand, was much more drawn to the contemporary repertoire. If it were possible, he wrote to Stanislavski on June 21, 1898, he would only do modern plays. Unfortunately there were not enough good ones to fill a season. What did not interest him was what he called 'great men's trivia'. These included *Much Ado About Nothing, Twelfth Night, Taming of the*

Shrew and the plays of Molière. What he wanted was a mixture of classic plays which had some relevance to contemporary problems and modern plays of evident artistic merit. The light comedies and vaudevilles Stanislavski wanted to introduce would, to his mind, do nothing to enhance the reputation of a theatre dedicated to serious drama. He also took the opportunity to make it quite clear when and where he would tolerate directorial licence. Stanislavski could do what he liked with the 'trivia', let his imagination run riot, as he showed every intention of doing, but:

'. . . it is essential from my point of view that it be taken as read that for a modern theatre with pretentions to any sort of significance, the plays of Hauptmann and even the less talented Ibsen are more serious and profound than the trivia by poets of genius like Shakespeare and Molière. For that reason I very much want to include in the repertoire *The Sunken Bell, Hannele,* and even *Lady From The Sea, Ghosts, Doll's House,* etc. . . .' (Nemirovich Danchenko, *Izbrannie Pisma,* I, p. 120, Moscow 1979.)

There was to be no nonsense here.

The long list of suggestions the two men threw at each other were whittled down gradually to a reasonable-sized repertoire. Nemirovich managed to scotch the idea of using the Sporting Club when, in June, he worked out the performance schedules and decided it was impractical to try and run two theatres simultaneously. It was no great loss to him. The Sporting Club meant a backward look to the Society of Art and Literature and he wanted Stanislavski to sever all his earlier connections in favour of their new partnership. In any case, as far as the members of the Society of Art and Literature were concerned, he had no high opinion of their talents. It was Stanislavski and Stanislavski alone that he wanted. As he wrote, 'You *are* the Society.'

Nonetheless, the Society served its purpose. Stanislavski amply justified his stand over staying in Moscow and using the Society as a springboard. The final season provided an attractive foretaste of what the Art Theatre would be able to offer. Two major new productions were presented, *Twelfth Night* and *The Sunken Bell.*

Twelfth Night opened on December 17, 1897. The production was well received. It seemed to the critic of the *Russkoe Slovo* that the cast played like a full orchestra under a great conductor. There was not one false note, not one harsh sound. It was neither too fast nor too slow. Stanislavski's Malvolio on the other hand, ran contrary to the traditional view, and was less well received. Like many twentieth-century interpreters he saw the dark side of the character. The same critic found that:

'. . . he made the audience pay attention to him rather longer than they should, endowing him with strong feelings. The pleasure Malvolio took in the letters he received and then his indignation and rage were too strong, too tempestuous for this insignificant pedant and so, instead of drawing laughter, Malvolio drew pity.' (*Russkoe Slovo*, January 6, 1898.)

His next interpretation, Heinrich in Hauptmann's *The Sunken Bell*, again split critical opinion. For some the interpretation was too down to earth, too 'unheroic' and cluttered with 'superfluous realism'. For others it was a performance of true poetry, of 'titanic character'. Nemirovich was unreserved in his praise.

On January 31, 1898 the *Moskovski Vestnik* speculated on the pleasure Moscow audiences would receive if Stanislavski and Nemirovich were to succeed in launching their new enterprise. A foretaste of that pleasure came from the Princess Elizaveta Fedorovna, who came to see the play three times. Support like this was important since the government had yet to make up its mind whether to permit the new theatre to open.

CHAPTER SIX

PUSHKINO

Five months were all that remained to pull the first season into shape. As the new theatre was to play in repertoire this meant working on four or five plays simultaneously – *The Merchant of Venice*, *Antigone*, *Hannele*, Aleksei Tolstoi's *Tsar Fiodor Ioannovich* and *The Seagull*. This meant tightly-interlocking rehearsal schedules, starting one play, going on to the second and the third and thereafter keeping them all going. There were designs to be prepared, materials to be bought and sets to be constructed. Stanislavski had engaged Viktor Andreievich Simov as his principal designer. Simov had learned his craft as a scenic artist in Mamontov's Private Opera Theatre. He had met Stanislavski in the autumn of 1896 and had thereafter been a visitor to Red Gates where he had seen and admired Stanislavski's own set models. He officially entered the theatre's employ on May 1.

Stanislavski attempted to solve as many problems as he could during the pre-production period. He had decided to open the season not with the best or most original play from the list but with *Tsar Fiodor Ioannovich* a spectacular director's piece. In mid-May he set out for Rostov, to visit museums and collect material, determined not to present the conventionalized Russia which could be seen on the Mali stage. At the end of June he took Simov and members of the company on a tour of Rostov, Yaroslavl and other towns along the Volga to try and soak up the atmosphere of Old Rus. Simultaneously he briefed Simov on the designs he wanted for *Merchant*.

Members of the company read for parts in *Fiodor*, *Merchant* and *Antigone* but basic casting was kept fluid until Stanislavski had tested the capacities of actors whom he did not know. He had not yet decided what he himself would play in *Fiodor*, Boris Godunov or Prince Shuiski. Nemirovich's view was that it would help the play if he were to play Boris but he settled finally for Shuiski.

He was working under great pressure and alone. Nemirovich had a novel to finish and was away from late spring to the summer, at his wife's estate and then in the Crimea. The two men kept up a voluminous correspondence settling details of casting and repertoire. They agreed that Stanislavski would write the production plans, do preparatory work with the company and then hand over to Nemirovich who would start detailed work with individual members of the cast, while Stanislavski went on to the next production. This suited Stanislavski. Writing to Nemirovich on June 12 he said:

'I shall be a happy man if you will start taking the individual actors through their roles. It's something I don't like and can't do. You're a master at it.' (SS, VII, p. 128.)

The same letter, however, contains a gentle warning to Nemirovich not to interfere in the process of writing the production plan or to press for quick results:

'Let me pour out, sketch the play as I see it . . . independently . . . then you can correct it if I have done something stupid . . . I am always wary of falling under any kind of influence . . . Then my work becomes uninteresting and hackneyed. Sometimes I can't put down what I dimly perceive . . . And often these passages are better than all the rest. If unconsciously, instinctively I stick at these places be patient with me, give me time to clarify my ideas and put them into comprehensible form. You know, these details, prompted by instinct, give a play its flavour. I feel there will be very many of them in *Fiodor* so that we can get rid of the usual things we are accustomed to see in so-called Russian plays. To play them in that manner is absolutely unacceptable . . . We must get away from it as soon as possible.' (Ibid.)

On June 14, the new company assembled for the first time in Pushkino, some fifty miles from Moscow. They were a mixed bunch, former pupils of the Philharmonic School, ex-members of the Society, Darski, an experienced provincial actor, brought in to add weight, even Boris Alekseiev's fiancée, Olga Pavlovna Polianska, who had been a pupil at the Society's school.

The decision to rehearse outside Moscow had more or less been forced on Stanislavski. There was simply no convenient space in the city. The rehearsal rooms he had in mind had been taken over by Lenski who had also just launched a new company and the Hermitage would not be ready until the autumn. Nikolai Arkhipov, a former member of the Society came to the rescue, offering a small theatre on his country estate. Pushkino was only a short distance from Liubimovka so while the company found accommodation locally, Stanislavski was able to live at home, coming over for rehearsals every day, often on horseback.

On the first day there was a short religious opening ceremony, after which Stanislavski made a speech which Meierhold described as being of 'great warmth and beauty'. To our more cynical age it sounds idealistic and romantic in tone but it left no one in any doubt as to why they were there and what was expected of them:

'Let us prize what has fallen to us, for fear that we should weep later, as a child weeps when a favourite toy has been broken. If we do not come to this enterprise with clean hands we will dirty and degrade it and go our separate ways across the face of Russia, some of us returning to our mundane, everyday tasks, others profaning the name of art in paltry little provincial playhouses and side-shows, just for a crust of bread. And remember this, should this happen we shall deserve to be ridiculed and abused, for the task we have undertaken is not just a simple, private affair, its nature is social.' (SS, V, p. 175.)

In his application to the Moscow City Council Nemirovich had been careful to state that they were aiming at middle- or lower-middle-class audiences. Stanislavski could afford to be more open in private.

'Remember, we are attempting to bring light into the lives of the poorer classes, to give them a few moments of beauty in the darkness that surrounds them. We are trying to create the first rational, moral public theatre and it is to this lofty aim we dedicate our lives.

It is for this aim we must leave our petty quarrels at home. Let us assemble here to work together not to settle personal differences and squabbles.' (Ibid.)

Working in the comparative isolation of Pushkino proved beneficial. The new company lived as a community. As there were no servants, they had to keep the place clean and fend for themselves. The general handyman who had been engaged failed to turn up. Stanislavski insisted on participating on the domestic side and to set an example to others he was first on the duty rota. He believed that a theatre should be orderly, that actors should have working conditions which were clean and comfortable. It was a sign of respect for the art. Years previously, when he directed his first professional production, he had staged an angry walk-out on a drunken impressario in protest against the squalor in which he and his cast were expected to work. By the next day the theatre had been scrubbed clean. Working now, with his own company, he intended to remain true to his principles. Unfortunately, conscientious though he might be, he was not very efficient. This was hardly surprising as it is highly improbable that he had ever swept a floor or filled a samovar in his life, but efficiency was not the main issue. Attitude was what counted. Application to domestic chores was part of a broader concept of the way an artist, an actor should behave, a concept of discipline and dedication which Stanislavski called his Ethic and which was the essential companion to talent.

The workload was extremely heavy and discipline was a practical as well as a moral necessity. Stanislavski introduced a day-book, in which a record of work, attendance, lateness and reasons for lateness was carefully noted.

Critical comments could also be added. Rehearsals began at midday and
went on until four. There was then a break for about three hours after
which work was resumed often going on until midnight. In addition to
preparing *Merchant*, *Antigone* and *Hannele*, the company looked at Ostrovski's *We'll do it Ourselves* and Diachanko's *The Governor*, which was planned for a special performance at Pushkino itself but which never took
place.

The company were slowly introduced to Stanislavski's working method,
reading, research and extensive, detailed rehearsals 'at the table'. The action
was defined before the play was actually moved or blocked. The general
opinion, Stanislavski wrote to Nemirovich, was that the atmosphere was
more like a university than a theatre. Some were disconcerted by this unfamiliar approach but Vladimir Lanskoi, a young actor recently graduated
from the Petersburg academy, described by Stanislavski as 'stupid but nice',
declared that he had learned more in one rehearsal than in three years'
study. That, Stanislavski commented, did not say much for the school.

During those few weeks at Pushkino Stanislavski and Meierhold forged
life-long bonds of affection and respect. Meierhold was already a mature
mind. Nemirovich later wrote that he arrived at the Philharmonic school
fully fledged. In a series of letters to his wife, Olga, Meierhold set out his
reactions to Stanislavski both as a man and as a director. On June 22 he
told her:

> 'He captures your interest with his explanations, creates the mood with his
> wonderful demonstrations which get him excited too! What artistic flair,
> what imagination!' (Meierhold, *Perepiska*, p. 18, Moscow, 1976.)

Six days later he wrote:

> 'Alekseiev isn't talented, no, he's a genius, this director-teacher. What a
> wealth of erudition, what imagination . . . (Meierhold, *Perepiska*, p. 19.)

Stanislavski returned this affection. On June 25, while giving Nemirovich
an individual comment on every member of the company, he wrote, 'Meierhold is my darling'.

Everyone was learning – and not merely the young and inexperienced.
Darski, who was to alternate the role of Shylock with Stanislavski, was
treated no differently from the rest.

> 'And how, you will ask, is Darski behaving himself . . .? Is it possible for
> him to knuckle under to unaccustomed discipline? The fact is that not
> only does he submit to external discipline, he is completely reworking the
> role of Shylock, which he has been playing for such a long time. Alexeiev's
> understanding of Shylock is so free from clichés, so original that Darski
> hasn't dared protest once, but dutifully, though not slavishly, (he's a

clever man) is relearning the whole part, getting rid of the conventional and overblown. He has played this part for eight years and several times a year. . . .

Alekseiev plays the part better, of course. He has been perfecting it for years.' (Meierhold, *Perepiska*, pp. 18–19.)

The company were also being introduced to a new world of design. They saw the set models for *Merchant* on June 15. Meierhold wrote to his wife, on June 22:

'*The Merchant of Venice* will be done à la Meininger, respecting historical and national accuracy. Old Venice will rise as a living thing before the audience. . . . On one side the old Jewish quarter, dark and dirty, on the other the square in front of Portia's palace, poetic, beautiful with a view over the sea. . . . There, darkness, here light; there despair and oppression, here gaiety and light. The set outlines the idea of the play all by itself.' (Meierhold, *Perepiska*, p. 18, Moscow, 1976.)

The sets for *Fiodor*, eleven of them, caused an even greater stir when Stanislavski read the play on July 7. They had been much more troublesome to produce. Stanislavski worked with Simov throughout June and July. He was extremely demanding, posing what seemed like, and sometimes were, impossible problems. But, as Simov noted in his Memoir, the man was so charming you could refuse him nothing. It was the set for Act Three, Prince Shuiski's Garden, that proved the most original. Stanislavski wanted the Kremlin in the background. Unfortunately, the view of the Kremlin with which all Muscovites were familiar contained the church of Ivan the Great, which did not exist at the time of the play. Complete authenticity would simply upset the audience. Stanislavski suggested hiding the church behind a convenient clump of trees. Simov, or so he claimed, took this idea and extended it, filling the whole stage with trees and introducing a cut-out front-drop of birches right across the footlights. Writing to his friend Ekaterina Munt, however, Meierhold credited Stanislavski alone with such a revolutionary idea:

'The Shuiski Garden . . . is Alekseiev's idea. And do you know what's original about it? Trees stretch right across the stage parallel to the footlights. The characters will move beyond these trees. You can imagine the effect. Through the trees you can see the porch of Shuiski's house. The stage is moonlit.' (In *V. E. Meierhold*, N. D. Volkov, I, p. 107.)

In his history of the Art Theatre Nikolai Efros stated:

'To [the company] this innovation appeared a complete revolution, delighting them by its truth and boldness . . . . In the other models for

Fiodor the director and his young army were delighted by the historical accuracy, the break with cliché in the treatment on stage of the ancient Russia of the Boyars.' (MXAT, 1898–1923, p. 127.)

It was soon made clear to the cast that the reality of their acting was expected to match the reality of the sets. There were to be no actors' tricks, no 'peasant' acting of the traditional kind. A truthful presentation of the people was essential to the meaning of the production. Stanislavski took the view that although the play might be called *Tsar Fiodor* the real centre of the piece was the Russian people themselves. The failure of the Tsar, good and kind but unable to live up to the people's needs, provided the dominant theme. The crowd scenes, non-existent in the spoken text, became central to the action. Stanislavski went to greater pains than ever to give each walk-on an individual character. Nowhere is this more evident than in the final act scene on the Yauza bridge. The stage direction, 'Across the bridge pass people of different condition', is the cue for 14 paragraphs of detailed character descriptions in the production plan. In some cases they are almost minor dramas in themselves:

'3.   At curtain rise a German (in foreign costume) approaches a barge and meets a stevedore, asks him something. The stevedore not wishing to answer starts to go, the German stops him afresh with his hand and questions him again. It is obvious they don't understand one another. (Scene lasts 15 seconds.) Having examined the sacks lying about he undoes one of them, takes some flour in the palm of his hand, examines it, tastes it. Then he crosses the plank onto the barge and only returns when the fight begins. Then he and his wife rescue their goods.

4.   The German's wife, heavily-built, stout, with a kerchief, humbly follows him. She patiently waits until her husband has finished speaking to the stevedore. When her husband is examining the flour she notes down the number and the quantity. For this purpose she has an inkwell round her neck and paper and a goose-quill in her hands. When her husband goes onto the barge, she sits on a log and patiently awaits his return.' (*Rezhissiorski Eksempliari*, K. S. Stanislavskovo, I, pp. 210–212.)

With *Fiodor* launched, there was a read-through, on July 21, of Hauptmann's *The Assumption of Hannele* which reduced everyone, except a sceptical Meierhold, to tears. He found the whole occasion too self-indulgent, with too much talk about form and 'beauty'. He wondered what had happened to the content of the play.

Although company morale was high and work was progressing well, Stanislavski was beginning to feel the strain. He had written to Nemirovich a month earlier to complain about the overload. He could not manage the business side and rehearse as well. He could see the money running out.

Certain essential repairs at Pushkino had gone over budget although the company had taken to do-it-yourself rather than employ outside labour. Money was being spent on sets and costumes despite the fact that not a single play had been passed by the censor. The most vulnerable was *Tsar Fiodor* which was just the kind of historical subject which aroused the authorities' suspicions. Would any of the ecclesiastical characters be cut? If they were, it meant changing the cast-list and that would have a knock-on effect on the casting of all plays.

Nemirovich kept a level head throughout. By his calculation income would cover expenditure and at most a further 10,000 roubles would be needed in the late autumn. He would raise a loan himself rather than bring in another shareholder. He arrived finally on July 24, much to Stanislavski's relief, and stayed at Liubimovka, spending most of August coaching his former pupils from the Philharmonic school. Stanislavski took the opportunity, on August 5 and 6, to make a shopping expedition to Nizhni-Novgorod to buy material for *Fiodor* – head-dresses, boots, skirts, kerchiefs, Persian silks, necklaces, aprons and plates, any kind of bric-à-brac that might seem useful. On his return he began work on the difficult task of preparing the production plan for *The Seagull*. Chekhov's play had been included in the repertoire at Nemirovich's insistence; he was determined to stage it and had fought hard to overcome Chekhov's absolute refusal to let it be seen in Moscow. The play's first run at the Aleksandrinski theatre in 1896 had not been quite the total disaster that subsequent legend has painted. It was underrehearsed but had a strong cast which included Vera Komissarzhevskaia as Nina. It was the first night that had proved catastrophic. The audience had come expecting to see their favourite comedienne, Elizaveta Levkeieva, in a benefit performance of a light comedy. They were not prepared for the half-tones and subtleties of Chekhov's text. By the time Komissarzhevskaia got to the opening of the speech, 'Men, lions eagles' they had had enough and erupted into jeers, catcalls and insults. Chekhov took refuge in a dressing-room and then roamed the streets half the night. None of the subsequent favourable comments, either from friends or in the press could erase the memory of that dreadful evening. He vowed that if he lived for seven hundred years he would never write for the theatre again.

The memory of that humiliation lay at the root of Chekhov's attitude to Stanislavski's productions. He loved the theatre and was fascinated by it but feared nothing so much as ridicule. The dread that uncomprehending actors and directors would expose him once again to the derision of an audience made him prickly and suspicious. *The Seagull* was performed in provincial cities but he had resisted all efforts to stage it in Moscow, although the Mali appeared to hold an option. Their intention was to present it at a benefit performance. When Nemirovich tried to put on the play at the Philharmonic School the Mali management had blocked him but had done nothing about the play since.

Nemirovich and Chekhov were friends. They used the familiar second person singular form of address in a way that Stanislavski and Nemirovich never did in forty years of collaboration. Nemirovich decided to use their friendship. On April 25, 1898 he wrote to Chekhov asking for permission to do *The Seagull*. In this and in subsequent letters he spoke of the production as his own, not Stanislavski's. He advanced his own superior claims to understand the play better than any other director. Chekhov refused. It took three more letters, two written on May 12 and one written on May 16, before he finally obtained Chekhov's consent. In his reply of May 31, he clearly stated 'So I am to direct *The Seagull*!'

Stanislavski is mentioned only once in Nemirovich's correspondence. On August 21 he wrote to Chekhov:

'Alekseiev and I spent 48 hours going over *The Seagull* and many ideas took shape as to how to create the *mood* (and that's so important in the play).' (Iz. Pis. I, pp. 143–44.)

It was a one-sided conversation. Nemirovich did the talking while Stanislavski took notes.

It may be that Nemirovich emphasised his own role as a stratagem, on the assumption that an already nervous Chekhov would not confide his play to someone he did not know, however, for Nemirovich to regard himself as the prime force behind the production would have been entirely in keeping with his view of the partnership. The interpretation of the play was his. Stanislavski would translate what he wanted into stage terms and he would then take rehearsals.

Stanislavski, for his part (and he was not alone) was bewildered by the script, which seemed to offer him nothing as a director. There was no action. Having listened carefully to everything Nemirovich had to say, on about August 10 or 11 he left for his brother Georgi's estate near Kharkhov.

'I went to the Kharkhov district to write the *mise-en-scène*. This was a difficult task, as, to my shame, I did not understand the play. It was only as I worked on it that, almost imperceptibly, I came to know it and fell hopelessly in love with it. I yielded to its charm, wanting to inhale its aroma.' (Sobranie Sochinenii. Vol. V, p. 331.)

Stanislavski worked hard. By the end of August he had completed the first three acts. On the 30th he sent them off to Pushkino though still full of doubts, the more so since he had reached a block on Act Four:

' . . . as I am not steeped in Chekhov the plans I am sending you may be completely unusable. I drafted them at random. . . . I got down to the last act. Nothing went through my head and I wouldn't dream of forcing it out. I am reading the whole play again in the hope that the three acts I have already sent (by registered post) will keep you busy for some time.' (SS, VII, p. 142.)

There was the question of what he himself should play. The general view seemed to be that it should be Dorn:

'I've started reading the part of Dorn. . . . The part interests me, if for no better reason that the fact that I have not played a character role for some time but one thing I don't understand or feel – why I should be Dorn. . . . I'm annoyed because I can't see what people expect of me in this part. I'm afraid I will be no more than adequate. . . . I can see myself as Shamraiev, Sorin or even Trigorin, I mean, I feel how I could transform myself into these characters. In the beginning you always think you can play any part but not those you have simply taken on . . . You have not time but perhaps someone else, Meierhold for instance, who, as you say, is steeped in *The Seagull* could give me a report on what was said about Dorn in the discussion and how he sees him, what his appearance is. I would be grateful to him for then I would appear the way you want me.' (Ibid., p. 141.)

Stanislavski may have been manoeuvring in order to be able to play the part of Trigorin. It is significant that in an extremely detailed production plan Trigorin's long speech to Nina in Act Two, beginning, 'What's wonderful about it?' contains no directions at all, almost as though Stanislavski thought them superfluous since he himself would be playing the part.

Stanislavski adopted the same basic approach in creating the production plan, the 'score' as he came to call it, as he had with *Fiodor*. He simply moved in closer. He gave each character an individual rhythm, a way of walking and moving, mannerisms: Sorin's laugh is 'startling and un-expected'. Arkadina, 'habitually folds her arms behind her back when she is angry or excited'; Konstantin is, in general, 'tense'; Masha takes snuff; Medvedenko smokes a lot. The production copy sets down every move, every gesture, exact facial expressions in almost cinematic detail. Small drawings show the physical position and relationships of the characters at key moments as in a story-board.

The detail is not present simply from a desire to reproduce the surface of life, or an adherence to what Stanislavski called 'vulgar naturalism'. The detailed physical action is intended to reveal personality, the inner state of thought and emotion. Writing in 1923, Efros recalled the impact of moments of silent action, citing a passage in Act Four where Chekhov asks for the sound of a piano two rooms away, playing a waltz. The text runs:

MASHA (*dances a few silent waltz-steps*). The important thing, mother, is to avoid seeing him. I just wish they'd give Simon his transfer and then, you'd see, I'd be over it in a month. All this is so stupid.

This Stanislavski expands into:

MASHA (20 – MASHA *sighs, takes a pinch of snuff. Snaps the lid shut vehemently.*) ... [DIALOGUE] .... (21 – MASHA *sighs again, waltzes over to the window, stops beside it, looks out into the night, takes out a handkerchief and unbeknown to her mother, wipes away one or two tears which are rolling down her cheeks. (Rezhissiorskie Eksempliari K. S. Stanislavskovo, II, pp. 138–9, Moscow, 1981.)*

Efros commented:

'Once you had seen it you would never forget it, the profound sorrow, the feeling of shock, almost of doom in your heart, that resulted from those silent, almost mechanical waltz-turns Masha performed, the complete hopelessness, as she heard the distant music coming from Kostia's room. She simply heard it and made a few turns to the rhythm ... That's all ... but you never felt more pain for her blighted existence than in those few silent moments.' (*Ezhegodnik* MXAT, 1944, p. 290.)

These silent moments acquired ever increasing stylistic importance. Chekhov stipulates a considerable number of pauses. Stanislavski added to them, although it did not prevent him from contradicting Chekhov at one point with a peremptory, 'No pause here under any circumstances.'

The use of sound is also developed: natural on-stage noise – a window shutting, the clatter of plates – to heighten the moment, to define it more closely; off-stage noise – frogs, crickets, barking dogs – to create 'mood', 'atmosphere'.

ACT ONE
The play opens in darkness. An (August) evening. A dim artificial lamp. Distant sounds of a drunken song, distant howling of a dog, croaking of frogs, the cry of a corncrake – help the audience to enter into the sad, monotonous life of the characters.' (Rezhissiorski Eksempliari K. S. Stanislavskovo II, p. 55.)

Stanislavski stipulated August because he calculated that the moon would have been at the right angle at that time for the performance of Konstantin's play. Meierhold, the original Konstantin, was in no doubt as to the essentially *poetic* nature of Stanislavski's intentions. Speaking nearly 40 years later he stated:

'You ask me if there were [elements of] naturalism in *The Seagull* at the Art

Theatre and you think you are putting a trick question... Probably there were individual elements of naturalism but that's not important. The important thing is that it contained the poetic nerve-centre, the hidden poetry of Chekhov's prose which was there because of Stanislavski's genius as a director. Up to Stanislavski people had only played the theme in Chekhov and forgot that in his plays the sound of the rain outside the windows, the noise of a falling tub, early morning light through the shutters, mist on the lake were indissolubly linked (as previously only in prose) with people's actions. At that time this was a discovery; naturalism only came into being when it became a cliché ...' (In 'Meierhold Speaks', *Novi Mir*, 1961, No. 8, p. 221.)

Nemirovich received the first three acts on September 1 or 2. On September 4 he sent his first reactions which were almost entirely favourable. But his own innate conservatism as a director made him cautious about some aspects of Stanislavski's plan. Wasn't he overworking the effect of actors turning their backs to the audience, particularly Sorin? Just as Stanislavski had put a line of trees across the front of the stage in *Fiodor*, so, in Act One of *The Seagull* he put a line of actors with their back to the audience. The effect, which Nemirovich seems to have missed, was effectively to link the real audience with the stage audience as they all watched Konstantin's play. Nemirovich was also concerned about the amount of attention paid to minor characters, he was afraid they might overshadow the leading roles.

On September 10 Stanislavski despatched the plan for Act Four with his reply to Nemirovich's comments:

'I repeat, personally I can't tell whether the plan for *The Seagull* is good or bad. I only know it is a talented and fascinating play but I don't know which end to start. I've come at it haphazard so do what you like with the plan. ...

I fully understand and am in agreement with your remarks that when Treplev's play is being performed the minor characters should not kill the major. It's a question of method. ... As is my wont, I provided a comprehensive sketch of each character. When the actors are on top of things I start taking away what is superfluous and select what is important. I go about it this way because I have always been afraid that actors will only come up with superficial, uninteresting ideas out of which you get nothing but commonplace puppets.' (SS, VII, p. 145.)

As to the number and variety of sound effects:

'Consider this, I put in the frogs during the play scene solely to create total quiet. Quiet is conveyed in the theatre not by silence but by noise. If you don't fill the silence with noise you can't create the illusion.' (Ibid.)

Continuous noise backstage and in the auditorium destroys the mood of a scene. Attention needs to be focused on deliberately created sound on-stage.

In 1938, when the production plan for *The Seagull* was published for the first time, Nemirovich paid homage to the greatness of Stanislavski's achievement:

'This is a supreme example of Stanislavski's *creative instinct* as a director. Stanislavski who was still indifferent to Chekhov sent me such rich, interesting, original, profound material for the production of *The Seagull* that it was impossible not to admire this blazing, masterly imagination.' (Quoted in Introductory Essay to production plan for *The Seagull*, *Iskusstvo*, Moscow, 1938, pp. 47–48.)

Chekhov, finally responding to repeated invitations to stay at Pushkino or Liubimovka, attended rehearsals on September 9 and 11 in Stanislavski's absence. He was put on the defensive before he had heard a line. When one of the cast informed him of the 'real' croaking frogs and barking dogs that were to accompany the action he commented sharply:

'Real . . . The stage is art. There's a genre picture by Kramskoi in which the faces are painted marvellously. What if you were to cut out the painted nose from one of them and put in a living one? The nose would be "real" but the picture would be a mess.' (Meierhold, *Teatr, Kniga O Novom Teatre*, Petersburg, 1908.)

Nor was he pleased when he heard of Stanislavski's notion of bringing on a number of servants at the end of Act Three, where the script leaves most of the confusion of departure off-stage.

' . . . the stage demands a certain artifice. You don't have a fourth wall. Above all the stage is art, the stage mirrors the quintessence of life, you need not bring anything superfluous onto it'. (Ibid.)

When he finally got to see what was actually being done most of his anxieties disappeared. Writing to Stanislavski on September 12, Nemirovich was able to report:

'Your *mise-en-scène* proved a delight. Chekhov was in raptures about it. We just altered one or two details in the interpretation of Treplev–Chekhov did, not me. . . . He soon understood how your *mise-en-scène* strengthens the overall impression.' (Iz., Pis., I, p. 154.)

On September 21 Chekhov, in typically oblique manner, wrote to P. F. Iordanov:

'If you happen to be in Moscow, go to the Hermitage Theatre, where

Stanislavski and Vl. Nemirovich-Danchenko are staging plays. The *mises-en-scène* are amazing, the like of which have never been seen in Russia. By the way, my ill-fated *Seagull* is being done.' (*Pisma*, VII, p. 272.)

Chekhov also managed to see a rehearsal of *Fiodor* and was impressed, as he wrote to Suvorin on October 8, by the intelligence and genuine feeling of art the company conveyed, even if there were no outstanding actors. According to Nemirovich it was at this rehearsal that Chekhov first noticed Olga Knipper.

On the 11th Nemirovich and Chekhov settled the question as to who was to play Trigorin:

'I asked whether Trigorin wouldn't benefit from having you in the part.
"Much better," Chekhov answered.
'So you see, I owe you an apology for having kept this role from you. The whole company, I gather, was expecting you to do it.' (Iz., Pis., I, p. 154.)

Stanislavski set out from his brother's estate somewhere around the 15th. Writing to Lilina he expressed his satisfaction at the change of casting:

'... I've been through Trigorin – the part is dearer to my heart than Dorn. At least there's something in it but in the other, nothing – and they expect God knows what.' (SS, VII, p. 149.)

It was the rehearsals of *Fiodor*, however, that demanded his immediate attention. The censor had finally licensed the play towards the end of August. Nemirovich had written on the 24th to announce the news and pass on the inevitable cuts. Stanislavski was irritated by the pettiness of the changes and set about trying to repair some of the damage to the verse which the censor had succeeded in mangling.

He arrived in Moscow on the 18th and went straight to the theatre to see what progress had been made in his absence. The first scene depressed him considerably but matters improved in the second and went better after that.

The role of Tsar Fiodor had still not been cast although the opening was less than a month away. Stanislavski could not make up his mind. He found Moskvin's playing extremely moving but Meierhold was a main contender and one cast list, written in Stanislavski's hand, ascribes the part to him. Meierhold himself was under the impression that he, Moskvin, and another young actor Aleksandr Platonov would play Fiodor, Shuiski and Starkov turn and turn about. The rehearsal with Moskvin finally settled matters:

'Konstantin Sergeievich summoned me to the director's table and, much moved, with tears in his eyes, told me that I would play Tsar Fiodor and

that we would start rehearsing the rest of the play the very next day.'
(Moskvin, 'My First Role', *Sovietskoe Iskusstvo*, October 26, 1938.)

Nemirovich later took credit for this final casting, maintaining that Stanislavski had originally intended Moskvin for the role but had mishandled the young actor during early rehearsals and then lost confidence in him. It was thanks to his own coaching that Moskvin was able to develop his performance and so finally land the role.

Stanislavski now set about polishing and tightening up *Fiodor* and *Merchant of Venice*. Any idea of his playing Shuiski was now quite impractical. He had no time to prepare his own performance. Everything inevitably was behind schedule. Between rehearsals Lilina used her skills as a seamstress to sew the elaborately embroidered costumes for *Fiodor*. Even Stanislavski's mother joined the common effort, dipping lengths of braid in coffee to give them the right period look.

Elizaveta Vasilievna's willing cooperation symbolized the end of any opposition inside the Alekseiev family to Stanislavski's ambitions. He had succeeded in opening the door to professional life not only for himself but also for his brothers and sisters. Anna joined the company in 1899 and remained with it until 1903. Boris spent the season of 1900–1901 with it, acting under the name of Polianski while, in 1903, Georgi took over the direction of the theatre in Kharkov, where he lived.

CHAPTER SEVEN

THE MOSCOW ART THEATRE

Moscow society awaited the opening of the new theatre and *Tsar Fiodor* with great excitement and not a little malice. They admired Stanislavski, he had been their idol, but they were also quite prepared to see him fall flat on his face. A failure would prove how stupid it was to transgress the code of one's class. On the other side there were those, the young, the intellectuals, who pinned their hopes on the new company. Stanislavski and Nemirovich knew there was only one answer – *épater les bourgeois*. They needed an unqualified success, a smash.

The audience on the first night, October 14, was a stiff one, with a large number of professional actors from the imperial theatres. Lenski and the young company at the rival New Theatre sent telegrams as did the pupils of the Philharmonic School. Stanislavski, who was not performing, was so nervous backstage that he upset the cast and had to be sent away before he produced complete hysteria.

The Art Theatre had not yet dispensed with the custom of taking curtain calls after each act. It was therefore possible to judge the way a performance was going as the evening progressed. The audience only thawed out slowly. There were not enough members in the company to make the opening scene really effective; the set for Shuiski's garden had a mixed reception, but after scene three the originality of the production, the combination of historical accuracy and theatrical splendour gradually won through and the final scene, at the Yauza Bridge, was a triumph.

Ermolova, who was present either at the final dress rehearsal or the first night – the young medical student who accompanied her could not later in life remember which –:

'. . . threw off a string of observations which brooked no objection. "That's acting! That's directing! Those are costumes! We put a padded jacket over our corsets and a fur coat and a peasant's head-dress and think we're boyars' wives. All we've done is dress up! We've got a lot to learn from Stanislavski."' (Letter from G. Kurochkin to Stanislavski, January 26, 1938.)

The press on the whole was favourable. There was admiration for the audacity of the young company in tackling such a difficult play. The combination of realism and theatricality was praised. Efros devoted two articles to the production in *Novosti Dnia* on the 18th and the 20th, concluding:

'There were two heroes at the first production of the Art-Open Theatre: the *mise-en-scène* and Mr Moskvin.'

The first hurdle had been passed but the theatre had to prove itself as a going concern – an almost impossible task. To present a season of plays, all of which needed to be more or less successful, with an inexperienced cast, and at the same time to break new ground was to invite disaster. And so it proved.

After *Fiodor* Stanislavski put all his energies into *The Sunken Bell* and *The Merchant of Venice* to the detriment of his personal affairs. He did not go near his factory. His efforts were not rewarded. *The Sunken Bell*, which opened on the 19th, was a revival and made no impact. Stanislavski's interpretation of Heinrich was once again criticized for being too prosaic. *The Merchant of Venice*, which opened on the 21st, was no better received. The audience was disconcerted by the fact that Darski, on Stanislavski's instructions, played Shylock with a Jewish accent. This was considered inappropriate for a 'tragic' role. The press, not understanding that it had always been Stanislavski's intention to alternate the role with Darski, announced that he would take over in order to justify his interpretation. In fact Stanislavski never played the role. The play had many fine moments but it was 'caviare to the general'. This prompted Nemirovich to quote Tolstoi: 'In art, subtlety and the power to influence are almost always diametrically opposed.'

A further blow came when, on October 27, *The Assumption of Hannele*, the next production, was banned after protests by the church. A visit to the Metropolitan Vladimir of Moscow, proved abortive. It was useless to explain that the translation the Metropolitan angrily waved at them was not the translation, duly passed by the censor, which was being used. The ban stayed. This was the first of many brushes with the authorities, frequently in the person of the Chief of Police, General Dmitri Fedorovich Trepov, a ruthless organizer of anti-revolutionary pogroms and later governor of the Winter Palace in Petersburg.

Ostrovski's *A Law Unto Themselves*, which opened on November 4, failed to arouse any interest. Audiences simply stayed away. This was critical. The launch capital of 28,000 roubles, barely adequate in any case, had been used up. Box-office receipts, the only source of income, could not cover costs. On November 30, Stanislavski received a demand for 3000 roubles in rent from the theatre's landlords. If payment was not made by noon on December 1 the contract would be considered null and void and legal action would be taken.

On December 2 Goldoni's *La Locandiera* opened together with a short Viennese piece, *Greta's Joy*. As the *Moskovskii Listok* commented, the theatre was half empty. The run of failures had destroyed its prestige. The Goldoni did nothing to stop the run of bad luck. Stanislavski received mixed notices as Ripafratta. Many critics found him too 'passive'. It began to look as though the theatre which had opened so successfully in October might well be forced to close its doors by Christmas. Everything now depended on *The Seagull* which was scheduled to open on December 17.

Stanislavski and Nemirovich marshalled all their combined talent and energy to ensure a success. Nemirovich made a number of changes to the blocking, which are noted in his hand on the production plan, and made a number of alterations to the décor. The play had 24 rehearsals, 9 of them taken by Stanislavski and 15 by Nemirovich. This added up to some 80-hours work, a great deal in contemporary terms. There were three dress rehearsals during which Stanislavski and Nemirovich examined every inch of the sets and checked and double-checked every lamp to make sure none of the effects would misfire. Stanislavski, nonetheless, considered the play under-rehearsed and insisted that the opening be postponed for a week. Nemirovich knew this would be a mistake and refused. Stanislavski then threatened to have his name taken off the posters but Nemirovich managed to talk him round although in later years he could not remember quite how he did it.

When opening night came a sense of crisis pervaded both stage and auditorium, which was by no means full. Maria Chekhova was so afraid of a failure, which she was convinced would be a death-blow to her brother, that she stayed away. Most of the cast were taking refuge in the contemporary equivalent of tranquillisers, Valerian drops.

'The house was poor. I don't know how the first act went. I only remember that all the actors reeked of Valerian drops. I remember how awful it was for me to sit in the dark with my back to the audience during [Nina's] monologue and that I unconsciously grabbed hold of my foot which had developed a nervous twitch.' (*Sobranie Sochinenii*, Vol. 5. p. 332.)

Nina's monologue, which had provoked catcalls in Petersburg, was listened to attentively and throughout the rest of the act the audience appeared to be concentrating. Dorn's final speech came, with Stanislavski's 'atmospheric' effects.

'DORN: How tense they all are! How tense! And so much love. . . . Oh that lake's an enchantress! (*Gently*.) [114. MASHA *Bursts into tears, kneels, buries her face against* DORN'S *knees. 15 second pause. The wild waltz grows louder, a church bell tolls, a peasant's song, frogs, a corncrake, the knocking of the night-watchman and other nocturnal sound effects*] But what can I do, my dear child? Tell me, what? [*115. Curtain*].

After the curtain there was a silence which seemed to go on forever. They had failed. But there are silences in the theatre which are more profound than instant frenzied reaction. When the clapping began, it was, in Nemirovich's words, like a dam bursting. He did not believe in grabbing curtain calls. He insisted that they be properly spaced so that it was possible to gauge the reaction more accurately. Three or four curtain calls taken slowly meant success. Act One got six.

For the audience the evening was a unique experience. The writer A. S. Lazariov wrote to Chekhov on January 19, 1899:

'I attended the first performance. In the first act something special started, if you can so describe a mood of excitement in the audience that seemed to grow and grow. Most people walked through the auditorium and corridors with strange faces, looking as if it were their birthday and, indeed, (dear God, I'm not joking) it was perfectly possible to go up to some completely strange woman and say: "What a play? Eh?" At all events, N. E. Efros, always so reserved and "respectable", rushed up to me in the stalls, as I was going back to my seat after the second act, stopped me at the entrance to the parterre and exclaimed so that practically the whole theatre could hear: "Ah, what a play A.S.! What acting! What passion!"' (Quoted in Introduction by S. D. Baluzhati to *The Seagull* Production Plan, *Isskustvo*, 1938.)

By the end of Act Three the actors were weeping with excitement and embracing one another. Nemirovich informed the audience that the author was not present and suggested that a telegram of congratulation be sent to Chekhov in Yalta. The suggestion was greeted with prolonged applause. There was still Act Four to go. That, too, was a triumph.

The press was unanimous in its praise.

'The directors completely understood what the author wanted; the actors completely understood the directors' ideas and created a performance which emerged not simply as an interpretation of the play but as its very embodiment.' (*Teatr i Iskusstvo*, January 10, 1899.)

There were reservations, however, about some of the performances, including Stanislavski's:

'The success of *The Seagull* was an extraordinary phenomenon. It explained much to us, it opened our eyes to many things. The performances of the actors of the Art Theatre in this comedy were far from being irreproachable. One of the play's leading roles, the author, Trigorin, was misunderstood and misinterpreted and the part of the heroine of *The Seagull* was simply distorted but nonetheless we forgave the artists their shortcomings. . . .' (*Russkaia Misl*, X, 1899.)

These criticisms were echoed by Maria Chekhova, who found Stanislavski 'limp' and Roksana, who played Nina, 'very bad'. When she attended the play for the third time, however, the following February, she was able to report to her brother that both were now good.

An article in *Russkaia Misl* in January 1899 drew attention to the social, the critical implications of the production:

'. . . you cannot "do" a play like this. You can only experience it with sadness of heart and extreme sensitivity towards the sickness and suffering which is destroying certain circles in our society.'

It was important to follow *The Seagull* with another success but this was not to be. *Hedda Gabler* which opened on February 19, failed to excite. Two other blows, considerably more serious, followed. On January 10 the theatre had given a special performance of *Locandiera* for factory workers, as a result of which Nemirovich was summoned by the Chief of Police, Trepov. It was explained to him that such performances needed special clearance by a fourth censor whose task it was to vet material intended for working-class audiences. The theatre had omitted this formality and could be in serious trouble. Nemirovich's attempts to talk himself out of it were brushed aside. It became quite obvious that the alternatives were conformity or prison. The notion of an 'open' theatre was being strangled by red-tape. In a very short space of time the word was dropped from the title and the theatre became simply, at Chekhov's suggestion, the Moscow Art Theatre.

Ironically, the worst blow seemed to come from Chekhov himself. The Art Theatre production of *The Seagull* had finally established him not only as *a* dramatist but probably *the* dramatist. He could be in no doubt of his success. His sister, who lived near the Hermitage theatre, could hear people talking excitedly in the streets after the performance. Levitan, Russia's leading painter, wrote to him on January 8, explaining that when he read the play he had not understood it. The Art Theatre production had revealed all. He had seen Lenski, who 'is in raptures both about the play and the production'. On January 9 Chaliapin sent a telegram of congratulation again both for the play and the production.

Chekhov was evidently pleased. On January 25 he wrote to a medical colleague, P. F. Iordanov:

'My *Seagull* is playing in Moscow to packed houses. It's a sell-out. They say the production is exceptional.' (Chekhov, *Pisma*, VIII, p. 47.)

It was natural, therefore, for the theatre to expect to be given his next play. It was obvious to everyone in the company that another Chekhov play was essential to bring in audiences. When Nemirovich was informed that *Uncle Vania* had been given to Mali, he felt betrayed.

Chekhov never explained or excused his behaviour. This has given rise to considerable speculation by commentators anxious to drive a wedge between him and Stanislavski, to the detriment of the latter. There are no grounds, however, for concluding that he refused the play because he was outraged by the staging of *The Seagull* and did not like Stanislavski as an actor. He had not seen the production nor Stanislavski's performance. Stanislavski's own explanation was that Chekhov played the two theatres off against each other, not wishing the play, which had a chequered history, to be performed. He told the Mali that he needed to rewrite and the Art Theatre that he needed actually to see their work before committing himself further. This does not fit the facts.

Having failed to exercise their option on *The Seagull*, the imperial theatres realized that the Art Theatre was a serious threat. In his diary, on February 4, the chief administrator, Teliakovski, noted that serious attention should be paid to the production methods of the new theatre and that whatever was useful should be taken over. It was a short step from there to luring away their most successful author. A few days later the principal director of the Mali, A. M. Kondratev, asked Chekhov if they could do *Uncle Vania*. Chekhov agreed. He was undoubtedly flattered by the offer. The Mali, after all, whatever its shortcomings, did represent official recognition, a success there would do something to compensate for the humiliation he had suffered in Petersburg. It is doubtful whether he was aware how important another sure-fire success was to the Art Theatre. There was also a simpler reason for letting the Mali do the play: money. On February 22, Chekhov wrote from Yalta to Ivan Orlov, a doctor friend:

'. . . Next season my play [*Vania*] . . . will be done at the Mali. Lucrative, that, you see.' (Chekhov, *Pisma*, VIII, p. 100.)

In the event the Mali ruined its own chance. Chekhov and Kondratev had reckoned without the stupidity of the Repertoire Committee. Chekhov was summoned like a tradesman and told that Act Three would not do and had to be rewritten. He was understandably outraged and withdrew his script.

Nemirovich, who was still officially a member of the Repertoire Committee although he no longer attended meetings, got wind of what had happened. In desperation, on March 26 he went to see Maria Chekhova: He again asked for the play which, of course, would be done without changes. Could Chekhov telegraph his permission so that they could finalize their repertoire and start casting? Maria Chekhova was sufficiently impressed to write to her brother for the second time that day. No immediate reply was forthcoming until late April when Chekhov handed over the play. Chekhov had still not seen a performance of *The Seagull*. On May 1 a special performance, in make-up and costume but without sets, was arranged for Chekhov at the Paradiz Theatre. His reaction was mixed but on the whole followed informed opinion: he agreed with his sister and the critic of *Russkaia Misl'*

that Stanislavski and Roksana were not good but endorsed the general view
that the production was outstanding. Chekhov was a man of widely fluctuat-
ing moods – an effect of his tuberculosis. Gorki records that on a bad
day Chekhov hated everyone. He therefore expressed various views in various ways to various people, depending on the moment. This has provided
more than ample opportunity for selective quotation. To Stanislavski he
said:

> – You act splendidly, but that's not my character. That's not what I
> wrote.
> – What's wrong? I asked.
> – He wears checked trousers and has cracked shoes.
> That was all the explanation A[nton] P[avlovich] gave me, for all my
> persistence. . . . I only solved this riddle six years later when *The Seagull*
> was revived.' (*Sobranie Sochinenii*, V, p. 336.)

Writing to Gorki on the 9th Chekhov was more brutal:

> 'I saw *The Seagull* without sets. I can't judge the play dispassionately since
> the Seagull herself was so awful, sobbing out loud all the time and Trigor-
> in (the bellelettrist) wandered about the stage and spoke like some par-
> alytic; "he has no will of his own", which the actor interpreted in such a
> way it made me sick to look at it. Still, on the whole, all right, thrilling.
> In places I couldn't quite believe I had actually written it.' (Chekhov,
> *Pisma*, VIII, p. 170.)

Chekhov's dominant impression of the overall production remained, nonetheless, positive. On the 15th he wrote again to Iordanov:

> 'In Moscow they performed my *Seagull* for me at the Art Theatre. The
> production is amazing . . . the Mali theatre pales in comparison, as far as
> *mise-en-scène* and production are concerned, as inferior to the Meininger
> as to the new Art Theatre, which is performing at the moment in very
> poor conditions.'

He confirmed his judgement when he wrote to Stanislavski on June 24:

> 'I learned from Luzhski, dear Konstantin Sergeievich, that you are in
> Moscow. I, too, am in Moscow. Could we see each other? The fact is I
> was in Petersburg and talked to Marks [his publisher] about bringing out
> the play with your *mise-en-scène*. He liked my suggestion – and now the
> rest is up to you . . . Perhaps we can have lunch at the Slav Bazar, if that
> suits you. I warmly shake your hand. Yours, A. Chekhov. (Chekhov,
> *Pisma*, VIII, p. 208.)

From Stanislavski's point of view the first season had been only a partial success. The director had to an extent obscured the actor. There had been no major acting triumphs. Trigorin had been a great disappointment. It must be said, however, that if *he* had taken the wrong line on the character then so had Nemirovich, the 'expert', who had written to Chekhov after the first night to say that Stanislavski had 'successfully captured the soft, weak-willed tone' – precisely the quality to which Chekhov took exception. Nowhere is there recorded any disagreement about the interpretation of the role. Stanislavski himself attributed his failure to his lack of knowledge of the literary world and the fact that he had no living model on which to base his interpretation.

His one real achievement, Lövborg in *Hedda Gabler*, went comparatively unnoticed, although it was appreciated by the more discriminating:

'An aura of genius surrounded Lövborg. This rarely happens in the theatre. Genius is talked about but not experienced. He made the audience feel it and not just take it for granted. And this to my mind was the most valuable aspect of the interpretation of Ibsen's character. Lövborg was a volcano of passion, he was all storm and whirlwind, he was all thunderstorm. And the actor was able to convey this element literally bursting out of its shell, tearing it apart.' (Efros. MXAT, 1898–1923, p. 56.)

An eye-witness at the final dress rehearsal described the effect on the audience:

'At the final rehearsal, Stanislavski, as the wild genius Lövborg, who had just lost his manuscript, rushed onto the stage like a thing possessed – "all storm and fury". It was such a shock that there was a stir in the auditorium. Several people leapt to their feet.' (Quoted by E. Poliakova in Stanislavski, Moscow, 1977, p. 154.)

All this was achieved without any obvious external characteristics, no conventional signs of 'genius', and almost without make-up. It was achieved by inner transformation:

'It was Stanislavski's face and yet also the face of the extravagant genius, Lövborg. As if the "make-up" came from within, was there under the skin of the face and so transformed it. The only make-up here was the soul.' (Efros, *K. S. Stanislavski*, pp. 88–89.)

Lenski could not have asked for more.

It is difficult to locate precise turning-points in an actor's career but it is worth noting that this performance follows immediately on the encounter with Chekhov and the demands his plays made on the actor's inner life. In subsequent seasons Stanislavski gave performances in which the psychological is emphasized rather than external appearance and technique. The accumulated lessons of the past were beginning to bear fruit.

As far as the theatre was concerned the outside world was not to know in what dire financial straits the company found itself. The losing battle to capture audiences was forgotten. The Moscow Art Theatre was pronounced a 'success'. Thus the *Novostni Dnia* confidently stated that Stanislavski and Nemirovich had:

> 'established their audience and achieved something unparallelled in the history of Russian theatre, a continuous series of full houses throughout a complete season, with three or four plays. Needless to say the Open Art Theatre achieved its position under a barrage of criticism from all those who stand for the hackneyed, the *status quo* in the theatre.' (*Novostni Dnia*, March 1, 1899.)

The foundations of the Moscow Art legend had been laid.

CHAPTER EIGHT

UNCLE VANIA

The shareholders approached the future boldly. Given the losses there might have been a temptation to cut back. But they were determined to maintain standards and were not prepared to compromise on sets, production values or the rehearsal period; on the contrary, they planned to build a new theatre and provide it with all the latest equipment. As the first season ended preparations for the second began.

The repertoire was much as before. The first production would be another historic drama by Aleksei Tolstoi, *The Death of Ivan the Terrible*. This would be followed by *Uncle Vania*, a revival of *Twelfth Night* from the Society of Art and Literature and Hauptmann's *Drayman Henschel*. In later July, Nemirovich suggested the inclusion of another Hauptmann play, *Lonely People*. Chekhov who was now following the theatre's activities with great interest from his 'exile' in Yalta, approved. He found the play 'intelligent and theatrical'. *The Seagull*, *Antigone* and *Fiodor* remained in the repertoire.

The full burden of creative planning fell once more to Stanislavski. It was a well-nigh impossible task, demanding total concentration of energy. The family business took second place. Always scrupulous in his affairs, at a shareholders' meeting on March 10, he proposed that since he was not providing a full service his salary be reduced from 5000 to 4000 roubles. Later that same month he took a so-called holiday with Lilina, actually spending the time working on the production plan for *Drayman Henschel*. As Lilina wrote to her daughter, Kira: 'Papa writes all day and thinks about his plan. I read.' Returning to Moscow in early April he began to work on *Henschel* and *Ivan*. The first readings of *Vania* took place at the beginning of May. This time round there was no question of preparing a production plan well in advance. It was written during rehearsals. This had the advantage of bringing Stanislavski and Nemirovich closer together in the early stages but it also increased the pressure. The casting of *Vania* brought Stanislavski a great disappointment. He had decided to play the title role, with Vishnievski playing Astrov. Nemirovich was not entirely happy but initially said nothing. Finally he managed to persuade the two actors to exchange roles. Writing to Chekhov he expressed his relief at having managed to get his own way at last, adding that Stanislavski would make an excellent Astrov.

For his part Stanislavski was more than a little worried. To have to struggle with a difficult role like Astrov, which he did not find at all sympathetic, while preparing three other productions, was an almost intolerable burden. Preliminary work continued and on May 24 Chekhov was able to see what had been done with the first two acts which he thought 'went splendidly'. Stanislavski decided to spend the summer in Moscow. Lilina and the children were sent to Liubimovka while he finished the production plan for *Vania*, rehearsed *Ivan*, sketched in the broad outlines of the production plan for *Henschel* and discussed the sets of *Vania* and *Ivan* with Simov. In mid-June he made a short trip to the Volga, with Lilina, buying materials for *Ivan* in Kazan. Finally, on June 29, he made what was now a regular visit to Vichy to take the waters, although this did not prevent him from continuing to work. Pressure of work now obliged him to appoint assistant directors and supervise preliminary rehearsals. The first of these was Aleksandr Sanin who had been his close collaborator at the Society. On July 21 he sent Sanin the production plans for the crowd scenes in *Ivan*. In that same letter he announced his final disillusion with French theatre after seeing a poor performance of Feydeau's *La Dame de Chez Maxime* – 'routine, routine'. Two days later he wrote again:

'I have once more experienced the negative side of theatre. I am returning with the firm intention to strive for truth and the most realistic action both in tragedy and in the emptiest farce. Only then can the theatre make a serious statement. Otherwise it is a toy (as in France) and a very boring toy.' (SS, VII, p. 163.)

He had written to his mother in even stronger terms.

'I impatiently await my return to Moscow as the West, with its bogus culture, its posturings and affectation, with all its marks of decadence, grates on my nerves appallingly.' (Letter to E. V. Alexeieva, July 20, 1899, Ibid., p. 160.)

He left Vichy at the end of July, stopping over in Berlin on his way to Sevastopol where he was to join Lilina and the children. Once there he was again on the look-out for any genuine objects or materials or clothing which might be useful for *Ivan*.

In spite of all the dissatisfactions he had experienced the break had done him good. Friends and colleagues had been seriously worried about his health and the pace at which he had been working. On July 23, Nemirovich wrote to him:

'You can't go on working the way you have been working ... you can't and that's an end of it'. (*Ezhegodnik* MXAT, 1949–50, p. 158.)

There were no concrete suggestions, however, as to how his workload could be reduced. Nemirovich, who was as usual spending the summer in Yalta, arrived in the middle of August and stayed for two days. He was relieved to find Stanislavski in good form, looking, as he wrote to Sanin on the 17th, better than he had for months. That same day he wrote to Stanislavski asking for help with *Lonely People* which he was working on. His talent was for keeping a tight grip on the structure and maintaining the integrity of the whole. He lacked capacity to visualize, to fill the stage with significant detail. Stanislavski had promised to help. Could he do so now?

> 'One hint from you and I've got a whole scene. . . . Just take some scraps of paper and write down the first thing that comes into your head – salad on a broken plate, physical attitudes, shouts, a departure by steamer . . .' (N-D Archive No. 1558.)

A few days later he outlined Stanislavski's workload for September:

> 'So, our work comes down to five plays. You've got to prepare the role of Ivan to perfection, get Astrov absolutely ready, direct *Ivan* in its entirety, tighten up *Henschel*, bolster up *Twelfth Night* and run over *Antigone* and *Fiodor*.' (Ibid., pp. 166–68.)

So much for his earlier concern about his colleague being overworked. He did, however, make one concession. Stanislavski would only play the opening performances of *Ivan*, then the title role would be taken over by someone else – in the event, Meierhold – while he rehearsed Astrov.

Stanislavski returned to Moscow on August 28 and on the 29th saw what work his assistant had done on *Ivan*. According to Knipper, Sanin was so nervous he practically bit his fingers down to the knuckle. Stanislavski took over and rehearsed for the next month, managing in the interim to provide Nemirovich with detailed plans for the first two acts of *Lonely People*. On September 8 there was a costume and make-up parade. The first dress rehearsals followed on September 10 and 11. The final dress rehearsal was scheduled for the 27th and the play opened two nights later.

Stanislavski had taken a strong line with Aleksei Tolstoi's play, expanding it into an epic, filling it with spectacle. Once again he insisted on the crucial role of the people. This meant, as before, expanding the crowd scenes, making them central to the action. But it was a very different crowd from *Fiodor*. As he had written to Sanin on July 21:

> 'In rehearsal concentrate primarily on keeping the voices down, emphasize the subjugation, the signs of starvation, famished people shaking with cold. In short the two dominant moods are cold and hunger. In two or three places the crowd rises to a pitch which demands a terrifying flash of power which immediately subsides into total nervous exhaustion.' (SS, VII, p. 161.)

In his own interpretation of the leading role he once more pursued the psychological. This was a many-sided Ivan which Stanislavski created single handed. Nemirovich, who was directing, simply let him get on with it:

'You managed to capture the most profound aspect of Ivan – his retribution for his whole life, for his tyranny, for all the vileness which filled his life and his character. You succeeded in painting a portrait that filled everything about it with horror yet also conveyed the human qualities in him that lead to destruction and inexpressible suffering. What must the sufferings be of a man who in his time condemned tens and hundreds of thousands of people to suffer for them to reconcile me, the audience, to him? How heavy the torment and the torture, of the most sincere and profound kind, that passes through me so that I can say to this fanatic: "God forgive you!"

... from the very first speech at the very first rehearsal I saw I was immediately satisfied with your interpretation. .... That is why I reserved my notes until the final rehearsals. ....' (*Izbranie Pisma*, I, pp. 190–191.)

These notes were confined to warnings about excessive pausing and against overdoing an old man's cough.

Chaliapin, who attended a rehearsal on the 25th, according to Knipper 'banged the walls with delight'. Efros, too, saluted Stanislavski's achievement in combining the Ivan of history, the myth-figure, and a real human being, in encompassing the heights of heroic tragedy and ordinary human drama. But the favourable judgements of the professionals were not shared by the public. True, Stanislavski was ill on opening night. Much against the wishes of the rest of the company he insisted that an announcement be made before the curtain went up. The audience froze. Nonetheless that cannot fully account for the overall failure of the production.

Stanislavski's own performance evoked the now familiar criticism that he had reduced a 'heroic' character to something commonplace. The public was simply not ready for his three-dimensional portrait although it was endorsed by Aleksei Tolstoi himself who ascribed the generally adverse reaction to the fact that audiences and critics alike insisted on clinging to their outdated notions of what the theatre should be. Perhaps nowhere was Stanislavski more modern as an actor than in his continued attempts to destroy the conventional, two-dimensional image of historic or heroic figures in order to reveal the difficulty of actually living history and the human cost involved. Stanislavski's Ivan was not the towering monster made famous later by Eisenstein but a decrepit shambles of a man, impotent where he had once been strong, guilt-ridden where he had once been ruthless. That was what the audience disliked. But Stanislavski the director had also overloaded the play, attempting to endow it with meanings it could not bear. He had stretched the material beyond its endurance, trying to transform a

minor play into an epic drama. That, combined with his own provoca-
tive interpretation, made it almost impossible for the production to
succeed.

He was very depressed. Nemirovich wrote to Chekhov:

'. . . The actor [in him] is aware that he has *lost* his audience but he still has
to go on performing. He spends an enormous amount of nervous energy
but it doesn't get across, the audience does not like his *conception*. I don't
know whether the audience is right or not. I'm so used to Alekseiev's
interpretation which I find absolutely satisfying . . . What is exhausting
for an actor is not so much the part as lack of success in it. And Konstantin Sergeievich is so worn out that he was not fit for work on the
day of *Ivan* or the day after. That's why so far he has not been near
Vania.' (*Ezhegodnik* MXAT, 1944, p. 119.)

The opening of *Vania* was less than four weeks away. *The Seagull* was
back in the repertoire; a matinée of *Twelfth Night* on October 3 was well
reviewed and *Drayman Henschel* opened on the 5th to good notices but
went on to play to poor houses. Stanislavski was still dogged by illness. He
put himself entirely in Nemirovich's hands as far as Astrov was concerned –
at least that is what Nemirovich claimed when writing to Chekhov after the
opening. The production plan represented an advance over *The Seagull*. The
sets Stanislavski had created with Simov looked as though they had been
lived in; the props looked as though they had been used over many years
and the costumes looked as though they had been worn. The action was
full of the trivia of life, the deadening trivia against which the characters try
to struggle in their attempt to remain spiritually and mentally alive. The
detail of daily life was an essential agent in the drama.

Stanislavski found his way into the character of Astrov with difficulty.
His method was still to work from the outside in, to establish a sequence of
actions in the hope that they would stimulate the right mood and emotion.
His insecurity in the early stages of rehearsal was indicated by his rest-
lessness, his inability to keep still. When actors are uncertain or do not feel
at one with their characters they become overactive, hoping that continuous
movement will disguise the absence of genuine thought or feeling. Thus he
wandered round the house and garden, noting everything, examining the
plants, picking the heads off dead flowers. Above all, he swatted mosquitoes.
He remembered how family and friends were tormented by these creatures
during the summer at Liubimovka. The production plan contains instructions to everyone to swat them and even, as an added protection, to put
handkerchiefs over their faces. Nemirovich was not at all happy with this
particular piece of local colour.

'I don't want any handkerchiefs on anyone's face to keep off the mosquitoes.

This is a nonsense and I can't accept it. And I can tell you for certain that Chekhov won't like it; I know his tastes and creative nature extremely well. I can tell you in all confidence that this particular detail doesn't introduce anything new. . . . It's one of those details that's just asking for trouble . . . and that's why I am asking you to drop it for my sake, please.' (Iz., Pis., I, p. 198.)

The letter also contained another complaint. Stanislavski, hardly surprisingly perhaps, was not sure of his lines. What's the point, Nemirovich asks, of his trying to discipline other members of the cast when the company's leading director and producer is setting a bad example? He received a curt refusal. Stanislavski could snap back when he felt artistically in a corner. So, for the time being, the handkerchiefs and the mosquitoes remained. Only gradually, as rehearsals progressed and confidence grew, did the welter of detail disappear. There were, however, more important problems of interpretation to be resolved, in particular the relationship between Astrov and Elena, the professor's wife. Stanislavski's original intention was for both characters to play at a high level of intensity. Nemirovich did not agree.

'You interpret the little scene between Vania and Elena (Act Two) as though she was genuinely afraid about his drinking. That's not in the play, on the contrary, for Elena to be afraid in these circumstances is *not at all in keeping* with her character.

– You've been drinking again today. What's the point?

The very structure of the sentence gives a much quieter tone, the languid tone which marks Elena's attitude to everything going on around her.' (Ibid., p. 199.)

Nemirovich was also worried about their final scenes in Act Four. So was Knipper. Stanislavski, she wrote to Chekhov, was playing the scene like a passionate lover, clutching at feeling like a drowning man at a straw. Chekhov, who resolutely refused to give explanations to actors when they met him, was willing to be categorical on paper:

'But that's wrong, absolutely wrong. Astrov finds Elena attractive, she captivates him with her beauty but in the last act he already knows that she is lost to him forever – and he speaks of her in this scene in exactly the same tone as he speaks of the heat in Africa and he kisses her simply because there doesn't seem anything else to do. If Astrov plays this scene vehemently it will ruin the mood of the whole fourth act, which is quiet and muted.' (Chekhov, *Pisma*, VIII, p. 272.)

Chekhov reinforced this view in the only comment he made to Stanislavski on his performance:

'Listen, he whistles. Uncle Vania moans and groans but *he* whistles.' (SS. VI, p. 342.)

Stanislavski was at first mystified, as he had been over Trigorin, but a short while later tried it out and realized that, of course, it worked.

Even if Stanislavski the actor had not yet found the right tone, Stanislavski the director, realized that Act Four as a whole was a problem. He confided his anxieties to Efros:

'The basic idea is in "they've gone". The director must make the audience feel clearly what their departure means – so everyone goes home depressed, as though the lid had been nailed down on the coffin and everything was dead for ever. Without that the act doesn't exist, without that there's no end to the play. . . . What would happen if the audience didn't feel they were really "going" but merely that the actors were wandering back to the dressing room to take off their make-up? Can an actor convey everything he has to with just one exit?

I'm told there are actors who can do this. I haven't seen them, I don't know them. During one rather tedious break in rehearsal while we were trying to work out an answer as it were, one of the crew who was tinkering with the set, started banging with a stick. And we . . . suddenly detected in that banging the clatter of hoofs going over a bridge. Why not make use of it, providing it conveyed the author's intention truthfully and expressively and gave us what we needed to achieve the aim of the production?' (Reported by Efros in MXAT, 1898–1923, pp. 232–33.)

The same, he added, was also true of many other details in the production. This statement again stresses the organic, functional nature of Stanislavski's production effects. They are there to illuminate the play and if necessary cover the deficiencies of the actors.

By opening night the problems had been ironed out. Stanislavski and Nemirovich could congratulate themselves on another effective and creative collaboration. On October 23 Meierhold wrote to Chekhov:

'The play is exceptionally well directed. What I note above all is the artistic restraint which is sustained throughout the entire production. For the first time the two directors fully complement each other; one, a director–actor, has a great deal of imagination but is inclined to go over the top; the other, a director–author, protects the writer's interests. And it's well for the latter to have the upper hand.' (Meierhold, *Perepiska*, p. 23, Moscow, 1976.)

As to Stanislavski's Astrov, it was considered by many to be his finest role in any Chekhov play, not excepting Vershinin in *Three Sisters* which he was to play a year later. Writing to Chekhov, Nemirovich described the line they had taken on the part:

'We present Astrov as a materialist in the best sense of the term, incapable
of loving, relating to women with elegant cynicism, scarcely perceptible
cynicism. There is sensitivity but no passion there. And all this in that
half-joking form women find so attractive.' (Iz., Pis., I, pp. 195–6.)

But there was more to Stanislavski's interpretation than that. His performance as Astrov revealed an inner tension born of struggle. The word 'tense',
'tensely' occurs frequently in Stanislavski's production notes. Astrov is a
man of strong convictions, if not of strong passions, but a man who under-
cuts himself with a deprecating remark as soon as he feels he has revealed
too much about himself. He drinks to deaden the pain and if he drinks too
much it is because there is too much pain. Late in life Knipper maintained
that Stanislavski's insight into the character sprang from an identification
of his own attempts to create a new kind of theatre with Astrov's attempts
to plant new forests. Astrov's frustrations were his frustrations. She also
recalled the depth and feeling with which he played his last scene with her
incidentally revealing the measure to which he had brought together into a
complex being the intense lover he had originally conceived and the cynic
Chekhov had described:

'. . . what a wonderfully poetic and courageous person he created in Astrov
and with such lightness of touch. And in the last act when he went over
to the map of Africa and looked at it: "Ah, the heat in Africa – it must
be dreadful." How much sorrow was packed into the experience of that
bitter phrase.' (Olga Knipper Chekhova, *O Stanislavskom* p. 266.)

The audience found a broader social meaning in the performance. For them
Astrov's struggle and suffering went beyond the personal to the state of
Russia itself. Efros placed Astrov in the line of the 'superfluous men', that
peculiarly Russian phenomenon – men of talent and ability who for one
reason or another never fulfil their promise and make no mark on their age,
effect no change and finally succumb beneath the dead-weight of history.
Astrov is on his way to join their ranks:

'All Astrov's traits emerged clearly defined and life-like in Stanislavski's
performance, all the elements of the image equally – the typical and the
individual. He plays the social and the psychological aspects clearly. He
revealed this man in his entirety. You could clearly feel the "wood-
demon" already running to seed, coarsening, yielding to the pressure of
"a way of life" but with brave hopes and thoughts still glowing under the
embers. You could feel the soul of a gifted poet, flying across the centuries, dedicated to the most far-distant dreams. You could see the broad
sweep of this soul, in which there was a great thirst for beauty. . . . His
interpretation excited, delighted the audience, saddened them, evoked in

them fierce protest against that form of Russian life which turns Astrov into a mere "crank", a new variation of "superfluous men", and little by little transforms great strength, great power of soul into everyday triviality.

Stanislavski's Astrov was fully realistic but it was also romantic. And with all that it was beautiful as a piece of theatre.' (Efros, MXAT 1898–1923 pp. 237–238.)

As for Stanislavski himself, he was astonished at his own success. 'I do nothing and the public loves it,' he remarked to Knipper showing he had yet to learn the supreme actor's art: 'doing nothing' to maximum effect.

The production did not enjoy the immediate success *The Seagull* had obtained. It took hold only slowly but established a permanent place in the repertoire which *The Seagull* did not. It was the capacity of the Moscow Art Theatre, through productions like *Vania*, to speak to its age, as, in the past, only great literature had done, that made it a focal point for advanced opinion.

In January 1900, Gorki saw a performance of *Vania* after which he confessed to Chekhov that although he was not exactly the sensitive type he had cried like a schoolgirl. The play, he wrote to Chekhov, tore him apart like a rough-edged saw. He went back for a second visit, arriving for Act Three, and wrote to Chekhov again. His praise for the production was high but not unconditional:

'Pity that Vishnievski doesn't understand Uncle but on the other hand the rest are a wonder. Stanislavski's Astrov in minor respects is not what it should be. Still they all play marvellously! The Mali theatre is unbelievably crude in comparison with this company. How aware and intelligent these people are, how much artistic flair they have! . . . All in all this theatre gave me the impression of being solid, serious and important. I'm sorry that I don't live in Moscow otherwise I would go to this marvel of a theatre.' (Gorki, *Sobranie Sochinenie*, XXVIII, p. 117.)

Chekhov's response was to invite him to Yalta in April, when the company would be on tour:

'You need to get nearer to this theatre and observe it so you can write plays.' (Chekhov, *Pisma*, IX, p. 67.)

Of his own experience, in November 1899 he had written:

'. . . I thank heaven that, sailing through the ups and downs of life, I finally came on such a wonderful island as the Moscow Art Theatre.' (Chekhov, *Pisma* VIII, p. 297.)

If the young Gorki was a visitor to the theatre so was the elderly and

now immensely venerable Lev Tolstoi. He saw *Vania* on January 24 and
was pleased with Stanislavski's performance and with the production as a
whole. On February 18 Lenin paid his first known visit to the theatre to see
Drayman Henschel. His endorsement of the theatre's policy and his approval
of its artistic practice were later to assure the company's survival. Even
Ermolova, who had spent her life at the Mali, talked of leaving and joining
the new company.

In the meantime, Hauptmann's *Lonely People*, with Meierhold in the
lead, had opened on December 16 to a huge success, although most of the
company were prepared either for a total flop or, at best, a lukewarm reception. But, here again, a skilfully orchestrated portrayal of domestic life,
presented in what was now the company's 'Chekhovian' manner found an
echo in the public mind. Although the debts were mounting, the future
seemed bright.

CHAPTER NINE

THREE SISTERS

By the time the season ended on February 20 Stanislavski was almost at breaking point. He had pushed himself hard, performing even when not in the best of health. He was exhausted yet could not sleep. Tension had been increased by his first serious disagreement over management with Nemirovich. Its subject was Savva Morozov.

Without Morozov the theatre would have gone under. Apart from his original investment, he had put up 21,000 roubles at the end of 1899 in order to extend the lease on the Hermitage theatre. He later subsidized the 1900–1901 season to the tune of 120,000 roubles. From time to time he would give money to actresses to buy the costumes they needed for modern roles. He was now a constant visitor to the theatre, attending rehearsals and generally taking an interest in the day-to-day running of the company. There was nothing malicious in this, no sense that Morozov was protecting his investment. He was simply passionately devoted to the Moscow Art Theatre and what it stood for. But Nemirovich suspected a take-over in which he would be the loser. The resentment he had felt against Morozov from the very beginning, and which he had found it increasingly difficult to keep hidden, burst out in an angry letter which he wrote to Stanislavski just before the end of the season:

'Did I start this business with you for some capitalist to come along and try to turn me into – how shall I put it? – a kind of secretary?' (N-D Archive No. 1571.)

Stanislavski, normally reticent in all personal matters, sent back a letter which was equally exasperated in tone. He had been here before. He had seen the Society of Art and Literature founder in a welter of pettiness and selfishness, just the sort of destructive emotions displayed in Nemirovich's letter. He had tiptoed a path through the rampant egos of colleagues, filling in the cracks, discreetly, where he could, often made himself look ridiculous in the process – for Nemirovich's sake. He had made financial sacrifices, denying his family essentials, and reducing his own personal budget. As to any artistic satisfaction, there was not much of that left:

'I have reconciled myself to the fact that (often) I neither play in nor direct things I long to do but act what I have to, not what I want to. In a word I am ruining myself financially and morally, without complaint as long as my nerves are not stretched to breaking-point. That's the stage we have obviously now reached and, as you can see, I have started to kick. . . . In fact I'm sick and tired that everyone else seems to have the right to talk about themselves but *I'm* not . . . and that's unfair. . . .

I will not remain in the theatre without you. We started it together and should lead it together. I recognize in you, of course, as in any human being, certain deficiencies but at the same time *I value your many good qualities highly* and especially the good relationship you have with me and my work. Without Morozov I cannot remain in the theatre *under any circumstances* Why? Because I value Morozov's good qualities. . . . Remember, I have no money, I have a family and moreover *have no right* to take risks with that part of my property. I believe . . . in Morozov's honesty blindly. My confidence in him is so rock-solid that I have no written agreement with him. It's superfluous. . . . In the future I'm not going to play a double game, trying, privately, to reconcile Morozov with Nemirovich and vice versa. If conflict is unavoidable then let it happen quickly and our enterprise be wrecked while it will still be missed, let us Russians prove once more that we are rotten to the core and that personal egoism and petty ambition will destroy anything worthwhile . . . (SS, VII, pp. 166–7.)

This exchange was the first of many similar arguments of the next few years. It marked perhaps the end of the pioneer days when everything was sacrificed to the common goal. Success was to bring its own problems. For the moment, however, Stanislavski's uncompromising tone put an end to discussion.

He took a short rest with Lilina although it was not long before he made an expedition to the Archangel area to study the northern landscape and collect material for Ostrovski's *Snow Maiden*, the by-now almost regulation 'spectacular' which was to open the 1900–1901 season. Rehearsals began in March but were interrupted the following month by a tour which had been arranged for Chekhov's benefit. His health did not allow him to come to Moscow and he had not yet seen *Vania*. The company therefore decided to take four productions – *Seagull*, *Vania*, *Lonely People* and *Hedda Gabler* – to Sevastopol and Yalta on the principle 'if the mountain won't come to Mahomet, Mahomet will come to the mountain'. The company were a little disconcerted to learn that many figures from the Russian literary establishment were to be present but set off on the two-day train journey with determination.

It was an idyllic 'month in the country' for all. Chekhov was pleased with

the production of *Vania* and impressed with Hauptmann's gifts as a dramatist, as opposed to Ibsen whom he did not rate at all highly – 'not a
playwright'. According to his sister, Maria, it was the happiest time he ever
spent in all his years of enforced exile in Yalta. He was constantly at the
theatre and even, one day, tried to teach the stage carpenter how to imitate
a cricket. Stanislavski, for his part, was fascinated by the conversation of
the literary men present at the many lunch parties. Chekhov, in particular,
brought books and literature alive to him in a way his schoolmasters had
never succeeded in doing. He also came to know two men who were to
become life-long friends, Sergei Rachmaninov and Maxim Gorki. He found
Gorki fascinating:

> 'For me centre stage was held by Gorki who immediately excited me with
> his charm. In his unusual figure, face, [provincial] accent, extraordinary
> way of gesticulating, revealing the peasant in him at moments of high
> emotion, in his bright, childlike smile, in the at times tragically heartfelt
> expression of his face, in his colourful, expressive speech, whether light-
> hearted or intense, there appeared a certain gentleness of soul and grace
> and looking at his stooping body one saw a special kind of physical
> expressiveness and outward beauty. I often caught myself admiring his
> stance and his gestures.' (SS, V, p. 345.)

Gorki was equally taken with Stanislavski. On May 1, as the party was
breaking up, he gave him a photograph with the inscription:

> 'To Konstantin Sergeieich Alekseiev a great and beautiful man, an artist
> and the creator of a new theatre. I wish, with all my heart, that every
> sensible man who meets you for the first time may love and respect you
> as I now love and respect you. . . .'

Rehearsals for *Snow Maiden* resumed in Moscow in May immediately on
the company's return and in the middle of the month work also began on
An Enemy of the People. There was a major casting problem in *Snow
Maiden*. Stanislavski could not find anybody he thought right for the role
of Tsar Berendei. It was finally offered to a young actor who was to become
one of the great stars of the Moscow Art Theatre, Vasili Kachalov. Not
that Kachalov had been enthusiastically welcomed into the company. In
March he had auditioned at Nemirovich's invitation, in the roles both of
Boris Godunov and Ivan the Terrible in *The Death of Ivan the Terrible*.
Stanislavski's reaction had been discouraging. He had said, quite frankly,
that he was not sure that he and Kachalov spoke the same language or that
they could use what he had to offer. On the other hand they did not want
to lose him because in time he might become a Moscow Art kind of actor.
What he was trying to tell Kachalov, discreetly was that he had too many
bad habits as an actor. The following day Nemirovich was rather more

blunt. Kachalov nevertheless elected to stay and for two months attended all the *Snow Maiden* rehearsals, watching and learning. His application was rewarded. One day Stanislavski came up to him, drew him to one side and explained that as everyone else had failed as Berendei he could try. Three days later he showed what he could do. This time Stanislavski applauded:

'That was wonderful! You are one of us! You've understood it all! You've understood the most important thing. The very essence of our theatre. Hurrah!' (V. I. Kachalov, p. 24, *Iskusstvo*, Moscow, 1954.)

Stanislavski was rarely lavish with his praise but when he saw something of real quality he was open-hearted in his generosity. He had recognized Kachalov's obvious talent at their first encounter. He was tall, slender, elegant, well educated, with a naturally musical voice. Indeed reference to his 'velvet tones' became a critical cliché. But he had come to Moscow convinced that he had nothing to learn and it showed. He was, he told his friends, 'a proper actor'. When he had auditioned in Petersburg he had turned up in a top hat and a vivid orange overcoat, very much the leading actor. Such an attitude did not suit Stanislavski. But now he had proved that he was both willing and able to learn. Hence Stanislavski's delight. He worshipped nothing so much as real, native talent but he would not tolerate conceit – 'Love the art in yourself, not yourself in art.' Kachalov had come through.

Work continued on *Snow Maiden* and *Enemy of the People* intensively throughout June so much so that on July 10 Nemirovich wrote insisting that Stanislavski should rest for the remainder of the month and the whole of August. Rest, in reality, meant simply being out of Moscow. Stanislavski continued to plan *Snow Maiden* and learn the part of Dr Stockman. Disillusioned by his previous year's visit to Vichy he stayed in Russia, going first to Essentuki to take the cure, then to Novosibirsk, from there to Yalta where he joined up with the rest of his family and thence to Alupka. As always, when absent from the centre of things, he engaged in a voluminous correspondence.

Being so near to Chekhov's home Stanislavski was able to contact him and finally to report to Nemirovich on August 9 with exciting news:

'*I am writing in terms of the utmost secrecy.* Yesterday I managed to drag out of Chekhov the fact that tomorrow he is going to Gursuf to write. He will be back in Alupka in a week and will read what he has written. He hopes to be able to deliver the play on September 1 ... He is writing a play about the life of military men with four roles for young women and 12 for men. I know that we can expect good parts for Meierhold, Knipper, Sheliabushskaia, Vishnievski and Kalushi ...' (SS, VII, p. 185.)

Great efforts had been made to persuade Chekhov to write another play.

It was essential for the new season. This time it seemed, the play would really be their own. *The Seagull* had been rescued, as it were, from theatrical hacks; *Vania* was a revision of an earlier piece; the new play would be specifically tailored for the company. Chekhov had in fact indicated to Knipper, soon to be his wife, that he wanted to write something for her. But work for him was an increasing effort and it was by no means certain that he would be able to deliver on time.

Stanislavski returned to Moscow at the end of August and saw the work which had been done on the first three acts of *Snow Maiden*. He was pleased with what had been achieved and took over rehearsals on September 4. Gorki attended rehearsals and brought with him Leopold Sulerzhitski who was to become Stanislavski's most devoted assistant, disciple and friend.

Immense care, attention and money had been lavished on *Snow Maiden*. Stanislavski had insisted on visual authenticity as usual but out of that Simov had created a magical world. The sets and costumes were dazzling. The production was full of imaginative detail but when it opened on September 24 it was a flop. Critical opinion was sharply divided. Gorki wrote a glowing letter to Chekhov on the quality of the acting. Efros praised the production for its richness and brilliance of invention but others found it overloaded. Kachalov was badly mauled by one critic for his interpretation of Tsar Berendei. Stanislavski immediately sent him a letter of support, taking full responsibility for the line that had been taken on the role and begging the young actor not to lose faith in himself. As for the audiences, they simply stayed away or, as Meierhold put it, slavishly repeated the carping criticisms which had appeared in the popular press.

It was Meierhold, in a letter to Chekhov on October 1, who put his finger on the true reason for the play's failure.

'... *Snow Maiden* is simply old-fashioned. It's obvious that in troubled times like ours, when everything is falling apart around us, a simple appeal to beauty is not enough. ... Gorki considers, I don't know why, that the public and the press are ignorant. Our critics are ignorant, that's a fact. ... But the public? Credulous it might be but it hasn't lost its instinct. Isn't the play, surely, beautiful but thin?' (Meierhold, *Perepiska*, p. 28.)

Meierhold's analysis was proved correct by the phenomenal success of *An Enemy of the People* which opened a month later. Stanislavski's Stockman was one of his greatest performances. It was also one of his most instinctive. His remarkable attribute as an actor was his capacity for physical transformation from within. Astrov had been pudgy, running to seed; Stockman was thin, wiry, stooping, with a characteristic gesture of the hand. Where Astrov had been all circles Stockman was all angles. Stanislavski even succeeded in making his giant frame appear small. He slid into the character with an ease he had rarely, if ever, experienced before.

Stockman's body and physical patterns were put together, mostly unconsciously, from various sources. The basic shape was derived from Rimsky-Korsakov. Much later, Stanislavski realized that the hands came from a German doctor he had seen in Vienna, and the jabbing gesture used when speaking directly to someone came from Maxim Gorki whom he had observed closely in April that year. The physical characterization impressed everyone who saw it. The hands, with their characteristic shape, were photographed from many angles and a statuette was cast, fixing for ever the combative figure of Stanislavski-Stockman.

There was more to the performance, however, than a brilliant physical composition. Many friends and colleagues saw considerable affinities between Stanislavski's own personality and Stockman's – the passionate idealism, the same commitment to truth, the same lonely struggle against falsehood and corruption. Kachalov maintained that everything that was best in Stanislavski went into his performance. Certainly there is something of Stockman's Act Five naïveté and courage in Stanislavski's own character. And the decision at the end to bring in the poor off the streets and educate them was the kind of impulse he understood. This was not, of course, the first time that Stanislavski had played the part of an individual against the mob and the production notes for Act Four recall the mob scene in *Uriel Acosta*. As in *Acosta* Stanislavski insisted that the crowd should be individuated, real people in real circumstances, people with whom the audience could identify.

In this production the skills he had acquired came together, the intimacy he had learned to project for Chekhov's plays and his capacity to orchestrate a crowd. As for the 'message' of the play that was left to Ibsen. It was not consciously played. All the effort went into making people and events as laid out in the script, the 'given circumstances', authentic. In terms of a Realist aesthetic a goal had been reached.

Letters poured in but intelligent public reaction was best summed up by Sulerzhitski who wrote to Stanislavski on October 21, after a dress rehearsal:

'You don't only work upon the senses but penetrate into the very soul, you enter life itself, to a man's very "holy of holies" in a way that only a close, understanding, sensitive friend can do. . . . Listening to Stockman I found corroboration of the fact that there is not and cannot be any other outcome except the acknowledgement of truth no matter where or when, without regard to the consequences of that acknowledgement. I was always conscious of that truth, of course, but you shifted it from the realm of consciousness to the realm of feeling, i.e., you did what was necessary for that consciousness to give living results, expressed in deeds and actions.' (K.S. Archive.)

The enthusiasm, the passions which the production aroused were unprecedented. Stanislavski experienced in full measure that electric flow of energy which passes from stage to auditorium and back not only when the performance is exciting but when ideas, feelings and convictions are shared.

Chekhov arrived in Moscow on October 23, in time for the opening of *Enemy of the People*, bringing with him the first draft of the script of *Three Sisters*. Work on the play started immediately, three months behind schedule. This was to be the first Chekhov play Stanislavski directed without any initial help from Nemirovich who was preoccupied with the final stages of rehearsal for *When We Dead Awaken*, his first venture as a solo director. The first reading took place on the 29th. It did not pass off without incident. In the discussion which followed Chekhov heard his play qualified as a drama or a tragedy, while he insisted it was a comedy. This could be sorted out. When, however, one of the more pretentious members of the company began a pseudo-philosophical discourse he quietly slipped away. Stanislavski went round immediately to his flat, where he found him in an angry mood but managed to calm him down. Nonetheless the conflicting views which Chekhov and others took of his last two plays was an acute problem and one which was never satisfactorily resolved. What did he mean by 'comedy'? Turgenev, indeed, had called *A Month in the Country*, with all its destructive elements, a comedy. Molière's *Le Misanthrope* for all its black moments is a comedy. In that sense *Three Sisters* is a comedy and, after much work, Stanislavski found sufficient positive elements to justify placing it in that category. The fact remains, however, that Chekhov apart, everyone else, his own family included, found a deep well of sadness in his work – *lacrimae rerum*. Chekhov recovered from his initial displeasure and remained in Moscow throughout November, meeting Stanislavski several times to discuss the production. Just before Christmas, when he could have been helpful, Nemirovich was obliged to take his ailing sister to Mentone. Gorki described Stanislavski's *Three Sisters* as 'music, not acting', thus providing the key to the formal pattern of the production. Writing to Chekhov in January 1901, Stanislavski outlined a symphonic concept of the play's structure, virtually allegro, andante, scherzo and finale:

'Act One – joyous, lively,
Act Two – Chekhovian mood,
Act Three – terribly tense, works on speed and nerves. Towards the end energy has run out and the tempo slackens,
Act Four – not sure yet.' (SS, VII, p. 205.)

The major theme of *Three Sisters* was once more the destructive effect of the trivia of life. In this play, however, no one plants trees, there is no positive reaction, no concrete investment in the future. There is only hope and stoical endurance. The Prozorov family is invaded by vulgarity, in the person of Natasha, that 'lower middle-class vulgarian' (*meshchanka*) as Masha describes her, and its members suffer physical and moral destruction (Andrei), the loss of loved ones (Masha and Irina) or the demoralizing effect of unrewarding work (Olga). Stanislavski's production plan clearly marked the progress of the action. The staging was an expression of the human drama. Stanislavski's eye was cinematic. He was aware of the effect of visual signals. He used the language of the theatre – sound, lights, props, setting – to reveal psychological states, shifts in relationships and social meaning. Everything was in the action. All that was lacking were the camera angles.

The setting for Acts One and Two, the drawing-room, was not an enclosed box set. Chekhov indicates a drawing-room with pillars upstage behind which is another large room. To this, in collaboration with his designer, Simov, Stanislavski added a small room with five windows downstage right, a 'Lantern', with three steps leading up to it, a hall upstage right, a staircase upstage left and the door to Andrei's room, downstage left. The life of the household went on all round. The drawing-room was a place people passed through on their way *from* somewhere *to* somewhere. And the house lay within a community, whose presence was continuously felt.

In Act One, the most positive in tone, spring was in the air. The tops of the trees, beginning to bud, could be seen through the windows of the 'Lantern'. The cooing of doves could be heard. By Act Two a fundamental change had taken place. The house was in the grip of winter; outside the roofs covered in snow, the windows frozen fast. The 'Lantern' was blocked off by the grand piano which had been moved in front of the steps. The entrance to the dining-room was covered by a felt-clad screen. The stove hummed. Later a mouse could be heard gnawing in the wainscot. Toys were scattered everywhere, including a clown with clashing cymbals. Natasha's influence was evident in all the changes. Her opening dialogue is concerned with the lamps. This Stanislavski carefully prepared. He also took the opportunity to make a statement about the marriage before the Act proper began.

'It is dark in the drawing-room, the fire is almost dead, there is only a beam of light from the open door to Andrei's room. From time to time Andrei's shadow flits across the beam of light. He is pacing his room, going over his lectures. We hear Andrei's footsteps, the drone of his voice, sighs, nose-blowing, chairs being moved. Then nothing. He has stopped by the table and is leafing through some exercise books (rustling of pages). There could be the sound of something like weeping. Then nose-blowing again, footsteps, a droning voice and his shadow on stage.

In the dining-room the lamp (hanging over the table) is about to go out.

It flickers then dies. The lamps in the hall cast patches of light (through the hall windows) on the floor. Beams of light in the dining-room from the half-open doors leading to the corridor. Municipal street-lighting (transparent) in the dining-room window. . . .' (*Rezhissiorski Ekzempliari*, K. S. Stanislavskovo, Vol. 3, p. 132.)

Into this comes Natasha, the obsessive 'good wife and mother', with her sense of what is 'right and proper', her unimaginative and insensitive conformity to what she imagines the 'rules' are. Within a few lines of dialogue the audience knows what has happened during the interval.

Later in the act Stanislavski used the children's toys to counterpoint the dialogue. Thus, when Irina dreams of going to Moscow, Vershinin plays with the clown and his cymbals. When Vershinin, on his side, suggests talking a little philosophy, Tusenbach plays with a music-box. The contrast between high seriousness and triviality was physically conveyed. Doubt is cast on the characters' capacity to achieve even part of their ambitions without explicit comment. Inside and outside the house there is always distraction. Act Three is filled with noises coming from the town as the fire rages. It is in moments of high emotion, such as Masha's farewell to Vershinin in Act Four, that Stanislavski deliberately strips everything down.

However good the plan, the actual process of rehearsal proved hard going. The cast were enthusiastic and worked well but the pace was sluggish and the play would not come alive. Stanislavski came to the conclusion that only an overall increase in tempo would get them out of trouble. He insisted that Act Three move along quickly and instructed the actors not 'to overdo the pauses'. He also, as Knipper reported to Chekhov on December 16, introduced moments of more general movement, as in Act Two, where he elaborated upon Chekhov's stage directions:

'Tusenbach swoops down on Andrei, sings *"Seni, moi seni,"*, everyone dances – Irina, Chebutykin. Then when Tusenbach plays a waltz Masha reaches out, first dancing alone, then she is caught by Fedotik but she pushes him away (he's no good) and Irina dances with Rodé and into all this racket walks Natasha.' (Knipper-Chekhova, *Perepiska I*, Moscow, 1934.)

By the time Nemirovich returned in January 1901, just two weeks before the opening, the play was in need of a fresh eye. Everyone's nerves were in shreds and Stanislavski was very tired. He was also locked in a battle with Knipper over the end of Act Three.

Knipper wanted to play her scene with Irina and Olga, when she confesses her love for Vershinin, on a note of high, almost desperate emotion – a penitent woman pouring out her heart. Stanislavski saw it otherwise. He insisted that by this point in the act exhaustion had set in. He wanted a much more low-key performance. So bitter was the disagreement that, it appears, he may well have thought at one moment of taking her out of the play. Someone had to arbitrate – Nemirovich. He approached the production very carefully, saw two run-throughs of the first three acts – Act Four had yet to be rehearsed – and came to the overall conclusion that the direction was cluttered, overloaded with detail. He cleaned up the action to release the play's forward movement. It became clear that a scene could be dull even though there might be nothing obviously wrong with the direction; the problem lay in its rhythmic relationship to the one before. The question of flow also emerged as one of cardinal importance. There could be no abrupt changes once the action had started. Transitions had to be incorporated into a continuous whole like a sustained melodic line.

This provided the key to the problems of Act Three. Nemirovich agreed with Stanislavski. Masha's scene needed to be quiet. In order to enable Knipper to do that, it was necessary to modify what had gone before. The whole mood of the act needed changing. This Nemirovich achieved by placing a *physical* control on the scene – the state of the characters, just before dawn, after a sleepless and exhausting night. Each would respond according to his or her temperament and, while there might be a certain edginess, there would be no high passion. Within this new context Knipper found it easy to play the scene at the right level and even to smile. This approach to the scene was approved by Chekhov in his letters to Knipper of January 20 and 21. He was, however, not at all sure about the high level of off-stage noise but it was difficult for him to judge at a distance what the effect would be in performance.

The end of the play was also proving problematic. In the original version, Tusenbach's body is carried across the stage after Olga's final 'If only we knew'. Chekhov was not sure that this would work but Stanislavski persuaded him to leave it in. When he got into rehearsal he realized this was a mistake.

'Chekhov must be made to understand that if we follow his version we shall have to put in a crowd scene and also the noise made by the people carrying the body, otherwise it will just become a ballet. If we carry his body across such a narrow stage the set will wobble. The crowd would make a noise with their feet. This will create a deadly flat pause. And can the sisters be left to stand indifferent as Tusenbach's body is carried past? We would have to find some action for them. I'm afraid that if we try to hit too many targets at once we shall miss the main point, which is to present the author's final, optimistic conclusion, which counterbalances the many heavier passages in the play. Carrying the body across will either be boring, dispiriting and artificial or (even if we did manage to overcome all the difficulties) terribly ponderous, merely adding to the general impression of heaviness.' (*Rezhissiorski Eksempliari*, K. S. Stanislavskovo, Vol. 3, p. 289.)

Serious casting difficulties were now becoming apparent which threatened the careful balance which both directors had worked for and by and large achieved. Neither Meierhold as Tusenbach nor Sudbinin as Vershinin were adequate. Knipper had seen the problem earlier. She had written to Chekhov on January 7, that Meierhold lacked 'vitality, strength, life – he's dreary.' Everyone knew that the ideal actor for the part was Kachalov but nothing was done. A dull Tusenbach accompanied by a heavy-handed Vershinin meant that much of the play's humour was lost, and with it those optimistic elements which are essential to counterbalance the more negative moments. The only answer was for Stanislavski to take over. About a week before the opening he read the part through for Nemirovich, who told Chekhov that it was 'more than interesting', and started rehearsals proper on January 23. The play opened on January 31.

Stanislavski's Vershinin, born of unforeseen circumstance, proved one of his greatest performances. Knipper remembered it with affection and admiration all her life. It was, once again, his capacity to give genuine life to the dreams and ideals expressed in the script, to make them vital rather than rhetorical, which impressed audiences and critics alike. The social meaning of the play, the implicit criticism of the corrosive effect of Russian life, had been made clear. Thus it was possible for a teenage boy to write:

'I shook with rage all over when I saw *Three Sisters*. I mean, what these people have been reduced to, so cowed, walled in. Decent people, the Vershinins and the Tusenbachs, those dear, lovely sisters, I mean, such noble creatures who could have been happy and made others happy too. On my way home from the theatre I clenched my fists so tight they hurt and in the shadows I seemed to see the monster to which we must deliver a shattering blow even if it costs us our lives.' (Quoted by Poliakova, *Stanislavski*, Iskusstvo, Moscow, 1977, p. 178.)

In Nemirovich's judgement nearly forty years later, the production was:

'. . . the Art Theatre's best presentation both for the perfection of the ensemble and Stanislavski's direction.' (Nemirovich-Danchenko, Iz *Proshlovo*, p. 218.)

Sooner or later the Art Theatre had to confront a different audience, the critics and public of St Petersburg, the seat of government. Moscow, for all its past glories, was more or less 'the provinces'. As soon as the Moscow season had ended on February 11 with a performance of *Three Sisters*, the company moved to St Petersburg.

They were in no doubt as to the reception they could expect from the critics – prejudice and snobbery – and their expectations were fulfilled. The bulk of the company were written off as nonentities, good as an ensemble but lacking outstanding individual talent. In response to an upset Knipper, Chekhov replied that he had never expected anything but muck from the St Petersburg press. Only Chekhov and Stanislavski emerged unscathed. The most grudging critics had to admit their overwhelming talent. By the end of the tour, Stanislavski was hailed as Russias's greatest actor.

Audiences were another matter. Their enthusiasm was more voluble than in Moscow. *An Enemy of the People* provoked the greatest excitement. At the second performance on February 26 the house went wild, applauding continuously during Act Four, the scene of the public meeting, and, finally, at the end of the play, rushing down to the front of the stage, trying to drag back the curtains so they could see the actors, with shouts of 'Thank you, Stanislavski' on all sides. A further and more significant demonstration took place at the performance of March 13. Earlier in the day there had been a demonstration of students in Kazan Square protesting against the implementation of a law which enabled the government to expel 'un-cooperative' students and force them into the army. The demonstration had been brutally broken up and many of the participants had been thrown in jail. In the evening they were released. It was a tradition after such events to go, en masse, to some congenial place, somewhere they would feel at home. They chose to go to people whom they considered soul-mates, the company of the Moscow Art Theatre.

'In the final interval there was a stir among the audience, there were whispers of "Students, students" on all sides.

People were uneasy. . . . What was going on? Which students? Nobody understood anything.

Suddenly, indeed, all the aisles, especially in the "gods" were filled with students, young men and women. It transpired they were demonstrators who had just been let out of "jug".

Hungry, exhausted, but happy and excited at suddenly being set free, the whole crowd had come straight from jail to the theatre they loved. Stanis-lavski gave orders for them to be given tickets. And then, in the last act, Doctor Stockman, who has returned from a hostile meeting, where he has been more or less manhandled, looks at the tears in his new frock coat and says: "When you go out to fight for freedom and justice you don't put on new trousers." . . . There was nothing emphatic in the actor's delivery, not a glance towards the audience but that sentence full of ex-pression and quiet simplicity and, at the same time, tragic humour caused a real electric discharge in an audience that was, in any case, already "charged up." In a single moment a contact had been established between actor and audience and the audience, without exception, immediately responded with a stormy, elemental explosion of feeling. . . . It wasn't applause but a genuine, stupefying and even frightening demonstration.

The character of Stockman had grown at an instant from an individual rebel into a figure of enormous political significance.

The manager and the box-office manager ran into the theatre. . . . The temperature suddenly rocketed.

– Well, we'll all be arrested and the play will be stopped – that's what went through the minds of all us students, who were inured to catastrophes of that kind. But the performance just went on to the end. Some invisible but powerful "hand" prevented police interference and the inevitable "scandal".' (Recalled by O. Bogolioubova. K.S. Archives.)

Ten days later, as the tour finished, a group of students, a 'family' of friends, wrote to Stanislavski with their thanks:

'. . . the tragic events of recent times have scattered that family. The brightest memories which our banished comrades took away with them to the darkness of the provinces were the artistic images and pictures which you created.' (Theatre Archives.)

It was responses such as these which further convinced Stanislavski, if, indeed, he needed further convincing, that the function of the theatre was, according to Tolstoi's principle, to make the content of art transparent, not to make overt ideological statements. He had spoken loud and clear to a new generation. What more did they need to be told, other than what they had seen on stage?

By the end of the tour even sections of the press were having to modify their attitude, although prejudice died hard. As for Stanislavski himself he had little time to enjoy his triumph. He immediately began work on Hauptmann's *Michael Kramer*. His mother was horrified. She felt he needed a rest, not all the nervous strain involved in this 'heavy and depressing play'.

CHAPTER TEN

THE LOWER DEPTHS

The theatre was now able to fulfil what Nemirovich regarded as one of its prime functions: the presentation of outstanding contemporary Russian plays or unfamiliar foreign plays dealing with important social issues. In addition to Hauptmann's *Michael Kramer*, the 1901–2 season included Ibsen's *The Wild Duck*. Over the next four years works by Chekhov, Ibsen, Tolstoi, Hauptmann were brought into the repertoire and Gorki, who had only published short stories, launched on his career as a dramatist. On October 30, 1900, during a performance of *Lonely People*, he suddenly announced his intention of writing a play. In the event, he started work on two simultaneously – *Small People* and *The Lower Depths*. In choosing to present works by a notorious rebel and former political prisoner, the Art Theatre was courting danger. The least it could expect were long battles with the censor.

The theatre was interested mainly in *The Lower Depths* but it proved the more troublesome to write. Gorki found that he could not control his material. His characters had taken over and he said, simply would not stop talking. *Small People* was finished first and delivered in October 1901. Stanislavski sent his impressions and comments, which Gorki gratefully acknowledged.

The play is concerned with a small, petit-bourgeois family, its narrow-mindedness and meanness both material and spiritual. In ideological terms the central character is the adopted son, Nil, typical of the progressive 'new man' whom critics like Chernichevski had insisted was an integral part of revolutionary literature. Both Gorki and Chekhov were convinced that Stanislavski should play the role. They were in one sense right. Nil is the lead role. It requires an actor of strong personality able to dominate the play; on the other hand, Stanislavski, at thirty-eight, with his upper-middle-class background, realized that he could not play a rebellious working-class train driver of 25. He was able to form strong personal and artistic relationships with turbulent young artists – Meierhold, Gorki, Sulerzhitski and, later, Vakhtangov – preferring to do battle with them rather than live in docile agreement with the less energetic and the less able – but it was quite another thing actually to try and play, or to embody this new generation, from which he was culturally and historically separated. He was convinced that you could not 'act' Nil. It was not a character part and that was what it would become in his hands. You had to 'be' Nil. He was afraid, as he wrote to Chekhov, that the audience would get Stanislavski in costume and not the character. In the event, the production suffered greatly from the fact that there was no one of the right age and of outstanding talent to take on the role. New actors were needed for new plays. They had to be created.

There was insufficient time to include *Small People* in the Moscow season. Nemirovich had only read the play to the company at the end of December and with the Petersburg tour due to open on the February 19 there was insufficient time for adequate rehearsal. Nemirovich's own play, *In Dreams*, which was less demanding, was put in as a stop-gap. Gorki made no secret of his contempt for the piece which failed badly. *Small People*, it was decided, would be given a try-out during the Petersburg tour while waiting for *The Lower Depths* which would, it was hoped, be ready by the autumn.

To stage Gorki in Moscow was bad enough but to do it in Petersburg, under the nose of the imperial court and all its ministers was something else. The authorities insisted on a dress rehearsal for a small number of government officials to assess the play. The theatre, at this moment, discovered a powerful and unexpected ally in the snobbish curiosity of Petersburg society, confident of its own position and waiting to be shocked and titillated by progressive ideas. Word of this 'private view' soon got round and a battle ensued among the great and fashionable for the remaining seats. The government decided, in response, that all the usual ushers should be replaced by uniformed police who would ensure that no undesirables gatecrashed the performance. This produced alarm among the audience. Nemirovich insisted that the police withdraw and leave the normal ushers to their task. During the course of the evening he was sent for first by the assistant chief of police, then the chief of police and finally by the governor of Petersburg himself. He resolutely refused to leave the theatre during the performance. He presented himself the next morning and explained his position. The governor, anxious not to ruffle the feathers of his fashionable masters, agreed that the sight of uniforms would, perhaps, be alarming.

On the first night the police were present but in full evening dress. Mounted police patrolled the streets outside. Nemirovich had, however, taken the precaution of appealing to the students beforehand not to make any demonstrations as they had during *An Enemy of the People*. Gorki's play, he explained, was important to the survival of the theatre. They could not afford to have it banned. The students complied and it was only at the final performance that one solitary cry of 'Down with the Grand Duke' was heard. As for the audience, they were far less concerned with Gorki's politics than with the strapping young actor, Baranov, who had been taken from the Moscow Art Theatre School to play the part of Teterev, the cantor.

They swooned with delight over this true son of the Russian soil. Here was another Chaliapin, they said. They praised him and lionized him. He stole all the notices. Success went to his head together with a not inconsiderable amount of alcohol, and he destroyed his own career.

By April, Gorki was able to show Stanislavski the first two acts of *The Lower Depths*. By July, it was complete and, during Stanislavski's absence abroad, sent to Chekhov and Knipper who were staying, at Stanislavski's invitation, in Liubimovka.

Knipper had fallen seriously ill during the Petersburg tour and had needed surgery. Stanislavski, she wrote to Chekhov, fussed over her as if she were his own daughter. Shortly after Stanislavski and Lilina went down to the Crimea, Knipper had a relapse. Chekhov stayed constantly at his wife's bedside and on their return Stanislavski and Lilina took turns to sit with him. It was only at this stage in their relationship that Stanislavski felt at ease in his company. The crisis and the intimacy of the sick-room brought them close together.

'Up till then, even though I had known Anton Pavlovich for a long time, I could not feel at ease with him, I could not establish an easy relationship, I was always mindful of the fact that I had someone famous before me and tried to appear more intelligent than I really am. This unnatural behaviour truly inhibited Anton Pavlovich. He only liked open relationships. My wife who established that kind of simple relationship from the very start, always felt more at ease with him than I. . . . It was only during those long days when I sat with Anton Pavlovich in the room next to the sick-room that I was for the first time able to discover that openness in our relationship. Those days brought us so close together that Anton Pavlovich would sometimes come to me with requests of an intimate nature about which he was very reserved. For example, having learned that I knew how to inject arsenic – I had boasted to him somewhat of my ability to perform that operation – he asked me to give him an injection. . . .' (SS, Vol. V, p. 359.)

The injections, given in the buttocks, formed part of Chekhov's treatment and had to be given regularly. It was agreed that, for the time being, Stanislavski would do them. He was, unfortunately, less expert than he had claimed and bungled the operation badly, causing considerable pain. Chekhov pretended not to notice and said thank you with a smile but Stanislavski was never asked to officiate again.

Stanislavski suggested that as soon as she was sufficiently recovered, Knipper and Chekhov should move into the house at Liubimovka where Knipper could convalesce while he and Lilina were abroad. The offer was gratefully accepted. Chekhov was already hinting at a new play and it was at Liubimovka that *The Cherry Orchard* was conceived. In late June Stanislavski joined Lilina and the children in Franzensbad and in July visited Bayreuth where he was taken back-stage by Cosima Wagner. There he had an opportunity to see how the wave effects were created for the opening of *Fliegender Hollander*. The copious technical notes he took on that occasion were later incorporated into the opening of his 1929 production plan for *Othello*. On August 19, the family returned to Liubimovka, where Knipper was still recuperating, and on the following day Stanislavski gave the first reading of *The Lower Depths*. On August 22 he discussed the play with Nemirovich and the company.

At the beginning of 1902 the lease on the Hermitage ran out. The Moscow Art Theatre Board signed a twelve-year lease on the Omon Theatre in Kamergerski Lane, formerly used for operettas and cabarets. The plan was to gut the interior and create a new auditorium, entirely plain, without the usual plush gilt, or anything that might distract attention from the stage itself. There was to be no orchestra pit, since neither Stanislavski nor Nemirovich approved of the practice of playing light musical interludes during the intervals. They were another hindrance to proper concentration. The very latest lighting and technical equipment was to be installed. The theatre would in every way be state-of-the-art.

This ambitious scheme was launched at a moment when the theatre was deeply in debt and when the existing shareholders were refusing to put in any more money. The cost of the reconstruction, some, 300,000 roubles, was borne by Morozov who not only supervised the work, particularly the electrical installations, himself but, when necessary, picked up a hammer and joined in. He leased the theatre to the company for a modest 10,000 roubles a year and guaranteed an annual subsidy of 30,000.

The time had come to reorganize the theatre's finances and create a new company on a new basis. In July 1897 Nemirovich had predicted that by 1900 the theatre should be sufficiently well established for the actors to share in the profits. Morozov now proposed that the actors should become shareholders and own their own company. He bought out the existing shareholders and then offered to lend any actor who needed it the money to acquire stock against a bill of hand. As none of the actors had private means they all borrowed from Morozov which meant that by the summer he was virtually the sole owner of the company.

It was strictly understood that shares could be acquired by invitation only and a list of potential shareholders was issued in January 1902. Some names were conspicuous by their absence: Sanin, Stanislavski's production assistant, and Meierhold. Nemirovich, it appeared, had written his former pupil off. An uncomfortable meeting of the new shareholders in February decided who among the actors were to stay and who were to go. Meierhold, who was already feeling at odds with the theatre's policy, did not wait to be pushed out but resigned, taking a number of other members of the company with him to form a theatre in the provinces. On February 24 he published a letter in the *Kurior* denying any financial basis for his departure.

There was a great deal of bitterness in the air. Knipper described the whole affair as 'disgusting' while Chekhov wrote a letter of protest to Nemirovich. He was particularly outraged by the departure of Meierhold, whom he respected not so much, as he admitted, for his talents as an actor, which had proved disappointing, but for the intelligence which came through in his performances. Whatever thoughts Stanislavski may have had he kept them private. He stuck to his resolution not to become involved in the theatre's finances. New articles of association were drawn up giving Morozov almost absolute power over the members of the Board and the administration. Current policy on repertoire was endorsed and a resolution was incorporated into the statutes giving priority to plays of significant social content, irrespective of box-office appeal.

This decision produced immediate conflict. Nemirovich, jealous of his control over repertoire, clashed violently with Morozov at a board meeting when Morozov tried to give pride of place not only to Gorki, of whom Nemirovich was suspicious, but to the circle of writers around him. Nemirovich considered these writers inferior and he refused absolutely to allow the theatre to be identified politically or artistically with any one school or tendency. A spectacular shouting-match ended with Nemirovich storming out, slamming the door behind him.

In October, despite all these tribulations, the Art Theatre finally moved into the premises it was to occupy for the next seventy years. Within a few months Stanislavski, too, had moved, selling Red Gates and acquiring a house on Carriage Row opposite the Hermitage Theatre.

He had a new theatre, a new home, but no new burst of creative energy. The theatre was in danger artistically. It was beginning to lose sight of the distinction between realism, which was its stated goal, and naturalism which it ostensibly rejected. Passion for detail, apparent in the early stages of *Three Sisters*, was beginning to take over and *Small People* was its first victim. With some 80 cuts imposed by the censor, the play opened on October 25 to a lukewarm reception. Watching the play in rehearsal, Gorki himself had found it 'staggeringly boring . . . long, boring and stupid.' Efros blamed the production:

'The dramatic essence of Gorki's play was lost in these trifles, the energy of the actors was stifled under the weight of contrived character traits, voices, grimaces and the audience's attention was diverted from what was essential and important to the incidental and the quaint.' (*Novosti Dnia*, October 27.)

The next production, Tolstoi's *The Power of Darkness*, suffered a similar fate. Stanislavski had wanted to do the play in 1895. Tolstoi had visited

1a Stanislavski's mother, Elisaveta Alekseieva, and father, Sergei Alekseiev.

1b The Alekseiev house at Red Gates where Stanislavski lived
from the age of a few months (1863) to 1903.

2a The Alekseiev children in 1875.

2b The theatre at the country estate in Liubimovka built when Stanislavski was 14 in 1877.

3a *The Mikado* 1887. Yum-Yum – Anna Alekseieva. Nanki Pu – Stanislavski.

3b Stanislavski as the Knight in Pushkin's *The Miserly Knight*, 1888.

4a Stanislavski as Ferdinand in the play *Kabale und Liebe* (Schiller). His wife, Lilina, as Louise.

4b *The Fruits of Enlightenment* (Tolstoi). Stanislavski, 1891.

5 *Foma* (Dostoievski/Stanislavski) Lilina, Stanislavski, 1893.

6a *Much Ado About Nothing* (Shakespeare)
Stanislavski as Benedick, 1897.

6b *The Last Sacrifice* (Ostrovski)
Stanislavski, 1893.

6c *Uriel Acosta*, 1895.

7a Chekhov with the
Art Theatre Company.

7b *Uncle Vania* (Chekhov)
Stanislavski as Astrov,
1899.

8a *Uncle Vania* (Chekhov) Act III. Stanislavski as Astrov, Olga Knipper-Chekhova as Elena.

8b Stanislavski as Vershinin in Chekhov's *The Three Sisters.*

Red Gates to discuss changes to Act Four and had agreed to rewrite it on the lines Stanislavski suggested to him. The production never materialized. Stanislavski had now reworked Act Four himself, combining two earlier versions, and in early May asked Chekhov who was living in the Crimea, near Tolstoi, to act as his intermediary and get approval for the revisions. Tolstoi's son, Sergei, approved the changes when he attended rehearsals towards the end of the month. Stanislavski made one of his customary trips with the wardrobe mistress, Grigorieva, to the Tulska district in search of materials and local colour. Sketchbooks were filled. They returned laden with shirts, coats, pots and pans, and they brought in a peasant couple to advise on manners and customs. The woman proved to have genuine dramatic gifts, and after she had filled in at one rehearsal for the actress playing Matriona who was ill, Sergei Tolstoi, carried away by the reality of her performance, suggested she take over the part. This was agreed. She was dropped, finally, because in moments of high feeling she abandoned Lev Tolstoi's text and insisted on improvising her own dialogue using language so foul no censor would possibly pass it. Stanislavski was loath to lose her entirely and put her first in the crowd, then gave her a moment on her own when she crossed the stage, humming a song. Even that destroyed the credibility of what came after; even when singing off-stage she eclipsed the rest of the cast. Anything and everything she did merely served to highlight the superficiality of the rest of the acting. In the end they recorded her singing a song and used it as background.

Writing to Sulerzhitski on November 28, Sergei Tolstoi commented:

'[The actors] worked very hard but nonetheless it is evident what a gulf there is between them and the peasants. At bottom only actors from the peasantry itself could play *The Power of Darkness* really well.' (V. V. Luzhskii, Archive No. 6396.)

The whole episode marked a giant step backward. Stanislavski had known ever since his experiments at Liubimovka, twenty years earlier, that 'real' truth and theatrical truth are of a different order. He had written in his notebook of the 'essential laws of the stage'. All that had been forgotten. Had he been able to draw less superficial performances from his cast, and from himself, he might have been less carried away.

Chekhov found the production, which opened on December 5, had 'a great many good intentions and affection for the task in hand', but nothing could hide the fact that it was all local colour and little else. The poetic insight of *The Seagull* had degenerated into mere stylistic mannerism. Stanislavski's own judgement in *My Life in Art* was categorical:

'Realism only becomes naturalism when it is not justified by the artist from within.

... the external realism of the production of *The Power of Darkness*
revealed the absence of inner justification in those of us who were acting
in it. The stage was taken over by things, objects, banal outward *events*
... which crushed the inner meaning of the play and the characters.' (SS,
Vol. I, p. 261.)

The play, nonetheless, enjoyed some success although Stanislavski's own
performance as Mitrich was a disaster. He applied mountains of make-up
and putty, bumps and protuberances but it remained a soulless, mechanical
exercise. He only gave three performances.

The Lower Depths was given the same careful preparation. Gorki provided
Stanislavski, who, as he had wished, was playing Satin, and Kachalov, playing the Baron, with biographical sketches filling in the background. Stanislavski felt that the usual analytical discussions were not enough. He needed
living models to stimulate his imagination. On the evening of August 22
therefore, the company, together with Simov, paid a visit to the Khitrov
Market. The assembled tramps and thieves were flattered to be visited by a
group of actors and impressed by the name of Gorki. Much drink flowed
and personal secrets were revealed. Stanislavski found what he was looking
for, an ex-officer who had gambled away a fortune. His manners were
perfect and, Stanislavski noted, despite his ragged clothes, his beard and
moustache were neatly trimmed. Simov made innumerable sketches. Later
he took a number of photographs of locations which would serve as a basis
for his sets.

The visit served its purpose. When rehearsals began in the autumn Stanislavski had a total picture both of the characters and of their environment.
The production plan is filled, as usual, with details of moves and objects, all
exactly and perfectly true to life. At one session he gave a virtuoso display,
demonstrating a string of characters, one after the other, almost without a
break between, to the students who were to play the small parts. Above all,
he insisted, there was to be no sentimentalization, no display of pity or
condescension to these people. They were what they were. Gorki's intention
was not to make the audience feel sorry for them but to provoke the kinds
of social change which would make their condition impossible.

Stanislavski had a great deal more trouble with his own performance. He
had his model, his gentlemanly ex-officer, and he had Gorki's biographical
notes. Gorki also indicated that he wanted a touch of Don Cesar de Bazan
in Satin's character. Don Cesar was a dashing Spanish grandee in a French
melodrama which had enjoyed considerable success in the nineteenth century and was a great favourite in Russia. Gorki had made specific reference
to it in *Small People*. At the same time, Stanislavski was acutely conscious
of the social message of the play. How could all these disparate elements be
brought together?

The play badly needed an outside eye. The individual elements of the staging, good in themselves, accurate, truthful, were not adding up to a performance. There were many trees but no wood. Stanislavski himself needed a director. Nemirovich once again stepped in and pulled the production together, giving it some much-needed pace. He more or less told Stanislavski to start again. A letter written during the autumn of 1902 begins gently but finishes on a much more hard-hitting note. Perhaps, he suggested, it was time for Stanislavski to do something different as an actor? Everyone in the company was all too familiar with his ways, the irritability and tension that reduced him to a state of exhaustion. Satin offered him an opportunity to be a slightly different actor from the one they knew. Why couldn't he relax a little?

'. . . you have great difficulty in just surrendering to a role and that is because you have no faith in the audience's intelligence, because you think you have to hit them on the head all the time. You want to make something out of practically every sentence and it becomes difficult to listen to you because as the dialogue proceeds I, the audience, have long since understood from your facial expression and gestures what you want to say or act but you continue to play some detail at me which is not going to interest me overmuch by being prolonged. This happens not only with individual lines but even in the middle of speeches and lines.' (*Izbranie Pisma*, pp. 306–7.)

The answer was to play against the tragic nature of the script. *The Lower Depths* would be played like Act One of *Three Sisters*. Not one tragic note would be allowed to creep in. This would bring something new to the stage.

In practical terms he offered the following advice:

'1. Don't thrust the part and yourself on the audience. It understands both it and you;
2. Don't be afraid the role won't exist in those places where a great deal of acting is not appropriate to the situation. If there's nothing to play it's almost a mistake to do anything and easy to wear yourself out prematurely; . . .
3. Learn the lines by heart;
4. Avoid excess of movement;
5. Keep the tone vigorous, light and vital, i.e., with vitality, *carefree and vital*. (Ibid.)

The letter was just what was needed. Stanislavski created a performance which was a mixture of imperiousness, malice, humour, arrogance and optimism and when he delivered the Act Four monologue 'Man is truth . . . Man is wonderful!' it had the right degree of panache and seriousness. Nemirovich had released the strain of broad theatricality which existed in Stanislavski without allowing it to become false, as in the past.

The play, which opened on December 18, had a huge success, equal to that of *The Seagull* and *Enemy of the People*. It made Kachalov a star and brought Stanislavski further accolades. Gorki was overwhelmed. He wrote:

'It was only at the first performance that I saw and understood the amazing leap forward that all these people, who were used to creating characters by Chekhov and Ibsen, had made. Something of themselves had been released.' (Gorki, *Perepiska*, p. 225, Moscow, 1986.)

Stanislavski himself was not so happy. Writing to Chekhov the day after the first night he could only say that despite all the praise he was dissatisfied with what he had done. He was full of praise for Nemirovich's achievement in finding the right tone for the play but the problem for him was that in playing Satin he was aware both of the character and of the play's social message. When he played Stockman there had been no such mental division. He had simply played the character and the social message had been conveyed equally well, if not better.

Stanislavski's mood was increasingly despondent. The theatre was stagnating. Nowhere could he see evidence of fresh thinking. Nemirovich's production of *The Pillars of Society* did nothing to encourage him. The rehearsal period was not happy. Everyone was depressed. Stanislavski found the production unimaginative and the set, which he had approved, a mistake. His disagreement with Nemirovich also extended to individual characterizations. Knipper reported that he and Nemirovich were fighting like cat and dog over her performance as Lona. Stanislavski found the role of Consul Bernick 'heavy-going and unrewarding'. He was uncharacteristically uncooperative in rehearsal, often insisting on working in French. Nemirovich kept a brave face on it writing to Chekhov on February 16:

'The more I fight with Alexeiev the closer I get to him, since we are both united by a fine and healthy love for the same things.' (Iz., Pis., p. 319, Moscow, 1979.)

The play opened on February 24, 1903, to good reviews and, as Knipper remarked, 'even Efros for once did not nit-pick'.

For all his brave words to Chekhov, Nemirovich was worried. He could feel Stanislavski drawing away from him. In a series of private letters he attempted to pull him back under control. His letters were concerned with practical problems but sooner or later he returned to Stanislavski's 'psychology' or 'artistic nature'. Stanislavski was treated as a talented but wayward child who needed occasionally to be disciplined. In the previous July, he had complained about Stanislavski's methods as a director: he would write a production plan, allow an assistant director to prepare an act and drive an unwilling cast along by his own energy, and then arrive and alter everything:

'The act is blocked. You arrive. You whisper to me that none of it is any good but that we must be supportive to the director and the cast. Then you go into your act, one which has caused great disappointment in recent time to directors who are still only apprentices, i.e., you praise them and thank them loudly for all their hard work. Then you arrange rehearsals and start to alter everything. . . . After two rehearsals there is nothing left of all the hard work that had been put in. Sanin and the actors begin to feel revolt welling up in them. . . . If [the director] starts to justify himself by referring to your own production plan, you answer – "Yes, yes, yes. It's all my fault. Don't let's argue about it. But this isn't right, we must rework it." Or – "Dear God, who knows what rubbish I wrote in that production plan. It's clear when you see it in rehearsal." And this really isn't a joke, it's an absolute disaster. . . . Therefore, it must be established once and for all, that . . . until the roles are properly under way, you must take the rehearsals. Then, when the act is set it can be worked on by a second director. Excepting . . . when your second director happens to be me.' (N-D Archive, No. 1578.)

Nemirovich might just as well have saved his breath, or his ink. For the next 36 years Stanislavski continued to drop, cut and alter until he was satisfied.

More fundamental divisions were beginning to emerge. For Nemirovich the basis of a production lay in a detailed literary analysis which was then, as it were, 'illustrated' by the staging; for Stanislavski, a production was created in the actual rehearsal period itself, through the active collaboration of actor, director and designer.

The production of *Julius Caesar*, which was scheduled to open the 1903–4 season, brought the differences between the two men into sharp focus. Stanislavski had not wanted to include the play but Nemirovich had insisted for two reasons: first, because he, too, thought the theatre was in a rut, playing safe, choosing to do *The Pillars of Society* rather than one of Ibsen's later, more difficult plays, putting on comfortable plays for comfortable bourgeois audiences; second, because he wanted to establish his reputation as a director equal in stature to his partner. The most effective way to do so was through a successful production of a major classic.

On May 31, Nemirovich left for Rome with Simov to prepare the sets. In his absence Stanislavski began making notes for the production. He gave his broad views on an approach to the play but provided much more detailed suggestions for the crowd scenes. The two men kept up a regular correspondence. By June it became obvious that Nemirovich was going his own way. Rome had had an enormous impact on him: the scale, the spaciousness of the ancient Forum, that was what he wanted to reproduce. Stanislavski pointed out that it would be difficult to create the impressions of a mob with a handful of actors if the set had a large open space in the middle. Nemirovich nonetheless insisted on his own way. He was equally insistent over the interpretation of Act Two in particular the scenes between Brutus and Portia and Brutus and Ligarius.

Once rehearsals began on August 7 there was no respite for anybody. Nemirovich poured all his energy into the production. According to Knipper the endless rehearsals, day and evening, the costume fittings, the make-up sessions, the crowd scenes were 'hell'. Nemirovich emphasized the broad political themes. What interested him was not individuals but the total situation, the death of a republic. This gave Stanislavski, as Brutus, little scope for psychological exploration. The result was a mis-match between actor and director. Stanislavski, realizing how difficult he had been during *The Pillars of Society*, which with his sense of discipline he truly regretted, buckled down and did his best to conform to the over-all production concept. He also collaborated in the staging of the crowd scenes, which proved the high points of the evening. But he disapproved of the production style which he found picturesque. His own instinct would have been to dirty the costumes and put patches on them rather than have a display of pristine whiteness. Nemirovich was aware of this, aware, too, that he was going against their agreed policy of 'artistic realism' but at the same time he was convinced that it was right for this particular play.

Nemirovich's slave-driving paid off. The play opened on October 2 to a generally warm reception. The production was much admired, not least for its historical accuracy. Parties of schoolchildren were brought to see the production to get an idea of life in ancient Rome. For Stanislavski, however, it merely confirmed all his worst fears concerning the artistic sterility of the theatre. His own performance as Brutus found little general favour and, once again, he was accused of being insufficiently 'heroic'. 'Nobody likes it', Knipper wrote. Even the usually sympathetic Efros wrote:

> '... there was neither a Brutus who was Hamlet-like, nor the Brutus as the artist apparently conceived him. The central bone-structure, the spine of the tragedy was approached coldly.' (N. Efros, *Teatr i Iskusstvo*, No. 41, p. 754.)

Sulerzhitski, however, took an entirely different view. He wrote to Stanislavski:

> 'Up till now I "knew" what Brutus was, I respected this "type", if I can so express it, but for me he was distant, alien and cold. He existed only in the mind, in the realm of abstract ideas. You, your performance, transformed that beautiful but cold classical statue into a living being, you clothed him in flesh and blood, you warmed him with tribulation and

brought him down from his inaccessible marble pedestal and into men's hearts. . . .

I do not write to Alekseiev, whom I do not know at all; I write, not as an acquaintance, but as a member of the audience, wishing to join the actor in sympathy for Brutus who died as all fine things must die in this life, where only lies can triumph. . . .

I write to Stanislavski, who more than once already had upheld and strengthened people in their belief in "man".' (Sulerzhitski, p. 433, Moscow, 1970.)

Another commentator, doubtless with the contemporary political situation in mind, noted:

'Shakespeare's Brutus is an abstract, ideal man, who in given historical circumstances, quite uninvited, like all useless dreamers, foists his freedom-loving dreams on the people, but Stanislavski tried to speak in the name of the people, as if those people had no other dream save democratic freedom.' (L. V. Goldenweiser Archive, MXAT Museum.)

Ermolova declared the performance 'beautiful'. Maria Chekhova, who apparently was present on one of Stanislavski's good evenings, thought he played better than anyone. Diaghilev admired him, too, in the Forum scene. A Petersburg correspondent, Kotlareievskaia, writing to Stanislavski on October 27, summed up the whole debate:

'On all sides I read and hear contradictory opinions: some condemn Brutus others praise it . . . I know your creative work and understand why 50% of the public condemn you, 40% don't understand you and only 10% understand and are delighted by you. It's very clear to me: you play in a tone and manner in which people *will* play but in which for the moment only you, the first, play. In twenty years they'll all be doing it your way but right now it's new, alien and incomprehensible.' (K.S. Archive.)

As for Nemirovich he gave Stanislavski's final performance his full support. It matched his political view of the play:

'His performance as Brutus, conceived as an ardent republican, was bold, interesting, beautiful and physically expressive. But it was totally removed from the Brutus established in the public's mind. And at that time, when the other actors became more and more mechanical from performance to performance, confining themselves within their own acquired technique, he, Konstantin Sergeievich, on the contrary, as it were, tried to surmount his lack of success and continued to work.' (N-D Archive, No. 127.)

It was, nonetheless, torture, made worse because being, technically, a heavy production, *Julius Caesar* had to be played in blocks and not in repertoire. There was, therefore, no respite, no time to recover lost energy. Stanislavski had to go on night after night, struggling through a performance he knew most of the audience did not want to see. The interpretation which had refused to come alive for him during rehearsal did not come alive in the actual playing. It was only in the following year, during the Petersburg tour, that there was some glimmer of light. For the moment it seemed to him that the very scenery was drenched in the sweat of his own useless endeavours.

It was not until three weeks into the run that he confided his unhappiness to Nemirovich. His comments, which appear mainly to have consisted of self-criticism, produced a violent reaction which threatened to destroy the theatre altogether. He voiced them in Morozov's presence and Nemirovich jumped to the conclusion that there was a conspiracy against him. He drafted a letter full of bitterness and anger, which he read to Luzhski, Vishnievski and Knipper on the day of the first meeting to discuss the casting of *The Cherry Orchard*. He was outraged to think that a production in which he had put the best of himself and which had achieved critical success could be dismissed as inartistic by the two other senior members of the management. Stanislavski had been equally negative about *The Lower Depths* which had been a huge success and had offered not one word of praise for *Pillars of Society*. His whole view of Nemirovich's work was negative. What rankled Nemirovich most was that while his own successes were passed over, Stanislavski's failures, like *Snow Maiden*, were cited as conclusive proof of his brilliance. All he got from Stanislavski were constant jeremiads that the theatre was going into a decline, that it was sliding down-hill and would end up like the Mali – the ultimate term of abuse in Stanislavski's critical vocabulary. It was a short step from defending his own qualities as an artist and reaffirming his own aesthetic beliefs to attacking his colleagues' abilities as a director. Nemirovich now reduced Stanislavski's ability to visualize scenes in concrete terms, so effusively praised in happier days, to a mere capacity to create incidental detail while the main thrust of the play was lost. In *Caesar*, he argued, Stanislavski had failed to appreciate the overall meaning, the *concept*, and had been principally concerned with the design and cut of a particular toga. The trouble once more was Stanislavski's fashionable friends who wanted something more 'spicy' and 'original'. With such major differences between them, Nemirovich ended, what was future of the theatre to be?

Stanislavski, in his equally emotional reply, called Nemirovich's letter 'a bolt from the blue.'

'In God's name what are you accusing me of, duplicity, conspiracy or just plain stupidity? . . . Calm down and try to understand what it really was I said. If I criticized anybody it was myself . . . I spoke so frankly because your role as a director is clear, well-established, acknowledged by everyone.' (K.S. Archive.)

He then drew attention to his own sacrifices and his genuine efforts to work in collaboration with someone else when for fifteen years he had been totally independent. More importantly, perhaps, the letter also reveals Stanislavski's view of his position in the theatre. It is surprisingly insecure but the insecurity is not without justification. Writing to Chekhov with her account of the quarrel, Knipper ends:

'Please God all this will be all smoothed over very quickly. But if Nemirovich goes I won't stay in the theatre. K.S. can't be left in charge. He's inept.' (Lenin State Library, Manuscript Section, F 356.)

Knipper's lack of confidence in Stanislavski's ability to run the theatre was shared. Whether in the main company or in the School, which, admittedly, he only visited intermittently, Stanislavski, was coming to be regarded as an outsider:

'Do you think I don't realize the extent to which my importance in the theatre has declined? Do you think I don't see that in a short while it will be reduced to nil? . . . One thing I prize greatly; the right to express my artistic "credo" openly. I am beginning to lose that right. Haven't you noticed how obvious this has become recently? I speak to Tikhomirov *purely privately* about the new things he is doing (Tikhomirov knows my position in the school – precisely nil) and they all declare that I am creating confusion and that students have left because of me. If I give any kind of advice or instructions they all shout "he's creating confusion!" and no one takes the least trouble to examine my ideas more closely. If I ask for someone to be fined – for blatant misconduct about which I would have created a scandal five years ago and had the theatre up in arms – now my words are quietly passed over in silence and nothing happens. If I give any kind of artistic advice "crank" is written over everyone's face.

My ideas have produced a worthless harvest and actors are praised for it and I suffer, witnessing the desecration of that which is sacred and precious to me. But I say nothing. . . . I will not lift a finger to create a new position for myself at the theatre. If I am on the slippery slope then the sooner I hit bottom the better. I am a very reserved man and say much less then I think. I hand over the theatre without a struggle. If I am needed then let me be treated with care and tact. If not, then get rid of me and (if it is inevitable) the sooner the better. . . .

Affectionately and devotedly yours, K. Alekseiev.
If I have in any way offended you I am sorry. It was quite unintentional.'
(K.S. Archive.)

Allowing for a degree of exaggeration, or even self-dramatization, the letter confirms the extent to which Stanislavski was separated, and remained

separated, from the daily life of most of the company. He might be called fami-
liarly Kostia behind his back but no one said it to his face. He remained
Mr Stanislavski – Konstantin Sergeievich. He was, of course, unlike the rest
of the company, including Nemirovich, in that he had a complete life outside
the theatre. There was the Alekseiev business and all the Alekseiev connections. He commuted between two worlds. His determination to create
good theatre was matched by no one but he was not economically dependent
on it and that made a difference. In personal habits he was perhaps rather
more conservative than his colleagues. He smoked heavily but did not drink.
He detested drink in the theatre and on one occasion was found weeping
because he had seen a member of his cast very much the worse for wear. He
was entirely faithful to Lilina and his attitude to relationships outside marriage tended towards the puritanical. He relaxed little. Possibly, too, he
distanced himself from the rest by his increasingly frequent assertions, at
the moment when the theatre appeared to be doing well, that things, in fact,
were going very wrong.

Nemirovich was deeply touched by this letter and regretted ever having
sent his own. The air, for the moment at least, had been cleared and attention could not be devoted to the production of *The Cherry Orchard* which
had to be prepared in two months if it was to be included in the current
season.

CHAPTER ELEVEN

THE CHERRY ORCHARD

It was the thought of *The Cherry Orchard* that kept Stanislavski going during the long misery of *Julius Caesar*. After three unhappy productions in a row he could only think what a blessed relief it would be to get back to Chekhov. Even one of his favourite roles had been denied him. It was not until mid-October that he was able to play Vershinin again. He wrote to Chekhov expressing his pleasure at being back once more on congenial ground, openly confessing his dislike of *Caesar*, and begging for the new play as soon as possible. When he went to collect it on October 18, although the most courteous of men, he did not even greet Knipper but simply put out his hand for the manuscript. He read the play at home on the following day and immediately sent Chekhov a telegram:

'. . . I think this is the best play you have written . . . . I feel and value every word.'

In a letter to her husband on October 20, Knipper confirmed:

'Konst. Serg., it can be said, has gone mad about the play. The first act, he says, he read as a comedy, the second he found thrilling, in the third act he was in a sweat and in the fourth he cried the whole time.' (Olga Leonardovna Knipper-Chekova, I, p. 307, Moscow, 1972.)

Stanislavski had personal reasons for being attached to this particular Chekhov play which did not excite the same enthusiasm from Nemirovich. It had been conceived at Liubimovka. Two of the characters were based on people he knew. Charlotta was inspired by a local English governess and Epikhodov had many of the characteristics of the family servant who had looked after Chekhov during his stay. Trofimov also had a local model. Even the Act One set, recalled the Alexeiev home:

'I drink coffee on the old sofa No. 1 [on the ground plan]; the sofa is placed just where it was at Liubimovka, in the connecting room, just by our dining-room. Remember?' (Ibid., p. 334.)

Chekhov was writing specifically for the company and had his own ideas about casting. He wrote to Knipper on October 14;

'Read this through when you've finished the play;

1. Liubov Andreievna [Ranevskaia] will be played by you, there's no one else . . .
2. Anya can be played by any young actress;
3. Varia, perhaps Maria Petrovna [Lilina] could take this role.
4. Gaev is for Vishnievski . . .;
5. Lopakhin, Stanislavski;
6. Trofimov the student, Kachalov;
7. Simeonov-Pishchik, Gribunin;
8. Charlotta – difficult question . . .;
9. Epikhodov, perhaps Luzhski would not turn it down;
10. Firs, Artiom;
11. Yasha, Moskvin . . .' (Chekhov, *Pisma*, XI, pp. 273–4.)

The first casting meeting took place on October 28, in the middle of the emotional exchange of correspondence between Stanislavski and Nemirovich. Whatever Chekhov might think, members of the company had their own ideas. Stanislavski was reluctant to play Lopakhin, although it had been written for him. Lilina was resolutely against his taking on the part. Also, quite inappropriately, she wanted to play the seventeen-year-old Anya, a part for which, in her mid-thirties, for all her talent, she was far too old, as Stanislavski later recognized. An exchange of letters followed, Chekhov urging Stanislavski to play the part he had written for him, Stanislavski indicating as tactfully as he could that he would rather play Gaev. Writing to Chekhov on November 3 and 4, he offered to look at both roles:

'I can't say which part I want the more . . . To tell the truth I am afraid of Lopakhin. It's said my merchants don't come across, or, rather seem theatrical and false. . . . Lopakhin is good, small – sweet-natured but strong. . . .

I like Lopakhin and will play him with pleasure but I can't yet find the right tone in myself. I'm trying hard and with great interest nonetheless. The trouble is that Lopakhin is not just a simple merchant, with their characteristically pushy manner. I see him exactly as you describe him in your letter. It needs great control over the tone so as to touch in the mundane elements of the character. All I'm managing to produce so far is Konstantin Sergeievich trying to be nice.' (SS, VII, pp. 269–70.)

The arguments are reasonable but unconvincing. There is an inner resistance behind the words. Stanislavski may not have wanted to be identified in the public mind with a class which, on the whole, he despised and from which, with a few exceptions, he had distanced himself. This would perhaps explain Lilina's attitude. But Stanislavski knew by now those characters with whom he could easily identify. In the space of a year he turned down

Nil in *Small People* and now Lopakhin, both a new breed. This had nothing to do with any political views he may have held. It may have had a great deal to do with an instinctive recognition that he belonged to a certain milieu and period, a certain historical moment, which prevented him from identifying *internally* with certain parts. He could produce an external characterization any time but that did not satisfy him. He could play middle-class and professional idealists (Astrov, Stockman, Vershinin) gentlemen on the skids (Satin) but not the young and rebellious (Nil) nor the upwardly mobile (Lopakhin). In the end, therefore, as everyone expected, he played Gaev.

There was another significant departure from Chekhov's casting, that of Epikhodov. When he came to write *My Life in Art* twenty years later Stanislavski stated that there was no role for Moskvin and that, since they could not waste a good actor, the part was assigned to him. He seems to have forgotten that Chekhov had suggested Yasha. The problem was that whereas Chekhov had described Epikhodov as fat and breathless, Moskvin was small and skinny. In the event Moskvin, who was brilliantly inventive, pulled off a *tour de force*, adapting the role to his own physique and personality, so well indeed that when a somewhat nervous company showed Chekhov the results he declared:

'That's just what I meant to write. It's tremendous, I tell you!' (SS, Vol. I, p. 267.)

Nemirovich announced the final casting on November 5. Rehearsals, that is preliminary discussions on the characters and their relationships, began on the 9th. Nemirovich, although listed as co-director, kept a discreet distance wherever possible. As he wrote to Chekhov, Stanislavski had to be given his head:

'First, he has staged nothing for the best part of a year and, in consequence, he has built up a great store of energy and imagination; secondly he understands you completely; thirdly he has left his whims a long way behind. But, of course, I shall keep a sharp eye on him.' (Iz., Pis., I, pp. 351–2.)

As for Stanislavski's understanding Chekhov completely, that was questionable. He had a basic disagreement about the essential nature of the play. Chekhov had become increasingly disturbed by the almost universal view that he was a pessimist. The truth was, as Gorki recognized, that he was clinically objective about his characters. The trouble was that audiences did not understand his diagnoses and interpreted them as hopeless resignation not as a call for cure. As a reaction, he tried to encourage a lighter, more ironic approach to his plays. Having called *Three Sisters* a Drama on the title page, he had insisted it was a comedy. Now he called *The Cherry*

Orchard a Comedy but insisted in a letter to Lilina (September 15) that, in places, it was almost a farce. Stanislavski's response to Chekhov on October 22 was equally unequivocal:

> 'This is not a comedy, nor a farce, as you have written. It is a tragedy whatever prospect of a better life you hold out in the last act.' (SS, VII, p. 265.)

Despite his essentially tragic view of the play he was anxious, however, remembering the slow pace of earlier productions, to keep the action moving wherever possible. Writing to Chekhov on November 23 he stated:

> "It seems that the whole play will go in a quite different tone from its predecessors. Everything will be light and cheerful . . . In short, we should paint everything in watercolours.' (SS, VII, p. 276.)

Chekhov knew, therefore, long before rehearsals began, what he could expect.

Stanislavski, Simov and Nemirovich spent a long time over the sets. On November 5 Stanislavski wrote to Chekhov saying he would like to play Acts Three and Four in the same set – the ballroom. Chekhov agreed. Stanislavski worked fast. The production plan for Act One was written in a single day, November 12, with a first rehearsal two days later. Act Two was ready by the 18th and in rehearsal by the 21st. On December 4, in spite of ill health, Chekhov arrived in Moscow and stayed until the play opened the following January. He sat in on rehearsals, staying modestly at the back of the auditorium, refusing to interfere directly in the work of production. Faced with Stanislavski's usual battery of sound effects he did, however, on one occasion, allow himself the remark:

> 'Listen, I shall write a new play which will open like this: "How wonderful, how quiet! Not a bird, a dog, a cuckoo, an owl, a nightingale, or clocks, or jingling bells, not even one cricket to be heard."' (SS, Vol. I, p. 270.)

This remark was pitched deliberately loud enough for Stanislavski to hear. The words registered but Stanislavski knew that he needed atmospheric devices to get his actors off the ground. Chekhov had, on the other hand, been delighted to learn in July that Stanislavski had recorded the sound of a shepherd's pipe at Liubimovka. It was a sound he had heard and liked. Not so acceptable was the idea of introducing a passing train in Act Two – an idea that was quickly dropped.

Chekhov, as Gorki reported to a friend, provided a considerable number of rewrites as work progressed. He even agreed to a major cut. Act Two originally ended with a scene between Charlotta and Firs in which they exchange reminiscences about their childhood, revealing their loneliness.

Stanislavski found this ending too downbeat. It was difficult to pick the play up afterwards whereas if the act ended with the exit of Trofimov and Ania the tone was much more positive. Reluctantly they asked Chekhov to take it out and after a very short hesitation he agreed. The scene did not appear in the published edition. Stanislavski reproached himself bitterly afterwards. He felt that his own inability as a director to make the scene work had resulted in the loss of a fine piece of writing.

For the first time the production plan contained notes on the motivations of the characters as well as details of the blocking. There are explanations of the psychological and social mechanisms at work. Nowhere is this more apparent than in Act Three, where he charts Lopakhin's behaviour after he has announced that he has bought the cherry orchard.

Stanislavski's staging is as follows:

RANEVSKAIA. Has the cherry orchard been sold?
LOPAKHIN. {*202. Guiltily, examining his handkerchief. Looks down. Doesn't answer at once.*} It has.
RANEVSKAIA. {*203. Pause, barely audible.*} Who bought it?
LOPAKHIN. {*204. Pause. Even quieter and more embarrassed.*} I bought it. {*205. Agonizing pause. Lopakhin feels badly and this arouses the beast in him. The awkwardness of his position starts to make him angry. He nervously pulls at his handkerchief. Ranevskaia just sinks down and remains in that position for some time. She takes nothing in, understands nothing. It is as if she has suddenly grown old. She sits still at the side of the table. For Varia, it is a huge drama. She is both depressed and outraged. Pishchik tugs at his beard, looking first at Ranevskaia then at Lopakhin. In the ballroom the guests are sitting round the walls listening to the recitation of the second verse by the Station Master (although he can't be seen). Varia breaks the pause. She steps forward, throws down her keys and goes downstairs. This exhausts Lopakhin's patience. He is irritated. His tone is bitter and insolent as he almost shouts.*} I bought it. {*206. Pause. Having shouted, Lopakhin tears his handkerchief in two and flings it away. He is still for a moment. He calms down. Then he gets up, covers his ears with his hands and crosses to the table. 207. On the cross.*} Excuse me a moment, ladies and gentlemen, my head is spinning, I can't say anything. {*208. Ranevskaia is motionless. She has shrunk even smaller. She looks vacantly at the floor. Lopakhin goes to the table. He wants to drink some seltzer. He up-ends two bottles – nothing. He pours some from a third bottle which Varia hasn't cleared and crosses, glass in hand, to the table with the semi-circular sofa, away from Ranevskaia. He sits. Pishchik closes the doors so that the guests can't hear what is going on. Having closed the doors Pishchik goes to Lopakhin and sits on the arm of the sofa. Now, at a distance from Ranevskaia, the feeling of*

pleasure and commercial pride leads them way over decent feeling of
embarrassment and Lopakhin begins to boast as a businessman does faced
with his brother's merchants or his assistants. 209. The account of the
sale (not small-minded) with artistic enthusiasm over his skill and ef-
ficiency. It is essential in order to justify Lopakhin that there should
precisely be this 'artistic enthusiasm'.} We got to the auction. Deriganov
was already there. Leonid Andreich [Gaev] only had fifteen thousand
and Deriganov immediately bid thirty thousand over the arrears on the
mortgage. I saw how things were going and pitched in with forty. He
bid forty-five. I bid fifty-five. He was going up in fives, you see, and
me in tens. So, it was all over. I bid ninety thousand over the arrears
and it went to me. Now the cherry orchard is mine! Mine! {*210. Gross*
guffaw. He clowns, leaning his head on the table, ruffles his hair, butts
Pishchik who is sitting next to him in the chest. Stands up, raises his
arms and beats his chest. He continues his speech as he does so. All this
clowning is explicable by the force of his character, his unbridled nature,
his ecstasy.} God Almighty, gentlemen, the cherry orchard is mine!
Tell me I'm drunk, or out of my mind, or that I'm imagining all this. . . .
{*211. Pause. He thumps the table and the sofa like a kulak. Laughs.*}
Don't you laugh at me! Don't you laugh, don't you dare! {*212. Sud-*
denly stops and changes tone. Now he is stern, imperious. The drink is
coming into its own. 213. He moves forward. Now he knows no mercy.
The drink has gone to his head. He cannot feel Ranevskaia's sorrow and
misery. Darkening malice and resentment towards the humiliations and
trials of his childhood have been aroused in him. All this will be accepted
if the actor goes at it boldly, powerfully, like a warrior not a bruiser.} If
my father and grandfather were to rise from their graves and see what's
gone on, how their Ermolai, their beaten, semi-literate Ermolai who
ran barefoot in winter, this same Ermolai, bought the property where
his grandfather and his father were slaves, where they weren't even
allowed into the kitchen. {*214. He strides boldly about the room. Ranev-*
skaia at this moment seems to have shrunk even more.} I'm dreaming,
this is just an illusion, lost in the mists of ignorance. {*215. Angrily steps*
on the keys and picks them up. 216. For a moment there is a touch of
remorse and if not love then some kind of positive feeling for Varia.} She
threw away the keys to show she's not mistress here any more. {*217.*
Pause. He thinks for a moment. The question of marriage flashes through
his mind but it is gone in a moment and he jingles the keys more angrily
than ever.} So what does it matter? {*218. Turns to the glass doors, opens*
them and shouts all his dialogue into the ballroom, standing on the thresh-
old. There is a minor commotion in the ballroom. All those sitting down
prefer to go and sit a little further off, Lopakhin.} Hey, you in the band,
play, I want to hear something! Come and see, all of you, how Ermolai

Lopakhin takes his axe to that cherry orchard and the trees come crash-
ing down. We'll put up villas and our children and great grand-children
will see a new life! . . . Let's have some music! {*219. The band strikes up
a trite little polka and Lopakhin dances backwards, bumping into Ranevskaia who has sunk onto a chair next to the table and is weeping bitterly.
Lopakhin's mood suddenly drops – at the sight of those tears the good
and sincere man in him and his tender love for the whole family and for
her especially is aroused . . . 220. He drops to his knees, kisses her hands
and skirt like a little puppy dog (the fact that he is drunk helps). He
weeps. The more sincerely and tenderly the better. Why then, if he is so
tenderhearted, didn't he help Ranevskaia? Because he is a slave to merchants' prejudices, because they would have made him a laughing-stock.
Les affaires sont les affaires.*} Why, oh why didn't you listen to me?
My poor, dear friend you can't go back now. {*221. Ranevskaia hugs
him and both weep. Pause.*} Oh if only all this could be over quickly. If
only our miserable mess of a life could somehow change soon. . . .
(*Rezhissioskie Ekzempliari*, K. S. Stanislavskovo, Vol. 3, pp. 422–425.)

By the end of the act, as if to mark the change, the trite little polka has
given way to a rough peasant dance.

The vision, as has been noted earlier, is cinematic; the psychology has the
details of the novelist. The very heavy demands both in terms of understanding and technique which Stanislavski placed on a still unexperienced company
are evident. There is also just sufficient contempt in his insight into Lopakhin's mechanisms to explain why he did not wish to play the part himself.

When the play opened, on January 17, 1904, it was inevitably under-
rehearsed, just as Nemirovich had feared. The opening night was combined
with a ceremony to mark Chekhov's birthday. This took place during one
of the intervals. Chekhov detested ceremonies of this kind and when one of
the worthy professors began his address: 'Dear and respected . . .' he gave
Stanislavski a sideways glance. Both men thought "book-case" – Gaev's
speech. But the real words, "Anton Pavlovich" came out. Chekhov's lips
twitched and the moment was over.

It is difficult to see how the play, which demands concentrated attention,
could have made its full impact, even if the production had been absolutely
ready on an evening which was half performance, half celebration. Success
was only moderate. Over the following weeks the production ran itself in
but Chekhov was not there to see it. He never, in fact, saw the production
in a finished state. He had to rely on second-hand reports. He was not
happy with the opening night. He wrote to Leontiev on January 18:

'My play was on last night and that's why I am in a bad mood.' (Chekhov,
Pisma, XII, p. 14.)

The day after he wrote to Batioushkov:

> 'It will be better if you come just before Lent. Because I don't think the actors will have come to their senses before then and play *The Cherry Orchard* with a little less confusion and vagueness than they are now.' (Ibid., p. 15.)

Faced with critical comment which, as he had feared, accused him of pessimism he grew more and more impatient with the production. He insisted again that the play was farcical. Much as Brecht was to complain later about the public's sympathetic attitude to Mother Courage, Chekhov insisted that Ranevskaia learned nothing, that she was incorrigible. The letters he received did not help. Members of Knipper's family reported, in March, that Act Four was appalling and that Stanislavski was dragging everything out. On March 29, in despondent mood, he wrote to Knipper:

> 'An act which should last twelve minutes *maximum* takes forty in your production. All I can say is, Stanislavski has ruined my play. Well, God be with him.' (Ibid., p. 74.)

Yet Chekhov had particularly praised Stanislavski's last exit in Act Four, during one of the final dress rehearsals and Knipper had written to her husband on the 18th that in everyone's opinion the production had achieved a better balance. What had happened? Probably, as so often in a production, unless the director keeps a tight rein on things, the performance had spread. As each actor discovers new depths in his role there is a temptation to linger, to play every moment to the full. Nemirovich had already criticized this tendency in Stanislavski's own work but it was, in fact, inherent in Stanislavski's total approach. The in-depth exploration of every moment was bound to slow, not to say bog things down. Writing to Efros in 1908, Nemirovich said that he had come to realize that at a certain point, when exploratory work had been done, a production had, as it were, to skim the surface. Stanislavski, for his part, remained quite unrepentant about his interpretation of the play as a drama:

> 'He [Chekhov] went to his grave without ever being reconciled to the fact that his *Cherry Orchard* is a tragic drama of Russian life. He was absolutely convinced that it was a light comedy, almost a vaudeville.' (*Ezhegodnik* MXAT, 1943, p. 130.)

Nemirovich agreed. He pointed to the number of times in the play there is the direction – he/she weeps. He commented, 'in a vaudeville you don't weep!'

At the end of June, Chekhov died in Badenweiler. Sulerzhitskii brought news to Stanislavski and Lilina at Liubimovka. On July 3 Stanislavski wrote to Knipper, describing their grief. They had, he told her, just kept talking to prevent themselves from breaking down.

Stanislavski and Lilina had little time to comfort one another. He was obliged to accompany his ailing mother to Contrexeville. On the journey he thought of Chekhov and nothing else – his ways, his voice, his gestures. From Contrexeville he wrote to Lilina:

'I never thought I would be so attached to him and that it would create such a yawning gap in my life.' (SS, VII, p. 293.)

An era had passed.

PART TWO

BIRTH OF THE SYSTEM

CHAPTER TWELVE

MEIERHOLD

Chekhov's death was not the only reason Stanislavski had to be depressed in the summer of 1904. Nemirovich had precipitated a crisis as a result of which both Gorki and Morozov severed their connections with the theatre.

Gorki had read his new play *Summerfolk* to the company on April 18 without much success. Stanislavski was cautious, reserving his comments. Nemirovich, still smarting from Gorki's contemptuous dismissal of his own play, *In Dreams*, which had flopped so badly, wrote a letter so scathing in its criticism as to be insulting. He accused Gorki of lacking respect for the Russian intelligentsia. He told him the play was shapeless and formless, having no centre or plot, in short that it was little more than raw material. Gorki was incensed. No theatre of which Nemirovich was the head, he replied, would be allowed to stage his plays. The breach was total. Nothing Stanislavski could do or say would make him change his mind. Later in the year, on December 12, he sent a telegram refusing to allow his latest play to be put on:

> 'Notwithstanding my personal liking for you, Nemirovich's conduct towards me obliges me to refuse to allow the theatre to produce *Enemies* and further to decline any kind of connection with the Art Theatre.' (G. S. Burzhdalov Archive, No. 689.)

Morozov was so angered by Nemirovich's behaviour that he resigned from the board. Only in the autumn did he agree to maintain an investment of just under 15,000 roubles while making it clear no further help would be forthcoming in the future. Stanislavski had lost a valuable ally and the theatre its main source of financial security. Nemirovich shed no tears.

The company was generally unsettled. Kachalov threatened to leave but could not bring himself to do so. His emotional and artistic debt to Stanislavski was too great for him to leave at a moment of crisis; however, his final decision to remain was not taken until late July so that Stanislavski only received the welcome news on his return from France, having spent the summer wondering whether in addition to losing his closest business partner and his best new playwright he was also to lose his best actor.

He was frustrated, too, by his failure to achieve his broader objectives.

He had not forgotten his aspirations of the 90s, when he had dreamed of creating a network of provincial theatre. Now he could see the Moscow Art Theatre as a potential power-base for a complete reform of Russian theatre but, given the derision his more idealistic attitudes excited among his colleagues, he realized that his ambitions could only be achieved through a new generation. He needed the energy and enthusiasm of the young. He began to look for possible future leaders in the School. In the winter of 1903 Boris Pronin, a student, was surprised to receive a summons to Stanislavski's dressing-room after a performance of *Julius Caesar*. He was expecting to be disciplined for having laughed during the scene in the senate.

> 'With a heavy heart he knocked on the door of Konstantin Sergeivich's dressing-room. "Come in" came the voice. He stepped through the door and recoiled quite involuntarily: Stanislavski was completely naked. That was his way of relaxing after the strain of playing Brutus. Konstantin Sergeievich with gentle affability invited him once more to come in and sit down. According to Pronin, in that mentally-complex giant there was a childlike simplicity as he stood there smoking. Thus, just as he could wear any kind of costume, he could wear his own naked flesh genuinely with the utmost Hellenic simplicity.' (Reminiscence of V. P. Verigna in *O Stanislavskom*, p. 357.)

Stanislavski, far from delivering the expected reprimand, asked Pronin home so that they could discuss plans for the future.

When Gorki set up a theatre in Nizhni-Novogorod early in 1904 Stanislavski saw it as the first of his projected network. He immediately provided it with the financial support he had always denied the Art Theatre and released Tikhomirov, who ran the Art Theatre School, and a small number of pupils to strengthen the company. Further financial support came from Morozov in April, once he had broken with the Art Theatre. It was a brave enterprise but everyone had reckoned without the hostility of the authorities, particularly the censor who managed to ban every play that was put forward. The project was abandoned in the early autumn.

Even had Gorki remained with the Art Theatre the problem of new repertoire would have remained. Tastes had changed. Realistic staging and, more particularly, the plethora of detail that had characterized the Art Theatre's recent productions was no longer acceptable. Progressives now demanded plays which dealt with more intangible aspects of human experience and which were more formally experimental.

The new avant-garde was represented by the Symbolists and their spokesman Valeri Briusov, who advanced his ideas first in an influential article, *Unnecessary Truth*, which appeared in the magazine *Mir Iskusstva* in 1902 and later in his book *Teatr: Kniga O Novom Teatr* published in Petersburg in 1908. The very notion of realistic staging was attacked. The more 'real' the sets, props and costumes the more 'conventional' they actually were. The 'real' actually was a convention. Why, Briusov asked, is night represented by an ingenious manipulation of light instead of a total blackout, which would indeed correspond to reality? The current compromise, elements of set, minimum of objects, does not solve the problem for against this conventionalized background all too palpable actors are moving and their attempts at physical and vocal artificiality are, at best, spasmodic. An extreme solution would be to replace actors by dummies with gramophones inside but that would remove the whole undertaking from the realm of art. It would put the theatre in the same relationship to the dramatist as typography is to the poet. The inescapable fact, Briusov maintained, was that realism and semi-realism limit the imagination of the audience and the creativity of the actor. The answer must lie in a return to Aristotle's definition of drama as the imitation of an action and to the actor as the creator and agent of that action. 'The art of the theatre and the art of the actor are one and the same thing.'

This was precisely the kind of radical challenge which Stanislavski needed. True to form he went from one extreme to the other, from the totally external to the totally internal. Even Chekhov, towards the end of his life, was moving in a new direction. He was interested in the Belgian dramatist, Maeterlinck, the most static and mystical of contemporary dramatists and, in the autumn of 1902, encouraged the Art Theatre to put on an evening of his one-act plays. The plot of Chekhov's projected last play, which he outlined to Stanislavski at their last meeting in May 1904, showed clear signs of this new influence.

'A husband and his friend are in love with the same woman. He went through the whole tragedy, the individual incidents of which were not yet clear, even to the author. The tragedy ends with first the husband, then the friend deciding to join a distant expedition. The last act, according to Chekhov, should take place at the North pole. Chekhov saw a ship lost in the ice, with the two heroes on it, the husband and the friend, who look into the far distance and see rushing by the ghost of the woman they both loved.' (Interview in *Rech*, July 2, 1914.)

Gorki had always recognized and respected the element of symbolism in Chekhov's work. It was logical therefore that in his search for change Stanislavski should accept the judgement of the two writers he knew best. He decided to act on Chekhov's suggestion and stage three short plays by Maeterlinck – *Les Aveugles*, *Intérieurs* and *L'Intruse*.

Finding a new style and a new method of approach was not easy. In May Konstantin Balmont, who had translated the three Maeterlinck plays into Russian, met the author to ask for his comments. As far as the dialogue was concerned Maeterlinck wanted neither romantic declamation, nor total realism but something in-between, expressive speech but understated. Stanislavski experienced enormous difficulty in getting a line on the production. How was he to 'make the untheatrical theatrical'? How was he to communicate the eternal, the intangible? Inevitably he exploited his skill as a producer, his capacity to manipulate effects, to fill the gaps. Maeterlinck's mysterious world was conveyed by a series of elaborate stage effects, which engulfed a largely static cast. He used a great deal of music – an excessive amount in Nemirovich's view – starting the evening with a five-minute overture by a hidden orchestra. But that did nothing for the actors. He realized that a new acting technique was necessary but his own experiments at home in front of a mirror, both vocal and physical, proved unsuccessful. In any case there was not time to retrain the company. He conveyed his anxieties to his cast, who struggled throughout August to come to terms with this unfamiliar material.

The final result was a hotch-potch of acting and production styles which when it opened on October 2, pleased nobody. The critics felt that Stanislavski had failed to capture the essence of Maeterlinck's symbolism because of his production technique; the public was simply confused both by the material and the apparent change of direction the theatre had taken. One medical student wrote a letter of protest against the total absence of positive values in the plays. The unremitting doom and gloom of Maeterlinck's texts were unlikely, in any case, to appeal to an audience already depressed by the news of Russia's endless humiliations during the Russo-Japanese War.

Both Stanislavski and Nemirovich felt that the new season must contain a tribute to Chekhov. Nemirovich directed *Ivanov* with Stanislavski in the role of Shabelski. The opening, which was scheduled for October 12, had to be postponed because of the death of Stanislavski's mother. When the play opened a week later Stanislavski turned in what was considered one of his best performances. His own success, however, did not reconcile him to Nemirovich's production which once again he found pedestrian.

Stanislavski's own tribute to Chekhov took the form of three adaptations of short stories under the title *Miniatures*. There was an opportunity here to attempt more experimental staging. In 1899 he had conceived the notion of a sequence of short dialogues and sketches by Chekhov and others which would be presented on a specially-constructed platform on the stage proper with elements of décor and props ready to hand. Scene was to follow scene without closing the curtain in a kind of cinematic rhythm. Unfortunately he did not follow the idea through. *Miniatures* was much more conventionally presented. The first night, on December 21, when the Chekhov pieces were accompanied by another one-act play, *At the Monastery*, which Nemirovich directed, was a total flop. Stanislavski said goodbye to 1904, which had been so disastrous in professional and personal terms, without regret.

The final production of the season, *Ghosts*, did little to raise his spirits.

He and Nemirovich were to co-direct but they agreed on almost nothing. Stanislavski described Nemirovich's mood as 'sour, as it has been all winter'. The sets gave endless trouble. In addition to Simov, Stanislavski called in a second designer Kolupaiev, and a design apprentice, Andreiev. Model followed model, some made by Stanislavski himself, and were rejected; furniture was continuously moved about to allow the actors freedom of movement. Nemirovich made no positive contribution at all to the discussions. Stanislavski admitted that he became thoroughly bad-tempered at his inability to give concrete form to the ideas that were running about in his head.

Building on his experience with the Maeterlinck plays, Stanislavski demanded a broader approach, less detail and more mood, in the early rehearsals. For the first time he publicly contradicted Nemirovich's basic method:

> 'We did a breakdown of the characters. [The cast] wanted to delve into every detail *à la Nemirovich* but I put a stop to it. What actors need initially is the general tone of their parts, the basic colour as it were. When an actor has discovered and feels at home with the overall outline, character and mood then you can show him various details and nuances. I have noticed that when Nemirovich is directing and goes into minute detail at the outset the actors are confused by the complexity of the material and get bogged down and the characters, even when the feelings are simple and straightforward, are vague.' (SS, Vol. V, p. 268.)

When Nemirovich took over rehearsals using the hastily-written production plan, Stanislavski sat on the side-lines providing more detailed explanations whenever he thought necessary. This, as so often, included graphic demonstration. Knipper, who was playing Regina, was having trouble establishing a definite speech pattern for the role. The character came and went all the time.

> 'Konstantin Sergeievich ran lightly onto the stage, stood in a corner and in silence in the space of about two minutes assumed the insolent coquettishness, the lust for life and the predatory essence of Regina's character. As Konstantin Sergeievich imagined himself as Regina, above all his eyes lit up in a special way, then a stream of fiery energy ran along his shoulders which were slightly hunched and raised. It ran down to his hands; his wrists came to life and the palm of his right hand, as though compressing the resistant air, landed in the palm of his left. The hands were tightly clenched, locking in the energy. The whole essence of Regina was contained there.' (Reminiscence of V. P. Verigna, *O Stanislavskom*, p. 350.)

Stanislavski had found a physical solution to a vocal problem. Rather than attempt to deal with speech patterns at a superficial level he saw the voice as part of a total physical characterization in which the body responded organically to inner impulses. His demonstration was the spontaneous response of an experienced professional, which he was not able as yet to analyse. He could not formulate in objective terms the principle which lay behind it. He insisted that the cast play against the tragic thrust of the play. He wanted firmness of tone and a good pace. By firm tone and good pace he did not mean superficial bravura and hack virtuosity but an actor's capacity, once he is confident in a part, to move swiftly from one extremity of mood to another. The key is in the notion of *tempo*. Tempo is not speed and rant but an ability 'to juggle easily with even the strongest emotions'. This is what audiences find exciting.

Stanislavski's dismissive attitude towards Nemirovich's working methods in this production was not an isolated phenomenon. He felt that the theatre had become too 'literary' and that his own creative development was being stifled by too great a subservience to the letter of the text.

This was clearly illustrated by his treatment of the opening *Ghosts*. When he came to plan Act One, he considered, somewhat arbitrarily it must be admitted, that Regina's first line to Ekdal, 'What are you doing here?' and Ekdal's own entrance were unmotivated.

> 'In Ibsen the carpenter enters the living-room without rhyme or reason and stands there doing nothing while engaging in a long dialogue. But we are in the theatre. It had to be changed. I decided on this: at the beginning of the act he is busy with the lock on the french windows. A steamer passes during the pause. He starts to hammer and Regina runs in. The scene continues with him working and her tidying up. Then everything comes alive. Only to do this we shall have to change the author's opening words and move sentences around. What else can we do? It seems to me not to do it is just pedantry.' (SS, V, pp. 263–4.)

Nemirovich could only find such an attitude deeply offensive.

Stanislavski had started to build a new circle of collaborators. Liubov Gurevich with whom he had been in correspondence since the first Petersburg tour, became his literary adviser, a role she was to fulfil for some thirty years. More than any other single individual she influenced the shape and structure of his writing. He then engaged Leopold Sulerzhitski, ex-merchant seaman, revolutionary, devotee of Tolstoi, as his personal assistant and paid for his services out of his own pocket. Nemirovich resented him deeply, as he resented anyone who came between himself and Stanislavski, and Sulerzhitski was never allowed to hold any official position on the staff of the Moscow Art Theatre.

Undeterred by Gorki's negative experiences, Stanislavski returned to the question of a general reform of the Russian theatre. On February 13 he called a number of senior colleagues to a meeting at his flat and again proposed a chain of provincial theatres under the general control of the Art Theatre. Members of the main company would be seconded to the new theatres and Art Theatre productions sent out on tour. The first theatre in the chain would open in the 1905–6 season. He might be prepared to put in 100,000 roubles of his own money. Stanislavski was without doubt thinking of tying in with Gorki who was planning to start a theatre in Petersburg with the former Art Theatre actress, Andreeva, and Vera Komissarzhevskaia, who had already considered joining the Art Theatre in 1902. Stanislavski had already been invited to become a guest director.

The meeting agreed that in general the scheme was a good one although, as usual with Stanislavski's schemes, some found it naïve and badly thought-through. It was Nemirovich who dealt the death-blow by raising all manner of practical difficulties. How, he asked, was a small undertaking like the Art Theatre, which was still not financially viable, to assume such a heavy responsibility? Where were the actors to come from? What would happen to the main company and its productions if its members were being sent into the provinces? How were the tours to be financed? These were, on the face of it, perfectly reasonable questions. What worried Nemirovich, however, was his own implied loss on control. If there was to be reform it would have to be on his terms, not Stanislavski's and certainly not Gorki's.

It was during these abortive discussions that Meierhold returned to Moscow. He had been working with his own experimental group. He claimed that he had the solution to the problem that had defeated Stanislavski – how to convey the ineffable. He had absorbed Briusov's ideas and made them work. He had passion, he had energy; he was extreme, he was intransigent – 'The theatre must be a hermitage and the actor forever a dissident'. Stanislavski responded to this outpouring of ideas with the enthusiasm of a man dying of thirst. He was not sure he understood his young colleague, or could say whether he was good or bad, a genius or a charlatan; he only knew that he needed him. Meierhold could be the right person to extend and expand the work of the Art Theatre and provide a way out of an artistic impasse. Meierhold was a man after his own kind, an artist who created in and through the theatre itself, not through literature. There was an affinity between the two of them which purely theoretical or aesthetic disagreements could not destroy.

Meierhold left Moscow again during the rehearsals for *Ghosts* but by April sent Stanislavski an outline scheme for a Theatre-Studio, a term which he invented himself. The scheme, based on discussions they had held earlier, embodies both Stanislavski's ideas for a wider social role for the Art Theatre and Meierhold's ideas on new theatrical forms. In May, Briusov agreed to give the venture his artistic support as literary adviser. The rest of the month was spent defining the artistic principles on which the Studio was to operate.

The company was composed of members of Meierhold's New Drama, members of the Art Theatre itself, pupils from the Art Theatre School, including Boris Pronin, and a number of actors from the Alexandrinski Theatre in Petersburg. Officially the Studio was attached to the Art Theatre; in reality it was subsidized almost entirely by Stanislavski. The main company were far from being sympathetic to the venture which many regarded as another piece of idealistic nonsense.

Stanislavski converted a barn at Mamontovka, not far from Pushkino, so that the company could rehearse during the summer. It seemed as though the Art Theatre, with all its early hopes and freshness, was starting all over again. He then lost his head, as he had when he created the Society of Art and Literature. He had intended to use the Hunting Club for performances, but instead he took on an empty theatre in Povarskaia Street, which Sergei Popov, a former associate in the Society found for him. It was a 1,200-seater, far too big for experimental work and in need of repair. He had the auditorium completely redecorated at his own expense. This cost him over 20,000 roubles. Having set the Studio up he did not interfere. Meierhold was given an absolutely free hand.

For his part, Stanislavski wanted to carry over the new artistic policy into the main company. He was due to direct Knut Hamsun's *The Drama of Life* in the coming season, an abstract, highly symbolic text. Discussing the play with Nemirovich he announced his intention to start rehearsals using improvisation, dispensing with all preliminary discussion and analysis, attempting to stimulate the actors' creativity through action. Nemirovich was outraged. He had concealed his dislike of the new Studio under a veil of politeness, sending a message of congratulation and encouragement to the new young company at its inauguration on June 3. But the sight of his colleague violating every artistic principle he held dear proved too much to take. Changing a few lines in *Ghosts* was one thing, now the whole supremacy of the text was in question. He attributed Stanislavski's behaviour to the malign influence of Meierhold whose interest it was to drive a wedge between them.

Between the 8th and 10th he wrote Stanislavski a huge 28-page letter with an almost equally long postscript in which he poured out his feelings of anger and resentment. He analysed the entire season. He brought up every disagreement, every imagined slight or insult. He attempted to apportion blame or merit for every aspect of the new productions. Yet the basic message was clear: it is thanks to me that you have become an effective professional; be guided by me or you will revert to the self-indulgent, capricious amateur you were when I met you.

'. . . in the last four or five years you allowed a number of restraints to be placed on your artistic temperament. You trusted, as it were, my *reason* and allowed that *reason* to govern, so that our theatre could enjoy real success. You saw from your own experience that with no one to control your temperament you destroy the best pearls of your own talent. Left to yourself you create with one hand and destroy with the other. There is not one single production to date, including *Three Sisters*, that would not have come to nothing had it not been for my control, not only literary but artistic. . . .

Now suddenly you seem to think that real art only existed at the Sporting Club where there was nothing to restrict your ideas. . . . You suddenly decided to give full rein to your own will, not realizing that your temperament would take over and ruin everything we have built up over seven years . . . Under the influence of Meierhold's absurd chatter on the necessity of rehearsing as the spirit moves the desire rose in you to exploit a method you have obviously been "thinking of for some time". This revealed very clearly a yearning to throw off "the yoke of reason".

In your serious moments you emerge as a teacher of the ethical view of art. Then you are a great man. But not when, unbeknown to yourself – because you are tired, artistic energy is beginning to flag – you transform serious matters into a personal plaything. Then you are no more than a talented but naughty child busy with trifles.' (Iz., Pis., I, pp. 391–412.)

Finally Nemirovich put a question almost too ridiculous to ask: was it possible that Stanislavski was jealous of him as a director?

In his brief reply Stanislavski, as in their earlier exchange, pointed to his own sacrifices and rebuked Nemirovich for his egotism, which was now doubly inappropriate, given the state of unrest in Russia. The country was still reeling from the shock of the massacre of innocent workers and peasants in Petersburg in January, on Bloody Sunday. It had suffered a series of humiliating defeats in the war with the Japanese. It was time to think of work, not hurt feelings:

'Dear Vladimir Ivanovich,
I admire your many qualities, your talent, intelligence and so on . . . And I am distressed at the deterioration in our relationship . . . I rack my brain over ways to improve it. . . . I don't think our relations can be improved by talking about them. . . . Instead of talk, work. That's your most powerful weapon against me. . . .

Let's say things are as you write. It's all my fault, my despotism, my whims, my obstinacy and the remnants of my amateurism. . . . I only ask one thing. Make life possible for me at the theatre. Grant me some kind of satisfaction, without which I cannot work. Don't let the time come when love and faith in our theatre will disappear *for ever*.

. . . at the moment, like everyone else, I am concerned for what is happening in Russia. Let us not talk of professional jealousy and pride. Dear God, I have finished with them forever. . . . I have never felt jealousy in my work as a director. *It is an activity I do not enjoy.* I do it out of necessity. In the realm of acting I have surrendered my pride, doggedly giving way to others and burying that side of me. From now on I shall only play so as not to lose the ability to demonstrate to others.

Try and appreciate the personal effort I have made. . . .

I do not value my success as a director but the theatre does. And that's the only reason I take pleasure in it. . . . Take my name off the posters once and for all. Think rather what it cost me to surrender my primacy of place as an actor to Kachalov and others . . . I have become . . . more demanding because of all that I have crushed in myself. I now have the right to demand full-scale, widespread theatrical activity throughout the whole of Russia. . . .

Perhaps I may come a cropper but I might also die in peace. . . . Let us work now as *at this moment* every *decent* man *must.* Do what I did. Kill your pride. Defeat me with the theatre and with work. . . .

Affectionately yours, K. Alexeiev.' (K.S. Archive, No. 5182.)

On June 28 Nemirovich wrote a conciliatory letter, backtracking on his pretensions as a director; there could be no comparison between himself and Stanislavski, but he could not help wondering if their collaboration had always been doomed to be transitory. Their paths had crossed briefly and there had been the illusion of unity. Then the momentum of their own artistic development had caused them to part. But a compromise was still essential for the good of the theatre and the people working in it. He would interfere less, although he reserved the right to express his opinion when it appeared absolutely essential. He appealed to Stanislavski to meet him half way, so that they could benefit from each other's gifts. Once again a truce was reached.

Stanislavski received the letter at the spa at Essentuki, where he was taking a much-needed rest while working on the plans for his production of *The Drama of Life* which he claimed would be 'revolutionary' in style.

Writing to Gorki on July 20 he shared his misgivings about the 1905–6 season. It was going to be 'difficult and dangerous'. He was to be proved right in more senses than one. For all that it might try to operate like a 1980s subsidized theatre it was still a commercial enterprise. There was the lease to be paid and production costs had already pushed them over budget. The new productions had been carefully balanced. The 'revolutionary' *Drama of Life* and the experiments of the Theatre-Studio would be counterbalanced by the greatest of Russian classic comedies, *Woe From Wit*, and Gorki's *Children of the Sun*. Gorki had agreed to set aside his resentment against Nemirovich and release the play when Stanislavski appealed to him, as a friend, for support. A Gorki play was a box-office certainty and as such was badly needed. Also included in the season was a revival of *The Seagull*, with Meierhold in his original rôle as Konstantin, and Stanislavski offering his new interpretation of Trigorin.

Stanislavski returned to Moscow in the first week in August with the production plan for *The Drama of Life* substantially complete. On the 7th, Gorki read *Children of the Sun*, for which Stanislavski was also to be responsible, to the company. Despite previous differences, Nemirovich was unreservedly cooperative. Apart from directing the Gorki and the Hamsun and playing in the *Seagull* revival, Stanislavski was scheduled to play Famusov in *Woe From Wit*.

On August 11 Stanislavski, accompanied by Knipper, Kachalov, Vishnievski and other members of the company went to Pushkino to see the work of the Theatre-Studio. During the course of the day they saw Hauptmann's *Schluck und Jau*, Maeterlinck's *La Mort de Tintagiles* and Ibsen's *Love's Comedy*. The Hauptmann was well received, and the Maeterlinck greeted with rapturous enthusiasm. The Ibsen was immature but nonetheless showed promise. Stanislavski returned to Moscow well-content and confident that the risks he had taken, both artistic and financial, had been justified. In early September he took a two-week break in Sevastopol, leaving Nemirovich in charge of rehearsals.

The Drama of Life and *The Children of the Sun* were diametrically opposed in production style. The Hamsun was an essay in abstraction. The production plan filled with sketches indicating physical attitudes. The body is the dominant medium of expression. The Gorki, on the other hand, was treated in the now familiar Art Theatre manner, with an excess of naturalistic detail. Yet Stanislavski saw the two leading figures, Kareno and Protassov, as essentially similar – naïve, quixotic, idealistic – but in this play, as in *Summerfolk*, Gorki was sharply critical of the intelligentsia. This Stanislavski failed to grasp. Gorki was by no means pleased with the overall approach. He successfully resisted Stanislavski's intention to bring on a real horse in Act Two but could not prevent the clarity of his intentions from being submerged beneath a welter of 'unnecessary truths'. Writing to a friend on September 25 he stated that the whole play had been distorted and would be a resounding failure.

The season started badly. *The Seagull*, which opened on September 30, failed to catch on. At the same time there was discontent among the young actors of the Theatre-Studio. They were worried about their future. They asked to be allowed to concentrate wholeheartedly on their work and their stated mission of creating new theatre. Back in Moscow, removed from the protective atmosphere and camaraderie of Pushkino, the latent hostility of many of the company had become apparent especially during Stanislavski's absence. It was to him they appealed for help.

From October 14–19 there was a general strike in which the Moscow Art Company participated. Despite an imperial decree, guaranteeing civil liberty, issued on the 17th, the secret police openly murdered a leading revolutionary figure, Nikolai Bauman on the 18th. There was further bloodshed at Bauman's funeral on the 20th, when Cossack regiments went into action. Apart from the troops, bands of right-wing extremists, the Black Hundreds, were also active, terrorizing, attacking and murdering known or suspected dissidents. Stanislavski put himself in danger. His signature – K. Alekseiev – appeared on the protest handed in to the Duma on the 21st.

Such was the political atmosphere when the public dress rehearsal of *Children of the Sun* occurred on the 24th. Everyone was expecting an 'incident'. It duly occurred.

'The audience was extraordinarily tense throughout the performance, expecting every possible kind of excess. And then, when, towards the end of the play the crowd – members of the company – broke through the hedge of Protassov's house, appearing as provocateurs, agitators and an "angry mob" and Germanova, playing my wife Elena, fired at the crowd, and I, as required in the action, fell to the ground, something completely unexpected and unimaginable occurred. The audience, not knowing who had fired at whom and why, took the actors rushing in for members of the Black Hundreds, who were breaking into the theatre to kill us and concluded that I was the first victim. There was an unbelievable uproar. Some women had hysterics. Part of the audience launched themselves towards the footlights, evidently ready to defend us. The rest went to the exit doors to cut off the escape. Someone leapt to where his coat was hanging to get a revolver from its pocket. Someone shouted, "curtain".

Vl. I. Nemirovich-Danchenko appeared before the curtain, asking the audience to allow the performance to finish, trying to calm them by telling them that the end was a happy one. When the curtains opened the audience had still not settled down. There were shouts of "Kachalov, get up! Get up, Kachalov!" I got up, showed that I was still alive then lay down again.' (Vassili Ivanovich Kachalov, *Iskusstvo*, 1954, pp. 39–40.)

One critic at least protested against being obliged to see on stage what he had already experienced in the streets.

At the same time the Theatre-Studio unveiled the final results of its work. Stanislavski needed the Studio to succeed and he had done everything he could to make success possible. Realizing that Meierhold was overworked he asked Nemirovich to replace him in *The Seagull*. He did not conceal the extent of his financial commitment and the consequences of failure. Nonetheless the Studio did fail and Stanislavski was too honest to pretend otherwise. Work which had seemed impressive in a converted barn proved inadequate in a fully-equipped professional theatre. Stanislavski contributed in a minor way to the fiasco. *La Mort de Tintagiles* opened in semi-darkness, with the cast almost in silhouette. After a while Stanislavski insisted that the lights be brought up on the grounds that audiences needed to see the actors' faces. He ignored protests. The increased lighting revealed the painful truth, the inadequacy of the young cast, who wavered between an uncertain realism and equally uncertain stylization. The evening demonstrated nothing more than a clever young director exploiting a group of actors to illustrate his own ideas. There had not, in Stanislavski's or indeed Briusov's sense, been a genuine breakthrough. The performance was brought to an abrupt end. Stanislavski disposed of the lease, paid off the carpenters and other craftsmen and gave the technical staff a year's severance pay. He had lost at least 20,000 roubles at a time when, because of political unrest, his factories were selling less and profits were plummeting. Any artistic disappointment was almost exclusively his. Neither Nemirovich nor other members of the company were sorry to see the Studio fold or to witness, once more, the departure of Meierhold.

The experience had not, however, been entirely unprofitable. Meierhold and Briusov both concluded that there could be no compromise with the Moscow Art style. There had to be a new method of training actors. This Meierhold set out to discover. Nonetheless Briusov made a crucial distinction – as did Meierhold – between Stanislavski, whom he saw as an enquiring, probing artist, and the Moscow Art Theatre as an institution. Thus it was possible for Briusov to write some months later:

'. . . I am ready with all my heart, as far as my strength and abilities allow, to assist you in any endeavours undertaken in the spirit of the former Studio. I ask you most earnestly, if there is a place for me in that work, to call on me.' (Briusov to Stanislavski, May 15, 1906, SS, VII, p. 711.)

Stanislavski, for his part, was left with a set of unanswered questions concerning his own art and his future. He could not return – much as Nemirovich would have welcomed it – to the methods the theatre now traditionally employed.

The political situation continued to deteriorate. In October there was another general strike followed by a Bolshevik-inspired revolution. Fighting broke out in the streets. Stanislavski insisted that rehearsals for *Woe From Wit* continue despite the gunfire outside. Nobody was sure how the cast could get home safely. In the end even Stanislavski's obstinacy had to give way and work was abandoned.

There was more than an artist's pride or pig-headedness involved in Stanislavski's persistence. True to his conviction that major classics were an instrument of progress, Stanislavski saw the production of Griboiedov's play as a contribution to the revolution:

'It occurred to me that the strike was a very good thing and even advantageous to the theatre. We had time to prepare *Woe From Wit* for without it the theatre could not continue to survive. In a word, I tried to demonstrate that *Woe From Wit* was the only play in tune with the revolution.' (K.S. Archive, No. 1093.)

The Drama of Life was shelved.

The revolution lasted one week before it was brutally and bloodily suppressed. Even the minor concessions to democracy that Tsar Nicholas had promised earlier were swept away. It seemed that all hope of progress in Russia had disappeared. It was a moment of black despair. Stanislavski was overcome by a sense of futility. Had art, he asked himself, any real function, or any contribution to make, in such circumstances? Would he ever realize his dream of a popular, open theatre? He decided, with Nemirovich, to close the theatre and take the company on its first foreign tour.

CHAPTER THIRTEEN

FIRST FOREIGN TOUR

Stanislavski left for Berlin on January 24, 1906, in advance of the rest of the company. The tour had been so hastily agreed that arrangements were still incomplete. The repertoire – *Tsar Fiodor, Uncle Vania, Three Sisters, An Enemy of the People, The Lower Depths* – reflected none of the company's recent experiments but productions which were now solidly established. *Fiodor* was no longer in the repertoire and had to be re-rehearsed.

In Germany the tour was given wide but dignified publicity. August Schultz, the German translator of Chekhov and Gorki, gave a lecture in Berlin on February 1 and the *Nationalzeitung* published an interview with Stanislavski on the 8th.

The season opened on the 10th almost inevitably with *Fiodor*. In the first-night audience were Gerhardt Hauptmann, Arthur Schnitzler, Eleanora Duse and the young Max Reinhardt. The performance was an immense success. The leading critic, Alfred Kerr wrote some years later:

'What I saw in that production was something first class. Unarguably first class. You may not possess any knowledge of the Russian tongue, no understanding of the individual details of the events but after two minutes you knew that this was first class.' (Alfred Kerr, *Das Mimenreich*, Berlin, 1917, p. 225.)

Writing under the immediate impact of the performance, on the 25th, he was in no doubt that he had seen 'a chunk of history', and his views were shared. To his brother, Vladimir, Stanislavski wrote:

'There are over a hundred newspapers here, some of which carry evening editions. All, without a single exception, published huge articles and were beside themselves with joy. I have never seen such reviews. It's as though we were the revelation. Nearly all end their articles with the cry: we know the Russians are over a hundred years behind politically but, dear God, how far they have overtaken us artistically.' (SS, VII, p. 335.)

On the 12th the legendary virtuoso pianist, Leopold Godowski wrote Stanislavski a letter of thanks for a performance which had given him more artistic pleasure than he had experienced for a long time. What struck critics and audience alike was the reality of the stage action and the presence of real characters quite unlike, as one writer put it, the posturings of the Meininger.

When *Uncle Vania* opened on the 15th, during one of the intervals Hauptmann declared loud enough for all to hear:

> 'This is the most powerful theatrical experience I have ever had, these are not people acting but artistic gods.' (Ibid.)

The Lower Depths opened on the 18th, with another personal triumph for Stanislavski:

> 'His Satin was unforgettable. . . . In any case, this man is a genius. The rest are capable indeed very capable artists, surrounding a genius.' (*Nationalzeitung*, March 3.)

Three Sisters followed on February 25 with equal success.

The Emperor, Kaiser Wilhelm II and his family attended a performance of *Fiodor* on March 6, thus setting the final seal of approval on the tour. Talking to the cast the Kaiser displayed a knowledge of Russian history which few of the actors, in their nervousness, could match. The Crown Prince was a constant visitor, attending as many performances as he could.

The Berlin season ended with *An Enemy of the People* which opened on March 7 and produced the only serious critical reservation to appear to print. Kerr found Stanislavski's Stockman unforgettable but not really Ibsen's character; he was not 'a Viking' – perhaps a somewhat Germanic judgement.

On March 12 the company left for Dresden, where they again met Duse. She suggested that the time had come for them to play in Paris and that they should come to an arrangement with Lugné-Poë. Nemirovich investigated further but concluded that a Paris season would not be financially viable. The idea was dropped.

On the 19th they were in Leipzig, the 22nd in Prague and the 28th in Vienna where, for the first time, neither the welcome nor the audiences were perfect. Vienna lived up to its reputation of combining a rare cultural tradition with pettiness and intrigue. If Stanislavski expected help from the Russian embassy he was disappointed. When he called there the day after his arrival to recruit extras for *Fiodor* he was not well received. On his return to the theatre he discovered that there was trouble with the fire department:

> 'Quite awful day . . . trouble and strife. . . . Visit Urusov [the ambassador]. His secretaries are nincompoops. Their reception was not very courteous. Urusov invited us all to breakfast. I declined.
>
> I returned to the theatre. Exhausted. There, more trouble. The police have taken the play off. The sets have to be fireproofed.

Lunch and then back to the theatre. Chaos, no make-up or wigs. Everyone exhausted. Reception feeble. . . . During the interval the police
daubed the scenery.' (*Notebook*, March 29.)

The performance was nothing like the success they had known elsewhere, a
large number of people left before the end in order to avoid being fined for
being out after curfew. There were also political tensions:

'Lay on the bed for hours. Read the reviews. Unexpectedly good notices.
The town and especially the audience divided. Hostility between the Slavs
and the Germans. Slavs 60%, ruled by 40% Germans. Germans stingy.
They pay 50 crowns for a box but they won't pay a fine of 10 pfennigs
for being out after 10 o'clock so at 9.30 many start leaving the theatre.
   Life is expensive; company is grumbling. The crowns just fly away.'
(*Notebook*, March 30.)

After Vienna the company returned to Germany, performing in Frankfurt
on April 10 and in Karlsruhr on the 11th. On the 12th, by special command
there was a gala performance of *Fiodor* in Wiesbaden. Ermolova, who was
staying in the town at the time, was also present. After the performance
both Stanislavski and Nemirovich were decorated with the order of the Red
Eagle, Fourth Class. From Wiesbaden, the company moved to Düsseldorf
on the 16th and Hanover on the 20th. While in Hanover Stanislavski received a letter from a group of émigré Russian intellectuals, thanking him
and the company for representing the spirit of Russian life and the free
spirit of art. The journey home began at the end of April, with a short
season in Warsaw, beginning on the 23rd. They finally arrived back in
Moscow on May 3.
   The tour had been long and exhausting but – Vienna excepted – an unqualified success. It marked the beginning of the company's international
reputation and influence. In contemporary terms the only comparison is the
impact of the Berliner Ensemble when it began to visit abroad. In a short
space of time the reputation of the Moscow Art Theatre spread throughout
Europe and beyond. The financial losses of the early part of the season had
been more than covered so that the theatre's future was assured – for the
time being at least. For German and Austrian writers the Art Theatre seemed
to offer a new way of thinking about acting and directing, a new concept of
the nature of the theatre itself. It opened up a range of possibilities.
   In Berlin, Hauptmann had given a rather chaotic lunch at his home at
which conversation was somewhat inhibited by Stanislavski's poor German.
Nonetheless the message Stanislavski received was clear:

'Hauptmann told us that he had always dreamed of seeing his plays acted
the way we had – without effects and theatrical conventions, with simple,

profound, rich, rounded playing. German actors had assured him that it could not be done, that the theatre, in their view, had its own conventions and its own demands which could not be denied. And now at the twilight of his literary activity it had been given to him to see what he had always dreamed of.' (SS, I, p. 292.)

Schnitzler, too, experienced the full impact of Stanislavski's thought and personality:

'That hour I spent with Stanislavski changed my whole inner life, my ambitions for ever. I finally found myself.' (Quoted in *Slovo*, Paris, Dec. 25, 1923).

Max Reinhardt went a stage further. Within a year he had opened the *Kammerspiele*, which was exactly modelled on the Art Theatre.

Not one of them realized that what they received so enthusiastically represented the Art Theatre's past. They picked up no hint of the aesthetic and philosophical debate, not to say the open war, which was going on inside the theatre. One negative result of the tour was to fix the Art Theatre in an out-moded brand image, as though everything had stopped in 1904. Subsequent foreign tours, when the public had to be given what it thought it wanted, reinforced this impression, giving rise to severely limited notions concerning Stanislavski's artistic thought and the development of his theatre practice.

The tour had produced a respite but the essential problems remained: the 'lost' season had to be reconstructed. Nemirovich and Stanislavski had still to come to an understanding and neither showed any signs of retreating from their fixed positions. Outwardly it was business as usual. Stanislavski put considerable energy into the rehearsals for *Woe from Wit* which began in late May, combining prescriptive directing and demonstration with an attempt to stimulate the actors' own imagination and creative force. At the same time he was working with the designers on the sets for *The Drama of Life*. But he was functioning in the midst of an overwhelming personal crisis. He felt as an artist he was dead. The feeling had overtaken him while on tour. According to an interview with the magazine *Studia* in April 1912, during a performance in March 1906 he suddenly became aware that he was acting mechanically. The outer shell of the character was there, the body moved, the voice spoke, few people apart from himself would have realized there was anything wrong but there was no life, no inner impulse or feeling.

There is good reason to suppose that the play in question was *An Enemy of the People*. The blow would therefore have been doubly heavy. Stockman had been one of his most spontaneous creations, a character which gave him deep satisfaction. The last two years had brought their problems and disappointments: Chekhov's death, the growing rift between him and Nemirovich, the failure of the Studio, his own inability to find a new artistic direction but the one thing which remained, and which he prized above all, was his supremacy and power as an actor and as a creator. Now, it seemed, that was gone. What could the future hold?

There can be no doubt that a major cause of this creative drying-up was sheer exhaustion. In the eight years of the Art Theatre's existence he had turned out one major production or performance after another. It was inevitable that the system would give out some time. This he realized himself. As usual he committed his thoughts to paper – his method of having dialogue with himself. He tried to analyse what was wrong with the company, starting with his own case. What he required was an exercise in honesty:

'I'll start with the good points. I have talent as a director and an actor, a middling intelligence, a passion for what I do, energy and purpose in art, in which I endeavour to strive without compromise. In quiet moments there is an ability to adapt to people, for tolerance and even [*illegible*] and a recognized portion of administrative ability. But my nerves are not good, I am very spoiled, my temperament lacks restraint. These faults dominate me when I am overtired, irritated or bitter. . . . The sickness of my whole system, my nerves, is a result of my abnormal way of life . . . from the enormous number of things there are to do. Hence exhaustion and the need to do less work and get more rest. The circumstances of my life have demanded a reduction of my work outside the theatre. That leads to the question of my activity in the theatre. Can it be controlled and reduced? Of course it can.' (K.S. Archive, No. 3464/2.)

These notes were written in late May, a few days before the Alekseiev family left for Finland, where they spent the following two months. But tired and demoralized though he was, this was not to be a holiday in the real sense. As Lilina wrote to Knipper:

'He [Stanislavski] is happy that the northern air and climate agree with him. But between ourselves he has a strange way of spending his time. He doesn't walk or swim or even take fresh air. He sits in a half-darkened room all day, writing and smoking.' (*Maria Petrovna Lilina*, VTO, Moscow, 1960, p. 203.)

What he was working on was a draft *Manual on Dramatic Art*.

The examination of conscience had become a full-scale review of his artistic views and practice. With him in Finland he had all his notebooks which contained his ideas on acting since 1889, a series of unconnected jottings, ranging from notions of theatre and professional ethics to advice on how to dominate back-stage noise and keep the audience's attention. The time had come to put his intellectual house in order.

'Through my experience as an actor I had gathered together a rag-bag of material on the technique of the theatre. Everything had been thrown in willy-nilly, no system. . . . Some order had to be created, the material had to be sorted out, examined, assessed, and, as it were ranged on mental shelves. Rough matter had to be worked on and polished and laid down as the foundation stones of our art.' (SS, I, p. 285.)

The failure of his experiments with Meierhold and the Studio, all concerned with form, Briusov's emphasis on the actor as the centre, and his own insistence on the notion of the actor-creator forced him towards a more thorough examination of the actor's process. If the play's meaning was to be realized principally through the actor then a prime concern must be to give the actor control over his creative method. That control, it now seemed, lay at the level of personal psychology. There had been hints of a new essentially psychological approach in his notes on Lopakhin. Since then he had gone a stage further. This is evident from the letter he wrote to his friend, the Petersburg actress Kotliarevskaia, on July 1, 1905, giving her advice on how to prepare the role of Charlotta in *The Cherry Orchard*:

'First of all you must live the role without spoiling the words or making them commonplace. Shut yourself off and play whatever goes through your head. Imagine the following scene: Pishchik has proposed to Charlotta, now she is his bride . . . How will she behave? Or: Charlotta has been dismissed but finds other employment in a circus or a café-chantant. How does she do gymnastics or sing little songs? Do your hair in various ways and try to find in yourself things which remind you of Charlotta. You will be reduced to despair twenty times in your search but don't give up. Make this German woman you love so much speak Russian and observe how she pronounces words and what are the special characteristics of her speech. Remember to play Charlotta in a dramatic moment of her life. Try to make her weep sincerely over her life. Through such an image you will discover all the whole range of notes you need.' (SS, VII, p. 315.)

This contains in embryo much that was to be developed later: the exploration of character through improvisation, setting the character in new, imaginary circumstances, not foreseen by the author, as a means of stimulating the actor's imagination. But is still *ad hoc* advice. If the creative process was not to be left to chance or the fickle inspiration of the moment, the only way forward was the systematic formulation of that 'grammar' of acting which he had dabbled with for years.

Stanislavski's determination to create that 'grammar' was not the expression of a purely theoretical concern. He always lived in a state of the provisional. He was and remained profoundly suspicious of 'the definitive statement'. Hence his difficulty in ever completing a manuscript. He had moved on almost before the ink was dry. But now he was driven by a sense of desperation. He had to create a survival-kit for himself as an actor.

The basis of his whole 'System', as he came to call it, was the conviction that in acting as in everything else nature, not the rational intellect, creates. What he had to discover was an artistic process in tune with the processes of the human organism at the level of the un- or super-conscious. By 'super-conscious' – a term which was to get him into a great deal of trouble later – Stanislavski merely meant those regions of the mind which are not accessible to conscious recall or the will. It had nothing to do with notions of latent content advanced by Freud, whose works he did not know. It followed therefore that whatever he proposed would have the status not of aesthetic theory or philosophical speculation but of natural law. Any grammar, method or system, however, was only useful as a stimulus to these organic processes. It was no more than a substitute for the instinctive, intuitive creation enjoyed by the truly great actors he had seen and of whom he did not count himself one.

Stanislavski undoubtedly over-romanticized great actors and insufficiently understood the difference between their working conditions and his own. In many cases they performed a limited number of roles to which they were temperamentally sympathetic and, like opera singers, took their interpretations with them wherever they went. The pressures of a working theatre like the Moscow Art Theatre were considerably greater. In any one month Stanislavski might be playing three or four major roles in the existing repertoire, creating new ones, directing new productions and discussing policy in addition to fulfilling his minimal but unavoidable duties at the factory. The problem was one of mentally changing gear. You could not expect to be able to walk into the theatre and automatically become Vershinin. Or, at least, he could now no longer expect it. Nor, as a company member could you always expect to like the parts you were assigned. More than ever now he needed a secure methodology, a new pattern of theatre practice.

Stanislavski founded his new 'grammar' on two basic principles. First, the actor's ability to use the totality of his experiences. If these experiences do not come into play automatically when starting work on a part then the actor must develop a method which will provide access to them, otherwise, in desperation, he will be thrown back on externals and theatrical clichés. Unfortunately the actor as Stanislavski saw him was a man divided against himself. On the one hand there was Kostia Alekseiev, with his mundane concerns and worries, his family, his meals, his children; on the other was Konstantin Stanislavski of the Moscow Art Theatre, who was expected to represent, nightly, extremes of human passion and feeling, to typify at the highest level, the human condition. The prime task of any method or grammar must be to bring the two aspects of the personality together in a creative relationship. For the moment, Stanislavski was convinced that the key lay in stimulating the will. The actor must arouse in himself the urge to create afresh each time thus bringing other psychological mechanisms into play.

The second principle involved the breaking down of a role into its component parts. Where a role was not grasped globally, in a single intuitive act, the creative process must be broken down into a series of smaller, more manageable problems, which could be studied and mastered separately and then brought together again to form the whole. Stanislavski derived this principle, in all probability, from his knowledge of industry. He was familiar with the theory of Taylorism, the break-down of complex manufacturing processes into a sequence of simple actions on a production-line. In his new approach to acting he transferred this theory to creative work.

He read his notes daily to Lilina and Kotliarevskaia in Finland. In Kotliarevskaia he found a sympathetic listener. Lilina was less convinced. On August 8 he returned to Moscow, knowing that he had done no more than lay down a programme of study. What he needed was a period of observation and analysis. He would watch actors at work and discuss their working methods with them.

CHAPTER FOURTEEN

A 'GRAMMAR' OF ACTING

The 1906–07 season began deceptively well. *Woe From Wit*, which had been abandoned in mid-rehearsal at the end of 1905, during the revolution, had its first public dress rehearsal on September 24. Stanislavski and Nemirovich worked together on the production although neither of their names appeared on the programme. Stanislavski, however, would appear to have the dominant influence.

Griboiedov's play occupies a special place in Russian theatre. It ranks in cultural importance with the greatest of Shakespeare's plays or, perhaps more appropriately. Molière's comedies. Written in a complex stanza form it has defied satisfactory translation and is therefore less well known that it should be. For Russian audiences, however, a new production of the play is comparable to a new *Hamlet*. Stanislavski was well aware of what he was taking on and of the expectations that the audience would bring with it. He met the challenge head on, making no concessions, sticking to the principles he had laid out in his letter to Besnard. Mrs Gurevich, writing in the spring of 1907 when the play was on tour in Petersburg stated:

> 'The Moscow people revolutionized the play; they blew all the expectations of the audience and the critics sky high.' (*Tovarishch*, May 10, 1907.)

Stanislavski repeated with this Russian classic what he had achieved in other standard works. He brought life out of literature. The tone was lighter; there was less bombast and rhetoric and more realism. The house in which the play is set was a place that was lived in, not a place where the actors recite verse. Professionals like Lenski, Ermolova and Fedotova were excited when the inexorable flow of the verse was broken up by the use of pauses in Act Three. Critics were suitably outraged. Nemirovich remarked that for the first time in Kachalov's performance Chatski, the rebellious young hero, was played as a human being and not as an illustration of every critical commentary ever written on the character. Stanislavski's own performance as Famusov, the merchant, was a triumph. He had again broken with tradition by playing the character not as an aristocrat, which was the practice at the Mali, but lower down the social scale.

Any feelings of euphoria were, however, short-lived. The differences between Stanislavski and Nemirovich broke out more virulently than ever and the gulf between them was patent for all to see. As Nemirovich wrote to Leonid Andreiev:

'We have finally reached agreement on the season. I shall be doing *Brand* and Stanislavski *The Drama of Life*. We rehearse separately and independently of one another, although simultaneously, me in the foyer, him on the stage – when I am on stage he is in the foyer. This is the first time we have drawn a demarcation line – a necessity in view of the continuing artistic differenecs between us.' (N-D Archive, No. 11303.)

There had been continuous argument since July over the order in which the plays were to be given and the casting. Nemirovich wanted *Brand* to have priority as he regarded it as a revolutionary play, a 'once in a lifetime work of genius', far superior artistically to the Hamsun, which was 'a talented question-mark'. He also wanted Kachalov for the lead in both productions, whereas it had been understood that Stanislavski would play Kareno. Both plays went into rehearsal on the 27th. Within weeks the company had divided into rival factions. Nemirovich's hostility to Stanislavski's method of rehearsing *The Drama of Life* was undiminished. He openly described it as 'crackpot'. The more he saw of *The Drama of Life* as it was shown to him act by act the less he liked it. As for the ideas on acting which Stanislavski brought back after the summer he took them as further evidence that his colleague had gone off the rails, as did many other members of the company who had no desire to change their working methods or to be treated as guinea-pigs in Stanislavski's research. Stanislavski on his side considered that Nemirovich had made a fundamental mistake in not playing *Brand* in prose. His decision to use a verse translation transformed the play into a fairy-tale or a piece of gothic tedium.

Nemirovich decided that in the interest of the future of the theatre he must take strong action and assert his authority in management. He could see no way of controlling his collegue and he became increasingly apprehensive that the theatre would become 'Stanislavski's club' as he later put it, rather like the Society of Art and Literature. He knew that commercially and financially the theatre could not succeed if Stanislavski were given a free hand: schedules would cease to exist and budgets would become a joke. Things finally came to a head in early November, with much manoeuvering among the shareholders. Nemirovich, having told Stanislavski on November 3 that he should not play Kareno, informed him on the 4th that the shareholders wanted him to take the part. He publicly humiliated Sulerzhitski, who was assisting Stanislavski on *The Drama of Life*, pointing out that he had no right to make any demands whatsoever on the management as his position was purely unofficial. Stanislavski reminded Nemirovich that they had agreed in private conversation that Sulerzhitski should become his personal assistant. He apologized for not putting in an official request and rectified the omission. He had no interest in power. All he wanted was a quick solution. He proposed that Nemirovich should become chairman of the board, if that was what he really wanted. The shareholders agreed.

He confided his sense of irritation to his journal on November 6:

'It's grotesque. I am paying Sulerzhitski with my own money. He is working all out and I still have to beg permission from V.I., who does nothing, to have his help. When Suler heard about it he almost walked out of the theatre.' (K.S. Archive, No. 746.)

Nemirovich took matters a stage further, writing on November 5, in response to Stanislavski's official request:

'Since you acknowledge me in your letter as chairman I will simply ask you to participate in a short meeting of the shareholders . . . so as to draw up the appropriate agreement. Then I will assume total *responsibility* for the current season and at the same time full *power* as chairman. . . . I ask you not to bring anyone to work in the theatre, even should it concern an assistant for yourself, without my permission or the permission of the management if any occasion should arise in the current season.' (November 5, 1906. N-D Archive No. 1627.)

At least one of the shareholders was critical of Nemirovich's behaviour. Writing to Knipper from abroad, Stakhovich accused him of being far to full of himself to do what he should, namely renounce his own ambitions, support Stanislavski, and cover his weaknesses.

Stanislavski's conciliatory attitude seemed to do little to improve the overall situation. Nemirovich continued to treat *The Drama of Life* and Stanislavski's new ideas with cynical disdain and made full use of the new managerial powers. He was, moreover, no more reconciled to Sulerzhitski than before. At the end of January Stanislavski was ill, with a high temperature. Sulerzhitski took over rehearsals, working alone for the first time. Nemirovich stayed away from the first dress rehearsal, something unheard of in the whole history of the company. Stanislavski was outraged:

'The worst insult I have received. Today when I was still very ill I went to the dress rehearsal of *The Drama of Life* after ten days in bed. The play was announced in the press last Saturday without my being asked. On Tuesday and Thursday performances were cancelled because of dress rehearsals. I was ill. Suler had charge of a play for the first time. Before it even began I learned that neither Vladimir Ivanovich [Nemirovich] nor Kaluzhski would be present at the theatre. They didn't even bother to inform us. This is theatrical filth, revenge. I can't stay in such an atmosphere any longer. I've decided to quit the theatre.' (K.S. Archive No. 746.)

This was not an idle threat. Stanislavski was now thoroughly disillusioned and sick at heart. He could not work in an atmosphere of intrigue or one that was not 'clean'. But for the moment he soldiered on with a production and a role that were now poison to him.

Nemirovich finally attended a highly-successful public dress rehearsal on February 6 and experienced a change of heart. The play opened on the 8th, when Stanislavski was still unwell. He wrote to Kotliarevskaia on February 15:

> 'The Drama of Life had the success I wanted. Half the people hissed, the other half were in raptures. I am satisfied with the results of a number of trials and experiments.
> They have opened up many interesting principles for us.
> The decadents are happy,
> the realists are outraged,
> the bourgeois are resentful.' (SS, VII, p. 364.)

His own performance as Kareno had a mixed reception. Efros condemned it as monotonous and boring and, on the whole, it did little to recommend his new ideas, his new grammar, to his collegues who could not see any positive result. His attempts to base the production on psychological action only, without gestures, conveying everything through the face and eyes, met with only partial success. There was still a basic contradiction between the production style and the ingrained naturalism of the acting. Even the faithful Suler, did not fully understand. His idea of 'psychology' was to whip the actors into a frenzy. Going into rehearsal one day Stanislavski found:

> '. . . a tragedian bathed in sweat, rolling on the ground and roaring with every appearance of passion he could drag out of himself, with my assistant sitting astride him, yelling at the top of his voice and pushing him with all his might. "More! more! Go on! Louder!" . . . 'Life, feeling! Feeling!" (SS, I, p. 310.)

Stanislavski was nonetheless determined to pursue his researches. The season was drawing to a close. After that there would be the by-now annual Petersburg tour. He had already fixed on the idea of directing Maeterlinck's Blue Bird for the following season. Among other projects were Byron's Cain and Oscar Wilde's Salomé.

It was at this moment that he learned that Nemirovich had been approached by Nelidov, the literary manager of the Mali Theatre, and offered the post of artistic director. He should not have been surprised. Nemirovich had threatened to leave in the previous November, a threat which Stanislav-ski described as cheap and vulgar. In fact there had been moves to combine the Mali and the Art Theatre in 1905 and Nemirovich had been party to the discussions. The authorities were worried by the decline in standards at the Mali, which was now not even a shadow of its former self. A fusion of the two companies would also give them an opportunity to bring the rebelli-ous Art Theatre under control. Both companies got wind of the scheme and were opposed to it. The whole idea was shelved during the revolution. Now it was being reconsidered. In fact, by the time Stanislavski learned of the new offer, Nemirovich had already turned it down. Nonetheless Stanislavski felt that it was time to resign for his own sake and for the good of the theatre, which must at all costs survive. With him out of the way, Nemir-ovich could pursue his own policies unopposed. On February 23 he drafted a letter of resignation in his Journal. It was never sent but reveals Stanislav-ski's state of mind and the low ebb he had reached. In it he refers to condi-tions, known to both of them, which would oblige him to leave the board of directors within a year. These conditions remain obscure. It is, however the deterioration in their personal relationship and its effect on the theatre which concerns him:

'The exceptional feature of our partnership has been our mutual respect for the work we have each contributed.
That has now disintegrated. We are pulling our enterprise in different directions and are tearing it apart. That is criminal.
Married people can divorce, lovers, friends can part so as not to make each other's lives a misery, Cannot we (condemned as we are to torture each other for all our lives) find some *modus vivendi* which will avoid the worst thing of all, ruining each other's very existence?
To create this new relationship we must, first and foremost, part.
I don't want to play on gratitude or be over-modest. . . . I should be the one to surrender because I am a director without responsibility and a shareholder without influence. If I relinquish these functions the theatre will not go off course for a single day. But if you go, the theatre will cease to exist. . . .
There can be no solution until what is unique and creative in our en-terprise is recognized. Regularize my position and everything will go smoothly, whatever position you envisage for me.
1. The theatre needs me as an actor in certain roles.
2. The theatre needs me as a director for one or two productions.
3. Sometimes it needs my tact and acumen in business.
All this will remain in a new role. . . .
As you see, I am not making demands but asking you, as a friend, to help me. . . .

Let us part friends, so that an enterprise of world renown may not, later, be broken up by its members.

It is our civic duty to support it.

To destroy it would be a barbarous crime.' (K.S. Archive, No. 746.)

In the event what he actually sent was a short, formal letter of resignation, followed some hours later by an even shorter letter asking Nemirovich to find some means by which it would be possible for him to retract.

Matters went no further but Stanislavski's scribbled draft accurately predicted both the timing of his departure from the Board, which took place a year later and the conditions of his future relationship with the company.

The Mali Theatre, however, did not give up so easily. On April 2, Nelidov made Nemirovich another official offer. Nemirovich insisted on seeing the director of the theatre, Teliakovski, and an appointment was arranged for 4.30 that afternoon. Teliakovski arrived half an hour late having been to see Stanislavski beforehand. The two men talked until 6.45. Nemirovich immediately went to see Stanislavski at his home but he was asleep and Nemirovich decided not to disturb him before the performance. After the performance he gave his colleague a full account of the discussions and of his feelings.

'I don't create at the Art Theatre, all I have really done is establish an institution where others create. If someone says to me: you founded a theatre, now found a state theatre, I can't do anything other than accept and try to bring the best artistic talents I can and exploit them. My attachment to one theatre, even one of my own creation, does not warrant my refusal, because that would diminish the progressive nature of what I am doing. It would be like a man refusing to go into parliament because he was a member of the local council. . . .' (Letter to his wife, April 3, 1907. N-D Archive No. 2088.)

Nonetheless he had suggested a year's delay. He had been quite blunt about the need for fundamental reforms at the Mali and had proposed that he should draw up a report outlining his conditions and that a final decision should be taken some time in 1908. There the matter rested. A few days later the company left for Petersburg where, on April 29, it gave the hundredth performance of *Three Sisters*.

The new productions were far more controversial. *Woe from Wit* caused a critical controversy of the first order, inciting the vituperation of conservative critics, *Brand* was condemned as socialist propaganda and *The Drama of Life* almost universally detested.

Returning to Moscow the company found itself in further trouble. The Synod banned Byron's *Cain*. Nemirovich, against Stanislavski's wishes, decided to replace it with Andreiev's *Life of Man*, a drama if possible even more abstract than *The Drama of Life*. Stanislavski directed it under protest, ultimately describing it as rubbish and not a play at all. The première which took place on December 12, was a success. This was almost entirely due to its production values and to Stanislavski's chance discovery during preliminary work on *The Blue Bird* of a method of making things appear and disappear as if by magic.

'I needed a piece of black velvet which I had just been looking at but it had disappeared. We looked everywhere, turning over drawers, boxes, tables, the whole room in fact – but no black velvet. At last we saw it, hanging right where we passed by, under our very nose. Why hadn't we seen it before? Because behind it on the wall, hung another piece of black velvet of the same size. You can't see black on black.' (SS, I, pp. 317–18.)

The result was a series of spectacular designs, considerably indebted to Beardsley, and effects, using the black velvet, which impressed the public. But Stanislavski wrote off the production. As far as he was concerned there was nothing new here, nothing that would provide the basis for experiment or for a more deeply inward acting technique. He wrote as much in the theatre's daybook straight after the play's hugely successful first night.

The production was, however, important in terms of artistic polemics. In late November, Meierhold who was directing *The Life of a Man* himself in Petersburg had delivered a lecture denouncing the Art Theatre as obsolete, bogged down in naturalism and literal realism. It was Efros' opinion that Stanislavski by his own, superior, production had given Meierhold the lie in the most effective way possible. Nor was Efros alone. A few months later Lunarcharski, subsequently to be the first Minister of Education after the Revolution, published a violent attack on Meierhold, denying that he was in any genuine sense revolutionary, accusing him of being fundamentally bourgeois and decadent in his thinking, and describing his writings as 'immature scribblings'. Andreiev himself was quite clear that Stanislavski's was the best version of his play available, although he would have preferred the designs to be based on Goya rather than Beardsley.

This was of little interest to Stanislavski who was now concentrating all his efforts on *The Blue Bird*. His obsession with Maeterlinck had not diminished. He was determined to solve the artistic problems which had so far defeated him. *The Blue Bird* was almost an international event before it got into rehearsal. Work had already begun in April 1907. After the first reading Stanislavski addressed the company, appealing for unity and criticizing the divisions and dissensions of the preceding few months. He reminded them of their mission to humanize an ignorant and insensitive mass and raise the level of moral awareness. His speech was sent to Maeterlinck and published in the *Mercure de France* on June 15. A Russian version, apparently translated back from the French by Efros, appeared in the *Stolichnoe Utro* on July 27.

'Man in his animal nature is brutish, cruel and vain. He kills his own kind, devours animals, destroys nature and believes that everything about him has been created solely for his pleasure. Man rules the earth and imagines he has captured its secrets. In reality he knows very little.

The most important things are hidden from him. People live among their material goods, becoming ever more remote from a spiritual and contemplative life.

Spiritual happiness is only given to a chosen few. They listen intently to the minute rustling of a growing blade of grass and turn their eyes on the mystical contours of worlds unknown.

Having seen or heard these secrets, they reveal them to people who look at geniuses with wide eyes, a cynical smile and a wink. Centuries pass and the clatter of the cities and villages drowns out of the tiny rustle of a growing blade of grass.

The smoke of factory chimneys hides the beauty of the world from us; industrial prosperity blinds us and moulded ceilings cut us off from the sky and the stars.

We fight for breath and look for happiness in the stench and grime of the world we have created.

Once in a while we catch a glimpse of real happiness, out there in the fields, in the sunlight, but that happiness, like the blue bird, turns black once we return to the darkness and stench of the town. . . .

Children are closer to nature from which they have but lately come. . . . Let *The Blue Bird* in our theatre delight the grandchildren and provoke serious thoughts and deep feelings in their grandparents. . . .

Let the old people cleanse their soul of its accumulated grime and perhaps for the first time in their lives look into the eyes of a dog and stroke it gently in gratitude for its dog-like loyalty to man. . . .

If we succeed in getting such a response from the audience, even in the smallest measure, I believe our dear friend, the author of *The Blue Bird* would be full of praise for us.

But the problem is how to get such a response from an audience a thousand strong? . . .

Things abstract are not easily accessible to the bulk of the bourgeois and that makes our task quite complicated. . . .

Luckily we have new methods which are the opposite of the old. Our theatre has become strong enough through the combined creative efforts of interpreters in all the arts and back-stage workers.

Creative effort of that kind is invincible. . . .

Directors have learned how to make a harmonious whole out of all the elements in a show. The theatre had become a strong thanks to this harmony. The new theatre is strong because of it. Through it we shall try to arouse the audience when the curtain rises on our new play. . . .

The dominant chord in that general harmony is you, ladies and gentlemen of the company. . . .' (SS, V, pp. 363–70.)

No such harmony was forthcoming, nor could it exist until some settlement had been found to the differences between Stanislavski and Nemirovich. Rehearsals for *The Blue Bird* started on December 16 but on the 19th Knipper was writing to her brother Vladimir expecting trouble. By the 28th Stanislavski was writing protests in the daybook about the lack of technical cooperation and the absence of the property-master.

Stanislavski, it is true, was making complex demands on the technical side. He wanted new methods, new materials. He set aside Maeterlinck's stage directions since in his view they would introduce the wrong kind of theatricality. He wanted neither gauzes, nor cut-outs, nor trap doors, none of the paraphernalia of the ballet but designs and sets that would be nearer to the child's vision. For the music he wanted new sounds and new combinations of instruments, not the usual symphonic orchestration. All in all, he envisaged several months of work and experiment before the play opened. These experiments included exercises and improvisations for the actors and the extras. On August 21 Nemirovich had written to his wife with cynical amusement that they were all imitating dogs, cats and cockerels and were mewing, barking and crowing all round a delighted Stanislavski. *The Blue Bird* enjoyed the longest period of rehearsals the theatre had as yet ever deliberately undertaken. It was an omen of things to come.

Stanislavski became increasingly isolated. The company, encouraged by Nemirovich, continued to regard his new ideas as an aberration potentially disruptive to the running of the theatre. The shareholders tried to get a grip on the situation before there was a total collapse. Early in February Nemirovich wrote to Stanislavski a letter, now lost, which was evidently intemperate in tone. On February 8, Stanislavski resigned:

'Dear Vladimir Ivanovich,
As our ten years of effort have ended with the letter I have just received, any belief in my *infinite* devotion and love for you, the theatre and our association can only be futile.
I ask you to take note that at the end of the current season I shall cease to be a shareholder and a director.
As to the future I offer my services, gratis, as an actor in my old roles and as a producer – under conditions of which you are aware. (K.S. Archive.)

What Stanislavski's conditions were is not clear.
The shareholders set up a committee of enquiry which met on February 15. Luzhski immediately raised the problem of the breakdown in relations

between Stanislavski and Nemirovich. Whatever Stanislavski might write in private correspondence, he was concerned to conceal the depth and rancour of the quarrel in public. The minutes of the meeting report him as saying:

'I understand Vasili Vasilievich [Luzhski], who has put his finger on a very sore spot. But I see no discord. I repeat, I am very fond of Vladimir Ivanovich [Nemirovich] and consider that it is impossible for us to split up under any circumstances. If there have been differences they in no way indicate a break. I repeat: should Vladimir Ivanovich leave I would not be long in following. . . .

Two years ago Vladimir Ivanovich said he felt crushed by me. It was essential at that time to go our separate ways so that later we could stimulate each other with what we had discovered through our individual work. That's not discord or splitting up, that's artistic freedom. . . . Can we close the theatre? No, that's not possible. Quite apart from the large number of employees in the theatre we must not forget its social significance. . . . The whole of Russian and even European theatre is centred on us.' (K.S. Archive.)

Methods of cutting costs were discussed. Stanislavski criticized the over-elaborate staging in recent – by which he meant Nemirovich's – productions.

Nemirovich condemned Stanislavski's scheme for a network of provincial theatres as an extravagance at a time when the theatre needed to reduce the number of productions and use the talents of its members more effectively.

The committee, which was unable to complete its business, was reconvened on the 27th. Stanislavski had failed in his attempt to play down his dispute with Nemirovich and the whole matter was raised once more. Stanislavski made a forthright statement on his artistic position and re-affirmed his view of the actor not as a passive interpreter of words but an active creator:

'The committee is wrong if it thinks that the director's preparatory work in the study is necessary, as previously, when he alone decided the whole plan and all the details of the production, wrote the *mise en scène* and answered all the actors' questions for them. The director is no longer king, as before, when the actor possessed no clear individuality. Work in the study can even be harmful and a positive hindrance. Even work on the décor and technical problems was impossible before general discussions. The director is accused of extravagance but he must, of course, want everything to be as good as possible. Above all the Art Theatre must not stop experimenting.

What is called the director's inefficiency is more often than not attributable to the cast. For instance the absence of method among those playing the major roles during rehearsals arises from *our lack of professional artistic ethics . . . .*'

Do not forget, the time has passed when the actor did not have to worry about anything – K.S. would teach. . . . and Efros would praise. It is essential to understand this – rehearsals are divided into two stages: the first stage is one of experiment when the cast helps the director, the second is creating the performance when the director helps the cast.' (K.S. Archive, No. 1098/4.)

The shareholders reached a decision on March 1. Stanislavski would be allowed to mount one 'experimental' production of his choice per season and would be required to direct no more than two other plays single-handed, although his help and advice might be sought for other productions. His work as an actor would continue. The present membership of the company was to be guaranteed for three years but responsibility for its administration would be handed over to a committee of five with Nemirovich as chairman. Stanislavski's conditions were accepted.

The question of a possible merger with the Mali remained. In September 1907, without waiting for Nemirovich's proposals, which had not yet been received, Teliakovski had made a direct approach to Stanislavski, who had stated bluntly that he was not interested. Following the shareholder's decisions, on March 6, Nemirovich wrote both to Yuzhin-Sumbatov and Teliakovski at the Mali saying that he could not leave the Art Theatre since that would entail nothing less than its demise.

The new managment structure, although it did not satisfy Nemirovich's desire for absolute control, was, in the long term, a liberation for Stanislavski. The kind of research he wanted to undertake could not be contained within the constraints of a theatre which had to be commercially viable. For the next thirty years he would work on the periphery of the Art Theatre, in one of its Studios or in opera. The whole pattern of his activities changed. His productions, highly successful as most of them were, were part of his research. The rehearsal process and the discoveries it produced became more important than the actual performance. Stanislavski never forgot that the ultimate purpose of his work was to have an effect on an audience, but to produce the *right* effect on an audience the actors had to produce the right truth and that could only be attained by the right methods which enabled the raw material of behaviour to be transformed into significant theatrical statements. It was the results produced by this search for human truth and the System, pursued for its own sake, that resulted in still even greater fame and recognition. Although he might, in strict legal or administrative terms, be on the margin of the Art Theatre there was no doubt in anyone's mind, in Russia or abroad, where the artistic and creative centre of that theatre lay. At the moment when his nominal power was being reduced at home he was becoming a world figure.

CHAPTER FIFTEEN

THE CREATIVE WILL

Stanislavski's 'grammar' of acting was beginning to take shape. It evolved slowly, not as a result of theoretical speculation but empirically, through rehearsal and the analysis of practice. It was as yet only the System as we know it in embryo. Indeed, the term 'system' did not come into common use until two or three years later.

Stanislavski pressed on with his *Manual*, developing the notion of the creative will conceived in Finland. In December 1907, he drafted a chapter in which he defined its nature, function and relationship to other elements in the creative process. At the same time he received fresh stimulus to his ideas from Isadora Duncan, who was giving a season of special matinées at the Art Theatre. Her impact was enormous. Even Suler, the dour revolutionary, came under her spell, taking to her, as someone put it, 'like a cat to cream'. Isadora was deeply impressed by Stanislavski's work and found his ideas on dramatic rhythm illuminating. On his side, he found her artistic energy and fresh approach revitalizing. At the very moment when he had rejected anything redolent of classical ballet for *The Blue Bird*, she came forward with a concept of physical expression and scenic movement which would release personal energy. They discussed the possibility of starting a school, attached to the theatre.

Isadora made no secret of her wish to take Stanislavski as her lover. He made it clear that he would always remain entirely faithful to Lilina. Fortunately, his rejection of her advances did not impair their artistic relationship. Isadora determined that Stanislavski and her ex-lover, Gordon Craig must work together and immediately wrote excited and somewhat exaggerated letters to Craig in Italy.

Stanislavski now began to put his notions on the creative will into practice during rehearsals for *The Blue Bird*. The urge to create, he decided, could be stimulated through the discovery of motivations. When an actor knew why he was performing a particular action his will to perform it would be aroused. The action would then become his.

He gave his actors a first indication of his notion of motivation, and the need to define what later became known as the 'task' or 'objective':

'The blocking is not understood. Everyone moves because the director has said "move" and because the move corresponds to the director's ideas. Nobody is digging around and so there is no search for inner motive. All the moves are false because they are unthinking. It's not enough to understand, you must take your positions and moves to your heart.'

'The will is perhaps only strong when there is a definable goal for it.' (Notes to *The Blue Bird* cast, January/February 1908, taken down by Sulerzhitski, K.S. Archive, No. 1392.)

As always he overestimated the speed at which his colleagues could change direction. They had achieved success by obediently following their master and now he was trying to push them out on their own. He was introducing unfamiliar ideas and expecting his actors to apply them without preparation. *The Blue Bird* was the wrong play with which to start introducing new acting techniques. It was a director's play and, as it turned out, a technical nightmare. By the time it opened on September 30 it had received some 150 rehearsals and generated a great deal of irritation. When at a final read-through on September 25, with full chorus and orchestra, the woodwind and xylophone failed to arrive, Stanislavski threatened to report the whole matter to the Board. Close to midnight on the 26th, still sitting at the director's table, he wrote a letter to Sulerzhitski, saying he had been shouting and yelling from eleven in the morning to eleven at night. New music had been provided which the cast must adapt to. He had been told that an effect he had been working on for six months would have to be scrapped. Small wonder then if he had behaved badly:

'*I* am the only one who is doing any thinking, *I* have to galvanize the will of every single actor. I am living for everyone, sitting here behind my table.' (SS, VII, p. 413).

Despite a first night when the intervals were too long, the audience's concentration overstretched and the atmosphere back-stage far from cheerful, *The Blue Bird* become Stanislavski's most famous production. In October, Beerbohm-Tree sent a request through the Russian ambassador in London, asking if his assistant, Stanley Bell, might come to Moscow and study the production. Tree's later presentation owed much to this visit. Sarah Bernhardt, who saw the play in December insisted that it be seen in Paris and, indeed, two years later Sulerzhitski was sent over to reproduce the production move for move for Réjane.

Stanislavski felt he had finally achieved his goal of expressing the abstract on stage, of moving beyond the literal surface, yet with the *The Blue Bird* he was not dealing with pure abstractions, or wholly symbolic figures, as he had in *The Drama of Life*. Maeterlinck's play provided a psychological framework – the mind of a child which, for all its capacity for fantasy, is essentially concrete, observable, reproducible. By insisting that the cast enter the imagination of the child and that the production as a whole should reflect that world, Stanislavski made the invisible comprehensible. He also arrived at a new and extended notion of Realism. *The Blue Bird* was his last 'spectacular' as a director and it was a fitting culmination to a brilliant series of productions. That phase was now behind him.

In his report on the tenth anniversary of the Art Theatre, which he delivered on October 14 he gave his version of the theatre's artistic trajectory and also stated the current position as he saw it:

'Having made a whole series of preliminary experiments and investigations into the psychology and physiology of the creative process we have come to a whole series of conclusions. In order to study them we shall have to go back for a time to simple, realistic forms of staging. Thus, having started with realism, having followed the development of our art, we have come full circle and are back to realism again, enriched by our work and experience.' (SS, V, p. 414.)

His approach to *The Government Inspector*, currently in rehearsal, amply illustrated not only his growing perception that motivation provided the impetus for truthful action on stage, but his intuitive conviction that an actor's past experience, his 'emotion memory', was a means of achieving that symbiotic relationship between the actor's personality and the character. The expression 'emotion memory' first occurs in a letter to Kotliarevskaia on May 5:

'I've got onto the track of new principles. These principles may turn the whole psychology of the actor's creative process on its head. I am making daily experiments on myself and others and have come up with some interesting results. What fascinates me most is the rhythm of feelings, the development of emotion memory and the psychophysiology of the creative process. With the help of these experiments I have managed to achieve much greater simplicity and strength in existing roles and I am able to fortify my creative will to such an extent that even when I am ill, or have a temperature, I forget about my illness and find energy on stage. As a result the company respect these new ideas and have stopped laughing at my experiments and listen to what I have to say with considerable attention.' (SS, VII, pp. 386.)

Chance brought Stanislavski scientific confirmation of what he had perceived instinctively. In July he went to Germany for the opening of the Chekhov monument and to take the water at Homburg.

'I met a very cultivated and well-read man, who, in conversation, quite by chance, produced this statement: You know that an artist's experience and creativity are based on affective emotion and memory? I said nothing but immediately wrote off for the literature dealing with the subject.' (Material for *My Life in Art*, K.S. Archive, No. 42.)

The books in question were Ribot's *Les Maladies de la Mémoire* and *Les Maladies de la Volonté* which had appeared in Russian in 1900.

Two of Ribot's notions were of particular interest. First, that the will has a positive role to play in the patient's recovery and that the rate of convalescence may depend on the desire to get better. Second, that all memories of past experiences are recorded by the nervous system and, although not immediately available to the conscious mind, may be evoked by an appropriate stimulus: a touch, a sound, a smell may enable a patient to relive not just one experience but a grouping of similar experiences which merge to create a single emotional state. The actor's problem was to remove the chance element and find a technique whereby his memories could be made available to him.

Stanislavski's marginal notes show his attempt to apply purely medical knowledge to a creative process. For the moment it was still the problem of the will which occupied him:

'Failures in creative art disappoint and in a given role produce the very same symptoms as in illness.'

'Automatic action is apparent in the daily routine of life.'

'Weakness of motive does not stimulate action. What must be the actor's motive – to convey the life of another person.' (Marginalia in *Les Maladies de la Mémoire*, *Les Maladies de la Volonté*, K.S. Archive.)

Apart from ideas drawn from or confirmed by Ribot, his own process of self-analysis had yielded results. Concerned as ever by the problem of relaxation and control on stage, he discovered that his own tensions disappeared if he concentrated his attention strictly on the specific action the production demanded. When his attention slipped physical tension returned.

Gogol's *The Government Inspector*, which went into rehearsal immediately *The Blue Bird* had opened, provided the perfect opportunity to draw these ideas together and work at an almost exclusively psychological level. Stanislavski made use of Gogol's notes on the play which he had studied twenty years earlier. A primitive terminology began to emerge. Actors were suddenly confronted with terms such as 'nail' – taken directly from Gogol and 'circle' – which in the final System become the through-line of action and circles of concentration.

Stanislavski did not wish to fall into the error of merely imitating external behaviour or the psychopathology of daily life. He noted in his journal:

'Explain the fact that every play needs the quintessence of life, not life itself. For instance: read some longwinded novel that doesn't appeal to you. You shut it at page ten. Cut the novel, leaving in what interests you and you respond. There's a great deal that is uninteresting in life. What interest is it to me how a man eats, drinks and washes, if he does not do it in a special way?' (K.S. Archive, No. 764.)

Gogol's play demands a kind of enriched realism which Stanislavski was anxious to achieve. He maintained that exaggerated external action could only be justified by a counter-balancing intensity of inner drive. The degree of his success is evident from Efros' review. Placed between the stage and the audience. Efros said, was a powerful magnifying glass. Everything was blown up but this exaggeration was not merely external, it encompassed the characters' thoughts and feeling. Everything Gogol had written, all his comments and stage directions, had been pushed to the limit. As for the moment when the central character, Khlestakov, crushed a bed-bug against the wall with the end of his nose, that was surely destined to cause as furious an argument among audience and satirical journal alike as the notorious crickets in *The Seagull*.

Nemirovich was certain this was a pivotal production in Stanislavski's development:

'I would say that no production at the Moscow Art Theatre up till now has been in the hands of the actors to such a degree. Not one production detail was allowed to get in the way of the actors. Stanislavski is no longer the kind of director he was previously, as, for example, in *The Blue Bird*, but has become a teacher. The essence of all the work on *The Government Inspector* consisted in deep psychological investigation of the characters and the rediscovery of direct, simple speech.' (Interview with Nemirovich in *Russkoe Slovo*, November 18, 1908.)

Nemirovich was right, although he could not have realized the far-reaching implications of such a change.

Stanislavski's concern indeed was now with research and teaching, with restoring creative control to the actor – but the actor had to be equal to the task. Stanislavski was depressed by the decline in standards of behaviour, the increased amount of drinking, the lack of discipline and sense of purpose. He had tried direct protest. Only a radical overhaul of working method, which included notions of personal and artistic responsibility, could turn the situation round.

On August 23 he had come home frustrated from a rehearsal of *The Blue Bird*. The cast had appeared neither to know their lines nor their moves, although the scene had been rehearsed at least ten times. Nobody seemed worried. He returned to his notes for the *Manual* and drafted a chapter on professional ethics. It was indicative of his isolation that he found the most sympathetic response outside the theatre in men of advanced ideas. Two days later on the 25th, he read his draft to Lunacharski. Discussion went on well into the night.

He tried, with varying degrees of success, to persuade his colleagues and contemporaries, the 'veterans', of the value of his new methods but it was increasingly to the up-and-coming generation and to young actors and directors in training that he turned his attention. He continued to play the parts he had made famous and to create the occasional new role, but the last thirty years of his life represent one continuous, deliberate effort to develop a set of training exercises and rehearsal practices, to produce an historical overview of various schools and theories of acting, and to apply his 'grammar' to the creation of new roles. Individual productions and performances, while important in themselves, take on their real meaning when seen as part of the evolution of the System.

CHAPTER SIXTEEN

THE SYSTEM EMERGES

Isadora succeeded in bringing Stanislavski and Gordon Craig together. Craig arrived in Moscow in October 15. He first greeted Stanislavski lying naked in a freezing cold bath in his room at the Hotel Metropole although there were several degrees of frost outside. With high romantic disdain for the vulgar realities of nature, he had turned up with only the light clothes he wore in Italy. His hosts, anxious to show him the city, the theatre and generally give him a good time, had first to express the warmth of their hospitality by fitting him out with a complete wardrobe, including a fur coat, taken from the stock of *Woe From Wit*. On the 18th he attended a performance of *An Enemy of the People*, accompanied by Stanley Bell, who had once again been sent over by Beerbohm Tree. Subsequently he saw *The Blue Bird*, *Uncle Vania* and *The Life of Man*, which, because of its unremitting black and white designs and claustrophobic atmosphere practically made him ill, as it had Isadora. Nonetheless his admiration for the theatre and for Stanislavski, despite basic aesthetic disagreements, was profound. Writing to himself in the guise of a fictitious correspondent, John Semar, he stated:

'The Art Theatre . . . is alive, is possessed of character and intelligence.

Its director, Constantin Stanislawsky(sic), has achieved the impossible: he has successfully established a non-commercial theatre. He believes in realism as a medium through which the actor can reveal the psychology of the dramatist. I don't believe in it. This is not the place to discuss the wisdom or folly of the theory. . . .

It is quite enough to say that what these Russians do upon the stage they do to perfection. They waste time, money, labour, brains and patience like emperors. . . .

They give hundreds of rehearsals to a play, they change and rechange a scene until it balances their thought. . . .

Seriousness, character, these two qualities will guide the Moscow Art Theatre to unending success in Europe or elsewhere. . . .

Less of a spontaneous whirlwind than Grasso, their first actor Stanislawsky is more intellectual.

This is not to be misunderstood. You are not to imagine that this actor is cold or stilted. A simpler technique, a more human result, would be difficult to find ... his performances are all remarkable for their grace. I can find no better word.

I have been most pleased by the performance of *Onkel Vanja*. ... In *The Enemy of the People*, Stanislawski shows us how to act Dr Stockman without being "theatrical" and without being comic or dull. The audience smile all the time that they are not being moved to tears. ... (Edward Gordon Craig, *On the Art of the Stage*, pp. 133–6.)

Stanislavski knew almost nothing about Craig, although Isadora had procured him a bad German translation of *On the Art of the Stage*. There could, in any case, be no question of their coming to an agreement on basic questions of principle. Both were far too committed to their ideas for that. But each could supply something of what the other needed. Craig was happy to have found a theatre that took theatre seriously; Stanislavski needed stimulus, a fresh mind, controversy, anything rather than the back-biting and derision to which he was so often subjected. In their correspondence various ideas for plays had been floated but both men harboured a desire to do *Hamlet*. On January 19, 1909 the Board decided to mount *Hamlet*, *A Month in the Country* and Leonid Andreiev's *Anathema*. *Hamlet* would be under the general artistic control of Gordon Craig. *A Month in the Country* would be directed by Stanislavski and *Anathema* by Nemirovich. The Turgenev and the Andreiev were scheduled for the 1909 season, *Hamlet* for 1910. It was agreed, however, that given the complexity of the undertaking, work on *Hamlet* was to begin at once.

Stanislavski's decision to work in tandem on two plays so disparate in style, the one intimate, domestic, subdued in tone, working in psychological hints and half-lights, the other spread across a huge canvas, combining intimacy with moments of extreme action and violence, the one in contained prose, the other full of intense and passionate poetry, was central to his purpose, which was to demonstrate that the System was a universal approach that could be applied to any play, whatever its formal demands.

Preliminary discussions and plans for *Hamlet* began immediately, prior to Craig's return to Russia in the Spring. Although Craig's designs were essentially geometric, made of blocks and cubes and giant screens, Stanislavski engaged a second designer, Egorov, who was sent to collect authentic material from Denmark, Sweden and Norway. The results of his travels were examined on February 24. On the 28th Stanislavski outlined his ideas on the play to the production team. Preliminary rehearsals began in March and on April 1 Stanislavski wired Craig asking him to be in Petersburg, where the company would be on tour, by the 15th. He also advanced two months' salary.

With Craig's arrival everything started all over again. He and Stanislavski went through the play scene by scene, building up a production plan, including basic blocking, sound and lighting, and then went over the text line by line so that Craig could check and if necessary improve the translation. Their discussions, all of which were scrupulously noted down, were conducted in a hotch-potch of English and German. While Stanislavski had no English, Suler was able to manage a little and acted when necessary as interpreter. Work continued in Moscow in May. Despite their agreement on matters of staging, divergences in approach and interpretation soon became evident. Craig's Hamlet was largely a self-projection, a pure spirit in a grossly material world. Stanislavski's Hamlet, also in part a self-projection, was another of his crusading individuals, a Christ-like figure sent to cleanse the world from corruption, – an active Russian Hamlet as opposed to the philosopher-Prince of German criticism. Stanislavski made it clear that whatever degree of abstraction or symbolism the production might ultimately achieve, he intended to rehearse, in the first instance at least, using the System. It was the only way to prevent the actors from falling back into their old habits and delivering standard, bombastic 'classical' acting. Their final discussion took place on June 2, before Stanislavski's departure for Paris. After that *Hamlet* would have to be set aside while he concentrated his attention on rehearsals for *A Month in the Country*.

He returned to Moscow in August and spent an evening going through the casting with Nemirovich who was pleased to report to his wife the next day that the atmosphere had been 'harmonious'. He was, therefore, not a little surprised when Stanislavski then virtually cut himself off for the next four months.

It was one of the rules of the Art Theatre that all rehearsals should be open. They were considered the principal means by which members of the company could learn. Stanislavski broke with this tradition. The rehearsals, conducted in the small rehearsal theatre, were closed. No one not directly connected with the production was allowed near it. This was neither pique nor paranoia. It was the direct result of his new working method.

Gone now was the carefully, minutely pre-established production plan. The sets were reduced to a strict minimum, just enough to suggest the milieu. Production values were not the main concern. The process of creating the performance depended on delicate collaborative work with the actor. For the first time Stanislavski's production book shows the action broken down into sections or 'units'. The rehearsal process consisted in finding the feelings, the psychological states, contained in those sections and in relating them, through emotion memory, to personal experience.

Stanislavski elected to work in a small rehearsal studio, rather than on the main stage, in order to emphasize the intimacy of the play. He further broke down the space into smaller rooms suggesting the house. He kept the actors under tight control, using what he was later to call the 'sitting-on-hands method.' They were not allowed to speak their text either in full or with full voice. Cuts were made in the longer speeches and used as sub-text, to be thought only. In this Stanislavski was influenced by certain notions drawn from yoga which had become fashionable. Great emphasis was laid on what is now called non-verbal communication. The actors were expected to 'radiate' their mental states. He was, in fact, as he was aware, returning to some of the experiments he had made when directing *The Drama of Life*. This time, however, the technique was to be applied not in order to convey the abstract and symbolic but the reality of psychological action.

'What we needed was a kind of invisible radiation of feeling and creative will – eyes, facial expression, fleeting elusive tones of voice, psychological pauses . . . We had once more to return to immobility, absence of gestures, we had to get rid of all superfluous movement; we had to cut down, cut out entirely all director's moves and leave the actors motionless on their chairs; let them speak, think and communicate their suffering to the thousands in the audience.' (SS, I, p. 326.)

This stripping down of the acting style was matched by the sets which were simple in the extreme. The interiors were symmetrical and unobtrusive.

Stanislavski provided a psychological outline for each character, not merely an overall profile, but the stages by which feelings and attitudes develop and change. Nowhere is this more evident than in his notes, made in late August, on the leading character Natalia Petrovna Islaieva, to be played by Knipper:

'Because of Beliaev's arrival she, above all, with increased energy, observes, notes and even criticizes in Rakitin and her husband things she let pass before. Not irritation but mild caprice. She is much more observant, concentrated, attentive. An outward smile.

She is concentrating and therefore seems outwardly distracted. Something has appeared in her which draws her into herself. When she is at her embroidery, she becomes easily lost in thought, but this love which she still does not recognize, does not disturb her and therefore she can remain entirely concentrated on herself.

. . . Must bear in mind that it is better for the actress to start the role quietly and keep the brighter colours for later. So for the moment there is no need to show irritation, nor excessive absent-mindedness, nor venom. All that is necessary, precisely to explain her state, but all in moderation. Only Verochka and Beliaev pay attention to her; the rest do not. So, these are the basic elements of her state, the starting point of her experience.

1) She has inward concentration, which is not disturbed by any thoughts which can draw her attention.

2) Nothing external can hold her attention, although it can attract it for a moment.

3) Critical attitude towards Rakitin (particularly) and to some extent her husband. They all become irritated, being interested in cards or the everyday things of life. She, as it were, is not disturbed by anything. Above all remind Olga Leonardovna [Knipper] of the restraint 'of being in corsets' (of the period). Olga Leonardovna may want to move towards external etiquette but in this case she can't. It is essential, that for her posture, she listen and answer very attentively (i.e., that she achieves "being in corsets" out of *inner concentration*).

. . . In the first act Natalia Petrovna loves Vera's youth. In the second act she becomes irritated by it and in the third act she hates it.' (K.S. Archive.)

He insisted on the essential charm of the woman. Knipper was still battling unsuccessfully with the role in October. Using his somewhat uncertain vocabulary of 'circles' Stanislavski explained the Act Three conversation between Natalia Petrovna and the young Beliaiev:

'[Natalia Petrovna] continues to probe him but the essential factor is jealousy. Having changed the circles of trickery, she wants to get from him a promise that the meetings etc., with Verochka will cease. All her lines, therefore, are tinged with that inward state of trickery. The outward appearance she gives is that she is mistrustful. Using in turn mockery, irony, an open and frank tone, the tone of a great and upright gentlewoman, with folded arms, she gets what she wants. All that is not a little dishonest, of course but it is also charming in a woman who is in love, who realises it is impossible not to fall in love with Verochka, who has no right to love another man, who deceives her husband and insults Rakitin.

This whole scene is about the agitation which the actress creates out of a desire energetically and clearly to change the circle of inner trickery.' (Directorial Notes, October 17, 1909, K.S. Archive.)

The intimate, analytical work, accompanied by exercises in focusing attention and silent communication, went on until the last ten days of October, when rehearsals had to transfer to the large stage. Stanislavski was aware that his System was on trial: Knipper and Nemirovich remained unconvinced of its value; even Lilina had made it clear during *Blue Bird* rehearsals that she did not find his new ideas helpful. The move from the small to the big theatre proved catastrophic:

'When we got onto the stage it wasn't rehearsal, it was hell. Everything just disappeared. What had seemed fine at the table, emerged as weak. They all spoke quietly, could not expand their voices . . . Knipper drove us mad with her obstinacy, Koroneva by her bad character. . . . Boleslavski out of inexperience turned into a complete idiot. The enemies of my system spread gloom and doom, said it was boring and brought the whole rehearsal down to a low point.

It's a long time since I have felt such torment, despair and a slump in energy (not since *The Drama of Life* and *The Life of Man*).' (Late October 1909, K.S. Archive No. 545.)

When Nemirovich attended a reading on October 31 he, too, was in despair. As he wrote to his wife, the play which had already been given 80 or 90 rehearsals, was nowhere near ready and what he had seen was totally feeble. He had decided to keep a tactful silence rather than try to sort things out and so revive all the old quarrels with his friend.

The main problem was Knipper. She had begun well enough but she was completely thrown when Stanislavski started to apply his new method. He had been in conflict with her before. He had accused her of being lazy, of never being ready on the first night. This was a little unfair since he himself was far from being a first-night actor. Indeed, his own performance as Rakitin did not fully mature until the Petersburg tour in the spring of 1910. But the difference between them was that he had a working method and she had none. She was an instinctive actress but her range was limited. When her instinct failed, as it had in this case, she was lost, and since she found Stanislavski's new ideas too 'intellectual' she was not prepared to be helped. She was attempting, as Stanislavski had suspected she would, to approach the role from the outside. Psychological analysis was lost on her. Of the 50 rehearsals that had taken place by the end of September, 19 had been devoted to Knipper privately in Stanislavski's flat.

Inevitably Nemirovich was drawn in. He had always had a close relationship with Knipper and when, on November 6, he arrived for a rehearsal in make-up and costume, matters came to a head. Knipper broke down in tears in Act Three and left the theatre. She had hoped that once she got into costume everything would come together. It had not. Her confidence was now completely undermined. Nemirovich crept out of the auditorium not wishing to become involved.

Stanislavski handled the situation with delicacy and tact. The following day he sent Knipper flowers and a letter, gentle in tone but offering no concessions. He expressed his affection for her and his respect for her great gifts. If he appeared cruel it was only because he loved her talent too much to allow it to be degraded. The letter contains an offer, a piece of advice and a criticism. First he proposes a painless, jargon-free introduction to the new method:

'If you need my help I will break your part down into sections. I promise not to frighten you with technical jargon. That's probably where I went wrong.'

Next he advises her to use her own personality, her own psychology as a base and stop thinking about her effect on the audience and whether they liked her or not:

> 'At every point in the rôle look for some desire which concerns you and you alone and banish all other, vulgar desires concerning the audience. You will quickly find this inward work will carry you away.
>
> Once that has happened you will turn from something which is unworthy of true artists, the desire to serve and ingratiate oneself with the audience.
>
> In the same measure that you are not logical in that instance, you will become logical by being carried away by genuine feelings.'

Finally he sugars the pills with a piece of flattery:

> 'You are lucky, you have a charm on stage which makes people listen to you and so it is easy for you to do anything you want.' (SS, VII, pp. 453–4.)

Above all he told her not to give up the fight since only through struggle could she achieve great art.

The letter had the desired effect. Knipper responded warmly and work began again. But the crisis was not over. A series of depressing dress rehearsals followed. Act Three was still weak. Yet when the play opened on December 9 it was accounted a success. Stanislavski and Boleslavski were much praised although Knipper's performance was accounted a failure. The favourable reception of the production as a whole was of the utmost importance to Stanislavski. He had proved the value of his new method in the most effective manner possible, by success.

The production nonetheless provoked criticism, in particular the accusation that there was an excessive concern with the trivial and the commonplace. A series of discussions took place in Petersburg in the first week of May 1910, during the annual tour. The production was compared unfavourably with 'true' theatre, as represented by Greek tragedy, which strove to create an 'event', something which had a liturgical and religious thrust. Could the Turgenev really be compared to that? Stanislavski avoided any theoretical response. He could only point, empirically, to the actual audience response the Art Theatre had experienced over the years. If what they did was insignificant, not an 'event', how did his interlocutor explain the stunned reaction of audiences in Berlin, when people had remained seated long after the curtain had fallen, still under the impact of what they had seen. Or how to explain the many hundreds of letters from appreciative theatregoers? Stanislavski was aware that he would always come under this sort of attack. As he wrote four years later:

> 'They will attack my system for driving conventions and clichés out of

art. . . . In order to discredit my opinions they will, of course, call me a realist–naturalist etc. They'll say I am a photographer, because I am dealing with the greatest of beauties, nature, while they, are refined people of culture because they work with all the errors which arise from copies of nature – actors' conventions and clichés.' (1912, K.S. Archive, No. 931.)

Stanislavski needed to prove the validity of his new method with a classic play. *Hamlet* provided him with the opportunity.

Craig returned to Moscow on February 15, 1910 so that he and Stanislavski could pick up rehearsals where they had left off. They would work together with the company until Craig returned to Italy at the end of April. Stanislavski would then work alone until the summer break. Craig would return in August and the play would open in November.

The company did not find rehearsals easy mainly because Craig did not know how to rehearse. He kept himself aloof from the company except for Alisia Koonen, to whom he had taken a fancy. This champion of the Übermarionette was prepared to allow the actors total freedom of choice in the means they selected to convey his abstract ideas. Thus, while the cast were willing to try anything he cared to suggest to them, he suggested nothing. Craig, like his hero, Hamlet, was pure spirit, dealing only in pure abstract concepts which somehow had to be materialized in actors' bodies. Similarly his designs took no account of practical issues. Many of his sets proved technically impossible to construct, although huge sums of money were spent, and wasted.

There was a mismatch between Stanislavski and Craig and the Art Theatre which events were to accentuate. Craig, unable to give any precise direction himself, found Stanislavski dictatorial and manipulative as a director, and merely complained that the acting did not match the mood of the sets. Stanislavski tried everything he knew to find a new approach demonstrating various styles of acting French, Italian, German, traditional Russian, none of which were to Craig's liking. Craig also created problems by his endless demands for money which he thought owing to him, whether he was present in Moscow or not. At one point he even took legal advice. Disaster struck in August when Stanislavski went down with typhoid. It became apparent that he could not return to work until the beginning of 1911 at the earliest. The whole production had to be postponed until the following season.

When he returned to rehearsal in April 1911 Stanislavski pursued his own line, applying the system. He made a number of cast changes. Craig had disappeared giving him a free hand, although he did, as far as he could, respect Craig's basic ideas. His fear was, as he had indicated to Craig at the very beginning, that the actors would fall back into a conventional style, that the speaking verse of the verse would become the mere mouthing of sounds, that the moves would be reduced to mere parading about in costume. The audience could all too easily, and willingly, become mesmerised by the visual aspects of the production and lose the meaning of the play. The actors must be clear as to the motivation and purpose of everything they said and did.

> 'The hidden essence of a soliloquy in verse can only be made comprehensible through clear and precise shaping of the units. Without that it is lost in a welter of rhetoric, elocution, rhythm and pounding metre.' K.S. Archive, No. 924.)

He accordingly broke the play down into units, with a specific 'task', or in the accepted translation, objective, and mood for each unit. When rehearsals resumed after the August break the company was still nonetheless confused, caught between Craig's abstractions and Stanislavski's own clear perception as to what the character of Hamlet was about. Kachalov had been brought to the point of nervous collapse by the conflicting direction he received. Any ambiguity was dispelled when, in a fit of exasperation, Stanislavski made his meaning clear in the most direct possible fashion, by demonstrating. During a rehearsal of Act Three scene two, the Players' scene, he leapt onto the stage. He seemed instantly to be transformed. The Hamlet he demonstrated was the active Hamlet he had conceived from the start:

> 'This was a brilliant Hamlet. Hamlet the artist, the teacher, the preacher, who knew so much more than those around him.' (Gzovskaia, in conversation with Chushkin, August 3, 1945.)

> 'This was not Craig's Hamlet, lit by the rays of death, striving to surmount his unreal, earthly existence. In rehearsal Stanislavski showed Hamlet to be so virile, full of human nobility and controlled passion. His demonstration obliged Kachalov to play Hamlet with enormous *spiritual* energy, with tragic élan ... Stanislavski's Hamlet was active and virile ... passionate, emotional, full of conflicting shifts of feeling, from tenderness and love for other men to angry sarcasm and hate.' (Chushkin, *Kachalov–Hamlet* Isskustova, Moscow, 1966, p. 31.)

On another occasion he demonstrated the scene with the recorders, venting his anger of his erstwhile friends, Rosenkrantz and Guildenstern:

> 'In the Third Act, in the episode with the recorders, he hurled himself around the stage, making them pursue him like foxhounds. He led this "chase" at a frantic speed and then suddenly came to a halt, throwing a line at them, so that Rosencrantz and Guildenstern, unable to stop themselves, crashed into him full tilt. In general, in Act Three, Stanislavski's Hamlet was full of tragic bitterness, enormous spiritual tension and strangeness.' (Ibid.)

Demonstration, however useful, was in a sense a return to old and rejected methods. The actors still had to be given a framework within which to work. Where necessary, therefore, Stanislavski broke the units down into a series of precise actions. Rehearsing the Mousetrap scene, he analysed the action for Kachalov, who was trying to be 'tragic' in the abstract and was getting nowhere:

'Kachalov puffed himself up, he tried to be subtle, merry, malicious, ironic. In a word he was playing results – despaired because it wasn't tragic.

STANISLAVSKI: This scene is a heap of pearls, sort them out individually and you will find:

a) Pearl number one. Hamlet is full of energy and therefore wants to cover the distance boldly and effectively; b) Hamlet wants the king to have a slap in the face but without revealing that it is a slap in the face; c) same thing for Polonius; d) same thing for Ophelia; e) Hamlet wants to watch the king unobserved (but you demonstrate that you are watching). Hamlet is afraid of alarming the king too soon; f) the king rises. Hamlet runs across and leaps on the throne, wanting to see the king; g) Hamlet shouts to the king "Why, let the stricken deer go weep" and very much wants him to hear; h) Hamlet runs downstage to get another glimpse of the king as he rushes out; i) Hamlet wants to get his cloak on quickly and properly (because he has a burst of energy and at such moments [people] act quickly and properly); j) Hamlet wants to declaim effectively; k) Hamlet wants to make Horatio tell what he has seen.

The tragic elements will arise from a series of simple, mechanical objectives.' (K.S. Archive, No. 912.)

Stanislavski was clear that under no circumstances was the play to become a series of set-pieces or 'arias', delivered for their own sake. A case in point was Hamlet's speech to the Players, which everyone knew and which could easily become detached from the main action and turn into an actor's credo. It had a dramatic function, a specific objective, and it was that which had to be played:

'This scene with the Players has a specific relationship with what has gone before and doesn't simply stand as a lecture on dramatic art . . . Hamlet pronounces his advice in the light of his main purpose, that "The Mousetrap" will be staged so truthfully, seriously and realistically that it will stir the conscience of the king. Without that Hamlet cannot discover the truth.' (K.S. Archive, No. 924.)

A major preoccupation in rehearsal was the relationship of the physical to the psychological. At this stage the psychological was pre-eminent and Stanislavski insisted on the primacy for the actors, as in the more intimate Turgenev play, of establishing contact with one another, mainly through eye-contact. The physical served mainly to illustrate and fix emotional states which the artist discovered, intuitively, under the director's prompting. Precise physical action was essential to prevent too great a variation from one performance to the next. The assumption was that once an emotional state was represented or realized in a physical action, the repetition of that physical action would evoke the emotion:

> The object of the director-artist is to be able to stimulate the actor's talent, to lead him along the right path.
>
> The creative process is unconscious. The most precious things about it are those flashes of unconscious inspiration. But inspiration is not enough, you must be able to fix those flashes.
>
> Otherwise the actor will play in an inspired fashion today and feebly tomorrow ... (Conversation with Stanislavski, *Rampa*, March 15, 1909, p. 171.)

If, however, the actor took premature refuge in conventional or theatrically false physical moves he could block the flow of genuine, authentic feeling. This is what happend to Massalitinov, who was playing Claudius, during the prayer scene. He got off to a bad start, falling immediately into a conventional posture:

'CLAUDIUS/MASSALITINOV: Pray I cannot.
STANISLAVSKI: You got down on the floor so conventionally, in such a clichéd posture that nothing can come of it but stagey conventions and not living truth. Honestly, aren't you yourself aware that only clichés of body, voice, rhythm, speech, diction habitually associated with such a clichéd posture can come if you do that? Try, instead, to discover for this mood – a tormented prayer – another, much more simple posture, far removed from any stagey picturesqueness, and you'll see it will result in a life-like body and a tone of voice and a manner of speaking which is habitually associated with that posture in real life.'
(*Massaltinov tries.*)
STANISLAVSKI: You see how much nearer you are to the truth. There are still some clichéd elements – root them out. The main thing is you are not living the reason for which Shakespeare wrote the king's words but the words themselves, you're spelling out their direct meaning. You illustrate "smells" and "offence" with a display of disgust but that prevents you from experiencing the truth fully. Don't live smells or offence but the impossibility of praying to God, the helplessness, the despair. Then you will experience the real truth inside and outside and will live it. ... You must abandon the periphery and go to the centre; external clichés are too firmly rooted in you. They are so blatant in their unnaturalness and falseness that they squeeze out the truth. Find the truth of inner feeling, then you can talk about external truth.' (K.S. Archive, No. 911.)

Stanislavski worked on remorselessly, obsessively, leaving the long-suffering Sulerzhitski to mediate between himself and Craig, ward off Nemirovich, who once again was becoming understandably worried, and sort out the many technical problems concerning the sets. When the play finally opened on December 23, it provoked, inevitably, a mixed reaction. Moscow had not seen anything like it, nor, for that matter, had anyone else. Craig's cubes and screens produced enthusiasm, bewilderment, irritation and derision. Neither audience nor critics were aware of his original intention to have visible set changes, with scene flowing into scene. The technical problems of constructing any sets at all produced a clumsy compromise.

The acting also encountered a mixed reception. Briusov, writing a year later pointed to the contradiction between the abstract design concept and the acting style. Knipper as Gertrude, Massalitinov as Claudius and Gzovskaia as Ophelia got bad notices and Stanislavski immediately thought of recasting. Of Kachalov's Hamlet there was no doubt. It was recognized as a genuine achievement, effacing the memory of Mochalov's turbulent, romantic mid-nineteenth-century peformance of which most people had heard but few had seen. The months of painful and sometimes despairing effort, under Stanislavski's mercilessly critical eye, had paid dividends.

The production received, in reality, few showings but its fame and influence spread across Europe, mainly because it was described in *The Times* and the French press as an unqualified success. Thanks to this legend, which Craig was careful to foster, it came to be regarded as a seminal event, influencing the whole history of production style, although as the years went by Craig took a more and more jaundiced view of the whole affair. As far as Stanislavski was concerned he had proved the relevance of the system to a major classical text. He now intended to move on, both as actor and director to another classic author, Molière.

CHAPTER SEVENTEEN

THE FIRST STUDIO

Even as he worked on his productions Stanislavski attempted to provide a coherent written account of what was now coming to be known as his 'System'. By 1910 a number of drafts existed besides the *Draft Manual* begun in Finland in 1906. The *Reference Book for the Dramatic Actor*, and *Practical Information and Good Advice for Beginners and Students of Dramatic Art*, date from 1907. The *Notebooks* for 1908 and after contain a series of individual entries on specific topics which were sorted out into some kind of order in 1913 under the following headings:

'Introduction, Hackwork, Performance, New Trend (General Foundation), Being [Experiencing], Truth, Logic of Feelings, Emotional Feelings, Roots of Feelings, Will, Muscles, Eradicating Clichés, Objectives, Desires, Communication, Adaptation, Kernel, Through-line of Action, Circles, Tempo, Characterization, Analysis, Self-analysis, How to Use the System, Annotation, Terminology.' (K.S. Archive, Nos. 906–934.)

Nonetheless, on March 8, 1909 he was sufficiently confident of the general shape of the System to deliver a paper to a theatrical conference. There is great emphasis here and in the later *History of a Character* (1915) on the use of emotion memory and on what came to be known as the Magic If. The actor knows, intellectually, that everything around him is false; it is wood and canvas and papier mâché. But *what if* it were true, *what if* the given circumstances laid down by the author were reality, how would he react?

In his preparatory notes Stanislavski sets out a six-stage process: first the stimulation of the 'will', the creation of a commitment to the author's text; second, the personal base, the inner search for psychological material; third, 'experience', the private process of invisible inner creation, when the actor comes to terms with a character, an 'image' which is not his own and merges his own personality with it; fourth, 'physicalizing', the process, still private, by which the actor gives the image bodily existence; fifth, the bringing together of the inner and the outer, the psychological and the physical, as a synthesis; sixth, making an impact on the audience.

The problem of implementing the System was still to be resolved. In

November 1910 he was able to give Nemirovich a summary of how far he had got:

> ... before you start work with my system you must:
> a) stimulate the process of the *will*; b) begin the process of investigation with some literary discussion (your expression) – how to maintain and develop these investigations, that I know: c) how to stimulate the process of lived experience – I know; d) how to help the process of physical characterization I don't yet know in detail but I am aware of the fundamentals and seem to be getting close to the right track; e) the process of *synthesizing* and *influencing* are clear.
>   Now I have to find a practical way to arouse the actor's imagination in all these processes. This aspect of psychology has received little attention, especially the creative imagination of the actor and the painter.' (Stanislavski to Nemirovich, November 16, 1910, SS, VII, pp. 484–5.)

In addition to working out the detail of the System he proposed to survey the art of acting and the theatre in general. Starting in 1909, he gave the work a number of titles, according to the draft he was working on: *Trends in Art*, *Two Trends and Hack-Work in Art*, *Introductions*, *Three Trends in Art* etc. He continued work on the manuscript, on and off, until 1922 when he finally abandoned it although most of the material found its way, later, in modified form, into the opening sections of *An Actor Prepares*. The manuscript is now published under the title, *Various Trends in Dramatic Art*.

The three trends Stanislavski defined were the school of the proficient or hack actor, the school or representation and the school of lived experience. To judge by the section on the hack actor there had not been much general improvement in acting style since Shchepkin's early days. There was still the same mechanical colouring of words: 'sad' was delivered sadly, always, 'love' amorously, always, without regard to context or real meaning. Words like 'big', 'small', 'tall', 'wide' were carved out of the air with the hands. As for stage movement it was always 'theatrical' and majestic:

> 'Let's start with the solemn, measured gait of the actors. They do not walk, they advance across the stage, they do not sit, they ensconce themselves, they do not lie down, they recline, they do not stand, they adopt a pose.' (SS, VI, p. 48.)

Magniloquence of speech and grandeur of movement were amply supported by stock gestures which were available to express all the important feelings:

> 'Agitation is expressed by pacing up and down the stage very quickly, by the hands being seen to tremble when a letter is being opened or by letting the jug knock against the glass and then the glass against the teeth when the water is being poured and drunk.

Illness – a hacking cough, the shivers or vertigo (theatrical medicine only recognizes consumption, fever and anaemia).

Death – clutching the chest or tearing at one's shirt collar (the hack actor only recognizes two causes of death, cardiac arrest and asphyxia)' (Ibid. p. 51.)

Many of the stock gestures were simply copies of copies of actions performed once by actors of genuine talent at dramatically appropriate moments, now slavishly imitated and handed on as law:

'One very famous French actor used a highly effective bow at the end of a costume play. A Russian actor who was with me at that particular performance remembered it and brought it back to Russia. Now this manner of bowing is taught in schools and is considered essential for costume plays, whatever the period.' (Ibid. pp. 54–5.)

The acerbity of Stanislavski's tone is attributable to the fact that even as he was drafting this section he was complaining to his colleague Leonidov that performances of *The Inspector General* had declined into mechanical hackwork.

The second trend, the School of Representation, commanded much more respect. Stanislavski identified it with the best in French acting which he had so much admired in earlier years. Its method consisted in finding emotional truths during the preparatory period, observing the external features of those truths and then reproducing them faithfully, technically, so as to give a perfect representation of feeling without actually experiencing it during performance. This is in essence the approach of Shchepkin's 'actor of reason'.

Finally there came the School of Lived Experience, the school of Shchepkin's 'actor of feeling'. Here the actor is required to recreate emotions and states of being afresh at each performance. This fell short of total identification with the role for, as Stanislavski pointed out later, actually to believe that one is someone else is a pathological condition. He never succeeded satisfactorily in defining the extent to which an actor identifies with his character and how much of the mind remains detached and maintains theatrical control. He was clear, however, that these schools rarely existed in pure form. In practice each performance was a mixture of all three trends. The crucial question was that of the proportion of one to the others. Only where the School of Lived Experience was dominant could there be real theatre. There could only be real theatre, too, when a company was dominated not by the author, as Nemirovich wanted, or by a single star actor who imposed his personality but by an ensemble of artists, working sensitively and responsibly together towards a common creative purpose.

As he worked on this manuscript over the years he felt the need to justify his opinions historically, to set his views against those of earlier writers. He undertook a further detailed study of Shchepkin's autobiography but wished to extend his reading further. In early May 1913 he approached his friend Mrs Gurevich for help. She was researching the history of acting, and placed her own considerable knowledge at his disposal, engaging a translator to produce quick versions of relevant foreign authors. Stimulated by this broad introduction, the following year Stanislavski embarked on an intensive reading programme, annotating as he went. The books he studied included: Luigi Riccoboni's *Pensées Sur La Declamation* (1738); Francesco Riccoboni's *Histoire Du Théâtre Italien* (1740) and *L'Art Du Théâtre* (1750); Rémond de Saint-Albin's *Le Comédien* (1747); Diderot's notes on Sticcotti's *Garrick Ou Les Acteurs Anglais* (1769); extracts from Ludwig Tieck's *Dramaturgische Blätter*, which dealt with the conflict between Mlle Clairon and Mlle Dumesnil in their respective *Memoires* (1798 and 1800) over the question of artificial and natural acting styles; *Lettres D'Adrienne Lecouvreur*, famous for the simplicity, intelligence and directness of her style. Stanislavski noted in the margin, that Lecouvreur 'was the first to relate to her partner and not the audience' and 'she instinctively followed Molière's advice: say your lines the way people speak.' Two other works, Doré's *Les Déclamations Théâtrales* (1771) and Fournelle's *Curiosités Théâtrales* (1859) further illuminated the conflict between the School of Representation and the School of Lived Experience. He made extensive notes on Coquelin's *L'Art Du Comédien* (1894). From Bram Stoker's biography of Irving he took over the notion of the Perspective of a Role.

At the same time as he was looking back, historically, he was also thinking forward to new forms, notably the effect of the cinema. Film was still at an elementary stage of development and he could see only a limited role for it. The absence of the live actor seemed to have a crippling effect:

'The theatre and the cinema belong to different spheres and the things by which the theatre excites, attracts and charms us can never be provided by the cinema. It is really naive to imagine that what currently has meaning in the theatre for audiences is outward form. That is not the life of the theatre. Theatre lives by the exchange of spiritual energy, which goes continuously back and forth between audience and actor; that contact of feeling that unites actor and audience with invisible threads. That will never and can never occur in the cinema where the living actor is absent, where the flow of spiritual motions is effected by mechanical means. In the theatre it is a *living* man who delights us, saddens us, disturbs us and calms us but in the cinema everyone and everything is *only apparently real*.

The cinema cannot replace the theatre, but it can, if it is understood and takes on board the questions of people's spiritual progress, introduce the popular masses to the generality of cultural life. Then it is undoubtedly an important and beautiful thing.' (Interview in *Peterburgski Kurier*, May 1, 1914.)

He sensed, nevertheless, that the screen would have an influence on acting technique and would, in fact confirm the superiority of the School of Lived Experience:

'You want to see the difference between the art of representation and the art of lived experience? – go to the cinema. The audience is beginning to understand the difference and very soon will be demanding it from actors. Are you ready for it?' (In *Voprosi Kinoiskusstvo*, 1962, p. 283.)

More new ideas came from Maxim Gorki. In December 1910 he suggested that Stanislavski complete his convalescence by joining him in the Mediterranean where he was living, for health reasons, on Capri. On December 18 and 19, Stanislavski read his notes and discussed the problems of training a new kind of actor. Gorki was sympathetic to Stanislavski's basic notions. He himself was fully convinced that a proper exploration of personal experience could lead to political insight just as well as abstract theory. Stanislavski's combination of the purely subjective with a concern for the historical and social was entirely in line with his own thinking. He suggested establishing a company of young actors who would devise plays through improvisation, working with a writer, just like the strolling players of the Middle Ages and early Renaissance. Strength was given to this idea when, on the 20th, the two men went across to Naples and attended a performance at a popular theatre, which was attempting to work in the *commedia dell'arte* tradition. There was no written script. The actors improvised. The performance captured Stanislavski's imagination but there was no time to see it again before his departure on the 23rd. Back in Moscow he met Efros and discussed the notion of this new way of creating plays and its implications for productions where the author's text was poor:

'If the words are poor, as for example in bad writers or translations and a talented artist finds his own words which are better and correspond to the objectives and the writer's intentions – why not take advantage of better words?' (*Notebook* 927.1 16.)

In January and again in September 1912 Gorki invited Stanislavski to come down with a group of colleagues and create a play. That was impractical. In any case it is questionable whether Stanislavski, who, despite his reservations on the supremacy of the author, remained devoted to the scripted and indeed the classic play, would have wished to go very far down this road. Gorki's ideas did, however, find an important place in the First Studio which was set up specifically to train a new generation of actors and directors in the System. It opened in the autumn of 1912 after a two-year battle with the Board of Art Theatre and with Nemirovich.

Having left the official management, Stanislavski's power to influence decisions or promote change had been seriously diminished. His reputation among the company for being something of a crank persisted and Nemirovich did little to discourage it. On the contrary, in private correspondence to Knipper and Luzhski, he made no secret of his own scepticism about the direction his partner had taken. But Stanislavski was not to be deterred. He made several attempts to promote his ideas among his colleagues. He gave a series of lectures outlining the System but soon realized that you could not compress an active process into one hour's talk. When he was directing, the cast attempted to use the System. They were compliant, if nothing else, when he introduced classes in Dalcroze's eurhythmics in 1911 and elements of yoga but on the whole they maintained a reserve. He came to realize that his main hope lay in the rising generation, but he had only limited contact with young actors. Having no status in the Art Theatre School he could only teach, privately, any student who showed interest. With time an increasing number of them came forward but there was no stability or continuity in the arrangement. As Sophia Gianitsova points out in her reminiscences, many young actors came upon the System by chance – in her case by finding some pencilled notes in a dressing-room. Misunderstandings and half-truths abounded.

By the beginning of 1910 Stanislavski felt that with the success of *A Month in the Country*, he had proved his point sufficiently to make demands. He wanted the opportunity and the facilities to teach the System officially. He drafted a seventeen-point statement to the Board which Stakhovich read to Nemirovich over a meal on January 19, 1910. It is highly personal, not to say emotional, and shows quite clearly how aware he was of his poor standing in the company:

'3. . . . I want total freedom for all those who are possessed of a pure and disinterested love of the theatre. Let whoever will make his own trials and experiments. I want the same right for myself.

4. . . . I am now persuaded as never before that I am on the right track . . . [and] will discover simple forms of words that will sum up everything and help the theatre to discover what is most important, that will point it in the right direction for many years.

5. I want not only to discover the fundamental principles of the creative process, I want not only to formulate its theory, I want to put it into practice.

6. The man who knows the difficult, uncertain, primitive nature of our art will be aware of the difficulty, scope and importance of this task. Perhaps it is insane arrogance. So be it! Then it will prove to be beyond

my strength and I shall get a broken head. And deserve it. . . . Perhaps I am a madman and a dreamer but I cannot be and do not wish to be otherwise. At my age your roots are your roots.

7. The task is complicated and long and I am not young in years . . . . At the very most I have ten years work left in me. . . . It's time to think of one's will. After all, every man wants to leave some small mark behind him. That's understandable.

8. I need material for my plan, I need help. It's impossible to count on everyone but there are a few people whom I have trained with great difficulty or who believe in my dreams. Of course I prize their help greatly.

9. The paths of our art are pitted with ruts and holes. They are deep and you can't get past them without falling. In moments like those you ought to help and pick up those who have stumbled and not think of them as already dead. . . .

10. . . . There was a time when there was not a single young person who was a real hopeful. Now there are such young people and our first task must be to teach them to find satisfaction in plain work, unless, of course, they turn out to be a real find – and there must always be a place for that in our theatre. . . .

12. I would like to forget just for a while many hurtful expressions used in respect of me – "scatter-brain", "a bundle of whims" – because they are unjust. I don't get into a mess all the time, sometimes I pull it off and my whims are not always unsuccessful.

13. If these expressions are dropped perhaps the result will be greater faith both in me and in the people I have trained to help me. . . .

15. It may be that the people I have chosen are failures, or that I have harmed them or that I am a bad teacher. If it is the case then it is better to tell me so straight out and not use hidden weapons against me. . . .

17. For my research I need a variety of material, not only what is artistic but also what is flawed. It is more difficult to eradicate faults than simply to develop secure talent. I need both people who are artistically dull, static, somewhat anaemic and weak and also those who are on fire. I can only verify the things I am working on with a range of differing pupils. . . . If you do not deny others the right to have pupils who are thick, I would also like to be allowed that privilege.' (SS, V, pp. 456–8.)

Nemirovich's response was to try and head him off with flattery. The theatre, he wrote, was enjoying great success, becoming internationally famous; box-office receipts were good; he was at the height of his powers; he had *Hamlet* – why bother with trifles?

Seeing Stanislavski's determination to follow his own path, Nemirovich decided he must, once and for all, take absolute control of the management

of the Art Theatre. He wrote to his wife that he was going to 'purge the
theatre of its Stanislavskiitis'. But such extreme attitudes were never real.
Nemirovich's feelings were never less than contradictory. He wanted nothing
better than a reconciliation but it would have to be on his own terms. He
saw positive aspects to the System but he could not believe that the process
of acting could be reduced to a series of single operations. It was too mechanical. Five years later, in a much less temperate letter, he charged Stanislavski with total incomprehension of the true nature of the actor's talent and
accused him of trying to replace an essentially mysterious and poetic process
with 'a crude, manufactured, artificial surrogate'.

On February 24, 1911 the Art Theatre management committee met to
discuss the future of the company. Kachalov, sensing a move to exclude
Stanislavski, reacted strongly. He stated, quite categorically that without
him the theatre would not be the same:

> 'Yes it would be a good theatre, the best of theatres but not the Art
> Theatre.' (N-D Archive, No. 2248.)

Finally he lost his temper and threatened to quit.

Stanislavski then submitted a document setting out in thirty-eight paragraphs the conditions under which he would work for the following three
years: a restricted work-load, proper holidays, a decent attitude towards his
immediate associates, particularly Sulerzhitski, and no more tragic roles.
What he wanted, he repeated, was the possibility to teach. He further made
it quite clear that he would, under no circumstances, assume any management responsibilities. This left the way open for Nemirovich and on May 7
new statutes were voted giving him full control. The powers of the management committee were reduced to a minimum. He was to all intents and
purposes only answerable to the full meeting of the shareholders. Stanislavski raised no objections.

Nemirovich had the good sense not to abuse his powers. It was in any
case clear that the theatre could only survive if his partnership with Stanislavski was seen to be working. He knew also that if he took a mind to it
Stanislavski could once again branch out on his own. The Art Theatre
would then collapse. He made a number of conciliatory gestures. On August
4, 1911, to everyone's surprise, during a rehearsal of Tolstoi's *The Living
Corpse*, he announced that the System was the official working method of
the Art Theatre. Then on September 5, he told the management committee
that Stanislavski should be given proper support for his teaching. These
moves in no way diminished his essential authority but they did give him
the opportunity to exercise a minimum of control. Any activity attached to
the Art Theatre still came under his jurisdiction. The teaching of the System,
as part of the Art Theatre's policy, could, therefore, be subject to his 'cor-
rectives' when he thought necessary.

Stanislavski's ideas had now taken firmer shape. He had decided, with encouragement from Gorki, to found not a school but a studio as he had done years earlier with Meierhold, a centre for learning, experiment and research. Rather than teach raw beginners he would form young actors who had sufficient experience of professional theatre to recognize their difficulties and know the problems involved but who were not yet fixed in their ways.

The obvious person to take charge of the Studio would be Sulerzhitski. Discussions on policy began:

'At one of the meetings Konstantin Sergeievich, explaining the purpose in establishing the Studio, said roughly the following:

The Studio exists thanks to the Art Theatre and for the sake of the Art Theatre, to help it.

It is concerned with the problems of the actor's creative process (system), the educational formation of the artist, providing him with a set of practices, help through daily exercises and, perhaps, in future, parallel performances.

... It provides new experiments on the creative process common to authors, actors and directors in the making of plays (Gorki's method). Experiments in décor, lighting effects and the possibilities of the stage. Experiments in mime for large-scale productions. Experiments on the management side. Research into proper methods of theatrical management.

... For that purpose, so as to learn who among the company of the Moscow Art Theatre wished to take part in these activities, Konstantin Sergeivich put up a list, on which each member of the company was to indicate his wishes by signing in the appropriate column.' (Sulerzhitski, Notes on the Studio, September 1912. Sulerzhitski Archive, No. 6477/47.)

Who were to be the founder members? Boleslavski was a natural candidate. Suler drew up a list of others. At the top came two names: Evgeni Vakhtangov and Michael Chekhov. Stanislavski added his own comments. Of Vakhtangov he said 'can turn himself into a good teacher and director. Forget him as an actor.'

Vakhtangov had entered the Art Theatre in March 1911 as a result of an interview Sulerzhitski had arranged with Nemirovich. He very soon attracted attention by the completeness and accuracy of the notes he took during rehearsals. He learned and mastered the elements of the System with amazing speed so that by August Stanislavski was using him to take classes and direct exercises with small groups of young actors who were involved in Tolstoi's *The Living Corpse*. Stanislavski, aware that allegiance to the System could be damaging to his career, and learning from Suler's unfortunate experiences, warned him of the intrigue which existed in the theatre, and put him under his personal protection. Stanislavski had auditioned Michael Chekhov in April, 1912 when he had seen two pieces – an extract from *Tsar Fiodor* and one of Marmeladov's speeches from *Crime and Punishment*. He had immediately asked him to join the company. Adding his comments to Suler's list he noted, 'talented, has charm. One of the real hopes for the future.' Also included on the list was Maria Ouspenskaia, who, with Boleslavski, was to found, in 1923, the highly influential American Theatre Laboratory. The original group of members was small but Stanislavski tried to open out the work of the studio as much as possible. He put up the following notice:

> 'Anyone wishing to give a reading, perform an extract, submit model sets, show the results of their research into stage techniques or offer some literary material for staging, should kindly inscribe their names in the book specially provided in the hall of the studio. The book is lodged with the porter, Baranov.' (In *O Stanislavskom*, p. 366.)

The new young company were subjected to a gruelling work-load. They had to fulfil their obligations to the main company, attend classes at the studio and rehearse any plays they wished to put on in whatever free time was left to them, mainly late at night. The facilities they enjoyed were modest: some rooms over a cinema, The Cinematograph (later known as The Lux). The theatre was tiny; a small stage on a level with the front row, a low ceiling, almost no wing space and a raked auditorium with room for about fifty people. But this time Stanislavski had judged the situation aright. He had succeeded in attracting major talent and provided the opportunity for a release of fresh creative energy. By the end of the season 1914/1915 the Studio had established itself as the centre for original work and sensitive expressive acting. Efros considered the adaptation of Dicken's *Cricket on the Hearth* to be the best production he had seen that year.

The Studio rapidly took on a life and character of its own, shaped by the talents of its members. New students, however, still needed training and it seemed to Stanislavski that he had to start afresh with each new generation; the Second Studio was created in 1916, the Third, which was in fact a school created by Vakhtangov, in 1920 and the Fourth in 1921. An Opera Studio was started in 1918.

Such developments had damaging side-effects on the Art Theatre proper. It meant that genuine new talent was being siphoned off. As for Stanislavski, he continued to act and to direct plays of his choice but his heart was with his students. His productions were, essentially, a way of teaching. For this reason, rehearsals from *Le Malade Imaginaire* in 1913 were conducted at the Studio rather than the main house. They were open to anyone interested in the practicalities of the System. Many actors not connected with the production did turn up. In a letter to Vladimir Gribunin, written in March 1916, Nemirovich noted ruefully that once he had a powerful ally in Stanislavski; now he had lost him to the Studio.

CHAPTER EIGHTEEN

PHYSICAL TECHNIQUE

Stanislavski the actor was not necessarily restricted to the System he taught. His own working method was more complex than his theories and his response to his own needs as a performer inevitably pushed him beyond anything he had formulated as a teacher. Even if justifiable claims can be made for the scientific nature of the System, the fact remains that its formulation depended on Stanislavski's capacity to analyse his own practice and that practice could not, except within certain general limits, be anticipated. It always produced change. There is a constant time-lag between personal practice as recorded in the *Notebooks* and the System as publicly proclaimed. The result of this evident discrepancy between words and deeds produced some sharp criticism, notably from Vakhtangov, who felt he was betraying his own ideals.

His first attempt to put the System into practice, as Rakitin in *A Month in the Country*, had been a psychological exercise. He had deliberately kept the character within narrow physical bounds. A year later, in 1910, he was confronted with a character, General Krutitski in Ostrovski's *Enough Stupidity in Every Wise Man*, which posed the whole question of the relationship of internal and external characterization. Stanislavski the actor could not get away from the highly developed visual imagination of Stanislavski the director. Despite his insistence on the supreme importance of the psychological aspects of a role he had a strong sense of any character's appearance and an exceptional capacity for physical transformation. Yet, knowing the errors a purely external approach had produced in the past he was suspicious of using it. Even so in October 1909, when preparing Rakitin, he had allowed Stakhovich to demonstrate the role to him and had then copied him. This had led him along a false path, away from Turgenev. In the end he had had to start afresh, using himself as a base. Yet he had been right in one important respect. Clarity concerning internal processes did not, as he had assumed, automatically lead to clear physical characterization.

He started work on General Krutitski in January with Nemirovich directing. The rehearsals followed Nemirovich's usual pattern: literary analyses, study of period material and photographs. Out of all Nemirovich's brilliant exposition Stanislavski only retained one phrase, a reference to Ostrovski's 'epic calm'. It was an expression he hung on to. He did his own independent research. He began to develop an external image but the part would not come together psychologically. The problem lay in the very first stage of the creative process as he then defined it: the stimulation of the will, the engagement of the actor's interest and personality. Yet the answer came not from psychological investigation or from Emotion Memory but, as so often in the past, from an accidental external stimulus:

> 'How many photographs, sketches portraits I was shown, how many did I find for myself that seemed to correspond with the external appearance of the role. We even managed to find out which general Ostrovski had taken as a model when creating Krutitski. But I did not know him and for all this material could not feel my Krutitski.
>
> Then the following thing happened. I had, for professional reasons, to go to what is called an "orphans' court". . . . The house, its customs, the people were bowed down under the weight of the ancient moss that covered them. In the courtyard of this institution . . . a small additional rickety, moss-covered building, and in it an old fellow (who did not look in the least like my make-up) writing, writing, writing, like General Krutitski, plans which were of no use to anybody. The overall impression I received from the building and its solitary occupant suggested to me what the face, make-up and bearing of my general should be. And there too *epic calm* had its influence. The external and internal forms of the role, which I had found by chance, came together, so that a role which had started following the line of "the interplay of forms and passions" was suddenly transformed into something else, following the line of "intuition and feeling", for me the only one of any value.' (SS, I, pp. 427–8.)

Once the block had been removed the historical and period aspects of the role fell into place. When the play opened on March 8 the role was recognized as one of his most significant achievements. Not only had he created the individual personality of this decaying general, who had power without sense, but had symbolized a whole era and a whole section of Russian society.

The role was also a masterpiece of physical transformation. In April, during the Petersburg tour, Mrs Gurevich met Stanislavski in the wings. She did not recognize him. She wondered who this old general, who was holding out his hand to her, could be. It took a short conversation to make her realize whom she was really talking to.

Yet Stanislavski could still go over the top on externals and this he did in his next production, *A Provincial Lady*, which formed part of a Turgenev triple bill. He was cast as Count Liubin, the sophisticate from Petersburg who goes down to the country and is humbled. He worked out the internal logic of the character's development in scrupulous detail but when it came to the make-up he allowed himself to be carried away. When the play opened on March 5, 1912, Efros commented:

> 'There was laughter all the time in the house. People had never laughed so much, or so it seems, at the Art Theatre. And the exaggeration was subtle, brilliant, with many exquisite details.
>
> Only Count Liubin's external appearance was overdone by Stanislavski. He had gone too far with the make-up so that the Count ceased to be a real character and the acting became laboured.' (N. Efros, in *Rech*, March 8, 1912.)

Stanislavski's difficulties became particularly acute when he was alone, preparing the annual production of his own choice. It was nothing new for him to work simultaneously as actor and director and negotiate the difficult balance of interests involved. Now, in addition he was attempting to justify, teach and verify the System. This meant that, at a moment when he was making more demands on himself as an artist, energies which should have been devoted entirely to the creation of a role were being dispersed. It also meant, more importantly, that he could not fulfil the primary objective of the System itself: to use conscious means to stimulate unconscious creative processes and then give them free rein. Involved as he was, inevitably, in endless verification and analysis, he was continuously inhibiting the free run of his imagination, or if his imagination was functioning he was unable to accept unquestioningly solutions which he had instinctively or intuitively found.

He was also beginning to confuse rehearsing and teaching, to the detriment of the production as a whole. Rehearsal was no longer work towards a performance but an end in itself. In Nemirovich's view Stanislavski wasted a great deal of time, and money, by turning every working session into an acting class. At the end of August 1911 he had come into a rehearsal where Stanislavski was working with a young actor, Sushkevich, on his one line in Tolstoi's *The Living Corpse*. It was a simple announcement but Stanislavski made his pupil speak it a dozen different ways, in a dozen different characterizations, from the adolescent to the senile, on the grounds that a creative actor should be able to offer the director a choice. Nemirovich made it clear that he was not interested in a gallery of characters but in a straight line delivered straight.

Having tried out the System on classic tragedy with *Hamlet*, Stanislavski turned now to classic comedy, *Le Malade Imaginaire*. He was still looking outside the company for other collaborators. An entry in his notebook in the autumn of 1907 advises him to keep an eye on Alexandre Benois and his group in Petersburg. The two men met in 1908 and, in 1909, discussed the possibility of working together. The interminable preparations for *Hamlet* and Stanislavski's illness kept the two men apart until 1912. When they did come together they had some initial difficulty in reaching agreement on the sets. Benois' preliminary sketches were too ornate, too 'theatrical' for Stanislavski's taste. They seemed to veer towards the School of Representation and the Molière 'tradition' he had been fighting for years. As with previous productions he refused to glamorize an essentially bourgeois milieu. Writing to his wife on September 15, 1912, the day of the first read-through, Nemirovich who was also to collaborate with Benois on *Le Mariage Forcé* which was to complete the evening, stated that he felt he had found a genuine ally. Benois put Stanislavski in his place much as from time to time he himself did. Nonetheless, although Benois was responsible for the staging of the last act, it was Stanislavski's views which prevailed.

As was now his accepted practice the play was broken down into units during the first session. Stanislavski's final units for Act One were:

1. Argan's exposition (analyses his illness);
2. Subjugation of everyone by the petty tyrant (Argan) to his illness;
3. Toinette's opposition;
4. Angélique's personal life counter to her father's life (revolution);
5. Despotism over daughter;
6. Exploitation of the petty tyrant (wife overcomes him; subjugation of petty tyranny by the insolence of the wife);
7. Conflict between two plots (camps) Toinette and Béline (Béline won, wife robbed);
8. Plot of second act – Toinette's campaign. (Rehearsal Day-book, January 19, 1913.)

As far as his own work as an actor was concerned, Stanislavski also developed a method of working within and through the units which would appear to show the influence of his conversations with Gorki. It consisted of a kind of personal, internal improvisation:

'Studying the text of a role. In the current year (1912–1913) I divide the work into *large units*, clarifying the nature of each unit. Then, immediately, in my own words, I play each unit, observing all the curves. Then I go through the experiences of each unit ten times or so with its curves (not in a fixed way, not being consistent). Then I follow the successive units in the book. And finally, I make the transition, imperceptibly, to the experiences as expressed in the actual words of the part.' (Notes, K.S. Archive, No. 1586/I.)

There remained the problem of physicalizing the role. Stanislavski turned once again, rather surprisingly considering his earlier experience, to Stakhovich, asking him to demonstrate the characteristics of French behaviour. Why Stanislavski, with his extensive knowledge of France and the French, should have needed this is not at all clear. It may simply be that as an actor in the throes of creating a role he needed some kind, any kind, of outside eye. The results were no better than before.

Towards the end of March 1913 he noted:

'Stakhovich showed me how to play a Frenchman (*Malade Imaginaire*). I easily seized on the external aspect from a visual impression and then during the process of experiencing the part in terms of my own personality I slipped over into an external imitation of Stakhovich. The result was clichés, everything became a muddle. To get back to a living state I had to 1) either cut free from Stakhovich and go back to myself or 2) capture in the French psychology Stakhovich had outlined for me what it was that made him [Argan] precisely what he was and not just wave my hands and rush about. . . . I tried to discover in myself, in my own individual psychology, fused with the role, and add to the common state (or kernel) [elements of] conceit and despotism. 3) I tried to discover in myself a completely different external image (Stakhovich portrayed an aristocrat, I was a bourgeois.) During subsequent attempts things came together by chance, i.e., the psychological side experienced earlier merged with the external image I had discovered quite separately. Image and character sometimes take shape from the psychological elements, i.e., from the internal image of a role, but at other times it emerges separately, from a purely external exploration of a role.' (K.S. Archive, No. 927.)

This recognition of the creative function of external elements, of the interpenetration between outward and inward, of the notion that an external action might subsequently be justified internally represented a marked shift of position. The System as taught to his pupils stated that physical action was always the reflection of a previously-discovered psychological truth. This move away from the purely psychological did not immediately get into the official version of the System.

The production as a whole ran into a more fundamental difficulty. Stanislavski had misunderstood the central message of the play, the Superobjective as it came to be known. It is the Superobjective which determines the contents of the individual units and the nature of the characters' motivations. Stanislavski saw the play very clearly as a mordant satire on the medical profession in Molière's time. He could not understand, therefore, why the production was increasingly plunged into gloom. The fact was that he had defined a wrong 'kernel', as he then called it, and taken the wrong through-line on his character:

'Initially we approached the play in a very simplistic fashion defining the super-objective as "I want to be ill". The greater my efforts to achieve that and the more I succeeded, the more it became obvious that we were turning a satirical comedy into a pathological tragedy about illness.

But we quickly grasped our error and defined the despot's super-objective as 'I want people to think I am ill'. With that the comic aspect of the play suddenly came alive, the basis for exploitation by a group of charlatans from the medical world had been created and a tragedy was suddenly transformed into a malicious comedy.' (SS, II, pp. 336–7.)

The play finally opened on March 27, 1913 to overall if not universal critical acclaim.

Stanislavski's own personal success as Argan, and Lilina's as Toinette, was immense. Reviewing the production on the 29th, Efros noted Stanislavski's capacity to exploit all the traditions of farce, to indulge in all the *bouffonades* and at the same time create a living character possessed of an inner emotional logic. He also considered the make-up and general physical characterization one of Stanislavski's finest achievements and, indeed, just as the skinny Stockman had replaced the overweight Astrov, so the scraggy Krutitski with his wispy hair and beard was replaced by a human dumpling. If there was a qualitative difference in the more recent performances it was in a move towards the realm of the grotesque but a grotesque which was inwardly justified and had nothing to do, as Stanislavski had written to Mrs Gurevich on March 14, with Meierhold's stylized offerings.

Stanislavski did not anticipate any personal difficulties with his next production, Goldoni's *La Locandiera*. He had already directed and played in it in 1898. His prime intention, as he had announced in April 1913, was to provide a show-case for Gzovskaia. The designer would once again be Benois while he himself would resume the rôle of the self-styled woman-hater Count Ripafratta. The 1898 performance had been a somewhat perfunctory affair, staged fairly rapidly. General critical opinion at the time had been that the rôle did not develop after Act One. Yet he assumed that he would more or less be able to walk through the part. He was wrong. Neither here nor in *Mozart & Salieri* of 1915 nor in the disastrous *Village of Stepanchikova* of 1917 did he have anything but an agonizing struggle.

He was happy with the first reading which took place in the first week of September 1913 and felt equally at ease during early rehearsals. He was taken aback when one or two colleagues, including Vishnievski, pointed out that he was merely producing clichés. His immediate, somewhat paranoid reaction, was to assume they were merely attacking the System but he had to admit, finally, that they were right. The System aimed at producing acting that was natural and simple but he had made the fundamental error of trying to play the results of the System and not its process. He was playing not the character but 'simplicity'. Just as he had discovered earlier that it is possible to gather together a set of clichés that superficially look 'natural' so it was possible to collect a set of clichés that looked 'simple':

'The greater half of our work was aimed at being simple, as in life, and nothing else.... When you want to be simple, all you think about is being simple and not the basic objectives of the role or the play and so you begin to act being simple. What you get are clichés of being simple, the worst clichés of all.' (SS, V, p. 521.)

He, no less than the rest of the cast, had to go back to basics. He had to establish a set of concrete objectives and look for elements of the character in himself, using emotion memory. This was not easy. He was a man who was fond of women and enjoyed their company. He did, however, recall an uncomfortable acquaintance of his wife's who had disliked overweight, over-bearing women. He also came to the conclusion that he could be very naïve when it came to affairs of the heart. But progress was slow and Nemirovich did not help the situation by coming in to the rehearsal and suggesting a quite different and from Stanislavski's view, quite unworkable, line on the part. Vishnievski suggested that the cast should familiarize themselves with the inn itself, its lay-out and contents. He also suggested to Stanislavski that he should rehearse the play in his own person, believing in the situation and believing himself actually to be afraid.

Many sleepless nights were spent going through the part, scene by scene, allowing the imagination to wander and suggest ideas. But all too often what had seemed clear in the darkness of the bedroom disappeared in re-hearsal. Recalling perhaps his encounter with the *commedia* three years earlier, he began to see the character in terms of Captain Spavento, the loud-mouthed but essentially cowardly soldier. Benois suggested that there were also elements of Don Quixote in the Count and provided him with a sketch which was half one and half the other. Stanislavski achieved the remarkable feat of combining both sets of characteristics.

At 51 Stanislavski was essentially too old for the part. He found a vocal solution, concentrating on the head-notes rather than the lower register to give the voice lightness and youth. Yet good as his work on his individual role might be, the play, like *Le Malade Imaginaire*, had ceased to be funny. The problem once more lay in the overall concept. Stanislavski needed to step back from his detailed work and redefine his through-line, his 'kernel' or super-objective:

'. . . at first we defined the superobjective as "I want to hate women" (misogyny) but this stopped the play from being either funny or effective. Once I had understood that the hero liked women and did not actually wish to be a misogynist but only appear so, then the superobjective became "I want to woo them secretly" (simulating misogyny) and the play suddenly came to life.' (SS, II. p. 337.)

By the time the play opened on February 3, 1914, it had received 112 re-hearsals, as opposed to 17 for the original production but the time, effort and struggle payed off. This time Stanislavski succeeded in making the character develop, presenting new facets with each succeeding act. His performance also gave the impression of being effortless. In a review in *Odesskii Novosti* on February 9, Efros described the performance as almost improvised, 'it sparkled with unexpected and beautiful comic details'. Stanislavski's application of his ideas was superior and more consistent than any other member of the cast's. Lvov, writing in *Novosti Sezona* on the 4th referred to a 'cascade of glittering nuances'. Instead of the usual loud-mouthed upstart, Stanislavski had presented a noble, simple man, 'a great big boy in his love for the lady of the house'. The reaction to the performance during the spring Petersburg tour confirmed his success. Whatever his private difficulties he still remained for the public the supreme actor of his time.

CHAPTER NINETEEN

THE VILLAGE OF STEPANCHIKOVO,
MY TRAGEDY

The period preceding the outbreak of the First World War was rich in promise for the theatre's wider, international reputation. While both Nemirovich and Stanislavski declared themselves depressed when they thought of the future, though for entirely different reasons, the rest of the world was still catching up with its achievements. Apart from staging its own productions the Art Theatre had served as host to concerts and musical evenings. Besides Rachmaninov and Chaliapin, who were already his friends, Stanislavski had attracted musicians of the calibre of the conductor, Serge Koussevitski and the harpsichordist, Wanda Landowska. All the people he drew to him shared one thing in common, high energy, drive, and an almost obsessive sense of purpose.

The Art Theatre increasingly attracted visitors from abroad. In January 1913 Beerbohm Tree arrived in Moscow specifically to see *Hamlet*, which he attended on the 16th, accompanied by Isadora. According to Lilina, who was still in correspondence with Craig, the performance was below par. Kachalov was ill and played very slowly. Knipper was also ill and had been replaced by an understudy. After the show Stanislavski gave a supper party at the Hermitage Theatre where Isadora improvised a dance with Scriabin at the piano. A year later H. G. Wells arrived and on January 21 saw Stanislavski, who was playing despite a very high temperature, in *Three Sisters*. Wells immediately tried to persuade the company to come to London on tour with a repertoire of Chekhov. This invitation was matched on March 12 by a telegram from Norman Hapgood inviting the Art Theatre to New York. In the interim Harley Granville Barker paid a visit, arriving on February 14, with the intention of studying the theatre's working methods. He held a long conversation with Stanislavski during which it was decided that he would send over two pupils. Significantly he chose to place them in the Studio rather than with the main company.

One can only conjecture what the history of western theatre might have been had these plans come to fruition, had not the war and the revolution intervened. In the event it was ten years before the Art Theatre went to the

United States and forty-three years before it set foot for the first time on a London stage.

When war broke out Stanislavski was in Marienbad with Lilina, Kachalov, Massalitinov and other members of the company. He was deeply worried:

> 'Kostia is in a panic, everything points to war with Russia tomorrow and how do we get back to Russia. . . . he's afraid of revolution in Russia. In a word he's in a state and has even forgotten all about the System.' (Letter to N. B. Litovtseva, July 1914. Kachalov Archives, No. 9611.)

His fears were proved right. On the 19th Germany declared war. On the 21st the group was dragged from the Munich train, not knowing whether they would live or die. If Stanislavski heard aright only lack of ammunition prevented them from being shot. As it was they were kept in a freezing refreshment room overnight and then, in the morning, told they would be allowed to go on to Switzerland. They were taken to Lindau and then put on a steamboat for Bern. They were held in semi-detention for three or four days before the Swiss authorities reluctantly gave them permission to stay. Life was difficult. They had little foreign money and exchange was already becoming well-nigh impossible. For the first time in his life Stanislavski, tired and worried sick about home and his theatre, experienced deprivation and oppression. He eventually reached home with his family by the steamboat, 'Equateur' which sailed from Marseilles to Odessa in the first week of September.

His reaction to this experience was one of patriotism and stoicism. According to Mrs Gurevich, on the night of July 21–22, in the train, Stanislavski spoke in a quiet, even voice of his reaction to the prospect of being shot:

> '. . . in that moment he could contemplate life from a kind of impersonal height and nothing seemed frightening. He said that events of recent days had given him a clear impression of the superficiality of all that was called human culture, bourgeois culture, that a completely different kind of life was needed, where all needs were reduced to the minimum, where there was work – real artistic work – on behalf of the people, for those who had not yet been consumed by this bourgeois culture.' (L. Y. Gurevich, in *Russkaia Misl*, Bk X, p. 153.)

Such an attitude was useful preparation for the upheavals to come.

Within two days of his return to Moscow on September 14, ignoring the fact that he had no real authority to do so, he called a special meeting, demanding that the theatre be even more strongly aware of its artistic mission. The repertoire must be examined and cleansed of all superficiality both in form and content. There was to be no running after cheap success just for the sake of making money. As chance would have it the new season was to include a revival of Russia's greatest classic play, *Woe from Wit*. The theatre's next patriotic contribution to the war was a presentation of a triple bill by Pushkin – *The Stone Guest*, *A Feast During the Plague* and *Mozart & Salieri*. Stanislavski, Benois and Nemirovich were to be jointly responsible for the evening.

Whatever difficulties Stanislavski might have had with his previous two rôles they paled in comparison with the problems he encountered with Salieri. His concern to research the System was having a damaging effect on his ability to perform. Nemirovich had seen the dangers. On November 10, 1914 he wrote to Stanislavski, pointing out that his performance as Vershinin had gone off because he was over-complicating the issue:

'. . . either I really don't understand your System or (*listen please*) you are so busy with the means that you lose sight of the end. Aren't you changing the role of prophet for that of a sacrificial priest?' (*Izbranie Pisma*, p. 321.)

A month later he was able to write again saying the performance was back to normal.

Stanislavski decided that the process of creating Salieri would form the basis of a book, *The History of a Role*, which would provide a practical illustration of his working method. He received almost no direction and consequently no challenge. Nemirovich was wholly occupied with *The Stone Guest*, with Kachalov, while Benois was concentrated on design. Between the beginning of January 1915 and the opening on March 26 Stanislavski worked steadily on the role, making notes as he went. First came the problem of the through-line:

'1. Salieri is a villain, a man of envy. Straight to the point – to hate Mozart, censure, cavil at everything about him. He turns out to be a theatrical villain.
2. A more subtle notion of envy. I want to be first and therefore I get rid of Mozart, although I have nothing really against him.
3. The most characteristic thing for Pushkin is defiance of God. Struggle with God.
4. An assault on injustice and therefore a desire (cowardly) to escape from oppression and injustice.' (SS, V, p. 527.)

He then created a history of Salieri's artistic development, defining his attitudes to other composers, based on material in the soliloquies, filling the rôle out by imagining the character's Emotion Memory of every incident. The result was a full biography, with every circumstance of the character's off-stage life vividly experienced. The subtext became so dense that it overpowered the text itself, which runs at most to a dozen printed pages, and it was the sub-text that Stanislavski tried to play rather than Pushkin's actual words. The text was shattered into fragments as he tried to motivate every single word and relive in performance the background material he had so carefully worked out. Pauses were heavy and long. By the time a sentence came to an end the beginning was lost. The fact was that in trying to live the character Stanislavski had ignored the means by which the life of that character was principally to be conveyed, Pushkin's subtle, finely-wrought verse.

He had become acutely aware of the inadequacy of his vocal technique. The mechanism could not take what he was trying to do and was suffering from it. On March 1 he even had Chaliapin, who was performing Rimski-Korsakov's operatic version, read over the part to him in an attempt to capture some of the true musicality of the verse but the singer's genius made him even more depressed.

For his part Stanislavski noted how difficult if not impossible it was in the theatre of living experience to be ready on the first night and went on working. In the end, after three months of struggle, it was an act of desperation, born of the actor's instinct for survival, which got him out of trouble. On April 1 he wrote to Benois:

'I felt so awful all day that I decided to go [. . .] for hypnosis. When I woke up in the morning and thought about the previous evening's performance I went red and was overwhelmed by a hot, burning depression. I stayed that way until they came to get me up. I acted the part all night, tormented by insomnia and the more I went through the lines the more I forgot them. During the day, in the street and in the carriage I wore myself out with the same relentless stupid repetition of the lines. During the day I was worn out, I lay down but could not sleep because I was still going through the lines. I arrived at the theatre completely exhausted. I made changes to the make-up in order to convince myself that I had discovered something and so give myself courage. I drank a double dose of drops and (horror of horrors) a secret glass of wine to cheer myself up. But I only needed to put on the white breeches to feel corpulent while the painted thinness of my face seemed like a caricature. My heart sank and I was in such total despair that I felt clumsy, superfluous, stupid, above all *ridicule*. God knows how I acted, I stumbled through the lines and almost came to a complete stop. The more I tried to overcome my apathy the more the audience coughed. Yesterday I went to the wardrobe in a state of nothing short of anguish and felt that I could not put on white breeches or, more precisely, could not bring myself to go out on stage. Confident in your basic agreement, I sent someone to get me some black breeches and stockings. After I had put them on I felt as though I had been set free. Confidence returned, gestures. With my inner plan in pieces I decided, in actors' jargon, to pull out all the stops, let fly physically and

9a *The Cherry Orchard* (Chekhov) Stanislavski as Gaev, 1904.

9b *Ivanov* (Chekhov) Stanislavski as Shabielski, 1904.

10 Stanislavski as Satin in *The Lower Depths* (Gorki), 1902.

11 Stanislavski, Gorki, Lilina. Yalta, 1900.

12a *Woe From Wit* (Griboiedov)
Stanislavski as Famusov,
1906.

12b *Woe From Wit*
Stanislavski as Famusov,
1914.

13 The house at Carriage Row where the Stanislavskis lived from 1903 to 1921.

14a *Le Malade Imaginaire* (Molière) Stanislavski as Argan, 1913.

14b Stanislavski as Cavaliere Rippafratta in *La Locandiera* (Goldoni).

14c *Enough Stupidity in Every Wise Man* (Ostrovski). Stanislavski as Krutitski, 1910.

15a Stanislavski
and Sokolova
at work, 1924.

15b Lunacharski,
Stanislavski and
George Bernard
Shaw.

16 Stanislavski.

vocally. And did I not!! It was so easy but I knew that only sheer desperation could push me to such shameful lengths. The audience listened to me
as never before. They even tried to applaud after the first scene. Moskvin
rushed round during the interval and said that this was the only way to
play it. I don't understand a thing.' (SS, VII, pp. 610, 611.)

The production was by and large savaged by the critics, both conservative
and avant-garde, and not even the sympathetic Efros could find anything
good to say for it. Stakhovich wrote an encouraging letter but his appreciation of the performance depended on his willingness to forget what
Pushkin had actually written. The one positive result of this unhappy period
was the recognition that formal, scientifically-based voice study was essential. Stanislavski turned to his colleague S. M. Volkonski whose book, *The
Expressive Word*, had appeared two years before in Petersburg and to Us-
hakov's book, *A Brief Introduction to the Science of Language*, which had
come out in Moscow at about the same time.

Relations with Nemirovich had not improved. They had quarrelled in the
upstairs foyer of the theatre after the one rehearsal of *A Provincial Lady*
Nemirovich had been allowed to see on February 14, 1912. Nemirovich
accused Stanislavski of misdirecting the play and distorting Turgenev's intentions. Stanislavski's reply according to Nemirovich's account, had been that
the part as written was not interesting. Nemirovich had tried, unsuccessfully,
to interfere during rehearsals of *La Locandiera*. They had clashed during
preparations for the revival of *Woe From Wit*, so much so that on May 1 a
leading literary historian, Professor Piksanov, had to be called to arbitrate,
or rather to lend support to Nemirovich's views and bring Stanislavski into
line, into literary line. Piksanov's view was clear:

'. . . it would be desirable to keep not only to the text of *Woe From Wit* but
also to the *author's comments*; highly desirable to adhere strictly to the
author's instructions.' (N-D Archive, No. 48/1–2.)

Two separate accounts exist of Stanislavski's reply. The substance is identical but in his own version Stanislavski supports his views by reference to
Gogol. He insisted on the creative function of the actor. The author had no
right to intrude in the actor's domain by laying down precise instructions.
He went on:

'Every established play, freely staged, done anew, is an artistic creation . . .
Gogol writes: take the best plays of Schiller and Shakespeare and put
them on in the way contemporary advances in art demand. And that
gives me courage to make changes, taking the essential inner experience
of the actor into account.' (K.S. Archive, No. 3328.)

Nemirovich's account omits all reference to Gogol. Stanislavski's views are seen as being entirely his own, unsupported by any more authoritative opinion. As a footnote it may be added that fifty years later Piksanov recorded his appreciation of Stanislavski's performance as Famusov.

Stanislavski's obstinate insistence on keeping literature, as literature, out of the theatre is nowhere better illustrated than in his complicated but amicable relationship with the symbolist poet Aleksandr Blok, whose play, *The Rose and the Cross*, set in the Languedoc at the time of the troubadours, was accepted by the Art Theatre in 1915, with some reluctance. At 35, Blok was the outstanding poet of his time. In his youth he had thought of becoming an actor but the publication of his first volume of poetry *Verses on a Beautiful Lady* set him on a literary career. His first play, *The Puppet Booth*, was staged by Meierhold in 1906 but the relationship, for both artistic and personal reasons, was an uneasy one. The following year he approached the Art Theatre in the hope that Stanislavski would take an interest in his work.

In May 1908 he read his new play, *The Song of Destiny*, to Stanislavski and Nemirovich. Stanislavski at first seemed enthusiastic, immediately suggesting some ideas for staging. He also made some suggestions for rewriting. On September 11 a revised version of the play arrived. Stanislavski did not answer until December 3 and his letter was full of polite reservations. He had read the play four times but while he appreciated the quality of Blok's poetry it seemed to him that, as drama, the play lacked consistency both of plot and character and often contravened psychological truth. With characteristic courtesy, however, he ascribed his failure to appreciate the play more to his own limitations. He was, he said, 'an incorrigible realist' and unable to go beyond Chekhov. This was manifestly a polite fiction since he had spent the last four years trying to do precisely that. He had, of course, in his recent tenth-anniversary speech proclaimed a return to an enriched realism but what Blok had to offer, apart from fine writing, did not offer then, or indeed later, any real advance in terms of Stanislavski's artistic search.

Blok did not give up. When in the summer of 1912 he completed *The Rose and the Cross* he refused offers from the Aleksandrinski and from Meierhold and again contacted Stanislavski. In late afternoon of April 27, the following year, during the Petersburg tour, he read his script to Stanislavski and Remizov. Remizov left almost immediately but Stanislavski stayed on until a quarter to midnight while the two men tried to come to an understanding. Blok has left a full account of their discussions in his diary.

Each man decided that the other needed educating at the most elementary level in the arts which they respectively practised. Blok found himself obliged to explain the meaning and the action of his play 'in more crude and simplistic terms' as Stanislavski had found it grey and monotonous. He was amazed that:

'. . . an intelligent man, in whom I have great faith, who has done important things (Chekhov at the Art Theatre) *understood nothing, "took in" nothing and felt nothing.*' (Blok, SS. Vol. VII, p. 246.)

Stanislavski, for his part explained in great detail the work of the Studio and, in explicit terms, what he thought Blok had to learn about writing for the stage. Blok's script was too allusive. Paying audiences wanted concrete action. Thus he suggested that the degradation of Bertrand, the principal character, should be established not by dialogue or description but concretely by his carrying out some menial task. He would be ordered to get rid of the slops. Down would go his sword and shield and he would pick up a bucket or even a chamber-pot. This was the way, Stanislavski assured him, to make the play work and offer an actor a meaty role. The arguments are deliberately pitched high in an effort designed to shock a lyric author out of his private world and bring him nearer the footlights. He was not and never had been confined to a world of slop-buckets nor was he indifferent to broader more philosophical issues. If anything, during the period 1915–1920 he was too concerned with the 'symbolic' and the 'cosmic', to his own detriment, but for him abstractions were perceived and communicated through a selective, clear, 'transparent' theatrical presentation of the living world. What he could not accept was the notion that it was sufficient to clothe ideas, however interesting and relevant they might be, in insubstantial forms which had no genuine, independent reality but were merely representative of different aspects of the author's own mind.

After the conversation Blok was not at all certain if he could or should go down the road of the overtly 'theatrical'. Two days later he did, however, have an opportunity to see the First Studio at work in *The Wreck of 'The Hope'*. He recognized and appreciated the working method Stanislavski had described. He saw the emotional effect on the audience. He still believed an understanding could be reached and kept the offer of the play open. He did not have a happy time. Stanislavski applied himself. He discussed the question of music with Rachmaninov, who suggested that his friend and fellow pianist-composer, Nikolai Medtner might be suitable. In the event responsibility for the production was bounced back and for the between Stanislavski and Nemirovich for three years, with constant changes of designer and design-concept. Rehearsals came to a halt during the October revolution but were picked up again with a complete change of cast the following year. The last rehearsal Stanislavski took was on December 3, 1918 after which the whole project was finally dropped.

In April 1917 it had become obvious to Blok that the play would not be staged and that Stanislavski, for all his protestations that he liked the play – 'self-deception' Blok called it – was finding the script impossible. Blok's diary entry for April 17, 1917 nonetheless contains a generous tribute to

Stanislavski whom he describes as, 'the only truly great artist in the Art Theatre' and in a letter to his mother, written the same day, he said that while Stanislavski might say stupid things from time to time he 'really loves art because he is art.'

No such generosity of mind was shown by Nemirovich. Relations, during this same period, did not improve. Early in 1915 Nemirovich wrote another letter, full of rage and frustration, going back once again over sixteen years of partnership. He complains that he is being shut out, that his contribution to the fame of the Art Theatre and to Stanislavski's own personal triumphs as an actor is being ignored. The cause is once again Stanislavski's impossible nature:

'Your monstrous ambition, which is supposedly burned out but isn't and never will be – intolerance of anyone near you.

. . . Why can't you come to terms with the fact that you are not God? That you are just a man? And that you are dear to us because we know your considerable human qualities and are happy to forgive your simple human failings?' (N-D Archive, No. 1703.)

It was in such an atmosphere that work began, in 1916, on Dostoievski's *The Village of Stepanchikovo*, which was scheduled for rehearsal alongside as Blok's *The Rose and the Cross*. Stanislavski was once again to play Colonel Rostanev, a role he had created in 1891, although this time it was Nemirovich who, in collaboration with V. M. Volkenstein, was responsible for adaptation. Rehearsals began on January 11. Stanislavski, who was directing with Moskvin as his assistant, allowed Volkenstein to read the play to the assembled cast so that they should have some notion of the script as it stood. The next day there was a discussion on the author and the tone of his writing. This was an evident demonstration of goodwill towards Nemirovich and his views, but little more than a token gesture. Stanislavski immediately turned the early rehearsal period into a course in the System. He was at pains, on day one, to stress his own concept of the actor-creator, distancing himself quite clearly from Nemirovich. The artist:

'. . . must experience the play not only in the terms laid down by the author but in all the circumstances which only his own imagination can create. It is that mastery of the inner, living spirit of a role which constitutes the actor's creative state. When a role is created in such a way it is better to avail oneself of the life laid down by the author than to create an inferior life for oneself. And then once more the author comes together with others who are creating the performance so that they flow together for ever, meet and can never again be separated. We start with the author's creation and come back to the author.' (K.S. Archive, No. 1351.)

He emphasized the relationship between the conscious and the unconscious and put a strict limit on the function of units and objectives. They were no more than a preparation:

'Only the creative objectives of a role should be conscious, the means by which they are attained are unconscious. *The unconscious through the conscious*. That is the watchword which should guide our coming work.' (K.S. Archive, No. 1353.)

The actor's approach to a role must be concrete:

'Put yourself in the circumstances of the character as portrayed and put the questions: what would I do in such a circumstance, what do I want, where am I going; stimulate your will. Answer them with verbs which express actions and not with nouns which express ideas and concepts.' (K.S. Archive No. 1388/1.)

Rehearsal, therefore, begins not with literary analysis but with an examination of the circumstances, the facts, the incidents, what happens. This acts as a stimulus to the imagination and the unconscious and evokes memories of personal experience:

'As an artist gets into a part, penetrates deep into it, unconsciously selects his feelings, the incidents, facts, which he knows and has experienced in daily life he becomes unconsciously entwined through feelings with the spirit and life of the part. With habit and time, believing everything he has been working on, the artist, unbeknown to himself, acquires, through proximity some elements of feeling and motivations which the part has implanted deep within him. This conjunction, person plus part, begins to live on stage as natural, lived life but is distinguished from his normal everyday life. The more the person approximates to the part the stronger, tighter, more compact this connection becomes. This transmutation seems like a wonder but at the same time it is quite simple and real and can be observed in life every minute.' (K.S. Archive, No. 1350.)

His statements, taken down by a young member of the cast during the series of lectures Stanislavski gave between January 11 and 16, represent a significant shift of public position. Whereas action previously had been taught as the expression of a previously-established 'emotional state', it is now action itself which predominates and is the key to the psychological. Indeed, within a few years, Stanislavski, somewhat perversely, was to deny having any knowledge of 'emotional states'. Throughout the rehearsal period the cast were given exercises to help the synthesis of the personal and the textual. It is important to note also that there is no suggestion of the premeditated use of Emotion Memory. Personal experience is brought into play unconsciously. Here, in embryo, is the System in its final form, the Method of Physical Action, which Stanislavski was to evolve in the last years of his life.

Stanislavski had similar difficulties recreating Colonel Rostanev to those he experienced with Ripafratta. In 1891 he had found immediate sympathy with the brow-beaten officer, who was bullied by his mother and exploited by the Tartuffe-figure, the evil, hypocritical servant, Foma. It had been one of those rare occasions when he had stepped straight into the skin of a character. Now matters were much more complicated. He was demanding greater psychological depth and insight. The world, too, had moved on and the political context in which the play was being staged was very different, the atmosphere was more highly charged. It was no longer a matter of presenting a gallery of Gogolian grotesques. The play was about the conflict of two principles, good and evil, Rostanev and Foma. But the search for the through-line that would express that conflict concretely in terms of character became more and more difficult and more and more complicated. In the earlier production he had been able to change in one crucial scene from good-natured compliance to towering rage. He had been able to reconcile the opposing tendencies in the character. But he now found it impossible to play a direct conflict between good and evil. At the January 18th rehearsal he stated:

'It seems to me that we made a mistake last time in trying to discover the through-line in conflict, in war.

Conflict, war against evil, the eradication of evil demands a strong Rostanev of which I am not capable.

The through-line may well be a longing for the idyll, simple love of life and a striving towards it.

That is on Uncle's [Rostanev's] side and on Foma's, the destruction of that idyll.

This newly discovered through-line essentially alters the objectives and the units we have established. I, Rostanev, do not even attack, I defend, I surrender to judgement – take me, devour me. I do not destroy evil, but defend the idyll. Striving for love of life and protecting it puts me in the position of defending goodness.' (Rehearsal notes, K.S. Archive, No. 1388/2.)

By 'idyll' he had in mind a Tolstoian notion, a longing for the preservation of peace, harmony, quiet and goodness, which he may well have derived from Suler. He began to see the character in Christ-like terms. Rostanev:

'. . . can say nothing but stands like Christ before Pontius Pilate.' (K.S. Archive, No. 9924.)

On the 19th he noted that perhaps the through-line was his love for his fiancée, Hastienka, and his desire to protect her. That would give the spine of the play. He felt that his imagination was more deeply engaged. However, by the beginning of February he had returned to his notion of the idyll but in a more active sense: it was the striving towards the idyll which was important.

The play was also beginning to acquire contemporary overtones. On January 22 he stated that Foma shared certain traits with Rasputin and, indeed, Dostoievski's text, published in 1859, is strangely prophetic in its description of the character. On March 18 he announced:

'The village of Stepanchikovo is Russia itself. It even has its own Rasputin. (Foma).' (Rehearsal Notes, K.S. Archive, No.1388/5.)

He worked in equal detail on Foma's through-line, helping Moskvin to build his performance, in counterpoint to his own.

Rehearsals went on right through to the summer break. For the first time in 12 years there was no Petersburg tour. What was the point, Stanislavski wrote to Mrs Gurevich, when they had nothing new to offer? The need for a première of some kind was becoming more and more pressing. Nemirovich hoped for an autumn opening but Stanislavski made it quite clear in a letter on August 11 that there was no hope of that. Too much time, he claimed, would be needed to revamp old productions that were being brought back into the repertoire. The fact was that he had no hope of being ready as he battled with the detail of his and other characterizations on the one hand and the philosophical significance of the play on the other. Matters were not helped when in the autumn of 1916 Moskvin was mobilized, although he was discharged not long after. Nemirovich was convinced that the play would never be ready. Stanislavski and Moskvin had taken 156 rehearsals between them and the end was still not in sight.

In February 1917 Nemirovich took over. For the next five weeks he and Stanislavski were at cross purposes. Not for the first time Nemirovich suggested an interpretation which went totally against everything that had been worked on previously. After more than a year's work Stanislavski was supposed to turn his whole performance round and adapt to Nemirovich's line on the grounds that it was more faithful to the author. Nemirovich wanted Rostanev played as a retired officer and a boor:

'. . . a fanatic, in that when there is talk of good he forgets everything, the agitation in the household etc., and is simply carried away by pleasure (the sense of goodness in caring for peasants.)' (Stanislavski, Note written after rehearsals, K.S. Archive, No. 1562.)

On March 8, 9 and 10 he worked alone with Stanislavski, with negative results:

'I'm often so ill at ease that the whole part is flattened out, it becomes muddy. We must [define] the through-line more clearly (in Dostoievski it is very clear). (Ibid.)

Three days later Stanislavski was both angry and frustrated:

'I may not be able to give birth to Dostoievski's Rostanev but I can to a son we both produce, who will bear many resemblances to both mother and father. But Nemirovich, like all literati, wants this mother and father to produce another mother and father in their own image. What's the point if they already exist? I can only give Rostanev/Stanislavski or at the very worst Stanislavski/Rostanev. Literary critics can give one Rostanev. He will be dead, like their critical essays. Let's absolutely not have that but something living. It's better than something that's identical but dead.' (K.S. Archive, No. 3174.)

By the dress rehearsal on March 28. Stanislavski had neither a fully prepared performance of his own nor had he adapted to Nemirovich's ideas. He was caught between the two and could not pull the role together. Towards the end of the play the other members of the cast saw him standing in the wings in tears. They waited for him to recover. Finally he said, 'On!' and the rehearsal was somehow completed. Immediately after the curtain came down Nemirovich took swift and decisive action. He removed Stanislavski from the cast and replaced him with Massalitinov. The cast waited for an explosion but none came. Stanislavski's iron sense of discipline prohibited any open disagreement. The deep hurt he felt was endured in silence, in public at least.

Nemirovich's action was so iron-fisted that the question inevitably arises whether he was settling old scores. Yet in taking the line he did he merely remained faithful to his own aesthetic philosophy: the author first, last and always. That Stanislavski was in part responsible for his own dismissal is undeniably true. He was asking too much of himself. Endlessly self-critical during rehearsal, never believing he had got it right, always searching for some perfect but perhaps unattainable theatrical truth, he prepared to go on until he did find it. Members of the cast who had watched the performance grow were convinced it was only a matter of time before it came together. But how much time? Nemirovich had been patient. In addition to the hundred and fifty six rehearsals already taken prior to his taking over, Nemirovich took forty more rehearsals before sacking Stanislavski. The play had to open on schedule if the theatre was to retain any credibility. Another season could not be allowed to go by without a new production. There was no time to wait for Stanislavski to get things right to his own satisfaction.

Yet if Stanislavski was asking too much of himself impossible demands were being placed on him. During the 1916 season in addition to rehearsing *Stepanchikovo*, he was playing leading roles – Vershinin, Gaev, Satin, Krutitiski, Ripafratta, Lubin – working on *The Rose and the Cross* and taking rehearsals for the Second Studio's opening presentation *The Golden Ring*. At the same time he dealt with an industrial dispute at his factory and coped with a walk-out of props men at the theatre. At a more personal level he suffered the loss of his beloved Suler who died on December 17 after a serious illness. At the funeral Stanislavski wept like a child.

In the circumstances, therefore, to succeed as Rostanev, Stanislavski needed sympathetic handling. But, as Stakanovich had remarked many years earlier, Nemirovich would always rather be one-up than help Stanislavski when he was in trouble. Lilina was in no doubt that Nemirovich's abrupt and in many ways insensitive handling of Stanislavski in rehearsal was the main cause of the catastrophe. In a letter to Mrs Gurevich, written after Stanislavski's death, she stated:

'I will give you a brief account of what happened. Vladimir Ivanovich wanted to instil something of his own attitude towards the role into a character that was already prepared, something very faithful from the literary point of view, but Konstantin Sergeievich really could not accept it or perhaps simply didn't understand how to deal with it and the whole part, or rather, all relish for the part was lost. The flavour was lost. But when he played without being told what to do, you could not watch his interpretation without tears in your eyes. The part was wonderful.' (In *M. P. Lilina*, VTO (1960)).

Stanislavski stayed away from the theatre and Nemirovich did not refer to the matter again until early September when he wrote justifying what he had done. He appears to have suspected Stanislavski of criticising him behind his back. He assured Stanislavski of his good will and reaffirmed the contents of the conciliatory letter he had written the previous January. As far as *Stepanchikovo* was concerned he had done what was necessary, in spite of personal feelings. Nonetheless he could not resist placing the blame for the whole unhappy business on Stanislavski's shoulders. Always the perfect manager, Nemirovich stated:

'Faced with an "affair" with a budget of a million, directors' vanities must give way.' (N-D Archive, No. 1724.)

Stanislavski, in reply, denied all charges of gossip, rebutted the accusation of vanity, expressed his pleasure at not being in the production but indicated that his days with the main company were perhaps numbered:

'I have no thought at all about future roles, there is nothing more I can do, not in the Art Theatre, at least. . . . Maybe I could be reborn in another sphere, another place. Of course, I am not talking about other theatres but about the Studios. *Othello free!* [in English in the text].' (SS, VII, p. 643.)

Later in the month Nemirovich wrote again, after the final dress rehearsal on the 24th, still, apparently trying to prove his point:

'This public dress rehearsal was a great success, especially with the literary part of the audience.' (N-D Arch, No. 1723.)

The same day all forty-seven members of the company, including Nemirovich, sent Stanislavski a letter, expressing sympathy and gratitude. A waxen-faced Stanislavski arrived at the theatre on the first night, September 26. He brought gifts for the young members of the cast. To each one he gave a parcel. It contained a large pear and an apple, rare treats in a period of war-time shortages.

Whatever the rights and wrongs of this complicated and unhappy affair, Stanislavski's career as an actor of new roles was over. His confidence was gone. Nemirovich's comment that he had been dropped because he had 'failed to bring the part to life' obsessed him and he would refer to it months after, in private conversation. He never again created a new character, although he took over the part of Shuiski in *Tsar Fiodor* during the 1923–1924 foreign tour. That, however, was a part he knew backwards. In his draft notes for *My Life in Art* there is a chapter-heading, *The Village of Stepanchikovo, My Tragedy*. It was never written.

CHAPTER TWENTY

REVOLUTION

Everyone connected with the Art Theatre's management had long been aware that while the Studios were flourishing the main company was in a state of crisis. The repertoire was stagnant. There were no new writers and no experiment. Much of the blame was conveniently put on the First Studio, which was demonstrating the dynamism the main theatre lacked. Not that it had always expressed itself in ways which met with Stanislavski's approval. In October 1913 Vakhtangov directed his first play, Hauptmann's *Das Friedensfest*. The production was extremely tendentious, stressing the negative aspects of the situation and presenting overt social criticism, violating Stanislavski's basic tenet that a play should always present counterbalancing forces and reveal its meaning to an audience rather than force it on them. After the dress rehearsal Stanislavski, white-faced and more furious than anyone had ever seen him, threatened to cancel the show. Sulerzhitski and Nemirovich supported him. It was only as a result of Kachalov's intervention that the production was allowed to go forward. Had Stanislavski believed less in Vakhtangov's talent his anger might perhaps not have been so great. The incident caused an artistic breach between them that was never fully resolved, although personal relations continued affectionate and they engaged in regular argument.

Nemirovich viewed the growth of the Studio with disquiet ever since in the autumn of 1914 it had moved into more spacious premises thus confirming its increased importance. Early in 1915 he formed a committee to monitor its activities calling a meeting on May 15. Stanislavski was not invited. Nemirovich had made it quite clear in a letter on January 9 that, given the poor state of their relationship, there was no point in their seeing each other. He would negotiate through formal channels. Luzhski's notes from the January meeting reveal the depth of resentment aroused by the success of the Studio. The general opinion was that it had done irreparable damage to the main company. It had to be separated from the main house and reorganized on a new basis. The hidden agenda was to get Stanislavski out of the Studio and back to the centre.

A meeting of shareholders was called for December 15 but Nemirovich's proposals foundered on Stanislavski's refusal to go back on his decision to quit management. A further shareholder's meeting was called in the following year on April 2, 1916. In the absence of any new arrangements, the 1911 agreement was extended for a further period. Nemirovich was re-elected managing director with full powers.

If the shareholders were unhappy, so was Stanislavski. On August 11, he sent Nemirovich one of the longest business letters he had written since their early days. He pointed out the ambiguity of his position. He had no formal power but nonetheless the theatre was identified with him both in the public mind and in the business world. Whatever formal arrangements might be made internally and however little power he possessed in reality he still had to underwrite certain financial liabilities since it was his name the banks trusted. The theatre was trading on his goodwill. He would continue to be supportive, but the theatre must be sound – and not just financially. It must be forward-looking, otherwise he would rather achieve his artistic ends elsewhere. At another level, it was he who suffered from gossip and adverse comment when the company got into trouble. Standards both back-stage and off-stage had reached an all-time low. Persistent heavy-drinking and general bad behaviour were beginning to provoke adverse press comments and the question being asked was why he, Stanislavski, allowed it? What was he supposed to do? The matter could be resolved by separating the Studio, which was his, from the Art Theatre for which Nemirovich was responsible, and by making that distinction clear to the public. He would base himself in his own studio at home. Nemirovich could come to him at any time to ask him either to take on a production or, in the event of a crisis, to provide financial support. Nemirovich still persisted in trying to persuade Stanislavski to rejoin the management and enter into a new agreement. This resulted in a sharp-toned response, written on December 4, in which Stanislavski absolutely and catergorically refused to sign any legal contract. He asked that the matter never be referred to again.

His answer to the problem of stagnation was precisely the one his colleagues would find least acceptable: the creation of yet more studios. In March 1917, he talked extravagantly of the need for fifteen of them. His many contacts abroad led him to the notion of creating an international studio bringing together artists from across the world to study the System. Jacques Copeau had written to him the previous October describing conversations he had had with Craig and others which had convinced him that there was much in common between the Vieux Colombier which he had launched in 1913 and the Art Theatre. There were, he said, too few people in the world who were unswervingly dedicated to art for them not to meet. Stanislavski wrote to him on January 1 1917 outlining his scheme. Copeau received the letter while on tour in the United States and replied offering his full cooperation. Between Stanislavski's letter and Copeau's response the February revolution occurred.

Stanislavski was not a political sophisticate. He had no conception of the ideological issues involved and no knowledge of Marxist theory. It was not, indeed, until 1926 that he even considered reading the basic texts of Lenin. But as an inheritor of the democratic aspirations of the nineteenth-century intelligentsia and as a patriot he believed that the revolution was in the best interests of his country and he welcomed it.

In a letter to the literary historian, Kotliarevski, on March 3, he described recent events as 'the miraculous liberation of Russia'. He regarded the overthrow of an absolutist government as an opportunity to realize the goals he had set himself twenty years earlier – new plays, new audiences the enrichment and enlightenment of the common people through art. That liberation however, involved a high degree of personal loss. The Alekseiev factories were taken into state ownership and within a short space of time converted to the production of steel cables. His private fortune was gone suddenly and he himself potentially suspect as a member of the propertied classes, one of the 'has-beens'. In May he wrote to Kotliarevski's wife that his house had already been 'done over' and he expected it would be again, this time thoroughly. He was looking for a new apartment not merely because he was about to be evicted but because he could no longer afford to live where he was. The rebirth of a nation, he wrote, inevitably involves disruption.

All Stanislavski had now was his salary from the theatre. Modest as his life-style had been in comparison with the rest of the *haute bourgeoisie* he could no longer maintain it. The stoicism he had developed when trapped in Germany in 1914 served him well. Just as he had then defined the patriotic duties of an artist in the war, so now, in the period of turmoil between February and October, he defined the duties of the artist in a new society. His notes for an article, *The Aesthetic Education of the Popular Masses*, gave a clear message to the leaders of the revolution: not by bread alone.

'Let there be no end to the opening of schools, people's universities, let there be general education classes and seminars, lectures etc., to encourage the intellectual development of the masses. But knowledge alone is not enough. It is essential to educate the people's sensibility, their souls. One of the most important human senses, one which distinguishes him from the animals and raises him to heaven, is the *aesthetic* sense. That is a divine spark planted in man. . . .

The aesthetic domain, that is our domain. Therein lies our most important work in the construction of Russia. It is in that domain above all that we must fulfil our civic duty.' (SS, VI, p. 23.)

Even in 1922, when as a result of the Civil War and the War of Intervention conditions were worse than ever, he was still resolute:

'Theatre for the starving! Starvation and Theatre!

There's no contradiction here.

Art is not a luxury in the lives of the people but a daily necessity. It is not something you can manage without but something absolutely essential to a great people. The theatre is not an idle pastime, or an agreeable plaything it is a cultural undertaking of importance. . . .

You cannot put the theatre in storage for a time, put locks on its workshop doors, bring its life to a halt. Art cannot go to sleep to be woken up when we feel like it. Rather it goes to sleep for ever and dies. Once stopped it dies. . . . And even should it rise from the dead that will be in a hundred years time. The death of Art is a national disaster. . . . Time will pass and famine will be conquered. Wounds will heal. And then we shall be thanked for saving Art in a time of martyrdom.

We are all the more happy that today we offer the Art which we are saving for the people to aid those same starving people.' (*Theatre for the Starving*, SS, VI, p. 118.)

In August he drafted plans for the new Union of Moscow Artists in which he set out a policy for all theatres. He was quite clear that the theatre's work must be limited to purely artistic activities. In November he successfully opposed a call by some colleagues for a token strike against the new government, maintaining that it would be detrimental to their work. Their task was to preserve Russia's cultural heritage and hand it on in living form to the people.

Where the February revolution had not even caused the theatre to change its schedule, the October revolution, like the revolution of 1905, brought about its temporary closure. A guest performance of *The Cherry Orchard* was given on October 26, at the Theatre of the Soviet of Workers' Deputies. The audience dispersed after midnight to the sound of gun-fire. In the streets outside the wounded were being carried away on lorries. The next day the theatre closed and the Studio was occupied by revolutionary forces. On November 5 the company assembled to consider its future. It was decided to send a representative to the Moscow Soviet to ask how the Art Theatre could best serve the people. The answer came back: start work again as soon as possible. The theatre reopened on November 17.

Stanislavski was convinced that without a radical change in outlook the theatre could not survive. Nemirovich had achieved the remarkable feat of paying off the debts and putting the theatre on a firm financial basis but in so doing he had abandoned the spirit of adventure which had characterized the company in its early days. The theatre needed revitalizing, rejuvenating. This would be difficult in view of the entrenched attitudes which prevailed.

On December 5, 1917 and at a later meeting on the 31st, Stanislavski and Luzhski presented a new plan to Board. All new productions, including those for the main house, should be prepared at the Studios. He proposed the partial separation of the First and Second Studio from the theatre and the creation of a Third Studio. He made it clear that he would neither prepare new roles nor direct new plays except under this arrangment. Nemirovich stood firm. The Studios and the main theatre were different establishments, with different methods. The Studios could never supply more than interesting experiment. They could not have the impact of the main house. Not all plays needed lengthy preparation. Rather unkindly perhaps he cited *Stepanchikovo* as an example of an unnecessarily time-consuming production. He also pointed to the adverse effect on the budget.

Stanislavski continued to formulate new plans and on May 22nd of the following year delivered one of his most critical speeches ever to the shareholders. The theatre had lost its soul, its sense of social purpose, it was complacent, concerned only with full-houses and the box-office and failing to keep up with recent artistic developments. Their task was to save Russian theatre. His solution was an up-dated version of schemes he had put to Nemirovich many years before and which Nemirovich had rejected. Whereas then he had proposed a network of regional theatres, under the aegis of the Art Theatre, he suggested now the creation of a 'Pantheon' of Russian theatre, with the Art Theatre at its centre, controlling a series of studios and youth theatres which would play in Moscow and the surrounding districts, go on tour, and teach by giving seminars for professionals.

Nemirovich's objections still stood: the theatre had not been able to spread its resources too thinly 13 years before and it certainly could not do so at a time of revolution, war and economic collapse when even the bare necessities of life were unobtainable. Stanislavski could not offer any practical suggestions as to how his plan might be implemented. He probably had not thought about it. As far as his colleagues could see he was once again displaying all the traits of character which had caused them to mistrust him in the past as an impossible dreamer, a 'muddle-head'. His idealism was impossible to live with but he made no demands on other people that he did not make on himself. He had accepted the loss of his privileges and property. He made constant efforts to make sure members of the company had food and fuel but asked nothing for himself, not even in 1920, when he was about to be evicted. He wept in private but made no application for the eviction order to be withdrawn. It was only when Lunacharski went direct to Lenin that it was agreed he could stay until he could be rehoused.

Justified as the theatre might be in practical terms to reject his ill-thought-through schemes, where was its alternative response to the situation created by the revolution? It was more vulnerable to attack than it had ever been. Meierhold had been an unrelenting critic over the years, never losing an opportunity to challenge the contemporary relevance of the Art Theatre's work. In May 1915 he attacked the First Studio's highly successful production of *The Cricket on the Hearth*, adapted from Dickens' story, describing it as 'key-hole theatre'. He followed that up by an assault on the Pushkin evening when Stanislavski played Salieri. Benois had, unwisely perhaps, gone into print in *Rech*, to defend the Art Theatre's style and approach to the three classic plays. Meierhold replied with a long and devastating article in which he deployed the full force of his intellectual gifts and polemical skill. But it was the theatre and, in particular, Nemirovich whom he loathed, that he attacked, not Stanislavski. He had told Aleksandr Blok very firmly in December 1912. 'I am a pupil of Stanislavski.' It was a position he maintained albeit not uncritically. Indeed, it was a standing joke among his friends in the Twenties that when he went to see Stanislavski he put on his best clothes like a schoolboy. Meierhold's insistence that theatre should be theatrical received support particularly among the younger members of the intelligentsia including, in time, Vakhtangov and members of the First Studio. A work of art should not attempt to present itself as 'natural', but should reveal itself as a human construct, as an artefact, making its means of communication evident. This aesthetic found its theoretical formulation in the work of Viktor Shklovski, who developed the notion of *ostranenie*, making strange, the precursor of Brecht's *Verfremdung*. By the 1920s the movement had emerged as Formalism.

Meierhold received, initially at least, support from another emergent director, Aleksandr Taïrov. Taïrov had founded the Kamerni (Chamber) Theatre in 1914 in a search for a style of presentation that was more formally structured and choreographed. His leading actress and also his wife was Alisia Koonen, who had left the Art Theatre in 1913 after playing a number of important roles including Myltyl in *The Blue Bird*. She had originally been scheduled to play Ophelia in the Craig *Hamlet*. Her greatest quality as an actress was expressive movement and she used this ability to give life to her husband's conceptions. By 1916 the Kamerni was using Cubist design, pointing the way towards developments in the Twenties. Taïrov and Meierhold collaborated in 1917–1918 on a production of Claudel's *L'Échange* and there was some discussion with Evreinov concerning the creation of a new left-wing theatre.

A new generation of critics was also to be reckoned with. Prominent among them were Mikhail Zagorski, later a close friend of Meierhold at the Meierhold Theatre, and Vladimir Blum who represented the sharp ideological edge of the opposition. Blum was uncompromising in his attacks on the Art Theatre, its Studios and all they stood for. Apart from a grudging recognition of Stanislavski's personal gifts as an actor, which he could scarcely deny, he had nothing positive to say. All the Art Theatre's opponents agreed on one thing, it was no more than a nineteenth-century relic, a monument to a now-outmoded naturalistic style, essentially reactionary in its attitudes. Blum summed up the general judgement in 1923:

'The Art Theatre died a natural death on that same night, the 25 to 26 October, when a mortal blow was dealt to that class whose finest essence its magnificent productions distilled. That theatre carried the banner of Russian bourgeois theatre high until the end of its days.' (*Zrelischa* 1923, No. 59, pp. 8–9.)

Such conflicts were, however, contained within a common set of cultural and aesthetic references; they assumed a certain historic context. But the Revolution had released forces of a much more radical kind, such as the *Proletkult*. The notion of the *Proletarian Cultural and Educational Organizations* had been launched by a conference of revolutionary exiles in Capri in 1909 attended by Lunacharski, Gorki and the philosopher and scientist Aleksandr Bogdanov who became its leader. It came into being officially early in 1917. The intention was to create an organization which would operate in parallel with revolutionary political groups and create a new, working-class, cultural consciousness that would match social and economic changes. For Lunacharski this new culture would be based on two major elements: the traditions of the past, rethought and restructured, and new creations springing from the as yet untapped creative potential of the working masses. There was, however, a hard-left faction within the movement which demanded no less than the total abolition of all prerevolutionary art and the creation of a new art which would spring from the masses and be comprehensible to them.

Proletkult was well organized and ready for revolutionary change. It moved fast. It held its first Conference in February 1918 when it drew up a programme for the creation of a network of Workers' Clubs and Studios based on works and factories. Where they could, they took over existing amateur groups. The intention was to train actors, directors and writers who would remain in vital contact with the masses and replace the current 'professionals'. The next fifteen months were spent implementing that programme as rapidly and effectively as circumstances would permit.

The leaders of the revolution, Lenin and Trotski, were not sympathetic to either of the tendencies within *Proletkult*. Lenin had already attacked Bogdanov and the Capri group for departing from orthodox Marxism in what he considered to be one of his most important works, *Materialism and Empiriocriticism* (1909). When he revised the work in 1920 he included a specific attack on *Proletkult*, mistrusting above all its claim to independence from party control. Trotski was equally sceptical of the notion of a 'proletarian' culture in a post-revolutionary, and therefore classless, society. How can you have 'proletarian' culture if there is no 'proletariat'?

Lenin was quite clear that audiences needed more than muscular slogans; they needed the lyrical, the poetic; they needed Chekhov. In conversation with Gorki he made it plain that of all theatres the Art Theatre had to be preserved. When Russian theatres were reorganized in December 1919, the Art Theatre, like the former Imperial theatres, was designated a state 'Academic' theatre with full independence, thus acquiring official, and subsidized, status.

During the two years following the revolution Lenin became a regular visitor, catching up with those productions which he had missed during his long years of exile – *The Village of Stepanchikovo*, *The Seagull*, *The Cherry Orchard*, *Uncle Vania*, and *The Lower Depths* which he found theatrical in the wrong sense and lacking in authenticity of detail. He particulary admired Stanislavski's performance as General Krutitski in *Enough Stupidity in every Wise Man* and in conversation after the show implicitly endorsed Stanislavski's refusal to indulge in didactic theatre:

> 'Stanislavski is a real artist, he transformed himself into the general so completely that he lived his life down to the smallest detail. The audience don't need any explanations. They can see for themselves what an idiot this important-looking general is. In my opinion this is the direction the theatre should take.' (Quoted in N. I. Komarovskaia's *Videnoe i perezhitoe, Iskusstvo*, 1965, p. 139.)

Nonetheless, Lunacharski, now People's Commissar for Englightenment, although fully aware of Lenin's private views, pursued a pluralist educational and cultural policy. His ambition was still a new culture which would be a fusion of the present and the past. The Communist Party was not yet committed to a particular line on the arts. The moment had not yet come when a word from a party leader could cause a work to be banned. Only in May 1925 did Lunacharski venture a preliminary statement on the party's attitude to literature and this amounted to little more than a warning against two dangers: at one extreme, statements that supported the idealist notion of universal human verities; at the other, attempts, for narrow ideological reasons, to muzzle genuine artistic expression. The battle for the artistic soul of the newly-created Soviet society was on and faction fought with faction in a struggle of almost Byzantine complexity. The Art Theatre was ill-equipped to engage in such ideological in-fighting. It had always been proud of its refusal to commit itself to any one tendency, political or artistic. It had relied on the superior quality of its product to assure its position. Where was that superiority now?

Unable to obtain any planned or coherent support from his colleagues or to drag them out of their inertia, Stanislavski pursued his own campaign of reform. He was inspired by his own idealism but, at a more personal level, it is clear that he was anxious to prove, as later letters to Vakhtangov and Luzhskii demonstrate, that he was not a parasite on the new Soviet state but was making a full contribution to its development.

*

In the years 1918–1922 Stanislavski was active on many fronts: he continued to play major roles particularly for new popular audiences, taught the System, directed or revived productions both at the theatre and in the Studios, launched an Opera Studio and was active in the new Professional Union of Moscow Actors of which he became chairman. All this in the worst possible material conditions.

The Revolution gave Stanislavski the opportunity to fulfil a life-long dream: to bring the classics to a wider, popular audience. Performances were now given for factory workers and the army. But they were often uncomfortable occasions. Early in the life of the Art Theatre Stanislavski had had to educate his largely well-heeled audience into his notion of the theatre as place that must be respected, a temple, persuading them to arrive on time and to listen. Now he had audiences who had, by and large, no experience of theatre-going. They talked noisily, ate and drank, seemingly unaware that they could be heard on stage. For once the illusion of the fourth wall was not helpful.

Stanislavski was driven to deliver a sharp rebuke. The day-book for February 15, 1920 records that after Act Two of *Uncle Vania* Stanislavski went out in front of the curtain in full costume and make-up and asked for silence during the action as the noise made it impossible for the actors to do their job. His little speech worked. The rest of the performance was heard in silence. In *My Life in Art* Stanislavski maintains that he made similar appeals on a number of occasions. The result was that as he arrived the schoolboy cry, 'He's coming!' could be heard and a respectful hush would fall.

He was similarly displeased by the audience's habit in cold weather of keeping their fur hats on. The fact that there was no heating made no difference. Hats are not worn in a temple. He endured it as best as he could but when he came across a company member, in November or December, wearing his hat he remarked that what might be tolerated among a largely uneducated audience could not be excused in someone who should know better. The offending garment was quickly removed.

Stanislavski saw the Studios as a means of creating a new generation of actors and directors who would take over the Art Theatre and all its related activities. A major concern was to ensure a proper organic relationship between the 'old brigade' and young talent. This meant teaching the System. It would be the means by which the older and younger generations could be welded together. A continuous tradition would be created, starting with Shchepkin and going through, unbroken, into the new Soviet society, guaranteeing for future generations the survival of Realism in its highest form.

In January 1919 he inaugurated a series of seminars at the Art Theatre, known as Creative Mondays, where broad issues of theatre aesthetics were discussed. He followed this up with a series of lectures on the System from

October to December. His notes reveal his implicit criticisms of the overall work and standards of his older colleagues. At the same time he lectured at the Second Studio, where he was also working on the *Blue Bird*. Significantly he did not attempt any classes at the First Studio which was resolutely, not to say aggressively, following its own line of development. He watched Boleslavski's rehearsals of a Polish play, *Balladina* taking one session but disappearing three weeks before the opening, apparently displeased.

His most consistent teaching, however, took place outside the ambit of the Art Theatre. Part of it was directed toward the members of the recently formed Habima Theatre, a company of Jewish Palestinian actors living in Moscow. He had seen a preview of their work on September 30, 1918, nine days before their official opening. He agreed to start a Studio for them and put Vakhtangov in charge. Vakhtangov had just, as it were, come back into the fold and his own studio had become the Art Theatre's Third Studio. Between September 1920 and April 1921 Stanislavski gave over twenty sessions at the Habima, sometimes dealing with specific aspects of the System, such as Units and Objectives, Role Analysis, Rhythm, and on other occasions using scenes from *Woe From Wit* and *The Merchant of Venice* as teaching material. The culmination of this work came in 1922 with Vakhtangov's internationally famous production of *The Dybbuk*.

The first comprehensive account of the system that has come down to us was delivered not to members of the Art Theatre but to young singers studying opera.

CHAPTER TWENTY-ONE

OPERA

In the autumn of 1918 Elena Malinovskaia approached the Art Theatre to see whether it could not collaborate with the Bolshoi and help raise the standard of acting there. She had been given responsibility for the Academic theatres in Moscow and was determined to protect and develop them. She was also concerned to train a new generation of singers. What she foresaw was the creation of a studio.

A gala evening was arranged for December 30. After dinner, members of each company performed extracts from their repertoire. The occasion was a considerable success. Both theatres seemed more than happy to cooperate. In the event the collaboration merely highlighted the deep division that existed between Stanislavski and the Art Theatre. Nemirovich worked consistently on major Bolshoi productions while Stanislavski worked on his own in the two rooms that were set aside for rehearsals at the house in Carriage Row. In 1919 Nemirovich created the Art Theatre Music Studio with which Stanislavski had no connection.

Stanislavski proceeded with caution. It was many years since he had worked in the musical sphere although his own musical culture had continued to deepen. He was not at all sure how welcome his ideas would be. One of his duties was to help the lead singers. He was aware that many established opera stars were convinced that all they had to do was open their mouths and allow a magical larynx to do the rest. They could be resistant. On January 20, 1919 he gave a demonstration-lecture to senior members of the Bolshoi company. Some were genuinely interested and participated in the exercises; others listened politely on the side-lines. A month later he gave a preliminary talk to the company's younger singers. As a result a small but dedicated group made great efforts in the most adverse weather conditions to get to his house for lessons. The work was fragmentary. It was impossible ever to get a complete group together because of rehearsal schedules; tenor, soprano and baritone were present at different times and the final result had to be patched together at the last moment. Malinovskaia, according to Stanislavski's account, watched over the whole enterprise like a mother.

Yet he still needed convincing that he could be of genuine use. The only means of proving it was to submit his work to critical examination. At the beginning of March he began rehearsing a series of extracts from Dargomizhski's *Rusalka* and Rimski-Korsakov's *May Night*. The results were shown at a small private performance in June before Nemirovich and the Art Theatre company. Members of the Bolshoi were, evidently, not invited. There was no doubt in anyone's mind that the results were positive.

Stanislavski agreed to continue his work but subject to certain conditions. The kind of improvised arrangements he had been working under would not do in the long term. He had uncovered the full depth of the problems young singers encountered. They had voices but no sense of theatre. The Studio must be properly organised, with a coherent and comprehensive programme. It would accept young singers from the Bolshoi and students from the Moscow Conservatoire, who, once they had proved their worth in class, would be allowed to perform. His teaching was based on the fusion of two masters, Shchepkin and Chaliapin. The System was the means, Chaliapin was the goal.

The study programme consisted of two main areas: exercises in the System and in technique, which took place in the morning, and work on repertoire for the rest of the day. He drew on the resources both of the Art Theatre and the Bolshoi to bring in teachers. Volkonski was invited to give courses on diction and Pospekhin, from the Bolshoi ballet, to teach dance and expressive movement. Stanislavski himself attended the classes as part of his own research and retraining. He also took the opportunity to bring in his sister Zinaïda and his brother Vladimir to teach and supervise the general running of the studio. His own contribution was a series of 32 lectures on the System delivered between 1919 and 1922.

The experience of working in music theatre revitalised him. He felt, as he wrote to one of his pupils, that he had been starved of music. Here was a chance to escape from the routine of the Art Theatre, to re-examine his ideas, to test them out on young artists who came because they wanted to and who were not yet caught up in back-stage or front-of-house politics. It was also an opportunity to refute the accusation that the System only had validity for 'naturalistic' plays. If it could be made to work in opera, that 'irrational entertainment' as Doctor Johnson described it, with its seemingly insurmountable conventions, it could prove its universality and its claim to be rooted in the real world of nature.

His objective was to create a synthesis of words, music, movement and gesture. Actions, motivation, he insisted, were to be found in the score not in the stage directions which were often added later, without reference to the composer and in blatant contradiction to the music. A bar by bar examination of the structure of the music, its rhythm and of the particular colour of the orchestration would supply the information needed for a truthful performance. It was essential above all for the singers to take the music into themselves, to experience its rhythm and tempo internally as their own. They were no longer to stand with their eyes glued on the conductor, waiting for his beat. They should feel the beat not watch it. At the same time, in an ideal company, the orchestra would understand the System and would be aware of the dramatic as well as the musical significance of the score so that there would be unity of intent throughout the company and the performance.

Such ambitions are not achieved overnight and Stanislavski proceeded slowly. A primary task was to make the singers sensitive to the full potential of the words they were singing. He began with scenes from *Onegin*. This opera makes two major demands. In the first instance the libretto consists almost entirely of lines from Pushkin's original poem and is therefore very demanding on diction and delivery; in the second, it is an opera of great psychological depth with solo and two-handed scenes where any failure of imaginative insight is cruelly exposed. Stanislavski explored the text as he would with a dramatic actor, refusing to accept anything that was vague or generalized, insisting that the words should have precise, vivid images behind them. To *Onegin* he added scenes from *Rusalka* and worked on both throughout the 1919–1920 season. At the end of June there was a final dress rehearsal in costume and make-up without a public audience.

The students were, however, pushed into a public appearance rather sooner than Stanislavski wished. As a teacher he was unwilling to force the pace, he always wanted more time but the original intention had been to bring the Bolshoi and the Art Theatre closer together. By 1921 it was important to show some results. On April 18 members of the First and Second Studios and of the Bolshoi company presented a Rimski Evening at the Opera Studio. This was followed, on June 9, by another Rimski Evening given by the students of the Opera Studio this time at the Art Theatre itself. Stanislavski wisely restricted his pupils to the presentation of songs, which he had prepared with the same meticulous attention to detail that he applied to full-scale opera.

At the same moment he began rehearsing Massenet's *Werther*. Here again the choice of material was crucial. Apart from a group of children, *Werther* contains no chorus and no big set-pieces. Instead there is close interplay between the characters and, as in *Onegin*, monologues and two-handed scenes. Work continued throughout June and July side-by-side with rehearsals for a Pushkin evening which was presented at the Art Theatre on July 16. *Werther* opened on August 2 at the Art Theatre for a run of six performances in a modest staging using drops and screens. They were out of season and attracted little attention. It was with a studio performance of *Onegin* in the following year that the Opera Studio really made its mark.

The study of scenes from *Onegin* had run like a thread through all the Opera Studio's work. Now Stanislavski decided he would stage the whole work. Circumstances provided him with the ideal setting. On March 5, 1921, after a great deal of official haggling, involving Lenin himself, Stanislavski was rehoused at number 6, Leontievski Lane, a modest but attractive building, constructed during the Napoleonic period. On the first floor there was a large ballroom, just across the corridor from what were to be the family's living quarters. At one end was a raised platform, originally intended for the orchestra, with four sets of double pillars. When Stanislavski visited the house in January his first comment was, 'It will be perfect for *Onegin*'.

The production was designed to fit within the space. It was to be a chamber performance. This meant that the peasant scene in Act One, with its singing and dancing was severely curtailed. Stanislavski did not consider this a loss as he found the scene something of a conventional set-piece which held up the action. He wished to concentrate on the human drama.

Clarity of diction and the meaning of the words were a major concern. He wanted the singers to be aware, during ensemble numbers, of the important line and to adjust the balance accordingly, holding back where necessary to let one single, as Stanislavski called it, the 'word-thought' voice emerge. Typical of this was the opera's opening number, a quartet, or rather a double duet, Larina and the Nurse, Filipievna, on the one hand, Tatiana and Olga on the other. Tatiana and Olga are singing a duet while the other two reminisce. According to the published score Larina and the Nurse are making jam. Stanislavski considered this quite specious and could find no justification for it in the music. On the contrary he invited the two to sit back and relax after a hard day's work – on the terrace suggested by the columns and not under a tree as indicated in the libretto – and listen to the young people singing. Vocally the problem was to make both the duet and the conversation of the two older women intelligible. The solution was to place Tatiana and Olga inside the house, invisible to the audience, giving depth and perspective to both sets of voices. This also provided Tatiana with a more effective first entrance. Rehearsal time was devoted to ease and naturalness of movement so that the music for all its complexity could emerge from credible behaviour. The audience would be at close range and would detect any hint of artificiality.

Full rehearsals had begun in November 1921, transferring in March 1922 to Leontievski Lane. The performance was previewed in May and opened on June 15. The accompaniment was provided by a grand piano placed in the body of the hall. There was the minimum of set, no costumes and no make-up. The singers were on their own.

The evening created another Stanislavski legend. Two years later the production transferred with full orchestra to the Novi Teatr. Stanislavski's staging survived many years and many changes of cast. As for the famous ballroom columns they acquired the status of an icon. No production of

Onegin anywhere in Russia was possible without them. They turned up in every set. So much so that in the 30s Meierhold remarked that if there was one thing he wanted to do with Tchaikosvski's opera it was to ditch them once and for all. As for the ballroom, from that time onward it became known as the Onegin Room.

Stanislavski's work at the Opera Studio had a decisive influence on the development of his own ideas and of the System, in particular on the import-ance he gave to the notions of tempo and rhythm. A musical score provides basic speeds, an inner impulse for each part or unit of the action. That impulse is integral to the scene. Stanislavski carried this notion over into the dramatic theatre and from this period onward he was increasingly con-cerned in rehearsal to find the appropriate tempo-rhythm for each moment in the play. His thinking on the subject is summarized in *An Actor's Work on Himself, Part Two*.

Stanislavski's activities at the Opera Studio during this period are well documented. Pavel Rumiantsev, who sang the title role in *Onegin* kept a record of rehearsals from 1919 to 1932, which was ultimately published in 1969. Another singer, Konkordia Antarova, who sang Charlotte in the 1921 version of *Werther*, took detailed notes of all of Stanislavski's lectures on the System and of the *Werther* rehearsals. They were intended only for her private benefit but in 1938 Stanislavski's sister, Zinaïda, tracked them down. They were edited by Mrs Gurevich and published the following year. Stanis-lavski delivered the lectures off-the-cuff, using the brief jottings which appear in the *Notebooks*. They are, nonetheless, even allowing for some tidying up by Mrs Gurevich, clear and coherent.

It does not seem to have occurred to Stanislavski to publish them. This was a pity since he could have saved himself a great deal of trouble had an accurate statement of his views been available. He was continuously at a disadvantage in the ideological debates that raged from 1917 to 1934 be-cause his opponents were for the most part working on hearsay or on half-understood, distorted summaries offered for the most part by people outside the Art Theatre. Everyone in the theatrical world knew about 'the System' and a minor industry grew up explaining it.

In 1916 Fiodor Komissarzhevski, the son of Stanislavski's old teacher, put out a volume *The Creative Actor and the Stanislavski Theory*. It was fullsomely dedicated to Stanislavski and, in the view of the dedicatee, totally misleading. Stanislavski's enraged comments are to be found in the margin. The word 'lies' makes more than one appearance.

Michael Chekhov had also gone into print in 1919 in the Proletkult maga-zine 'Gorn' with a short article which was equally unsatisfactory. Stanislav-ski did not respond publicly. It was left to Vakhtangov who delivered a sharp attack on both writers in 'Vestnik Teatra' accusing them of inaccuracy and of treating isolated elements of the System out of context. It would take, he remarked prophetically, several volumes to describe the System in its complete form. Nothing deterred, however, in 1921, Smishlaiev, an actor at the Art Theatre and also at the First Studio, published his *Theory of Stage Production*, also published by Proletkult, in whose central Studio he worked. Stanislavski jotted down his adverse comments but did not make them public. He noted that Smishlaiev was simply an inadequate and backward pupil.

The scope and volume of Stanislavski's activities and the attention paid to his ideas merely served to emphasise the inertia of the Art Theatre itself. Between 1917 and 1922 it staged one new production and that was Stanislavski's. Initially, while relations with the First Studio were still tolerably good, he worked there, supervising and revising productions prepared by young directors. The revolution of February 1917 put him in a mood of determined optimism and his work is characterized by a search for positive elements. In May 1917 he saw work-in-progress on *Twelfth Night*, directed by Shushkevich. The production was in a lamentable state. Both cast and director were depressed. The play was shrouded in gloom. Stanislavski took over rehearsals and rebuilt the production stone by stone, continuing his work in the autumn. He insisted that the play was light, youthful, without a shadow in the sky. He imposed a rapid pace on the whole performance, driving his young actors to a state of near exhaustion. For the first time in his productions the action spilled over into the auditorium, with characters appearing behind the audience and running down the aisles. It was an overt display of 'theatricality'.

Vakhtangov, who had not yet come under Meierhold's influence, was both shocked and bewildered by Stanislavski's almost exclusive emphasis on the externals of the staging. What had happened to the System? Where was the inner psychological truth to justify the outer action? He felt that the image of the First Studio had been tarnished. At the same time he did not doubt that the production would be a huge success. And so it proved on the opening night, December 25. Three years later Lunacharski could still recommend it to Lenin as the best show in Moscow.

A similar determination to find positive elements in established works was evident in the reworking of *The Seagull* which was in rehearsal at the same time as *Twelfth Night*. Stanislavski was concerned to reverse the view of Chekhov as a pessimist. He took a much less negative view of Konstantin. For the first time he introduced the comparison between Konstantin and Hamlet. It must, of course, be remembered that he saw Hamlet as an active moral force and not as a melancholic intellectual.

'S. suggested an analogy between Hamlet and Treplev. For both of them at a difficult period in their lives there was only their mother. [The more his mother] was dear to him [Treplev] in that moment, the more he desired to reform her and the more he controlled himself. He decides to kill himself not because he does not wish to live but because he passionately wants to live, he snatches at everything that would enable him to root himself firmly in life but everything collapses round him. For him – an aesthete – there is nothing in life to keep him back [from death]. His through-line: *to live* to live beautifully, aspiring to Moscow, to Moscow. Chekhov was a man of action, he was not a pessimist. Life in the 80s was such that it created Chekhov's heroes. He himself loved life, aspired to a better life, like all his heroes.' (Notes by P. F. Sharov, production assistant, in the rehearsal Day-book, September 12, 1917, K.S. Archive, No. 4328/1.)

After *The Seagull* there was nothing. 1918 and the first half of 1919 were consumed by the vain struggle to push the theatre forward into the future. In October 1919, *Pravda* announced:

'The Art Theatre, which has not offered a single new production in the last three years, has decided to present Byron's *Cain* with L. M. Leonidov in the title role.' (*Pravda*, October 1, 1919, No. 218, p. 2.)

The decision to put on an obscure example of romantic drama, unknown even to British audiences, as a response to the post-revolutionary situation in Russia might appear strange. Stanislavski had originally planned to stage Byron's play in 1907 but had been prevented from doing so by the church. This poetic expression of revolt suited him temperamentally. The initiative to take the plan off the shelf did not, however, come from Stanislavski himself but from Leonidov to whom the lead role had originally been promised. On April 19, 1917 he wrote to Stanislavski asking for permission to stage the play at the First Studio. His intention appears to have been not only to play the title role but to direct as well. Boleslavski would play Abel and act as assistant director. A full cast-list was supplied. Naturally it was hoped that Stanislavski would give all the help he could.

No reply from Stanislavski is recorded. In the autumn of 1918, however, Leonidov read the play to the First Studio by which time Vakhtangov had taken over. He had written to Stanislavski in July with a final cast-list, slightly different from Leonidov's original. Ideas on staging had begun to form in Vakhtangov's mind. In his diary entry for November 24 he noted the importance of putting the play on. Interest in the project spanned the generations. This Mystery, for all its religious connotations, was felt to be relevant to current conditions. But in August 1919 the play was taken away from the First Studio and transferred to the main house. Stanislavski later, in *My Life in Art*, described the whole production as 'doomed from the start' and 'an abortion'. On June 1 the bulk of the Art Theatre company, including such key figures as Kachalov and Knipper, had started a tour of the Ukraine. They were immediately cut off by the Civil War and could not get back. They spent the next three years touring Europe. An emergency meeting was called for August 6. Stanislavski travelled back overnight from Kimri, near Moscow, together with Moskvin and Vishnievski, the only senior company members left, arriving at eleven in the morning. They had to walk across the whole of Moscow to get to Nemirovich's office. Decisions had to be taken as how best to deploy the theatre's remaining forces.

Under the circumstances it would have been logical to merge the studios with the main house and form one company. But Nemirovich had no wish to go cap in hand to the First Studio which he continued to regard with suspicion. As for the Studio itself, it was split into warring factions. The result was a stand-off: on the one hand, the Studio waiting to be asked to help, on the other, the Art Theatre waiting for help to be offered. Inevitably the two companies remained apart. The Art Theatre took its fate in its hands and decided that Stanislavski should direct *Cain*. Work was to begin immediately. Stanislavski retired once more to Kimri to work on the production plan.

He saw Byron's Mystery play, like *Stepanchikovo*, as a conflict between the cosmic principles of good and evil and his intention was to bring out the contemporary relevance. God is conceived as a 'conservative' and Lucifer as an 'anarchist'. The problem was, as with the Dostoievski, that he was trying to make the text bear more than it could reasonably carry and so, despite his statements early in rehearsal that what was needed was not theological discussion but a factual analysis of the action, as work progressed more and more time was spent on philosophical issues. In September Stanislavski read I. A. Ilin's book, *The Philosophy of Hegel as Doctrine of the Concrete Nature of God and Man* making extensive notes as he went along. The central issue was the origin of evil. If God is perfect and His creation is perfect, how does evil come into being?

Cain is conceived as the archetypal rebel. He is dominated by a feeling of injustice and futility, of marking him off from his family. His sense of alienation is the counterpart of Lucifer's own opposition to God, the opposition of the spirit of absolute freedom to the spirit of compromise. God simply wants to side-step the problem of the origin of evil:

'. . . God says: No, good and evil have to be, i.e., we must allow compromise. Lucifer responds: compromise begets rules and regulations, etc., which diminish and destroy freedom. There must be truth and freedom. Though mankind should perish and the world fall apart, when all is said and done, they will come to the truth and know everything. God affirms that such freedom leads to egotism and only through goodness and non-resistance to evil etc., can goodness come through. Lucifer affirms that

but for the existence of good and evil there would be bliss, paradise.'
(Rehearsal Notes, September 5, 1919, K. S. Archive.)

In Stanislavski's concept of the play, Cain and Lucifer enter into a symbiotic
relationship:

'. . . in that moment when the first man appears asking intelligent questions,
saying "Why?", Lucifer (*lux ferus* the bearer of light) appears. Lucifer is
an extension of Cain. That is "Why", "What for". Those spirits who
created the earth with God, having created it, could not agree as to what
it should be. Lucifer wanted to people the earth with gods but God created Man. And this Lucifer approaches, goes to Cain. . . . Don't you feel
what that encounter means when a man is approached by a super-being,
how he fears it, how he recoils from it, how he is drawn to it even though
there is no enticement. [Lucifer shows him] all the beauties of the world,
the boundlessness of space and leads him to the highest ecstasy. . . . And
then Cain comes to life again. He is now someone quite different. He is
filled with the spirit of denial.' (Stenographic record, November 21, 1919,
K. S. Archive, No. 834.)

There are therefore two fundamentally opposing views in the play: those
who like Adam, Eve and Abel say, 'Wonderful are Thy works, O Lord' and
those who, like Cain and Lucifer reply, 'Not so, the world was created
imperfect.' The extension of the conflict between Cain/Lucifer and God is
the conflict between Cain and his brother Abel. If Cain's through-line is
'Why?', Abel's is, 'I believe':

The secret lies in this, that for Cain the most important thing is cognition
(the tree of knowledge), for Abel it is life as it happens to be.
    The fact is there are two truths. For Cain the truth is in enquiry, for the
others the truth is absolute. (Ibid.)

It was important not to see Abel as a purely passive or a weak character.
Gaidarov, who was playing the role had his own views:

Gaidarov (Abel) detects in Abel hints of the future Christ. Abel's last words
– of reconciliation – are Christ's own words ('they know not what they do')

'Oh God! receive thy servant and
Forgive his slayer for he knew not what
He did – Cain, give me – give me thy hand. . . .' (Ibid.)

From this flowed the idea that mankind is descended from Cain, since Abel
died childless. Abel returns in the form of Christ.

These theological issues had then to be translated into political terms.
Lengthy discussions took place on the nature of revolution and the class
war. These discussions, in turn, had to be expressed in the performance.

Despite all the metaphysics the actors were given concrete, practical objectives. Stanislavski insisted that thought must be a direct, lived experience, an idea must be a 'living vision'. 'Thought,' he stated, 'cannot be understood by thought alone.' This was crucial in a play such as *Cain*, which is set in the childhood, the innocence of the world, when sophisticated intellectual processes did not exist. There was no sense, except for Cain, of today and yesterday. Everything was a permanent now. There was no division between what was thought and what was said. In consequence he ruled out any question of sub-text. Impulse and expression were directly linked. Equally he ruled out a suggestion from Shakhalov, who was cast as Lucifer, that he should play the character as more than human. An actor, Stanislavski replied, could not escape his human status. A superman could only be an extension of a man.

In his attempt to make the play relevant, particularly to the Civil War, Stanislavski would provide contemporary analogues. In Act Three, towards the end of the play, Eve has a climactic scene in which she realizes that Cain has murdered his brother and curses him:

'Let us assume that a depraved German soldier raped you during the offensive and then vanished. Having given birth to a child you try to forget the appalling truth, you pray, you resign yourself. The child is your first born. All the time, all your life you fear that the German will come out in him. Finally, one beautiful day, with your own eyes, you see in your son that very German in whose face you could not spit. Therefore you curse not the son but his father.' (Rehearsal notes, September 4, 1919, K. S. Archive.)

If the cast entered happily and willingly into the complicated rehearsal process, the atmosphere on the technical/design side was far less happy. Although, in *My Life in Art*, Stanislavski claims that he was aware of the need to be cost-conscious the production was conceived on the grand scale. He intended to use a full orchestra and chorus but to keep expenses down by having one adaptable set. The theatre, including the auditorium, was to become a cathedral. The actors would be dressed as monks performing a Mystery play. The set would be elaborately architectural, with statues of saints and gargoyles. The flight of Cain and Lucifer through space would be represented by their climbing a large staircase while the stars and planets would be represented by lamps at the end of poles held by the officiants. Changes of time of day or night would be indicated by the light which filtered through giant stained-glass windows. A huge tree with shining fruit would represent the tree of the knowledge of good and evil with two stones on either side to serve as an altar.

The idea had to be scrapped. There was not enough money either to build such a set or to employ the number of extras that would be needed.

Stanislavski and his designer, Andreiev, then came up with another approach. They would make use of one of Stanislavski's favourite earlier devices, black velvet. Against this background architectural elements for Act One and movable statues for Act Two would be set.

'In the scene in Hell the tormented spirits of the Great Figures of the past who had lived in an earlier world, were represented by huge statues, three times life-size. . . . We found a very simple method of making these movable statues. Andreiev modelled heads with torsos and arms. We placed them on the end of long poles and draped them in ordinary scenic canvas of a yellow very close to the clay from which statues are made. The material fell in large folds and spread out on the floor.

When these statues were placed against the background of black velvet, by dimming everything down and lighting them in a special way they seemed transparent and produced a weird impression. To show the flight of Cain and Lucifer, in the second act we built high platforms covered in black velvet which were in consequence invisible against a background of identical material. When Cain and Lucifer were on them the audience had the impression that they were floating between the ceiling and the stage floor. Extras dressed in black carried huge lamps of translucent mica on the end of long black poles to represent dead planets. The black extras and the black poles disappeared into the background of black velvet so that the planets seemed to float in the air.' (SS, I, p. 380.)

Even this proved impossible. There was simply not enough black velvet in the whole of Moscow to black out the entire stage. It had to be replaced by black canvas. Unfortunately canvas does not absorb light in the way velvet does. The carefully calculated light-effects did not really work.

If Stanislavski's frequent complaints are to be taken seriously, there was a lack of coordination on the technical side which meant the sets were not ready. People were not consulting each other. By the end of December Stanislavski was threatening to decline responsibility for the production and only to answer for the acting.

Even the acting, however, was proving problematic. There was a serious lack of discipline. Worse, the sets, compromise though they were, had the effect of highlighting the technical inadequacies of the cast, with the exception of Leonidov. A high standard of diction was achieved, with clear incisive speech, but the giant statues, and such architectural structures as could be managed for Act One, revealed the serious limitations of the actors' bodies and their inability to extend out from mere day-to-day movement into a more poetically expressive dimension. If there was one serious flaw in Stanislavski's training at this period it was in the area of physical expression. Despite his experiments with yoga and Dalcroze eurhythmics he had not studied the problem systematically enough. It was precisely in this area that younger directors, Meierhold, Taïrov and Vakhtangov were making advances. The hastily assembled cast, particularly the younger and inexperienced members, had no skills with which to respond to the demands of the production.

In *My Life in Art* Stanislavski claims that the play was put on before it was ready. In reality it was he who forced the issue. He was fully aware that another season could not be allowed to go by without a new production. In January he wrote in the rehearsal day-book:

'For the salvation of the theatre and its children it is *imperative, imperative, imperative, come what may*, for *Cain* to go on in the immediate future.' (Day-book, January 13, 1920.)

Cain opened on April 4 and survived eight performances. The audience was simply bewildered. Stanislavski had made a futile attempt at a public dress rehearsal on the 2nd to explain the play's relevance; from the opening music and chorus to the end the audience sat in numbed silence. Stanislavski tried to blame the production's failure on the audience who consisted largely of workers and peasants but then why did the cultivated people, the 'intellectuals', stay away? The fact remains that the decision to stage the play had been a huge error of judgement on everyone's part. The critics were hostile. The theatre seemed once more to have proved its irrelevance to contemporary life and its incapacity to break with its 'bourgeois' past. Zagorski concluded that not only was the Art Theatre incapable of 'revolution' it could not even achieve 'evolution'.

Meierhold came to Stanislavski's defence. In an article, *The Isolation of Stanislavski*, published in the spring of 1921, he described the production of *Cain* as a tragic failure but saluted Stanislavski's attempt to stage something large-scale and ambitious. He was still the Michelangelo of theatre art. If only he had chosen something else, not *Cain*. Meierhold spoke with the experience of another kind of Mystery play behind him. In the autumn of 1918 he had staged three performances of Maiakovski's *Mystery-Bouffe*. Shunned by professional actors, put on with the help of almost anyone who made themselves available, Maiakovski's aggressive, irreverent, iconoclastic text, bristling with contemporary allusions made its mark. In its 1921 version it was destined to become one of the classics of early Soviet theatre. Lenin might call it 'hooligan communism' but it spoke to audiences in a way that *Cain* could not. Meierhold argued that Stanislavski was a genius whose flair and originality were stifled by the mediocre ambitions and petty atmosphere of the Art Theatre. There was a theatrical animal waiting to be released. The price of salvation was for him to go it alone.

Meierhold was not alone in this view. Among Stanislavski's younger associates and pupils there was a growing sense that he must somehow be rescued. In conversation in November 1921 Vakhtangov expressed the need to get Stanislavski to break with the main house and move permanently into the First Studio. Someone had to open his eyes but who was that person to be?

The following year Vladimir Volkenstein published an eighty-page monograph, *Stanislavski*. Volkenstein had been at the very heart of the Art Theatre's affairs. He worked there as a dramaturg and had been responsible, with Nemirovich, for the adaptation in 1917 of *Stepanchikovo*. From 1913–1921 he had charge of the literary department of the First Studio after which he became Stanislavski's secretary. The book caused Stanislavski acute embarrassment. It underplayed Nemirovich's contribution to the Art Theatre and the final sections, 'A Spiritual Portrait of Stanislavski and Stanislavski's Fate', depicted him as a lonely figure, isolated in his conflict with Nemirovich and shackled by a dead realism. Volkenstein provides a graphic description of Stanislavski sitting alone on social evenings, like a votary, with a yawning void all round him. Stanislavski felt impelled to write to Nemirovich to disassociate himself from what his secretary had written. In his letter of September 22, 1922 he told Nemirovich that he had discussed the problem with several professional colleagues and had been advised that it would be a mistake for him to reply directly as it would only inflate the whole business further and make it seem as though he was putting on a rather coy display of nobility. He suggested that someone should be found to write a suitably sharp review. Yet Stanislavski was perhaps less embarrassed by the truth or falsity of the Volkenstein's statements, which were not entirely without foundation, than by the fact that his often bitter quarrel with Nemirovich, which both men had resolutely tried to keep private and 'within the family', had suddenly become public knowledge.

After *Cain* no further new productions were scheduled for the foreseeable future. The Art Theatre had to fall back once more on restaging old productions. Yet it was with Gogol's *Inspector General* that Stanislavski was able to re-establish his right to be heard in the debate on new theatrical styles. Officially it was a revival of the production of 1908 in which Kachalov had scored such a great success, but in reality it was a complete reworking of the whole staging. It was essential in Stanislavski's view to rethink the play in terms of changed circumstances. With Kachalov still abroad, the lead was given to Michael Chekhov. The 1908 production had been considered remarkable in its time for the degree of exaggeration it had displayed. By the early Twenties the obsessive preoccupation with non-'naturalistic' acting focused on the concept of the Grotesque, defined by Vakhtangov as acting that was both tragic and comic but which went beyond normal 'character acting' to extend into new dimensions of fantasy. An alternative definition was Imaginative Realism. His approach was demonstrated in Strindberg's *Erik XIV* which opened on March 29, 1921 with Michael Chekhov in the lead. The style was typified by the exaggerated, non-realistic make-up. Stanislavski wanted to demonstrate his own view of the Grotesque, which he had passionately advanced to the sick and dying Vakhtangov late in 1921. In 1929 Stanislavski, who was then ill, dictated an account of this discussion to his doctor, now published under the title *From the Last Conversation With Evengi Vakhtangov*.

His view was that the grotesque is a rarity, something only experienced and highly-talented actors can achieve, not a style that can be applied indiscriminately to any text. It has to be the expression of enormous creative energy, springing from the unconscious.

'. . . . real grotesque means the vivid, external, audacious justification of enormous inner content, which is so all-embracing as to verge on exaggeration. Not only must human passions be felt and lived through in the full vigour of all their essential elements but they must be concentrated and made manifest, graphic, irresistible in their expression, outrageous, bold, going to the brink of over-acting.' (SS, VI, p. 256.)

Without a compulsive inner drive the grotesque is

'. . . a pie without filling, a bottle without wine, a body without a soul.' (Ibid., p. 257.)

Gogol is an author who can withstand, indeed demands the grotesque and in Michael Chekhov, Stanislavski had an actor of genius who could achieve it without losing his essential humanity to become a mechanical clown or a gesticulating puppet. Chekhov had an exceptional ability to invent and execute stage business. Stanislavski cut all this away. All effort went into the creation of inner objectives, motivations, which would generate extraordinary, eccentric behaviour, the Grotesque as he understood it. To most people the performance seemed endlessly improvised; no one could tell what he would do next. Nemirovich found himself endlessly checking the script as one new reading after another came at him. Gogol's text was untouched.

For the rest of the cast, Stanislavski conceived the play as a study in mass hysteria, a madness which overtakes a whole community and swamps its reason. That he intended this interpretation to apply to his contemporaries is clear from one effect which he introduced at the end of the play. On the Mayor's line, 'What are you laughing at? Yourselves, aren't you?' the lights came full up not only on the stage but also in the auditorium. Moskvin threw the words straight out front, to the audience.

The production which opened on October 8, 1921 provided a much-needed success. For the first time in many years an Art Theatre presentation provoked a serious public debate. This was conducted in the tradition of the old 'thick' magazines in the pages of the first issue of the newly-created *Teatralnaia Moskva* and in the *Vestnik Teatra*, once an innocuous journal but now, under Meierhold's influence, the voice of the radical left.

It was Michael Chekhov's performance that was the most widely discussed and *Teatralnaia Moskva* launched the debate by calling attention to the wide and unremitting coverage it had received in the Moscow Press, most of it highly favourable. The counterattack was led by the *Vestnik Teatra*. One critic described Chekhov's performance as that of 'a total non-etity, insolent, loudmouthed, without a brain in his head'. An equally negative judgement came from Vladimir Blum who defined the performance as 'the same old snub-nosed little idiot Petrushka'. Earlier in the year he had described it as one of the most unpleasant spectacles the European theatre had put his way in the last eight to ten years. One positive voice was that of Meierhold's collaborator, Zagorski. He found the performance 'stupendous, awe-inspiring, Hoffmanesque, like a chimera' and at the same time 'joyful, endearing, full of light and fascination'. Meierhold himself disliked the production as a whole but confided to a friend that Chekhov's performance had provided a revelation of new methods of achieving the grotesque in acting. Just how many people realized the contribution Stanislavski had made to Chekhov's success is not certain.

Four days after *The Inspector General* opened Stanislavski began work on a revival of Tolstoi's *The Fruits of Enlightenment*, hoping perhaps to repeat his success but despite several months of effort he could not discover a line on the play which could speak to a modern audience and the production was abandoned.

CHAPTER TWENTY-TWO

AMERICA

By January 1921 Nemirovich had to admit that the Art Theatre was almost defenceless in the battle against what he later described as near-hooliganism. He himself had made a serious tactical blunder and provided fresh ammunition to his enemies by opening his new Music Studio in the summer of 1920 with a French operetta, *La Fille de Madame Angot*. Meierhold gave expression to the contempt felt by the avant-garde:

> 'Now we know what the Moscow Art Theatre audience consists of, leftovers of the bourgeoisie who couldn't manage to get a boat out ...' (*Vesnik Teatra*, Nos 834/4, 1921.)

Maiakovski too had added his powerful voice to the opposition. In 1920 he wrote an open letter to Lunacharski describing the theatre of Anton Chekhov and Stanislavski as 'putrescent'. In the Prologue to the revised *Mystery-Bouffe* he proclaimed the virtues of overt theatricality and, with a direct quote from Meierhold, poured scorn on the Art Theatre:

> For other companies
> real theatre doesn't matter:
> for them
> the stage
> is just a key-hole.
> Sit down, shut up, relax now
> straight or skew
> we have a slice of life for you.
> Listen, look at
> Auntie Mania
> Uncle Vania
> sitting on the sofa whining.
> But we don't give a hoot for
> aunt and uncle?
> Uncle and aunt you've got at home.
> We can show you real life too
> but now
> transformed by theatre into a super-show.
> (Maiakovski, SS, IX, pp. 107–8.)

He was not to know, nor was anyone at the time, how disenchanted Stanislavski himself was with Chekhov, how irrelevant he felt him to be. He kept his feelings to himself but finally, from the safe distance of Berlin, in the autumn of 1922, unburdened himself to Nemirovich:

'. . . It would be ridiculous to take pleasure in the success of . . . the Chekhov productions or be proud of them. When we play the farewell to Masha in *Three Sisters* I am embarrassed. After all we have lived through it is impossible to weep over the fact that an officer is going and leaving his lady behind. Chekhov gives no joy. On the contrary who wants to play him?' (SS VII, p. 29.)

When Efros tried to defend the Art Theatre as a living and valuable tradition he was accused in the *Vestnik Teatra* of 'demonstrating his White [anti-revolutionary] nature'. Even Lunacharski was attacked by Vladimir Blum for 'propagating bourgeois culture'. Taïrov entered the fray, publishing a collection of his writings, *A Director's Notebook*. In it he distanced himself both from Meierhold and Stanislavski. He could not accept Meierhold's reduction of the actor to a mere mechanical function. On the other hand he was not willing to endorse Stanislavski's thesis of a necessary connection between emotion as experienced in life and emotion as experienced on the stage. Stage feelings were essentially imaginative creations. Nor was there any conscious, systematic way of evoking them; they were spontaneous and mysterious. What he sought was a freely creative imagination contained within a tightly choreographed stage pattern. Stanislavski, as usual, contented himself with writing caustic comments in the margins, Meierhold went public with a critical article.

For a time, it seemed as though Meierhold's views were to be translated into political reality. In the autumn of 1920 he assumed charge of the Theatrical Section (TEO) of the Commissariat for Enlightenment. He was one of the few members of his profession to have experienced the Civil War at first hand. Caught by the hostilities in southern Russia where he was convalescing, he had been imprisoned by the White Army. He was subsequently liberated by the Red Army and joined its political section. Lunacharski then called him to Moscow. He arrived in September with a radical plan of reform to eliminate the Academic theatres and replace them by popular, non-professional and Red Army theatres – a Theatrical October – a term invented for him by Vladimir Blum.

The time seemed right for a tactical retreat. Nemirovich approached Lunacharski with a plan to split the Art Theatre company into three. One group would remain in Moscow, another would tour the provinces and a third would take advantage of the many outstanding invitations to Europe and the United States, some of which dated from before the war. Yet even as the far left seemed to be triumphing, Proletkult's claims to independence were being undermined. Its attempts to create a network of studios and clubs had failed, mainly for practical reasons, and the tendency now was to centralise its activities in a workers' theatre. At its first All-Russia Congress Lenin had pushed through a series of resolutions bringing it under the control of the Commissariat for Englightenment.

Lunacharski had not by any means given a free hand to Meierhold whose authority did not extend to the Academic theatres. Within three months of his appointment they were in public disagreement. The December issue of *Vestnik Teatra* carried articles by each of them, published side-by-side. In a response to his detractors on the left, Lunacharski made it plain that whatever Meierhold's other qualities he was the last person to be entrusted with the preservation of the treasures of the past. The tone was heavily sarcastic. Meierhold replied with an article entitled *J'Accuse*. He was caught in a double bind. On the one hand, he was rapidly losing sympathy for the Proletkult. Despite his populist ideological flourishes he was never really interested in the kind of open-air and street theatre Proletkult advocated. As an artist he was interested in professional theatre of the highest standard. On the other hand, the professional, the Academic, theatres were outside his control. On February 26, 1921 he resigned.

Nemirovich took the view that he had, in fact, been dismissed. By the summer he was claiming, over-optimistically, that the left-wing bubble had burst. This apparent improvement in the overall situation did not induce him, however, to abandon all his plans. The original idea of three groups had been scrapped but the foreign tour remained. Although Lenin and Lunacharski had agreed to the scheme in principle there was considerable mistrust lower down the line. What guarantees were there that once out of Russia the Art Theatre would ever return? If the so-called Kachalov group could not be persuaded back why should their colleagues? Even the young Boleslavski had slipped out of the country, disheartened, so he said, by the increasing level of political interference in artistic matters. His production of the Polish play *Baladina* which had originally been well received came under attack when Poland invaded the Ukraine and was withdrawn. Boleslavski and his wife managed to get through the lines and made their way to Berlin.

Nemirovich continued to press for official approval. There were practical reasons for his persistence. The beginning of 1921 saw the introduction of the New Economic Policy, whereby market forces were allowed limited play within a hitherto state-owned economy. One consequence was the withdrawal of all subsidies to theatres. The result was a financial nightmare. The running budget of the Art Theatre and the Studios was just under 1.5 billion roubles and could not possibly be covered by box-office takings which, despite full houses, were only in the region of 600 million. As Nemirovich saw it the company could stagger on for a while but with no new productions on the stocks the outlook, in competitive terms, was bleak. A tour would at one blow reduce expenditure and allow time for reorganisation. A successful tour abroad might also be profitable and bring in foreign currency at a time when the rouble meant nothing on the world market. Therein lay the cause of Stanislavski's constant and, for him, exceptional preoccupation with finance throughout the tour. The restoration of subsidies to the Academic theatres in November 1921 changed nothing. The company still had to regroup.

A tour and any restructuring of the theatre was, however, impossible without the return of the Kachalov group. In July, October and November 1921 Stanislavski wrote pleading letters to his colleagues, setting out all the difficulties they were encountering at home, both financial and political, but at the same time painting a picture of economic recovery and improved conditions. On April 2, 1922 in desperation he sent a telegram: the tour was under active preparation, an immediate answer was imperative. On May 21 the whole company, residents and exiles alike, met for the first time in three years. The pleasure of this reunion was quickly overshadowed, for Stanislavski at least, by the fact that his favourite pupil, Vakhtangov, died a few days later at the tragically young age of 29.

In the chapter *Departure and Return* in *My Life in Art*, written in 1925 for the Russian edition, Stanislavski describes the opposition to the Art Theatre in purely artistic terms. He either did not see or chose to ignore the political issues involved. His tone is rather that of a disappointed teacher faced with a set of talented pupils who have steadily gone astray. He saw that in their ideological zeal these talented young people were mindlessly rejecting the past and trying to run artistically before they could walk. They were simply not willing to admit that work in the theatre demands long and patient preparation and training. They were always trying to jump a stage. As a result, actors were being manipulated by new directors, each apparently more green than the last, who simply made them jump through the latest theoretical hoop. How could a revolutionary theatre be developed without major new writers and performers of talent who were treated with respect? In the days when the Art Theatre had appeared as a revolutionary force it had had Chekhov. Where was the new Chekhov? He could not create another literary genius but he could bring the company back to some semblance of its former self. His prime task was to rebuild it, to marry the 'old brigade' with the new, to restore the sense of ensemble. His main fear was that the younger members of the Kachalov group who had not been given a basic grounding in his working method would have acquired slick and facile habits. There were just over three months to put together a repertoire that consisted of *Tsar Fiodor, Lower Depths, Three Sisters, Uncle Vania, Cherry Orchard* and *A Provincial Lady*.

On September 14, 1922 Stanislavski, his wife, his son, Igor, his daughter, Kira and his granddaughter, Kirilla boarded a train for Petrograd where they took ship for Riga. From there they went by train to Berlin. The rest of the company was to follow on a few days later, travelling by ship from Petrograd to Stettin. After Germany the full company planned to go to France and from there to the United States. The projected tour of England had not materialized.

Stanislavski arrived at Berlin Freidrichstrasse at 9 a.m. on September 18 after a day and a half of travel. There he had his first real taste of the American publicity machine. The US tour was being arranged by Morris Gest, a Russian-born impressario, who was interested in promoting cultural relations between his native and adopted countries. He had been promoting the tour ever since the spring and had succeeded in getting a long article in the September 17 issue of the prestigious *New York Times Book Review*. His brother Simon was waiting at the station in Berlin with a battery of photographers and cameramen. Stanislavski was then initiated into the first law of news reporting: once for real and once for the cameras. As he came down the steps from the station to a fairly moderate round of applause he was duly filmed and photographed. He got into a waiting car and drove off. The car immediately had to be turned round again. The reporters wanted pictures of his wife and family. His son, Igor, was with him but Lilina and his daughter had stayed over in Riga because his grandchild was ill. Publicity mattered more than truth and Stanislavski found himself suddenly saddled with a stand-in wife and daughter and had to repeat his descent down the station steps with bows, applause and flowers as before. This polite fiction was screened both in Germany and the United States.

He had been booked into a suite at the palatial Fürstenhoff, as befitted his status. Everything had been laid on to make him feel welcome, flowers, delicacies, great baskets of fruit but all this attention merely served to embarrass him. In any case, the splendour of his surroundings contrasted markedly with his own shabby appearance. This once elegantly turned-out man kept to his room rather than show his torn overcoat in public. However, there was a great deal of work to do. A management team had arrived for Moscow to tackle the intricate problem of preparing to transport a company of sixty, plus costumes, sets and props across Europe to America. At the same time extras had to be found and rehearsed, mainly for *Tsar Fiodor*.

Stanislavski set out on the tour in a state of high tension and that tension persisted throughout. He was always doubly nervous abroad. He was the ambassador of Russian art and whatever was presented must be of the highest quality. He was aware of the Russians' reputation in western Europe as strange, wild, essentially unpredictable people beneath a veneer of civilisation. To that now had to be added the suspicion with which the new revolutionary Russia was regarded and the revulsion of the execution of the Romanov family.

The tour began with tantrums and crises. Stanislavski was having trouble with his voice which was now quite husky. The cause may simply have been tiredness and physical tension. He turned for help to two Russian singing teachers living in exile. His vocal exercises were not appreciated by his neighbours at the Fürstenhoff and there was a certain amount of banging on connecting walls until Stanislavski toned down the volume of his exercises. Rather more seriously, the company were delayed by storms in the Baltic. Five days went by before news came that they had finally disembarked at Stettin. When they reached Berlin they were in no fit state to work. Valuable rehearsal time was being lost. When work did begin conditions were not ideal. The Lessing Theatre, where they were to play, had to be shared with another company. Max Reinhardt came to the rescue offering his workshops for morning rehearsals. Stanislavski kept everyone hard at it from 9 a.m. to midnight. It would be idle to pretend he used the patient, exploratory methods of the System to achieve his results. He whipped the company into shape. The correspondent of the *Berliner Tageblatt* wrote that he was like a conductor with an orchestra and, indeed, employed musical terms. It was hard work breathing new life into old productions. *Tsar Fiodor*, with which the season was to open, was 24 years old and it showed. In addition Kachalov had to be rehearsed into the lead. *Cherry Orchard* was in not much better shape. Things came to a head at the *Fiodor* technical rehearsal on September 24. The largest of the bells which formed part of the chimes to greet the Tsar's exit from the Kremlin had been deliberately left behind. It would have been impossible to transport; it weighed about 1600 kilos. At the appropriate moment all the other bells pealed out. Suddenly Stanislavski's voice came from the auditorium, 'And when are we going to hear the real chimes?'. When the situation was explained to him he exploded. All his anxiety and tension were displaced onto the missing bell. Suddenly nothing else in the production mattered. Emergency meetings of the Moscow Art team and the Lessing Theatre management were called and all manner of musical instruments tried out. Stanislavski rejected them all. His parting shot at the end of the day was, no bell, no performance. A member of the stage management team came up with what must be one of the most original solutions in production history. He located some eight or nine circular saws in a nearby factory. They were suspended, tried out for sound. The most appropriate of them was selected and two double-bass players were invited to play on it. Backed up by a gong they provided the necessary deep tones. The crisis was over.

The play opened the next day to great acclaim. In the audience was Jacques Hébertot, who had come especially from Paris to see the show. That evening a contract was signed for a season of eight performances in Paris at the Théâtre des Champs Elysées from December 2.

Cherry Orchard opened successfully on September 28 but *The Lower Depths* which opened the day after made the greater impact. *Three Sisters* followed on October 2. On the 3rd, between Acts Two and Three of *The*

Lower Depths Stanislavski gave his first interview for the American press. He was very cautious in all his statements, side-stepping specific issues. He was not prepared to make facile observations on complex artistic matters for the sake of a quick quote. Neither was he prepared to discuss the situation back home. He simply declared himself politically illiterate and kept his own counsel. It was a wise policy although it did not keep him out of trouble.

The last performance of the Berlin season took place on October 10. A sudden decision by the Americans to postpone the US tour, planned for October or November, to the following January meant that there was a gap to be filled. Logically, after Berlin, the company should have gone to Vienna as they had in 1906. Stanislavski would have welcomed that. Whatever his private anxieties, success in Berlin had almost been a foregone conclusion. The company were celebrities before they arrived. The city was full of Russian émigrés all of whom claimed to be ex-members of the Art Theatre and Stanislavski's pupils. A band-wagon was rolling. Vienna was another matter. An Austrian tour, unfortunately, made no economic sense. The schilling was too unstable. They would simply lose money they could ill afford. On the 17th the company took the train for Prague.

The tour was arranged at great speed and with considerable warmth and generosity. Schedules were rapidly reorganised to make room for these unexpected visitors. The company were given a rehearsal room in the magnificent National Theatre. The season opened with four plays on four successive nights starting as usual, with *Fiodor* on the 20th. It ended with *The Lower Depths* on the 31st.

Brief as his stay was Stanislavski found time to attend a rehearsal of Janacek's opera *Katia Kabanova*, based on Ostrovski's *Storm*, which was about to have its première. His reactions are not recorded. What he saw of the dramatic theatre, however, he found disappointing, too many '-isms', too many sterile experiments, too great a concentration on production values which distorted actors' work and pushed it back into the past. It was much more rewarding and profitable to watch ordinary people going about their daily business, to note their characteristic tempi, their rhythmic patterns and ethnic differences.

On November 3 the company travelled to Zagreb where they played until the 20th. There Stanislavski took over the role of Shuiski, which he continued to play in Paris. It was his first 'new' part since *Stepanchikovo* and his last. From Zagreb they returned to Berlin, travelling, as always now, third class. There Stanislavski had to say goodbye to his family. Lilina, Kira and Kirilla returned to Russia. Igor, who was suffering from tuberculosis, went on to Switzerland for treatment. On the 29th the company took the train from Berlin to Paris. The sets and costumes had already been sent on separately, direct from Zagreb. The cart arrived at the Gare du Nord at 1 a.m. on November 30. Jacques Hébertot, Lugné-Poë and Jacques Copeau were there to meet them. Stanislavski gave a brief press interview. On the 2nd he visited Copeau and the veteran André Antoine whose work at the Théâtre Libre and the Odéon had frequently, and superficially, been compared to his own. After lunch with Hébertot and Louis Jouvet, at which they discussed the creation of an international centre of theatre art, all three went to visit Isadora Duncan at her studio.

The cordiality of the welcome offered by leading members of French theatre was not matched by the authorities who disapproved of the presence of dangerous subversives. The tour, in fact, had only been made possible by a considerable amount of string-pulling and legal evasion. The whole operation was now threatened, however, by a crisis far more serious than the absence of a single bell. All the sets, props and costumes had been lost somewhere between Zagreb and Paris and no amount of telephoning to stations along the line could locate them. Stanislavski was concerned that the sets should be as impressive as possible. He had counted on touching-up the backcloths on their arrival. They had been deliberately painted in very broad basic strokes. Any elaborate over-painting would have flaked off during the journey. The answer was to do it after their arrival. He was aware of the high standard of scene-painting in France and was anxious to avoid unfavourable comparisons. The opening could not be postponed. The company saw no alternative to cancellation at a disastrous financial loss.

This time Stanislavski kept his head. A telegram arrived to confirm that the sets were on their way, although nobody could say when. The build-up to the first night, December 5, was gathering momentum. There were tributes on the 4th in *Paris-Journal* from Georges Pitoëff and Jouvet and in *L'Eclair* from Lugné-Poë who described Stanislavski as 'the apostle of all daring'. Lugné-Poë had also cancelled the performance at his own theatre on the 5th so that the cast could attend *Fiodor*. On the evening of the 4th there was a welcoming ceremony at the theatre and still the sets had not arrived. Despite pressure to cancel Stanislavski stood his ground. If there was a chance that the sets might arrive in time, as he had been assured there was, they would go ahead.

The ceremony was long and elaborate, including a lecture on the foundation of the Art Theatre as well as formal tributes. When it came to Stanislavski's turn to reply he was already nervous, wondering how, under the circumstances, the company could live up to their reputation. At the crucial moment in his speech as he planned to draw to a fitting close, he dried. He began to improvise. He was more than surprised to hear his own voice inviting everyone present to the opening performance the following day. He recovered control in time to warn them that the sets and costumes had not arrived but promised that the play would go ahead without them if necessary. The audience responded warmly, his colleagues less so. They had already drawn up a notice announcing cancellation. At that moment, as if on cue, a dishevelled, dusty figure arrived to announce that the sets were in Paris. After some telephoning it was established that they would be at the theatre by 10 a.m. the following morning.

At four in the afternoon there was still no sign of them. At 5.30 news arrived that the trucks were stuck in a traffic-jam. The first van arrived at 6.15. There was a panic to find costumes, get dressed and made-up. The technical staff finished the set-up in record time but the curtain was delayed for thirty minutes by which time the audience was demonstrating its impatience by clapping. There had been no time for a lighting rehearsal and all the elaborate effects had to be sacrificed. The entire performance took place with the lamps full up.

The first act was well received. The company stuck to its practice of not taking a curtain and Stanislavski used the time to rehearse the crowd scenes with the hastily-recruited extras who had not even seen the sets before. During subsequent intervals Picasso, Prokoviev, Stravinsky and Kussevitski came round to offer congratulations. After the performance Stanislavski sent Nemirovich a telegram:

'Colossal success, general acclaim, fantastic press.' (*Ezhegodnik* MXAT, 1943, p. 504.)

The Lower Depths followed on the 7th and *The Cherry Orchard* on the 13th with equal success. On the 15th there was a special performance of the Gorki for the profession when the cast was once more greeted with speeches and flowers. Such honours were, of course, very flattering but there was considerable discontent within the company. There were more performances than the eight originally scheduled and lead actors, like Leonidov, were feeling the pressure. Junior members were complaining that they were underpaid and underfed.

Stanislavski continued to study the theatre around him. Prior to the opening of the tour he attended performances by the Italian tragedian Ermete Zacconi. What struck him most was the economy of effort displayed by an artist who was used to touring. There were moments of psychological truth which were genuinely inspiring, moments when the role was experienced, there were others of technically masterful imitation, moments when the role was represented. There was a marked qualitative difference between the two approaches although given the technical accomplishment of the actor there was never anything that was less than satisfactory. The essential lesson to be learned was that of planning, to know when and where to switch the approach so as to conserve energy and apply it when it was most needed.

He kept in close touch with Jacques Copeau and on the 21st there was a midnight reception at the Vieux Colombier. Just before his departure for the United States he once again discussed the possibility of an international studio, a society 'for the preservation of European theatre.' Copeau gave a

dinner at a restaurant next to the Vieux Colombier to which he invited
Firmin Gémier, who had created the first Théâtre National Populaire, was
director of the Odéon, and who had introduced plays by Gorki and Tolstoi
to French audiences. Also present was Harley Granville Barker who had
come over especially from London to see the Art Theatre. There was unanimous approval of the idea in principle but, as ever, there was the problem of
finance. America might be the answer.

Stanislavski and the Art Theatre company sailed from Cherbourg on
December 27 on the R M S Majestic. The extremely rough crossing took
nine days and many people's thoughts turned to the fate of the Titanic. On
New Year's Eve Mr Stanislavski and Mr Kachalov played, or rather, as
Stanislavski put it, yelled, their way through a scene from *Julius Caesar* as
part of the ship's concert. It was with great relief that they sailed into New
York harbour late on January 3.

Stanislavski was besieged by newsmen and reporters. Indeed, he was kept so
busy that he missed seeing the Statue of Liberty. Again he was wary in his
answers. He felt that questions concerning the choice of repertoire were loaded:

' "Why did you choose these particular plays for inclusion in the repertoire?
I mean *Tsar Fiodor, The Lower Depths* and Chekhov?", asked one re-
porter. I understood right away what was behind the question, recalling
what had been said and written in Europe, that we had chosen *Tsar
Fiodor* to show a weak Tsar, *The Lower Depths* to demonstrate the
strength of the proletariat and Chekhov to illustrate the feebleness of the
intelligentsia and the bourgeoisie.

"We've brought precisely the plays that were precisely asked for and no
others", I answered firmly. "And they were asked for because they are
typical of an earlier period of the Art Theatre and because we performed
them in Europe in 1906 and just recently. America wants to see what
Europe already knows." ' (SS, VI, p. 182.)

Stanislavski went through immigration and customs on the morning of
January 4. He was apprehensive. Hostile articles had already appeared in
the press. He could be refused entry or, even if he were let in, the tour could
still be a financial disaster. As if to confirm his fears the planned quay-side
greeting was a masterpiece of mismanagement. Gest, blissfully ignorant of
the political consequences, had invited a Russian bishop or some other
spiritual dignitary to come down in full canonicals. Fortunately the invitation was refused and Bertenson who was part of the Art Theatre management
succeeded in persuading Gest that a religious display of any kind would not
be helpful. He had also intended the Mayor of New York to present
Stanislavski with the keys to the city but that had been mistakenly arranged
for the 3rd. Everyone was at an important meeting on the 4th. The boat
was so long docking that the officials who had arrived with gifts had to

leave. The presents were piled into Stanislavski's car but later taken away for the inevitable photograph after which they disappeared. Perhaps, Stanislavski wrote to Lilina, they had simply been hired. On the positive side, however, there were friends to meet him, Rachmaninov's wife and daughter and Boleslavski, who, after a stay in Paris had come to the United States on tour. A letter from Stanislavski asking him to act as assistant director had enabled him to extend his visa. Later that day Stanislavski met his nephew Koka, who was an official member of a Soviet trade delegation, at a special performance given at the *Chauve Souris* theatre, run by an émigré and former colleague, Baliev.

Some adjustment was necessary to American theatre practice. Stanislavski had not realised that when you rented a theatre that was precisely what you got, an empty building, nothing else. On his arrival at the Jolson Theatre on 59th Street he walked onto a bare stage with a solitary working light. It was soon apparent, moreover, that there were problems with the backdrops and larger pieces of scenery. Although the auditorium held two thousand the stage and wings were small and storage space inadequate. Dressing-rooms were difficult to reach, some of them located on the tenth floor. The technical problems of the get-in were complicated by the extremely rigid demarcation lines that operated among the back-stage staff. Once they had been briefed no one else was allowed to interfere. Stanislavski was impressed nonetheless by the cheerfulness and efficiency of the American crew as he was to be throughout the tour. He rehearsed where he could but it was difficult. Individual scenes could be worked on at his hotel on West 56th Street, very near the theatre but the major problem was the crowd scenes for which Luzhski was responsible. Boleslavski had recruited the walk-ons locally.

The New York season finally opened on January 8 after three days of chaos. The first performance of *Fiodor* was marked by a minor mishap when the curtain went up too soon on the second scene revealing stagehands trying to adjust the ceiling and actors scurrying to their places. The actors froze, the audience laughed, and the curtain came down again. A white-faced Stanislavski gave a few quick words of encouragement and the curtain went up once more. The incident was soon forgotten and the evening was, as Stanislavski wrote to Lilina, the greatest success the Art Theatre had ever known. There were flowers and telegrams from Rachmaninov and Chaliapin and the veteran director David Belasco, Gest's son-in-law, constantly shook Stanislavski's hand. The next day he sent a telegram of congratulation – 'the world is proud of you'.

The Lower Depths opened on the 15th and was a triumph. A special matinée was given for the profession on the 19th, with John Barrymore in the audience. Knipper wrote to a friend that the papers were saying that Rembrandt, Hogarth and Shakespeare himself would be bowled over by

such perfection. On the 20th the New York press published a letter from
Barrymore to Morris Gest stating that he had the greatest theatrical experience of his life. He had left the theatre shaken and intoxicated and with a
very modest opinion of his own abilities. The same day the *New York Times*
published an open letter from David Belasco to Gest thanking him for his
initiative in bringing the Art Theatre company over. There was a further
special matinée of *The Cherry Orchard* on the 26th.

Stanislavski repaid the adulation he received by seeing as much American
theatre as he could fit into a busy schedule. As he wrote to Nemirovich, any
notion that there were no actors of the first quality in the United States
must be abandoned. He saw Komissarzhevski's production of *Peer Gynt* in
which Joseph Schildkraut, who was later to make a distinguished and un-
dervalued career in Hollywood, played the title role. There was not his
equal, he wrote to Nemirovich, in the whole of Russia. He found David
Warfield in Belasco's production of *The Merchant of Venice* the best Shylock
he had ever seen. As for Barrymore's Hamlet, it was not ideal but 'absolutely
spell-binding'. In a later interview he did, however, express the worry that if
Barrymore did not learn to pace himself and control his nervous energy he
would burn himself out.

It is impossible to overestimate the impact of the company on the profession. In those brief weeks in January and February 1923 a seed was planted
that would come to fruition in a new approach to acting in America and
one which would ultimately feed back into Europe. Actors went to performances, Bertenson reported to Nemirovich, to study and learn. But they also
wanted more concrete information. With Stanislavski's permission Boleslavski gave a series of lectures on the System, which were later published in the
October issue of *Theatre Arts Monthly* as 'Acting, the first Six Lessons'.
These lectures established Boleslavski's authority as a teacher and launched
his career in America. Yet while Stanislavski was by now placing greater
emphasis on physical objectives and physical actions, Boleslavski stressed
the importance of Emotion Memory, developing the technique beyond
Stanislavski's original practice. His teaching laid the grounds for a bitter dispute ten years later between those who emphasised the personal, emotional
basis of the actor's craft and those who advocated the use of physical action.

One direct result of these lectures and the interest the Art Theatre tour
aroused was the American Laboratory Theatre, which Boleslavski created
with another Russian colleague, Ouspenskaia. An early member was the
twenty-two-year-old Lee Strasberg. The impact of Stanislavski's acting decided Strasberg to go into the theatre. He saw both Stanislavski and Kachalov play Vershinin and realised that whereas Stanislavski *was* Vershinin,
Kachalov, for all his accomplishment, still had a trace of the actor about
him. Moreover, Strasberg did not share the popular opinion that Stanislavski
was unable to play tragic roles.

In late January Stanislavski was approached to make a film of *Tsar Fiodor*. He started work on a script, more to see whether he could do it than anything else. He intended to combine *Fiodor* with *The Death of Ivan the Terrible* in a single epic, *The Peoples' Tragedy*. He had always taken the view that the popular masses were the principal characters in Aleksei Tolstoi's plays and this was the basis of his treatment. It became apparent when he met the producers on February 22 and March 5 that, in the best tradition of film moguls, they wanted the people as the background to a 'love-interest' that would be written in. The project was quickly abandoned.

Stanislavski had mixed feelings about New York, set out in long letters to Nemirovich and his brother, Vladimir. In his imagination he had conjured up a city like Fritz Lang's *Metropolis*. The reality was much more mundane. He was bewildered by traffic lights and almost got himself killed by standing in the middle of the street and examining them. The American people he took to immediately. He found them open, vital, impervious to social distinctions, free from snobbery and above all ready and eager for the new. On the other hand, he soon recognised the power of the success-ethic. It was wonderful to be successful but God help you if you flopped.

Musical life impressed him greatly. The opera was superior to anything he had known and the orchestras were outstanding, in particular the Philadelphia under Stokovski, which realised all his ideals of the perfect ensemble performing with commitment and energy. His old friends Rachmaninov and Chaliapin added to the riches available. At the end of February Rachmaninov, who had been away on a concert tour, returned to New York. On March 1 he attended a performance of *A Provincial Lady*. On March 13 Chaliapin, who was in town for a recital, saw *The Lower Depths*. In return, on the 25th, the entire Moscow Art company went to hear him in recital at the Met. It was not only the classical repertoire, however, that interested Stanislavski. As he came to know America better he became interested in popular songs and dance music. The syncopated rhythms were unknown in Russia and before he left in 1924 he asked friends to collect suitable recordings for him to take back to study.

The New York season closed on March 31 with a performance of *Three Sisters*. Artistically it had been all that could have been hoped for. Its success was due in part to the publicity campaign Gest had mounted with its endless flow of press releases and photographs. Full scene-by-scene synopses had been included in every programme. Everything had been done to attract audiences. Gest himself appeared very satisfied but the sad fact was that the company had made no money.

On April 1 they travelled to Chicago, going from there on the 23rd to Philadelphia and then on May 6 to Boston, where they encountered for the first time a hostile press campaign.

CHAPTER TWENTY-THREE

MY LIFE IN ART

In Boston Stanislavski signed a contract with Little, Brown & Co, to write his autobiography. He had been urged to do so by Oliver Sayler, one of the few foreigners to have worked with the Art Theatre. But Stanislavski had been under pressure to publish before and the only one to get a positive response had been Efros, who had been allowed to print the first section of *Various Tendencies in Theatre Art* in *Kultura Teatra*. The publishers and Gest were anxious to cash in on the tour's success since it had already been agreed that the company would return in the autumn. They wanted to rush the book out early in 1924 in the wake of what no one doubted would be a second triumph. The deadline for delivery of the manuscript was fixed for September 1. Stanislavski had to start work immediately, writing at the same time as performing, managing the tour and rehearsing a new repertoire. Igor needed treatment in Switzerland and that was expensive. Stanislavski, like the Art Theatre, needed dollars. He agreed to the impossible schedule. *My Life in Art* was partly written in long-hand, partly dictated to a secretary, sometimes at two in the morning when Stanislavski had a burst of energy. Work began on the Laconia in which Stanislavski sailed to Europe on June 7. Stanislavski worked full out but he had written 60,000 words before he even got to the creation of the Art Theatre.

It had been agreed that there was no point in returning to Russia. Stanislavski would therefore join his family at Freiburg in the Black Forest not far from the Swiss-German border and pay a visit to Igor at Wernwald. Knipper joined them and together they visited Gorki who was also in the area. On July 29 he travelled to Berlin and in August met Nemirovich at Waren. Stanislavski learned that the Studios, including the Opera Studio, were in a poor state while he had to report discontent among the company, who seemed unwilling to learn or develop. Kachalov was restless, complaining that the tour was preventing him from tackling new roles.

Work on the book continued past the September deadline. On September 13 he travelled to Berlin and from there, on the 18th, to Paris where they played a second season. By now rehearsals were upon them. They could not simply repeat the previous year's offerings. New plays had to be added to the repertoire. These were *La Locandiera* and *The Brothers Karamazov*. Stanislavski drove the company hard, reverting to his old practice of demonstrating, even to experienced actors like Kachalov, to get quick results. Nemirovich's adaptation had originally been spread over two evenings and it soon became apparent it was too long to be squeezed into a single performance. Stanislavski made drastic cuts three days before the opening on October 13. As if to repeat the *Fiodor* cliff-hanger of the first tour the sets for *La Locandiera* were lost on the way from Berlin. Stanislavski immediately contacted Benois, the original designer, now living in Paris, to see whether substitutes could be rushed together. The sets arrived on the 18th in time for the opening on the 20th. The performance was received with less than rapture. Some critics accused the cast of vulgarising Goldoni, of not being 'Italian'. Stanislavski on his side, was disenchanted with Paris. He found it corrupt. The rate of inflation and the cost of living consumed any profits. Writing to Morris Gest he confessed they were in debt to the sum of $25,000.

On October 31 the company sailed once more to New York on the Olympic. They arrived on November 7. There was much less ballyhoo than had greeted their first season and Stanislavski had the impression that Gest was skimping on publicity. Rehearsal conditions were poor but work began on *An Enemy of the People* which was being added to their repertoire. This was a painful experience for Stanislavski. He had to hand over Stockman, his favourite part, to Kachalov. He was now 60 and could not do everything. He drove the company mad, demanding all the time that they sharpen their objectives and discover the precise rhythm for each unit. *Karamazov* opened on November 19. Duse, now very old, who was in New York playing in *The Lady for the Sea* came for the first act but left immediately after as she needed to rest before her performance the following day. Reinhardt was also in town with *The Miracle* and made contact.

Locandiera opened on the 21st and, in marked contrast to Paris, was a 'smash'. *Enemy* opened on December 3, *Enough Stupidity in Every Wise Man* followed two days later and rehearsals for *Cherry Orchard* began, although not without incident. Knipper's unwillingness to rehearse a role which she thought she knew all too well provoked a furious outburst from Stanislavski who was not prepared to allow anything to endanger the success of the season. His letters to Lilina give details of box-office takings, show by show, indicating his preoccupation with finance.

The tour went on remorselessly. First Philadelphia where Rachmaninov, anxious to do all he could for his friend, arranged seats so that Stanislavski could hear Stokovski and the Philadelphia with Joseph Hoffman as soloist. But there were now political rumblings at home. The second season had confirmed all the suspicions that the company, or some of its leading members, would not return. Stanislavski felt obliged to emphasize in an interview for the *Novoe Russkoe Slovo*, published in New York, that he had every intention of going back to Russia, where his heart and duty lay. The satirical magazine *Krokodil* however, published, on October 28, what purported to be an interview with Stanislavski in which he is supposed to have said:

'What was our horror when the workers invaded the theatre with dirty clothes, uncombed, unwashed, with dirty boots, demanding the performance of revolutionary plays.'

A worried Nemirovich asked for an immediate denial and on November 24 *Pravda* published the following telegram:

'The report of my American interview is lies from beginning to end. Repeatedly, and before hundreds of witnesses, I stated the very opposite about new audiences, boasting about, taking pride in their sensitiveness, citing as an example the philosophical tragedy *Cain* which was splendidly understood by a new public. I thought that my forty years of activity and my longstanding dream of a people's theatre would have protected me against scurrilous suspicions. I am deeply hurt, cut to the quick.'

The allusion to *Cain* is quite at variance with the facts but Stanislavski's private perceptions did not always coincide with the real world outside. Stanislavski was tired of the political crossfire. On December 28 he wrote to Nemirovich:

'Moscow accuses us of disloyalty. But we get even blacker looks abroad. France just about let us in. We only managed to get a favourable result by circumventing French law. In Paris a considerable amount of people, both French and Russian, boycotted us because we came from Soviet Russia and therefore were communists. Now they won't let us into Canada, officially declaring us Bolsheviks, and all our plans have collapsed. Who knows how many more difficulties lie ahead of us? You only have to think of recent persecution in the press stirred up in the Boston papers . . .

Here we are attacked by both Russians and Americans for using our theatre to glorify present-day Russia. In Moscow they are slinging mud at us because we are preserving the tradition of bourgeois theatre and because plays by Chekhov and other authors of the 'intelligentsia' are successful with Russian émigrés and American capitalists; they think we are rolling in dollars while in fact we are up to our ears in debt. Believe me, it's not for my own pleasure that I am spending almost two years going from place to place, from city to city with absolutely no time for the things I love and dream about and that I am losing what remains of my health. My spirits are low, I'm depressed, I've almost lost heart and at times think of giving it all up . . . .

Seeing all the abuse that's heaped on me in Moscow I am refusing all kinds of good offers coming my way from Europe and America and yearn with all my heart for Russia . . . .' (December 28, 1923, K. S. Archive.)

One of the offers to which he refers was an invitation to found a Studio in the US at a salary of $1500 a month plus a percentage. He did, however, later express a willingness to teach a group of American students if they came to the Art Theatre. It was, he explained, a question of providing a proper working atmosphere. That was something which took years to create; it could not be drummed up overnight. It was Moscow or nothing.

The New Year brought fresh political embarrassment. The company returned to New York on January 13, 1924, which they had left on the previous December 30 to play Boston, New Haven and Hartford, Connecticut. On the 18th, against his better judgement, together with Knipper and Luzhski he attended a fund-raising bazaar in aid of unemployed Russian émigré artists in the USA, organised among others by Rachmaninov's wife. Stanislavski knew almost nobody present but asked for and received an assurance that no photographs would be published. On the 20th he received an anxious telegram from Nemirovich stating that a photograph had appeared, showing Stanislavski and Knipper in a group with the caption 'What White émigrés are up to', and an article referring to the sale of valuables smuggled out of Russia. Would he please explain? Stanislavski was so shaken by the incident that he began to be worried by chance encounters in the street, particularly when the odd Kodak camera appeared. As he wrote to Nemirovich on February 12, it was not unusual for people to come up and talk to him. For the most part he had no idea who they were. What was he supposed to do?

Public and even official appearances could not be avoided. On February 15 he was invited to the studios of Famous Players. He was taken onto the set where Rudolph Valentino and Bebe Daniels were filming *Monsieur Beaucaire*. His hosts, knowing that he had at one time been involved in textiles, pointed to the care that had been taken to obtain the right materials from Lyon and Paris. Stanislavski only half heard his interpreter and thought they were asking his opinion of the acting. He answered in one word, 'Abominable'. He was particularly incensed by Valentino. He was unable to put on his 'full-dress' smile but launched into an angry commentary on the importance of learning how to wear costumes properly, to make them your own. The interpreter, sensing a possible incident, toned down Stanislavski's remarks in translation and the visit passed off without further embarrassment. At all events the cast seem to have been unaware of any adverse criticism since they sent a signed photograph expressing their respects a few days later.

On March 16 the company travelled to Washington having given performances in Brooklyn and Newark, New Jersey. On the 20th they were received by President Coolidge at the White House. This was something of a coup since the newly-created Soviet Union did not enjoy diplomatic relations with the United States. The visit was arranged by Herbert Hoover, then Secretary of Commerce, who had worked as an engineer in Russia and knew the Art Theatre well. At the reception Stanislavski met his future collaborator, Elizabeth Reynolds Hapgood. Mrs Hapgood spoke good Russian and had been invited to perform the introductions to the President since no one in the White House could pronounce the actors' names. Stanislavski evidently took to her immediately since, to while away the time as they waited their turn to meet the President, he began to demonstrate to her elaborate eighteenth-century ways of greeting – perhaps he still had his encounter with Valentino in mind. It was Mrs Hapgood's husband, Norman, who had first suggested the Art Theatre might come to the United States in 1914. At all events, a firm foundation was laid to a friendship and to a collaboration without which Stanislavski's account of the System would not have been published.

After Washington the company travelled to Pittsburg on the 23rd, Cleveland on the 30th, Chicago on April 6, Detroit on April 27 and finally back to New York on May 4.

My Life in Art appeared in Boston at the end of April with a print-run of 5000 copies. It had been brought out at exceptional speed. Stanislavski was still working on the manuscript in February writing as he put it, 'in intervals, on trolley-cars, in restaurants, in the street'. He himself was under no illusions about the quality of what he had done. Seeing the handsome appearance of the first edition he remarked that the binding was better than the contents. It was a botched job, as far as he was concerned and he immediately started work on a revised version for publication in the Soviet Union.

On May 17 the company set sail for Europe on the Majestic, reaching Paris on the 22nd. From there he travelled to Switzerland on June 9 to see his son, Igor. On August 8 he was back in Moscow to a much-changed world.

CHAPTER TWENTY-FOUR

THE THEATRE OF THE REVOLUTION

Lenin was dead. The years of turmoil were over and the new state was attempting to consolidate itself. The Soviet Union had formally been created. In the arts the avant-garde seemed unstoppable. Painting, sculpture, architecture, posters, new ideas were bursting out with the force of energy long pent-up. The theatre was swept along in the general movement. The new cult was Constructivism and its high priest was Meierhold. The dominance of the Art Theatre was, or so it seemed, a thing of the past.

Nemirovich had watched the growth of Meierhold's influence with alarm. He had sent anxious letters to Stanislavski and other colleagues warning them of the new situation. His initial response to the danger had been a managerial one. He and Lunacharski discussed a reorganization of the Art Theatre and its Studios. Nemirovich wrote to Stanislavski in July setting out the plan he and Lunacharski had agreed: the First Studio was to become entirely independent and take the name of Second Moscow Art Theatre; the Third Studio was also to go independent while the Second Studio was to be merged into the main company. Stanislavski gave his agreement in a letter written on the 10th. His animosity towards the First Studio – 'that long-standing sickness of my heart' – was now considerable. His only objection was that it should be called the Second Art Theatre since it had betrayed every basic principle the original Art Theatre had ever stood for. He was also quite happy to see the Third Studio go. Privately he thought of the Studios as Lear's daughters: the First was Goneril; the Third, Regan; the Second was his true Cordelia. But on June 25 the Third Studio wrote to Stanislavski proposing he and Meierhold should run the Studio together. Essentially this was a revival of Vakhtangov's plan of 1921 to 'rescue' Stanislavski from the deadening clutches of the Art Theatre. Meierhold followed this up with a letter on June 25 offering his help.

Within a week of his return, between August 15 and 19, he held long discussions with the Third Studio. He was diplomatic, concealing the deep suspicion that he felt. He told them he welcomed the idea but how was it possible to abandon old friends and colleagues? Privately he could not see himself finding common ground artistically with Meierhold. And yet, younger colleagues, the second generation as Stanislavski called them, could see the potential of bringing the two men together, and this was not merely motivated by a sentimental attachment to an old and respected teacher. Perhaps they were more perceptive than they knew.

In the event, certain members of the Third Studio chose to come over to the Second. Among these was Nikolai Gorchakov who became an assiduous if not always reliable chronicler of Stanislavski's rehearsals. The newly-combined group was then transformed into the Dramatic Studio and School with Stanislavski in charge. The students at the Studio were to be involved in main-house productions, playing small parts and walk-ons. Just how open Stanislavski's teaching methods were is indicated by the fact that there was no fixed syllabus nor was there ever, although certain classes were always given.

These reforms put an end to ambiguities concerning artistic policy by getting rid of 'dissident' elements. The Art Theatre was stripped down for action. But what action? The tour had given the Art Theatre a respite but none of its essential problems had been solved.

The apparently inexorable progress of the avant-garde had not, it is true, gone unchallenged. On April 13, 1923, at the celebrations to mark the centenary of Ostrovski's birth, Lunacharski had reasserted the importance of the realist tradition with the slogan, 'Back to Ostrovski'. Meierhold made a defiant response a year later with one of the most revolutionary productions of *The Forest* ever staged.

Stanislavski's first concern was to reaffirm his artistic problem. This meant, in the first instance, revising *My Life in Art* for a Russian edition. He regarded the original American edition as mainly anecdotal, intended for the unitiated reader. The Russian edition would discuss artistic problems seriously. He made it quite clear, in September 1924, in response to an enquiry concerning a possible German edition, that any translation would have to be made from the revised version when it appeared. He gave a similar response to Gaston Gallimard in 1928 when a French translation was under consideration.

He turned once more to Mrs Gurevich for help. Immediately before leaving Russia in 1922 he had given her the keys to the cupboards where his notes and manuscripts were kept, asking her to put them into some sort of order. Now, with her help, he resectioned the book, moving chapters around, cutting passages, notably his reminiscences of Chekhov, removing religious references that were likely to cause trouble but, above all, adding new material. The few paragraphs devoted to *Cain* were expanded into a full chapter. He maintained his conviction of the play's relevance for contemporary audiences and still harboured ambitions to restage it. More than anything he attributed the failure of the production to lack of rehearsal time and the endless compromises over the sets. The chapter is a refusal to admit a mistake. In the new chapter *Departure and Return*, the penultimate in the Russian edition, he gave his assessment of the developments in the theatre that had taken place during his absence. He acknowledged the advances made in physical aspects of acting, the field where he himself was weakest. The expressive possibilities of the body had been explored and its physical vocabulary expanded but what was required, he argued, as he had argued with Vakhtangov, was a combination of physical skill and psychological depth. This part of the chapter was, in fact, a development of material he had prepared for the American edition and then withdrawn. He had originally intended to include an open letter to a former pupil, perhaps Meierhold or Vakhtangov, who had turned against his teaching. According to J. J. Robbins, the translation of the letter was already on its way to the publisher when Stanislavski sent a telegram stopping it. The chapter that finally appeared in the Russian edition, however, was certainly directed against Meierhold, bio-mechanics and associated techniques. The revisions were complete by January 1925 although the book itself did not appear until September of the following year.

As to the Art Theatre, itself, it had to be relaunched. Stanislavski proposed one or two plays which Nemirovich accepted. The material fell into two categories: first plays which examined human responses to specific social circumstances, either contemporary or historical; second, plays which provided material helpful to the actors development. Broadly speaking the plays in the first category fell into two groups, those that showed a corrupt pre-revolutionary society and those that showed reactions to the new world of the Soviet Union and all the difficulties of adapting to it. In the second category he was willing to go to melodrama or even vaudeville. In 1925 there was only one new production, Treniov's *The Pugachov Rebellion*, which Nemirovich directed. The play, which was concerned with a revolt against the Tsar in the eighteenth century, opened on September 19 and was well received. It was seen as the Art Theatre's first step towards ideological acceptability. By October 16 Nemirovich was in Berlin with the Music Studio, at the beginning of a tour that was to take them to the United States, including the West coast and Hollywood. He did not return for two years. This meant that the burden of reestablishing the theatre as a significant force rested entirely on Stanislavski's shoulders. Between 1925 and 1928 he was responsible for nine productions, including three new Soviet plays, as well as four operas. A tenth play, Aeschylus' *Prometheus Bound*, was abandoned after more than a year's rehearsal. It was obviously impossible for him to undertake such a work load single-handed. Productions were assigned to young directors whose work he supervised, modified and, if need be, as in the case of *Prometheus*, scrapped.

His new programme was an ambitious one. During 1925 he laid the foundations of four new productions, all of which were shown during the following year. His young team of directors started rehearsals while he himself undertook a tour across the Soviet Union between April 27 and July 3 which included Baku and Tiflis in the south and Kiev in the Ukraine.

The first production to be seen was Ostrovski's *The Burning Heart*, generally considered a minor work. Stanislavski took over rehearsals from the young director Ilya Sudakov. The production was his response, to 'Back to Ostrovski' and a further investigation of the problem of the Grotesque. The play was previewed on January 22, 1926 and opened the night after. It was received, the left-wing critic Zagorski apart, with an enthusiasm reminiscent of the theatre's early days. Nemirovich, who was in New York with his Music Studio, sent a telegram of congratulation. Meierhold shocked many of his supporters by turning to the audience at a performance of Tretiakov's agit-prop drama *Cry, China* and expressing his delight at the production by the 'wizard', Stanislavski, adding that young directors could not hope to equal the mastery the Art Theatre had shown that day. This was the second time he had made a public show of his support for Stanislavski. The first was in April 1923, at the jubilee to celebrate his own 25 years in the theatre, when he had insisted that a telegram of congratulation be sent to his old master in New York. This latest expression of his esteem, however, was too much for critics like Vladimir Blum who spoke of 'treason' against the avant-garde.

The problem of finding good new plays by new authors on contemporary subjects was still unresolved. *The Burning Heart* was a classic and *Pugachov*, in Nemirovich's words, a romantic historical drama. The task of finding new material fell to the young and exceptionally brilliant Pavel Markov who, with Nemirovich's departure, suddenly found himself in charge of the Literary Department. Markov, the most outstanding critic and teacher of his generation, was to the reborn Art Theatre what Efros had been to the old. His gift was his capacity to understand and to write about the art of the actor. Stanislavski, though retaining the final veto, treated him with respect and consideration, always publicly referring to him any manuscripts he was sent. Out of the authors whose work he knew and the hundreds of manuscripts he received Markov selected four writers, Ivanov, Leonov, Kataiev and Bulgakov.

Two instalments of Bulgakov's *The White Guard* appeared in the magazine *Rossia* early in 1925. The third and final instalment was not published as the magazine was closed down. The incomplete novel was nonetheless sufficient for Markov to propose a stage adaptation. Bulgakov was approached in April 1925 and agreed to start work on a script. By September a first draft was ready. It was overlong and without proper dramatic shape. Not surprisingly Bulgakov had tried to preserve as much of his original novel as possible. He spent the next three months reworking the script, with a great deal of advice from Sudakov, who was to direct, and other members of the production team. Sixteen scenes were reduced to seven. By January 1926 a rehearsal script was ready and work began on the 29th. The play very soon became the property of the younger members of the company. The members of the 'old brigade', like Vishnievski, who had originally been cast, fell by the wayside. Stanislavski was by no means averse to this; he wanted to see his second generation grow to maturity.

Rehearsals, according to Markov, were pure joy and very soon the spirit of Pushkino was being freely invoked. It was all happening again after almost thirty years. Bulgakov emerged as a second Chekhov and *The White Guard* as another *Seagull*. Like Chekhov, Bulgakov had a certain ironic detachment and a disconcerting sense of humour. He liked to debunk and had a propensity for what Markov described as 'philosophical sarcasm'. Unlike Chekhov, however, he was more than willing to discuss the content of the play. He could supply a biographical background for every character. A natural actor himself he was able, where necessary, to demonstrate what he meant. On March 26 Stanislavski saw a satisfactory run-through of the first two acts and sketches for the set of Act Three and urged everyone to work as fast as they could.

In the meantime he had two other productions to see through, *Nicholas I and the Decembrists* by Leonov and *Les Marchands de Gloire*, Marcel Pagnol's first play written in collaboration with Paul Nivoix. *Nicholas 1* was another historical study of an abortive revolt against imperial power. It opened on May 19 and its success was in no small measure due to an outstanding performance by Kachalov, in the title role, which found favour not only with the critic of *Izvestia* but also with Vladimir Blum. Pagnol's play, premiered only a year previously at the Théâtre de la Madeleine, opened on June 15. This study of corruption in the local council of a small provincial French town, where the war-dead are exploited for commercial purposes, was a subject to which Stanislavski instinctively responded. The production was a further example of his extended realism, first developed in the pre-war production of *The Inspector General*, where a truthful portrayal of character and milieu expanded into the grotesque. Here, though, Gogolian satire was given the quicker, sharper rhythms of the French. A rival version which had opened at the Korsh Theatre in February appeared superficial and conventional in comparison. The Art Theatre presentation contained darker, more tragic undertones. *Pravda* praised it as an exposure of bourgeois hypocrisy, of a world of 'shady dealings and rogue politicians'.

Stanislavski now struck a blow for the rehabilitation of Chekhov, whose place in the repertoire had been the subject of considerable debate ever since the revolution. A revival of *Uncle Vania* opened on May 11 with Stanislavski once again as Astrov. His performance was described as staggering. It seemed to have acquired more deeply tragic dimensions. The System was now bringing personal dividends. At the age of 60 he still continued to improve as an actor and develop roles he had been playing for twenty years. Nemirovich had noted how much better his performance of Famusov had been in the 1925 revival of *Woe From Wit*.

From the company's point of view the reaction of a new generation to Chekhov was of paramount importance. If Chekhov could be justified then the artistic policy of the Art Theatre could be justified. Positive articles appeared in *Vecheriaia Moskva*, *Izvestia*, and *Komsomolskaia Pravda*, which remarked that the time had come perhaps for the theatre to step out of its bombastic showcase and follow the path of more human and humane creation. The Art Theatre appeared to have found its ideological place.

Some time in late May or early June Stanislavski started attending rehearsals of *The White Guard* again to see what work still had to be done. He was the most transparent of audiences; it was possible to tell what he was thinking at any given moment. He would laugh, cry, occasionally bite his hand when he was uncertain. Over the years, these nerve-racking occasions where Stanislavski would give his yea or nay acquired a certain format. After the run he would give his comments, he would thank the company and list the things he liked. Everyone then waited for the 'But', which at its worst could mean 'Scrap the lot and start again'. On this occasion he merely commented, 'Well now, tomorrow we can start acting.'

Stanislavski was able to walk in and take over, even make radical changes, because the group he was working with employed a common method, the System. He could assume that basic problems of creating a character had been solved before he arrived. But problems of character-creation are not, as had often been assumed, the central issue of the System. The central issue is the structure and meaning of the play itself. It was therefore problems of the through-line both of individual characters and of the action, of dramatic rhythm, tempo, that occupied him most. His major criticism of Act Three scene two was that it was emotionally self-indulgent – a constant danger of the System misused. Actors were sentimentalising their own feelings when they should have been thinking of positive, active responses to their situation:

'Well now ... what's false here? You're playing feelings, your own suffering, that's what's false. I need to see the event and how you react to that event, how you fight people – how you react, not suffer .... What's the rhythm of this scene? You started playing it like a funeral .... You play a scene in which nice, kind, sensitive friends gather at home. The way you do it, they comfort their weeping hostess who is fast becoming hysterical and whom they all love very much. To do that you shed tears and suffer. To take that line on the scene is to be passive and sentimental. See everything in terms of action; *what we have here is an impassioned bitter argument* ....' (V. Toporkov, *O Tekhnike Aktiora*, VTO, 1958, pp. 25–7.)

Other problems, however, were beginning to surface. The free debate of the first years after the revolution was beginning to disappear. A new bureaucracy had been set up with its attendant abbreviations and acronyms. In its concern to establish a new art to reflect the new society the Soviet state created a Central Repertory Committee, *Glavrepertkom*, to vet all new productions. Inevitably its methods were cumbersome. It did not pronounce judgement until a play was at dress-rehearsal stage. Months of work could be lost if the judgement went the wrong way. At some time during March or April it would seem that the Art Theatre grew apprehensive about the reception that might be given to a play with a White, and therefore, *ipso facto*, anti-revolutionary family at its centre. An alternative title was needed. Anything with the word 'White' in it was difficult. Bulgakov seems not quite to have appreciated the point since of the four suggestions he made – *White December, 1918, The Taking of the City, White Storm* – two contained the word, white. In May the management committee of the Art Theatre suggested *Before The End*, which both Bulgakov and Stanislavski disliked. Changes in the script were also asked for, presumably to head off any possible ideological criticism. Bulgakov could be strongly defensive about his work. On June 4 he sent a curt letter to the management refusing both the new title and the suggested changes, and threatening to withdraw the play altogether. The play was shown, unrevised, to the repertory Committee on June 24. One of the principal spokesmen for the Committee on that occasion was Vladimir Blum. The play was banned.

In August Stanislavski took a short break, staying at a dacha near Moscow. He had to prepare for the reopening of the Opera Studio which was now to bear his name. Most of his time, however, he spent working on a book which, he wrote to a friend, was called *Work on Oneself, A Pupil's Notes. My Life in Art* now had an international reputation. Ellen Terry called it her constant companion. Given her own motto, Imagination, Industry, Intelligence, it was hardly surprising that she found a kindred spirit in Stanislavski. The new book was one of three about which he had written to Little, Brown & Co, in May 1925 – *Memoirs of a Journey to Europe and America, The Diary of a Student at a Drama School* and *The History of a Production*. He was uncertain which he would write first. The *Memoirs*, based on a journal he kept during his travels, were started but abandoned. They break off half way through the first American tour. The *History* was an old project for which there were many notes. It was the *Diary*, now *Work on Oneself*, on which he decided to concentrate, having now finally opted for a semi-fictional form rather than straightforward exposition.

He returned to Moscow on August 27 determined to get *The White Guard* on, not so much for Bulgakov's sake, it must be said, but because he considered it essential for the rebirth of the theatre; his Second Generation needed it. If the play did not go forward he would resign. He reworked the whole production, taking into account the comments of the Repertkom and managing to persuade Bulgakov to rewrite certain scenes along the lines he suggested. The result was inevitably an historical and ideological fudge but with luck it would be an acceptable fudge.

Arrangements were made to show the play to the Repertkom again on September 17. Only on the 16th was a new title agreed – *The Days of the Turbins*. Once again the play was rejected but the door was left open for possible approval. Stanislavski now went direct to Lunacharski. On the 23rd a closed performance was given for the press, a limited number of the public, and members of Repertkom. On the 25th it received approval subject to further, minor changes. Even so Lunacharski was aware how tricky the situation was and defended his decision in a public statement:

'*The White Guard* is an ideologically inconsistent and in places politically-false play. However it comes together in the production and soviet audiences appreciate it as its true value.' (*Vecherniaia Moskva*, October 1, 1926.)

Maiakovski, happy to repeat an earlier joke and take a swipe at Stanislavski, replied:

'I think this is a proper logical culmination. They started with Auntie Mania and Uncle Vania and they end up with *The White Guard*. (Laughter) For me it's a hundred times better for it to come to a head and burst out in the open than to hide under the banner of apolitical art. Take that celebrated book of Stanislavski's *My Life in Art*, that renowned book for connoisseurs – it's the same thing as *The White Guard*.' (*Nove o Maiakovskom*, AN SSSR, 1958, p. 40.)

The play opened on October 5. It was an immediate success. Box-office receipts went up and the theatre was once again solvent. The critics almost universally condemned it, displaying an animosity which may well be unique in the annals of the theatre. Nor did it diminish with time. Over the years Bulgakov counted 301 reviews, 298 of them hostile, their tone achieving, at times, an almost eighteenth-century scurrility. Against the nuanced complexities of *The Turbins* the critics set the 1925 production of Treniov's *Liubov Iarovaia* at the Mali, a much more straightforward piece, offering a conventional love/duty dilemma where loyalty to the Bolshevik cause comes into conflict with personal emotion. The play is an exercise in reassurance; its end is never in doubt. Nothing is left unresolved; there are no loose political ends to disturb. A public debate on the relative merits of the two plays was held at the Meierhold Theatre on February 7 1927.

Two weeks later Lunacharski chaired a conference on the future development of Soviet theatre at the People's Commissariat for Enlightenment. Stanislavski held a number of preliminary meetings at home with Michael

Chekhov, Meierhold and Markov, possibly in an attempt to find some common ground. If that was the case the attempt failed. He was called on the 21st. His speech was fully reported later in the journal *Zhizn Iskusstva*. His former pupils and younger colleagues were anxious for his approval and he would have given almost anything to be able to oblige but he could not. In February 1925 he had attended a performance of *The Flea* at the Second Art Theatre. He left the theatre in silence but was accosted by a student who was appalled that he should simply walk out without saying anything. 'That was splendid', Stanislavski replied, 'but now we go our separate ways'. In October of the same year he had paid his first visit to Meierhold's theatre. The final act of his production of Nikolai Erdman's *The Mandate* impressed him. Not only did the stage revolve but so did the walls of the set. Meierhold had achieved, he stated, something he had dreamed of doing. But it was a moment of rare satisfaction. Michael Chekhov's Hamlet a month later upset him profoundly, although he readily admitted, as ever, Chekhov's extraordinary talent. As for Meierhold's production of Gromelynck's *Le Cocu Magnifique*, which he saw on September 26, 1926, it left him frustrated and disappointed.

The Day of the Turbins had revealed the division between popular and critical reaction. Audiences had received the play as an illumination of their own lives, of history as experienced at the human level. At one performance a member of the audience, in a voice choked with tears, shouted 'Thank you'. Such reactions were anathema to the ideologues, for whom history was a matter of abstract forces, progressive or reactionary, with which one could identify or not. They demanded that a play provide a clear-cut, not to say simplistic statement of position, pro-revolutionary and therefore, of course, invincible. What was required was political tidiness.

Stanislavski could only restate his total opposition to such schematized views. He did not accept that avant-garde experiment was synonymous with revolutionary art or, more properly, with the art of the revolution. He had witnessed, he said, his colleagues' attempts to create theatre according to a series of formulae, of -isms, either artistic or ideological. The result was sterile propaganda. It produced ideological tidiness by exploiting stock responses and hack acting. The crucial question was what was to happen when the new writers of talent, the real poets of the revolution appeared, writers who would be able to confront the complexity and depth of the revolutionary experience in human terms? Such writers would require actors of genuine creative ability with a proper internal and external technique. 'We do not intend to kill that kind of actor and put a mere hack in his place', he concluded.

In reality Stanislavski's attitude to the work of younger directors was less oppositional. In conversation with Pulitzer prize novelist Theodore Dreiser, he admitted that something might come of Michael Chekov's and Vakhtangov's experiments. Stagnation was the real enemy. Behind this comment lay his disappointment that he had not been able to persuade the Art Theatre to establish an experimental group or laboratory.

About the same time as *The Days of the Turbins* was having its première, the newly-named Stanislavski Opera Studio opened. Rimski-Korsakov's *The Tsar's Bride* had its first performance on November 28, followed in January by Cimarosa's *Il Matrimonio Segreto*. Both had been in preparation for several months. Opera, happily, was less contentious than straight theatre and Stanislavski's productions were considered purely on their artistic merits. What struck critics about his production of the Cimarosa was his capacity to breathe life into works which were apparently only of historic interest.

His production of *The Tsar's Bride* was seen by the young Otto Klemperer, the doyen of Russian composers, Alexander Glazunov and Rimski-Korsakov's son-in-law Maximillian Steinberg who taught composition and orchestration at the Leningrad Conservatoire where he counted Shostakovitch among his pupils. Klemperer was impressed by Stanislavski's capacity to marry truth of character to musical form with proper theatricality. Steinberg felt that the production was faithful to everything his father-in-law had ever wanted both musically and dramatically.

After *Matrimonio* he turned to Puccini's *La Bohème*, which opened on April 12. This he updated from the 1840s to the turn of the century. Puccini's *verismo* suited him. The score contains many purely orchestral passages which accompany stage action. Stanislavski was able to push home the point that the motivation and shape of the moves were to be discovered in a careful study of the score.

The one production of the 1926/7 season for which Stanislavski took absolute responsibility was Beaumarchais' *Le Mariage De Figaro*. He worked as usual with assistants but of the 300 recorded rehearsals he took 82, an exceptionally high proportion. Work had started at the end of 1925, continued throughout the whole of 1926 and occupied the first four months of 1927. It opened April 28.

Stanislavski's purpose was twofold: to present a classic play which was relevant to contemporary audiences and to direct it in such a way as to reaffirm his aesthetic principles. A battle of words was no longer enough. He had once challenged Nemirovich with the words, 'defeat me with work'. Now what he required was a spectacular, prestige production with a clear post-revolutionary message and equally clear pre-revolutionary production values. He had frequently expressed his misgivings at the disappearance of the artist-designer who created a visual world specifically for each play, helping the actors to believe in the given circumstances. This had now been replaced by a mechanical, constructed world, essentially a style in its own right, making statements in its own right, reducing the actor to a function of the set. He suspected, moreover, along with Lunacharski, that after the rigours of scaffolding and walk-ways audiences were ready for something more lavish.

His view of the play had been expressed as far back as 1915 when he had seen Taïrov's production at the Kamerni. He had disagreed with the interpretation. In his notebook he commented:

'Figaro is ... a democratic play and certainly not decadent.' (K. S. Stanislavski, *Iz Zapisnikh Knizhek*, II, Moscow, 1986, p. 146.)

The action was to be seen through the eyes of Figaro and Susanna, not Count Almaviva, and set in a real not a theatrical world. The characters were not to be played as 'types' more or less derived from the *commedia dell'arte*, as they had been in the Mali production of 1920, but as individuals with historical and social roots:

'*Figaro* is a democrat, he's in the opposition, he's a rebel .... We know that he isn't a hero in the sense of our own recent turbulent revolutionary times but we won't "bring him up to date". But for his period he is a rebel, a representative of the people. And that's the effect he should produce today.

Susanna is Figaro in petticoats. Not a soubrette but a proper serving-maid who can work hard, spin, sew and cook – and she does it all easily and happily. Don't forget, she's the gardener's niece, a daughter of the people.

The Count is an egoist and a windbag but he's not stupid. A handsome man who knows he's handsome, the terror of all the girls in the district .... Inwardly amoral but outwardly attractive .... Even Susanna finds it difficult to resist his refined advances ....' (N. Gorchakov, *Rezhissiorski Uroki Stanislavskovo*, Moscow, 1951, p. 360.)

Figaro's attempt to deny the Count that last, degrading vestige of medieval privilege, the *ius primae noctis* is a symbolic act of revolt. In defining Figaro's through-line Stanislavski insisted that it was not, 'I want to be married' but 'I want to be married in order to be *free*.' He decided to transfer the action from 'Carmen's Spain' to pre-revolutionary France to show the people immediately prior to social upheaval.

The ruling idea behind the production was provided by the play's sub-title, 'la folle journée', the day of madness. This provided the rhythm of the action and the method of staging, which needed to be fast and free-flowing. From this decision others followed. He demanded of his cast that the 'Frenchness' of the play should be achieved by the quickness of their thinking, their nimbleness of mind, not through some vague notion that the French wave their hands a lot. This meant changes in the script. The same number of words takes much longer in Russian than in French and can appear heavy. He had the translation revised, cutting and condensing, while retaining the essential meaning, bringing the dialogue up to the lightness and pace of the original. He also insisted that Figaro's name should be pronounced, as in French, with the accent on the last syllable.

He decided to break Beaumarchais' five acts and five sets down into eleven scenes, moving freely throughout the house and grounds by means of the revolve. The last act, set in the garden, had four different revolve settings. The external pace with which the settings changed was to match the pace with which the inner action moved. As he told the cast, 'something new happens every second'. His use of the revolve may well have been influenced by Meierhold's production of *The Mandate* which he had admired a few months earlier.

For his designer he selected Aleksandr Golovin. Golovin belonged to the same school as Bakst and Benois; his designs recalled the splendour of Diaghilev's Ballets Russes. In 1910 he had provided opulent sets for Molière's *Don Juan* which he brought forward to the late eighteenth century and in 1917 he had designed Lermontov's *Maskerad* set in the same period. His palette was sumptuously polychrome. Stanislavski asked him to provide a contrast between the luxury of the salon and the poverty below stairs. To reinforce this contrast he also decided to change the location of Act Four, transferring it from one of the main state rooms to the servants' quarters. Golovin originally designed a splendid banquet with a table lavishly set. This is replaced by a small, shabby room with broken plaster. It is here that the wedding of Figaro and Susanna takes place.

Figaro brought two important developments to the System. Stanislavski began working in terms of broad physical objectives, well illustrated by the Wedding scene, in Act Four, where the entire household assembles for the festivities. Gone were the carefully choreographed movements and groupings with every pause timed, the cast were simply asked to respond truthfully to the cramped nature of the physical space. The action proceeded in three phases. Phase one: the servants were provided with a basic objective: find yourself a good place. This left no room for the Count and Countess. Phase two: make room for the master and mistress but still keep the best place you can. The question then arose, where were the Count and Countess to sit? Phase three: find two chairs and place them suitably. The scene staged itself through the identification of a series of basic physical problems, each requiring a new adaptation to changed circumstances but, from the servants' point of view, with a single objective running through, to gain and keep an advantage.

Stanislavski then elaborated the notion of the Flow of the Day. An actor's performance is constructed from a series of logically-connected actions, justifiable in terms of probability. The naturalistic actor, concerned only with the imitation of the surface can, if need be, create the performance out of sequence, in isolated fragments. For the realistic actor, concerned with inner justification, this is not possible. What is seen on stage is only moments in a continuum which is the 'life' of the character. It was the actor's task to have a thorough and clear knowledge of all off-stage moments, so that when he comes onto the stage he comes *from* somewhere and is on his way *to* somewhere.

Figaro has been recognised as one of Stanislavski's most remarkable achievements. It owed its quality mainly to its rhythmic unity, which bound all the disparate elements together. It was the organic cohesion of thought, speech, action and scene change which gave the play its drive and force. It was also the last production for which he was totally responsible.

The opening night was a success with ten curtain calls. Some thought the production would run twenty years. Others voiced criticism which was redolent of the theatre's early days. There were those for whom the play was still essentially a light comedy; they were disturbed by the way in which the dialogue was broken up with realistic pauses; they found the production a little heavy. Stanislavski did not demur. He merely pointed out that a play of this kind takes time to settle down; it has to be run in. The production received the inevitable thumbs-down from Vladimir Blum who accused it of failing to mark the class conflicts sufficiently. Stanislavski's principle of finding the good in an evil character and the evil in a good character – an essentially dialectical notion – meant nothing to Blum. He thought in crude ideological categories. It was simply unacceptable to him for Almaviva, the class enemy, to be presented as in any way sympathetic. First the *Turbins*, he wrote, now *Figaro* – the Art Theatre was incorrigible.

CHAPTER TWENTY-FIVE

THE ARMOURED TRAIN

The tenth anniversary of the October Revolution was approaching. Lunacharski attended the second night of *Figaro* with a number of colleagues and discussed plans for the jubilee celebrations. Stanislavski had decided ideas concerning the Art Theatre's contribution. He rejected an evening of dramatised extracts from contemporary writers. He wanted a single play, and a contemporary play, to contrast with the classic *Figaro*. He felt that while the theatre had presented works which dealt with the reactions of the privileged and middle classes to the revolution, it had not shown the lives of the people who had actually made it. There were apparently no new talented dramatists who could fill the gap. He was, however, attracted by a collection of short stories dealing with the partisans during the Civil War and, in particular, by Vsevolod Ivanov's *The Armoured Train* No 14–69. The story deals with the capture of an armoured train from counter-revolutionary troops by the partisans and with the transformation of the central character, Vershinin, from a politically-indifferent peasant farmer into a hero of the Bolshevik cause.

He asked Sudakov and Markov to collaborate with the author on an adaptation. They were to concentrate on the human content but at the same time to strip away any superfluous naturalism in order to achieve 'simplicity raised to the level of a clear symbol'. Having set the project in motion he turned it over to Sudakov, who was to supervise the production, and Litovtsieva, who was to take rehearsals. He was himself committed to a tour in Leningrad. During his stay in Leningrad Stanislavski was introduced to the painter Chupiatov, whose designs for a ballet he had admired. The artist's work seemed to open up new possibilities. It was three-dimensional and made interesting use of perspective. The original intention had been to engage Simov to design *The Armoured Train* but now Chupiatov seemed their man. He worked on the preliminary sketches throughout the summer.

A script had been ready in late June and a reading given at the Bolshoi on the 21st. In Art Theatre terms the play was a rush job. It received only 76 rehearsals, less than one third the number for *Figaro*. Everything needed to go like clockwork. It was inevitable at this point that things went wrong.

Chupiatov delivered his preliminary sketches in August when the play was well into rehearsal. Stanislavski was disappointed. They seemed very flat and lacking in energy. Above all they did not provide the opportunity for the dynamic staging in which the Art Theatre specialized. He made the necessary excuses and told Sudakov to contact Simov. There were barely two months to go to opening.

There were, however, more serious difficulties. The Repertkom was once again expressing its hostility. On August 12 Fiodor Mikhailovski, a member of the management team, wrote to Stanislavski, who was at a sanatorium in Kislovodsk, in Georgia, informing him that *Turbins* had been categorically banned and that a large number of changes were required in *The Armoured Train*, including a complete reworking of the final act. There were, furthermore, suggestions that *Uncle Vania* should be replaced by *The Cherry Orchard*. In other words the season as planned was on the rubbish heap.

On September 13 Stanislavski wrote to Lunacharski, asking for help.

'The presence of *Turbins* in our current repertoire would act as a guarantee that other new plays would come forward. Now we must either risk not being able to mount a show for the jubilee of the October Revolution or deliberately suffer financial losses.

I would like also to inform you that *Armoured Train* has still not been finally approved. We need extensive and complicated changes from the author who is abroad on holiday. We have sent him a telegram and all we now await is his arrival.

It is almost impossible to rehearse a much-needed show when there isn't a final script. Uncertainty is the worst enemy of work in the theatre; it saps energy and creates difficulties and delays by the minute.' (K. S. Archive, No. 6424.)

Early in October he was asked when it would be possible to arrange a showing for the Repertkom. On October 3 he wrote, displaying admirable restraint, to the Department responsible for state academic theatres informing them that he would be able to oblige once the author and Repertkom itself had agreed the two final scenes; the first seven were ready. He was careful to assure them that he would personally assume responsiblity for the final rehearsals and for the performances. On the 13th he received a letter from Lunacharski assuring him that there were unlikely to be any difficulties over the script for *The Armoured Train* and that the problem of the *Turbins* had been resolved – 'for this year at least'.

Lunacharski was right to put in the proviso. In the end the opposition to the *Turbins* triumphed and, in 1929, the play was taken off but the idealogical zealots were themselves wrong-footed. In 1932 it was discovered that Stalin not only liked the play but had actually seen it fifteen times. He detected no ideological problems. The play, in his opinion, finally proved the invincibility of the Bolshevik forces. The production was immediately revived and remained in the repertoire for the next nine years.

Stanislavski took over the production of *The Armoured Train* in September. He was then out of action for almost three weeks with a severe chill. He returned at the beginning of October and saw a run-through of several scenes on the 3rd. He was apparently pleased with what he saw. He made a speech of thanks for the good work done. The first complete run-through, staged for the benefit of the Repertkom, took place on October 31 in the foyer without costume or make-up; the sets were still not ready. Again Stanislavski seemed satisfied.

But, as on so many occasions, the more he became involved the less satisfied he became. The play was not progressing. The opening scene worried him particularly. Litovtsieva, he decided, had taken the wrong line. It needed to be tougher, harder, to set the tone for the rest of the play. What he was getting from senior members of the company like Knipper and Vishnievski was a kind of Chekhovian softness as a group of dispossessed White refugees considered their fate. It was the *Turbins* all over again, with the cast becoming involved with their own emotions rather than thinking of positive actions. What he wanted was murderous hate but the cast were unwilling to appear unsympathetic. Rather than adapt themselves to the characters, the actors were toning them down. Their unwillingness to show aggression was expressed in the over-relaxed physical action. At the root of the problem lay a degree of political anxiety. They did not, as artists, wish to be identified with the characters they were playing, something which is not unknown. Stanislavski understood but would have none of it:

> 'I'm not asking you to justify the characters either in political or human terms, far from it. What we're dealing with here is actors' feeling, a lack of courage to show the audience a so-called 'negative' character. You've got to get over that.' (N. Gorchakov, *Rezhissiorski Uroki Stanislavskovo*, Moscow, 1951, p. 481.)

The fact is the cast wanted the scene cut.

A long discussion ensued on the political and dramatic function of the scene but in the end Stanislavski resorted to a favourite strategy: he created a physical problem. He made them fight the furniture:

> 'Close in the greenhouse walls, pile all the furniture, crates and bundles on top of each other. Now I want you to clamber up on anything you like – the back of a chair, the piano crate, a pile of books. Help Olga Leonardovna [Knipper] onto the back of this armchair – it's strong . . . .
>
> KNIPPER: Look here, this is very uncomfortable.
>
> KS: That's just how it should feel. The others are uncomfortable too.

KNIPPER: But really I do feel a bit of a fool.

KS: Good. They all feel they're in a ridiculous situation. Only you hide the fact that you feel silly from everyone and so you say the lines about how you're going to line this barn with silk.' (Ibid., p. 484.)

The strategy worked although a few days later Stanislavski complained that the cast had adapted to the piles of furniture. If they had been in any way artistically adventurous they would have made life difficult for themselves again to keep the scene alive and push it forward.

The crowd scenes suffered from the same lack of focus, in particular the scene known as the Bell Tower. What Stanislavski was getting was undifferentiated peasant 'rhubarb' instead of genuine reaction. The cast knew perfectly well what was expected of them. They had discussed it in detail with Sudakov. Rather than indulge in further talk Stanislavski set them an exercise. He used a device which was later to become one of the principal features of his rehearsal method, the technique which came to be known as Here, Today, Now. The actor is asked the question: what would you do, as a private individual, if such and such happened? In the case of the *Armoured Train* he set them the following problem: what would they do if Lunacharski unexpectedly turned up at rehearsal and said:

'Comrade actors of the Art Theatre, in order to defend the Soviet state against the most recent attacks by our capitalist enemies, you must go with me immediately to the broadcasting station and tell the whole world that the rumour in the bourgeois press that the Art Theatre has refused to play *The Armoured Train* is a base, common lie. Who's coming with me?' (Ibid., p. 507.)

Stanislavski's imitation of Lunacharski was sufficiently impassioned and convincing to produce a equally impassioned and spontaneous response. The block to the scene had been cleared.

Stanislavski continued to pull the production together, making cuts, changing sets, clarifying objectives and the through-line. As always for him at this stage it was the dynamic, the forward drive of the play as a whole which mattered. After the first preview on November 3 he decided that the closing scene was too down-beat. He asked for more positive playing and again made changes to the set. The play opened five days later in a gala performance. Of the 76 rehearsals Stanislavski had only taken 11, 7 working on individual scenes and 4 run-throughs. There was, nonetheless, no doubt in anyone's mind as to who was responsible for the production in its final form.

Critics on the left apart, the production was received with enthusiasm both by the public, young and old, and by the authorities. For Lunacharski the Art Theatre had finally proved itself and demonstrated its ability to use high art to illuminate the revolution. *Izvestia* published a favourable article, rejecting the attacks of Blum and his colleagues. The *Vecherniaia Moskva* of December 13 reported that the Young Communists, the Komsomols, had warmly welcomed the progress the Art Theatre had made in moving ideologically from the *Turbins* to the *Armoured Train*. For Markov the System had proved its relevance:

'Through the revelation of the psychology of character it leads to the revelation of the social nature of that character. It reveals the period through man.' (P. Markov, Aktior Oktobriaski revolutsii, *Sovremeni Teatr*, 1927, No. 12, p. 179.)

Stanislavski surprised many of his colleagues, and shocked some, by working on a blatant melodrama, *Les Soeurs Gérard*, at the same time as *The Armoured Train*. This seemed ideologically inconsistent. He was, however, no artistic snob and he insisted that working on melodrama was good for actors. As a form melodrama relied almost entirely on plot. This forced the actors to make clear decisions about their sequence of actions. It also obliged them to use their imagination to flesh out the bare bones of the script and conceal the mechanics. At one rehearsal he gave a remarkable demonstration of what he meant. In the course of the action Constable Picard is meant to drug an old man, Martin. Stanislavski took over from the actor playing Picard and began to improvise with the actor opposite, Vladimir Mikhailov. A simple moment in the action was transformed into a ten-minute improvisation as each character tried to outwit the other. Stanislavski's point was not that such an exercise would ever be shown to an audience but that the logical pursuit of a goal, an objective, and adaptation to another character's reactions produced a richness of feeling and behaviour which would inform the final performance. The actors were no longer playing plot but situation.

After the success of *The Armoured Train* Stanislavski turned his attention to Rimski-Korsakov's opera *May Night* which had been in rehearsal for several months. It opened on January 19, 1928 though not before he had staged a walkout from rehearsal apparently over the uncooperative attitude of the cast. The reviews in *Pravda* and *Izvestia* were excellent. The Stanislavski System had, once again, according to *Izvestia* proved its value.

The next two productions at the Art Theatre, however, dispersed much of the goodwill which had been created. *Untilovsk*, by Leonov, set in a remote community in Siberia, had been in rehearsal for some time but had been set aside during the latter stages of *The Armoured Train*. Stanislavski took the unusual step of holding a public reading before an invited audience of writers, officials and critics which was followed by a discussion of the play's merits. That seemed a wise precaution. Nonetheless when the recently reorganised management committee saw a preview on the 14th they disapproved of the play on ideological grounds. So, when it opened three days later, did almost everyone else. On March 14 Lunacharski published an article in the Leningrad journal *Krasnaia Gazeta* stating that the play marked a step backward. Everyone agreed the production was full of fine touches and the acting excellent but they could not save the play. Stanislavski was fully aware of the political deficiencies of the script but it offered good parts for actors from which they could learn.

Equally adverse reaction was encountered by Kataeiv's *The Embezzlers* which opened on April 20. The play dealt with corruption among government officials in search of a good life during the early days of Lenin's New Economic Policy. The social themes of the play were denounced as superficial, as was the writing which, it was stated, offered trivial material for the actors to work on. The general view, expressed at an internal post-mortem discussion on April 16, was that the script could not bear the wealth of detail Stanislavski had lavished upon it. For his part Stanislavski could only ask what he was to do. New plays were thin on the ground. He had one, Bulgakov's *Flight*. What was better, to encourage young, inexperienced writers or to go on reviving classics? He lost the battle and the play was taken off after eighteen performances.

The failure of two productions produced a fresh wave of criticism. On May 5 an article appeared in the *Rabochaia Gazeta* accusing the Art Theatre of failing to give sufficient place to working-class groups and their interests, and of undervaluing the work of young actors. Particular criticism was levelled at Podgorni, of the literary department, and Yegorov one of the business managers. Stanislavski replied with an open letter in *Pravda* on the 16th which was also published by *Izvestia* and the magazine *Sovremeni Teatr*. He rebutted the criticisms and reaffirmed the theatre's concern for the future. That future, however, was no longer directly in his hands.

On January 22, 1928 Nemirovich had returned from the United States but the handover of responsibility does not appear to have taken place until May when the theatre's management committee was once more reorganized. The two-year period of Stanislavski's control had scotched the myth of his inefficiency. There was no talk of his being 'inept' or 'muddle-headed'. The fact is that with Nemirovich out of the way Stanislavski thrived and so did the theatre with him. The company were fully aware of their dependence on him and largely resented his involvement with the Opera Studio. They asked him more than once not to take on too many outside responsibilities. With Nemirovich back in command he was gloomy about future prospects and in May confided to his notebook:

'I cannot guarantee the further growth of the company and the actors' (K. S. Archive, No. 814.)

He had set a number of projects in motion. Work had started on a produc-

tion of *Othello* with Leonidov in the title role. He had proposed a stage
version of Gogol's *Dead Souls* which Bulgakov was to adapt. Bulgakov's
second play *Flight* was also scheduled.

In the field of opera he was already working on Moussorgski's *Boris
Godunov* which he intended to stage in the composer's own second version
with the original orchestration rather than the popular revised version by
Rimski-Korsakov. Moussorgski's score had just been published and it would
be the first time it had been heard since the 1880s. Stanislavski was on the
look-out, too, for modern operas. He had seen Berg's *Wozzeck* at the Mali
opera theatre in June 1927 and more recently had been interested in a one-
act opera by Kurt Weil, *Der Tzar Lasst Sich Photographieren*.

From mid-June to mid-July he was on tour in Leningrad. He left soon
after his return to Moscow for what had become a regular summer visit to
the sanatorium in Kislovodsk. He was being advised to slow down; he was,
after all 65. He stayed in Georgia until September 10 when he returned to
Moscow. On the 15th, he went to Berlin. While there he held his
last serious discussion with Michael Chekhov who had left the Soviet Union
in 1927, having fallen foul of the authorities. Stanislavski tried to persuade
him to return but to no avail. Chekhov never set foot in Russia again.
Their conversation, he recalled, centred on the function of an actor's own
personal emotions in the creation of a role.

Stanislavski also made contact once more with Max Reinhardt and on
September 19 saw his production of *Die Artisten*. Reinhardt had been trying
to persuade him to stage a play in Berlin for two years, suggesting either
The Dybbuk or a Chekhov. There were other offers. Leopold Jessner, the
Intendant of the Staats und Schiller Theater invited him to stage *Figaro*
with a German cast as part of the Berliner Festspiel in May 1929. There
was also a plan to make a film to illustrate *My Life in Art*. He did not
commit himself.

On the 22nd he left for Badenweiler where his family joined him. While
staying there he received a telephone call from Leonidov telling him that
Reinhardt had just spent 30,000 marks on a magnificent car which he intended giving him as a gift. Was he, he wrote to Podgorni on October 5,
supposed to drive to the theatre in it on the thirtieth jubilee in October?
Kind as it was of Reinhardt the car was an acute embarrassment. How
was he to get it to Moscow? What about the customs? What, more importantly, about running costs? Once back in Berlin he attended a reception
given by Reinhardt at which the car was ceremoniously presented. Stanislavski gave a credible imitation of surprise, joy, gratitude and allowed himself
to be driven back to his hotel, accompanied by Michael Chekhov. The car
was not entirely wasted. In the event it served to chauffeur Reinhardt round
Moscow on his next visit.

Stanislavski returned to Russia on October 16. He approached the forthcoming celebrations with a sense of foreboding. It would mean a heavy round of receptions, official ceremonies, meals, on top of what he had lived through in Berlin, getting to bed at three in the morning. He was also unhappy once again about the atmosphere in the theatre. He suspected that Podgorni and Yegorov, who had been so heavily criticized in the press earlier in the year following the presentation of *Untilovsk*, were now working against him. Greetings began pouring in from all over the world. Reinhardt made him an honorary member of the Deutsches Theater. *Izvestia* reported messages from Gordon Craig, Mary Pickford, Douglas Fairbanks, Charlie Chaplin, Gloria Swanson. But even this happy event was overcast by ideological shadows. Stanislavski's address to the company on the 26th, which was no more than his usual idealistic appeal for dedication and openness to the future, was criticised for failing to reflect the contemporary mood.

On the 29th the theatre celebrated its jubilee with a gala performance consisting of extracts from its major productions. Stanislavski was due to appear as Vershinin in Act One of *Three Sisters*. He had once said to an actor, 'You can die on stage but you can't miss an entrance'. Like Molière he remained true to that principle. His performance, according to eye-witnesses was exceptional despite the fact that he suffered a massive heart-attack. Years later he recalled:

'. . . I come on, applause, I say the lines and suddenly I feel faint. I nearly collapsed but got a hold of myself, pulled myself together and finished the act. However, going upstage (as indicated in the promptbook), you remember, to the dining-room I sent for my doctors. They were both in the audience. Finally the act came to an end, I came out for two curtain calls and . . . I collapsed, they were already carrying me away. The audience knew nothing although they were surprised that I didn't take any more calls.' (Stanislavski's account, taken down by B. V. Zon, August 11, 1934. In B. Zon, *Meetings with Stanislavski*. K. S. Archive.)

He was driven home. As he wrote to his doctor later he realised he might not actually reach there alive:

'I remember that fatal evening of the jubilee performance when you took me home in the car. I remember how you, in your dinner-jacket, took care of me, looking into my eyes searchingly and affectionately to see whether I was ill or already dead.' (K. S. Archive, No. 5103.)

He never appeared on stage again.

CHAPTER TWENTY-SIX

OTHELLO

Stanislavski lived the last ten years of his life on borrowed time. The heart was enlarged, he had emphysema, brought on by years of heavy smoking, and arterio-sclerosis, although the brain was not affected. Whatever his physical weakness his mental capacities were unimpaired but he could not carry through his ideas in practice. He suffered from periodic bouts of breathlessness, diagnosed as asthma. His natural propensity to colds, chills and flu meant that during the bad winter months the apartment was practically hermetically sealed. When he could he went abroad. At Leontiev Lane he had a nurse in constant attendance to make sure he took his medicine and did not overstretch himself. There was also the formidable Ripsime Karpovna Tamansova, 'Ripsi', his diminutive secretary, known to the outside world as Little Napoleon both on account of her stature and her fierce devotion to her employer.

His relations with the outside world were filtered through his entourage, domestic and professional; work was done at home, either in the flat itself or in the Onegin Room. Later, in the Thirties, he was able to make occasional visits to the theatre. If the doctors had had their way he would have retired but life without the theatre was nothing to him. He came alive when he could talk about the theatre or work on a scene, finding fresh reserves of energy. He did not reduce the scope of his interests – plays, opera, teaching, writing – but everything was done in snatches, often over long periods – the production of Bulgakov's *Molière,* from delivery of the manuscript to final showing, was spread over five years. His life became even more of a mosaic.

His health was a matter of national concern. On November 18 *Izvestia* published a bulletin giving details of his temperature, night and morning, and his pulse rate. They gave an assurance of general progress. He was confined to bed for three months. His attitude was exemplary. He was as disciplined a patient as he was an actor, almost as though he were being directed in a play, *The Sick Man.* He took the exact number of drops required and when he was finally allowed up asked how many steps a day he could take. Eventually he was allowed to go out for short walks. A chair was placed at each turn of the stairs so that he could sit down if he needed. These excursions were kept secret for fear that he should be approached by a colleague and get overexcited.

By the beginning of December he was well enough to write to the theatre to say what he thought should be done. He wanted work on *Othello* to continue with Leonidov in charge. He stipulated that there should only be a strictly limited number of performances, no more than one every fourteen days. He also directed rehearsals should continue for Bulgakov's *Flight*. Work had begun in October but was abruptly terminated in January of the following year in a shower of vituperation from the authorities who had seen a run-through. For the rest, his thoughts turned back to the early days. He remembered with nostalgic pleasure the sense of ensemble among the original group, now the Old Brigade. In contrast to what he had said in the recent past and what indeed he was to repeat not much later, he stressed the importance of revivals to weld the old and new members of the company together.

By the end of the month his condition had deteriorated, causing great anxiety. At the New Year Rachmaninov wired his good wishes from New York but the theatre's traditional celebrations were held under a pall.

As soon as he had recovered a little, he was asked to collaborate with Lunacharski and the new magazine *Iskusstvo* to try and solve one of the most difficult problems in Marxist thought, the development of an adequate aesthetic to counter crude sloganizing. Stanislavski's contribution would be his knowledge of the past and of the Realist tradition. A French publishing house La Renaissance du Livre requested permission to bring out a translation of *My Life in Art* with a preface by Jacques Copeau. Morris Gest renewed his invitation for another US tour to include the West Coast. Stanislavski was still writing up the System and was able to read Leonidov draft chapters on *Faith and a Sense of Truth* and *Emotional Memory*.

There was no question of his undertaking any rehearsal work, not even coaching actors or singers at home but the production of *Boris Godunov* which he had planned and in part supervized opened on March 5 at the Stanislavski Opera Theatre. Moskvin had seen the work through its final stages. Stanislavski was telephoned between the acts and told how the performance was going. It was an unquestioned success. The experience of recreating the realities of Russian history displayed for so many years in *Tsar Fiodor* was transferred to the operatic stage.

By April he was working on a production plan for Tchaikovski's *Queen of Spades* and discussing sets for *Othello* with Golovin. *My Life in Art* had its third printing in as many years. At the beginning of May it was decided that he was well enough to travel and on the 2nd accompanied by his family and his physician, Dr Chistiakov, he left for Berlin. While there he received an invitation to give classes for an eight-month period at Boleslavski's American Laboratory Theatre. All activity was brought to an abrupt halt when he went down with flu.

He was well enough to travel to Badenweiler, the spa where Chekhov had died, on May 28, where he began work with his son Igor on a production plan for Rossini's *Barbiere Di Seviglia*. In July, Knipper arrived, as did Elizabeth Reynolds Hapgood and her husband, Norman. Stanislavski read them extracts of the *Pupil's Diary*.

Mrs Hapgood like many others had been anxious, ever since the American tour, for Stanislavski to write a definitive version of the System. Now, when he was unable to act or direct, seemed the ideal opportunity to get the book into final shape. The commercial possibilities in the United States were considerable, a fact which continued to bear heavily with Stanislavski. Igor still needed treatment and that meant dollars. Undemanding on the whole for himself, he had always been careful, ever since he ventured into the theatre as a professional, to defend his family's material needs. Now he had a translator, Elizabeth Hapgood, with whom he could work on a day-to-day basis and an experienced critic and editor, Norman Hapgood. The Hapgoods were full of ideas about pre-publicity and suggested the appearance of the book should be preceded by the publication of extracts in leading American papers. They had also found a new publisher, Yale University Press.

Stanislavski did not, however, devote his energies full-time to the book. His main concern was still the production of *Othello*. In June he had renewed his invitation to Leonidov to supervise rehearsals and on September 23 wrote to Nemirovich asking for the production to continue on the lines he had laid down. His health was not helped by the fact that he was now restless, knowing that the Opera Studio was starting work again and wondering what was happening in his absence. Lilina was obliged to write to Moscow to ask for an extension of their leave. Stanislavski was not ready to brave the cold and damp of a Moscow winter, although he was worried lest such a request should seem disloyal or be interpreted, once again, as a sign that he was turning émigré. In November he succumbed to flu once again and on the 28th left for the more congenial climate of Nice where he worked simultaneously on the production plan for *Othello* and a production plan for *Rigoletto*. He also dictated to his doctor the article *From the Last Conversation with Vakhtangov*.

While in Badenweiler he had learned of radical changes in the Art Theatre management. To the two nominal directors, himself and Nemirovich, was now added a 'political' director, Mikhail Sergeievich Hertz, who would ensure that the theatre was on the straight and narrow ideological path. Stanislavski had given his reaction to this decision in a long letter to Leonidov on September 15. He had no objections in principle to the appointment of a political director. It was not the man's politics that worried him. What he was afraid of was an ignorant lay-man who would not understand the way theatres work and decisions are taken. He rejected Leonidov's notion that they would be better off with a second-rank official whom they could control. If there was to be a political appointee Stanislavski wanted someone with clout who could defend the theatre in the upper echelons of government.

Lilina was now worried. On December 19 she wrote to Ripsi that she was quite happy for Stanislavski to be sent news of rehearsals but she would prefer that bad or disturbing news be suppressed. Her good intentions misfired. On January 22, 1930 Stanislavski wrote to Ripsi complaining that he had no news and no response to the Hapgoods' plans for marketing the book:

'... Some time ago I sent you a list of American newspapers in which extracts from my forthcoming book might be published. There will have to be a lengthy correspondence. Elisaveta Lvovna [Mrs Hapgood] is waiting impatiently for a decision as to which of these papers we can give an answer to. I think you are holding back on this because you are afraid that I will publish something that has not been vetted by Liubov Yakovlevna [Mrs Gurevich] or that I will sell it too cheap. Don't worry, nothing will be done without Liubov Jakovlevna's being involved. The book has been sold for a fixed sum so that I'm not dependent on actual publication – that's a matter of how the book sells. My main concern is that nothing should be printed in the papers that might seem improper to the powers that be. If a reply is too long in coming then misunderstandings can arise, so please hurry!

But the most important thing I want to know is, the University of New Haven [Yale] would like to bring out my second book and any others. . . . Find out as fast as you can and write whether Elizaveta Lvovna can start negotiating with you. There's a Theatre Faculty at the university over there and they need my book. . . . (SS, VIII, P. 218.)

His statement that he had sold the book outright is not borne out by later contracts since his heirs, Igor and Igor's daughter, Olga, continued to collect royalties for many years after his death.

He was now working hard on *Othello*, sending the production plan to the theatre, scene by scene, as in the early days. Although Sudakov was the nominal director it was to Leonidov that Stanislavski sent his plan and indeed the bulk of it is more or less addressed to him direct. Act One arrived in Moscow on December 24. Act Two was despatched in two parts the following January, Act Three and Act Four scene one, on March 15 and 18. Stanislavski kept up a long and detailed correspondence with Leonidov, trying to help him through difficult moments. A major problem was Act Three, scene three, the pivotal point in the play for Othello. In his production plan Stanislavski broke down the duologue between Othello and Iago into ten units but in a letter February 10, 1930 he explained Othello's psychological progression in greater detail. What he offered Leonidov was a more elaborately worked-out version of the line he himself had taken on the scene in 1896, when he moved slowly towards the final oath of vengeance:

'Let us establish the circumstances as experienced by Othello. He has been indescribably happy with Desdemona. His honeymoon has been a dream, the ultimate height of passionate love. This ultimate height has been little presented by actors playing *Othello*, the writer himself gives little attention or space to it and yet it is important if we are to show what Othello is losing and what he is saying farewell to. . . . This scene marks, in essence, the dividing line. From here on Othello goes downwards. Can a man suddenly renounce the happiness he has known and to which he has become accustomed? Is it easy to acknowledge what one has lost? When a man loses the very thing by which he lives, he is at first bereft, loses equilibrium, then begins agonisingly to look for it. Once there was happiness, how can one go on without it? A man going through a crisis goes over his whole life in agony and sleepless nights. He weeps for what he has lost, values it more highly than before, and compares it to the future as he now imagines it. What must a man do to accomplish this huge inward task? He must go deep into himself to test out the past and to imagine his future life. Small wonder then that a man in such circumstances does not notice what is going on around him, that he is absent-minded and strange and that when he returns once more from the dream-world to reality he is even more horrified and disturbed and looks for a pretext to pour out the bitterness and pain that has built up while he was deep within himself.

That is Othello's situation in the scene as I see it. And that was the reason for the set. That is why Othello flies to the top of the highest tower as in this scene . . . to live the moment when he says "Ha, ha, false to me!". . . .

I don't think that Othello is jealous. The petty jealousy with which Othello is usually portrayed belongs more to Iago. The fact is, I now realise, that Iago is basely and vulgarly jealous of Emilia. Othello is an altogether nobler being. He cannot live in the world in the knowledge of the injustice men cause one another, to ridicule and debase with impunity the sublime love that lives within them. And that under the mask of an ideal beauty, almost of a goddess of heavenly purity and innocence, of unearthly goodness and tenderness! All these qualities are so cunningly portrayed that you cannot tell them from the real thing!

And so, in relation to this scene, I think it is not a question of jealousy but a pathological disappointment in the ideal of a woman and a man the like of which the world has never seen. It is the most profound pain, unbearable sorrow. Othello sits hour long in this attitude, eyes staring at a fixed point, delving into his innermost being, trying to comprehend, believe the possibility that such a satanic lie could exist. And so when Iago comes up from below, cautiously, unseen, like a snake, and says, with unusual gentleness, like a doctor to a patient, "Why, how now,

General! No more of that", Othello begins to tremble in anticipation of the pain this torturer is preparing for him. . . . Most actors playing Othello fall into a rage here. In reality it is still the most excruciating pain. It hurts so much that the illusion of joy he had before now appears to him as real joy. He compares this illusion of joy with what is happening now and begins to bid farewell to life. There are only two passions in the world for him: Desdemona and the art of generalship, as with great actors whose life is divided between the love of women and art.

So, "Farewell the tranquil mind! Farewell content!" etc., is a farewell, a lament, a lament for his second passion and not at all a sentimental panegyric over a life of war, as it is usually played. I will applaud you loudly if you remain in some attitude or other, motionless, oblivious to the things around you, and survey with an inner eye the total picture that is so infinitely dear to a master of the art of war. Sit still, wipe away the tears that are running down your cheeks in great drops, hold on to yourself so as not to sob out loud and speak in a muted voice, as people do when talking of something important and intimate.

This speech might be broken up by long pauses during which he sits there and silently surveys the picture of what he has lost. In other pauses he might bend forward over a stone and sob a long time unheard, shaking his head as though he were saying farewell. This is not emotional enthusiasm for war but the tears shed before impending death. Once he has bound up the wounds of his heart with this farewell, he feels the need to pour out his torment to somebody else. So he begins to reveal his pain to Iago. And when he has grabbed him and well nigh thrown him off the tower, he takes fright at what he might do and runs up the stone platform, throws himself down, racked with silent sobs. There he lies, like a boy, in a child-like posture, on this rock, and asks forgiveness and pours out his sorrow to Iago who is standing below him. And at the end of the scene, when it is almost dark and the moon and stars are appearing in the sky, Othello is standing on the upper platform and calls Iago to him and, up there, between heaven and the sea, outraged in his deepest human feelings, he calls the moon that is sinking below the horizon and the stars to witness and performs a terrifying ceremony, i.e., an oath of revenge.' (SS, VIII, pp. 221–4.)

What Stanislavski could not know when he sent the last set of notes on the 18th was that the play had already opened four days earlier, on the 14th. A telegram from Heitz informing him what had happened was concealed. It was not for another week or so that he learned what a failure the production had been. To make matters worse he also learned through the French and German press that the Opera Theatre's production of Tchaikovski's *Queen of Spades* had also flopped.

The reasons for the failure of *Othello* are complex. It was perhaps foolish to imagine that someone else could interpret and stage Stanislavski's detailed plan. The early days when Nemirovich had exploited Stanislavski's ideas could not be recreated. Sudakov was not Nemirovich and, in any case, the plan for *Othello* was qualitatively different from the plan for *The Seagull* which was like a story-board from which a moving picture could be made. The plan for *Othello* contained some indication of blocking but for the most part consisted in psychological analysis and methods of approaching a role. It could only truly be realised by the person who had created it.

The theatre was under pressure to get the play on. Nemirovich was busy with other projects. Leonidov had more than enough to cope with playing the leading role, Golovin was too ill to come to Moscow and had to turn his designs over to other hands. The full weight of responsibility fell on Sudakov who decided to cut his losses, use Stanislavski's plan as a guide, and for the rest follow his own judgement. Golovin's designs were similarly modified. To make matters worse Leonidov was ill. He had impressed Stanislavski during preliminary work in 1926, rehearsals had been more than promising, the previews, the second attended by Stalin, gave every reason to hope, but he suffered from agoraphobia which now extended to a fear of open space of the auditorium. His performance deteriorated steadily during the later previews and by the official opening was only a shadow of its former self. The first night was ponderous and overlong. The play came off after eighteen performances.

Knipper's view, as she wrote to Bertenson, was that the theatre should not have attempted to go off at half-cock. They should have got in a new designer and simplified the presentation to something they could manage. That, at least, would have been less damaging to Stanislavski whose name was still on the posters as the play's director. She simply did not know what to write to him.

Ripsi broke the bad news in a long letter on March 20. In it she spared him no details of the changes made both to the sets and the staging. She summed up the attitude in the theatre:

'. . . for the moment let the show go on as it is. When Konstantin Sergeievich comes back we will rework the whole play.' (K S, Archive, No. 10686/1–2.)

Stanislavski did not answer Ripsi's letter until April 9. He was still bitterly angry.

'I am appalled! Why put on *Othello* like that? What's it got to do with me or my production plan? It's pure ignorance. I took on *Othello* precisely to try and correct such ignorance and now it has emerged worse than ever. Where's the new here? Where is there any sign of Stanislavski's production plan? I go hot with shame when I think of it? Can't somebody do something to make sure my name is taken off the posters? Send me a poster and the reviews (of *Othello* and *Queen of Spades*). The French and (apparently) German newspapers are reporting that *Queen of Spades* was a failure. I know nothing, I'm being hoodwinked. I'm being made to look a fool because I don't know what's going on in my own theatre, others do but I, the director, don't. I'm not terribly fond of idiot parts. Send me the reviews, open all letters. Consult [Podgorni] as to how my name can be taken off the posters but without offending either Leonidov (I know what he's going through) or Moskvin (who worked on it). On the other hand why should my name be linked with a pot-boiler? Poor Golovin. . . . How low the theatre has sunk. . . .

   Don't tell Leonidov how upset I am. Get him to write to me. But please tell me how his health is.' (SS, VIII, pp. 242–3.)

A new word had entered Stanislavski's glossary of abuse, *kaltura*, pot-boiler.

A month later the failure still rankled. He had set such store by this production. While on tour in the United States he had written to Nemirovich of his ambition to direct Shakespeare:

'. . . as he appears to me in dreams, as I see him with my inner eye and hear him with my inner ear, Shakespeare on the basis of harmony, phonetics, rhythm, feeling for words and action, on the natural sound of the human voice, on the basis of the simple, rewarding, step-by-step logical development of feelings and the course of the action.' (*Sovietskaia Kultura* 1/XII, 1962.)

Othello had been intended to serve several purposes: it would wipe out an early failure; it would prove his ability to stage Shakespeare, the one major author who had eluded him; it would provide valuable teaching material for his books on acting. According to Mrs Hapgood he even considered centering all his writing on acting around the play. This appears to have been no more than the result of passing enthusiasm. *An Actor's Work on a Role* (*Creating a Role*) does, however, contain a section on *Othello*, including improvisations.

Othello seemed the ideal choice not only because he had a life-long fascination with it but because of the intensity and the elemental nature of the passions it involves. The major roles in *Othello* demand that access to inner resources, the unconscious, which the System is designed to supply. The production plan of *Othello* repays careful study. It was the last time that Stanislavski committed to paper his detailed thoughts on a play. Separated by thousands of miles from his collaborators he had to spell everything out. The result is a portrait of a man who, at 67, on the one hand sums up earlier experience and, on the other, shows that he is on the brink of yet another radical break with the past.

Act One starts with a set of instructions on the creation of wave effects taken direct from the notes he made in Bayreuth in 1902 when Cosima Wagner showed him round the set of *Der Fliegende Hollander*. There are signs both in this opening scene and, later, in the Senate, of earlier concerns with naturalistic effects – the lapping of waves and the beating of oars, the scratching of quills on parchment, which punctuate the dialogue – but these are the superficial aspects of a production plan which looks forward to the Method of Physical Action which he was to develop on his return to Moscow but which he never set down in complete form on paper. The essence of the approach is contained in the letter sent to Nemirovich in 1923, quoted above, the 'step-by-step, logical development of feelings and the course of the action.' He had now come to the firm conclusion that when the actor was not able to identify instinctively with a situation, emotion should not be approached direct. An assault on the unconscious produced a block. Emotion Memory had too often produced hysterics or self-indulgence. It is not possible to play Love. On the other hand, by recreating the stages by which a person falls in love, it is possible to induce feelings of love. The actions constitute the 'decoy-duck', as he called it, which lures the emotions.

In attempting to explain his new working method Stanislavski often used analogies of locomotion – trains, aeroplanes:

'Remember how an aeroplane takes off. It starts by running along the ground for a long time and then lifts off thanks to the momentum it has built up. A movement of air is caused which lifts the wings and takes the machine upwards.

The actor, too, moves and, so to speak, takes a run-up, thanks to physical actions and gains momentum. At that moment with the aid of the given circumstances and the Magic Ifs he spreads the invisible wings of belief which carry him upwards to the realm of the imagination in which he sincerely believes.

But if there is no runway and no aerodrome how can you take a run-up or rise into the air? You can't, of course. Our first concern, therefore, will be to construct that aerodrome and runway paved with physical actions which are strong in truth.' (*Rezhissiorski Plan 'Othello'*, Iskusstvo, 1945, p. 233.)

Stanislavski's experience in the period 1924–1928 had produced a shift of position, concerning not basic notions of training but methods of rehearsal and working on a role. Different productions had spotlighted different elements of the total process. Coming in at a late stage in rehearsal, after the ground-work had been done, he had developed a growing concern with the overall structure and dynamic of a play. He was conscious of the dangers of breaking a text down into too many small units. While constantly emphasising the importance of 'little truths', particularly to students, he was also aware of the importance of larger truths of which the little truths formed a part. What he was now anxious to emphasize was the distinction between the artist who *plans* and the actor who *performs* even though they are one and the same person. What an artist playing a major role must do is establish its dynamic, its 'economy', the curve of the action – where to hold back, where to play full out, as he had seen Zacconi demonstrate in Paris in 1923. The artist knows the end of the play, knows what happens next. When the actor, however, walks on stage he only *knows* one step at a time. The surest path, it now seemed to him, lay through a concentration on physical action. This he could only explain through his production plan and so, for Leonidov's benefit, he tried to pull all these emergent ideas together and summarize the process by which he now considered a role was created:

'When playing a role, especially a tragic role, you should think as little as possible about tragedy and as much as possible about simple physical objectives. Thus the plan for the entire role will consist roughly in 5–10 physical actions and the plan of the scene will be ready. In all five acts there will be 30–50 major physical actions.

Coming on stage the actor must think of the immediate physical act or the few immediately physical acts which fulfil the objective or a complete unit. The others will follow of themselves in logical succession.

Let him remember that the sub-text comes of itself, that when he thinks of physical actions he thinks, independently of any act of will, of the 'Magic Ifs' and 'given circumstances' which have been established during the working process.

. . . Physical actions which can firmly be fixed and are therefore useful for the overall plan, actually contain, independent of the actor's will, all the given circumstances and Magic Ifs. These are, in fact, the sub-text. Therefore, progressing on the basis of physical actions, the actor, involuntarily, at the same time, progresses through the given circumstances.

Don't let an actor forget to use this approach only in rehearsal. With it he establishes, firmly grounds, develops that line, the line of physical actions. Only in this way can an actor master the technicalities of a role. The actor possesses a number of possible lines, as, for example, the line of the plot, the lines of psychology and feeling, the line of pure stage action and so on. But there are lines which are often forgotten which are nonetheless necessary to an actor's technique and lead to a proper approach.

The line of physical action, truth and belief is one of the most important lines out of which is woven the so-called 'line of the day'.

'The Line of the Day' is the external physical through-line. The line of physical actions is the line of physical units and objectives.' (Ibid., pp. 230–31.)

Scenes are therefore analysed in terms of broad physical objectives. In the opening scene of the play Iago and Rodrigo have a single purpose: to create as much noise as possible and draw attention to themselves. The others in the scene appearing at doors and windows are trying to find out what is happening and why. Stanislavski insisted that the scene in which Desdemona looks for the handkerchief should be dominated by the act of searching and nothing else. Other scenes, such as the passage in Act Three scene one between Othello and Desdemona or Act Three scene three between Othello and Iago are broken down into smaller, more specific units.

Characters are also provided with a full biographical background. In Act One scene one a full explanation is provided of the circumstances which have brought Iago and Rodrigo to this point. The material which Stanislavski provides is an imaginative extension of hints and references within Shakespeare's text. Throughout the plan the off-stage action, the action between the scenes, is sketched in to establish the flow of the day.

The insistence on the physical, that moments of highest tragedy needed to be rooted in a simple physical objective, did not imply an indifference to the language of the play. Far from it, language is paramount. Language is stressed as the supreme form of integrated physical action. The prime consideration for an actor was the mastery of the text, of the 'active word':

'To achieve them [the objectives] (something extremely important and something actors always forget) he needs words, thoughts i.e., the author's text. An actor above all must operate through words. On stage the only important thing is the active word.' (Ibid., p. 232.)

It is possible to understand Sudakov's despair when faced with such a complex document. There was enough material here for a year's work or more, not the three months allotted him.

Stanislavski was now desperate to return home, fearing that the Art Theatre and the Opera Theatre were on the downward path. That, however, was out of the question. Only the book, as he told Ripsi in his letter of May 11, made his enforced stay endurable.

Work was progressing rapidly, although Igor's poor state of health caused periodic interruptions. On April 23 he wrote Ripsi a detailed letter of the manuscript material he was sending, including a list of chapters for the first volume and their order. This is shorter than the final published version and indicates the work that remained to do. It is clear that the *Diary of a Pupil* was to appear in two parts, *Experience* and *Physical Characterisation*.

Norman Hapgood had felt, rightly, that there should be one single volume on an actor's preparatory training, the current An Actor Prepares and Building a Character as one book, giving the internal and external elements as one continuous process. The fateful decision to split the book into two parts was taken because of the large format of Soviet publishing house 'Academia'. A single volume would have run to 1200 pages, which was unmanageable. Stanislavski was worried by this decision. To Ripsi he stressed the importance of seeing the System as a whole. There were three volumes planned: *The Diary of a Pupil, I* and *II* and *Work on a Role, The Creative State and the Unconscious.*

'It is important that the book begin with an overview of the whole scheme. i.e., all three volumes. Otherwise I think it is impossible for the book to appear in separate parts. The fact is that when the first book appears (*Diary of a Pupil, Work on Oneself, Experience*) it could appear as though experience was of an ultra-naturalistic nature and the book would therefore be reviled. It there is an overall plan at the beginning of the book and it is made plain that the whole book leads to superconscious creation the naturalism of the initial stages is justified.

Now, of course it will be said that all the books should come out together. In that case the earliest that could happen would be in five years time and in the interim anybody can catch hold of the "System" and publish it.' (SS, VIII, p. 244.)

The letter was all too prophetic. The accident of publication, the 14 year gap in America and the 17 year gap in the Soviet Union between the appearance of the Parts One and Two of the *Diary* has led, in the West at least, to an overemphasis on the 'naturalistic' aspects of the System and to the assumption even among the well-informed that *An Actor Prepares is* the System.

It is clear from the letter to Ripsi that another, albeit minor, editorial decision was still to be taken. When opting for the semi-fictional form Stanislavski had decided to give the characters generic names, rather in the manner of Jonsonian or Restoration Comedy. Thus the teacher is called Tvortsov (Creator) from the word *tvorchestvo* – creation. Other characters represented other abstractions – Chuvstvov from *chuvstvo*, feeling, Rassudov from *rassudok* reason. These were subsequently modified, though without entirely losing their etymological roots. Tvortsov thus became Tortsov and Chuvstvov, Shustov.

The day before Stanislavski wrote to Ripsi he had reached a formal agreement with Mrs Hapgood. On April 22, 1930, on a sheet of writing paper headed Vista Bella, Menton, France, he signed a document, in English, granting Mrs Hapgood power of attorney to negotiate contracts for the translation and publication of a sequence of books he was writing – four at

the time of drafting – in all languages, including Russian, and also to negotiate magazine, serial and motion picture rights. She was also to hold in safe-
keeping any royalties which might accrue to him. The document is signed
Constantine Stanislavski. The following day the American Consul in Nice,
George Armstrong, issued a Certificate of Acknowledgement of Execution
of Document confirming the legal status of the paper Stanislavski had
signed. In fact the assignment of rights within the Soviet Union was not
legally enforceable.

Mrs Hapgood's position and that of her heirs, as agents, was confirmed
subsequently in various duly-attested papers and letters signed by Stanislavski's son and daughter, Igor and Kira, and by his granddaughter Olga in
Rabat, Paris, Geneva and Moscow. Mrs Hapgood acquired the copyright
to *My Life in Art* in 1948. Later, in a document dated July 29, 1964, submitted to and accepted by the Copyright Office of the United States of America,
she claimed *co-authorship* for herself and her husband of three books, *An
Actor Prepares, Building a Character* and *Creating a Role* as well as other
undesignated works.

The claim for co-authorship is presumably based on the working method.
She would translate from Stanislavski's Russian; Norman Hapgood would
then cut and edit and suggest alternatives which Mrs Hapgood would then
translate into Russian for Stanislavski's approval. Stanislavski freely admitted in a letter later in the year to Mrs Gurevich that the book in its final
form owed much to Norman Hapgood's editorial skill and red pencil.

Certainly it is questionable whether the book, for which an English title,
An Actor Prepares, had now been agreed, would ever have reached publication had it not been for the Hapgoods' strong line. The trouble in Moscow
was that Stanislavski was a victim of too much deference. No one was
prepared to pull him into line. The Hapgoods' approach was this side of
idolatry, sympathetic but professional. They established a routine. There
can, however, be no question of Mrs Hapgood, or her husband, contributing
anything conceptually to the formulation of the System. Neither was a working theatre professional, neither had seen the System in action, or, indeed,
attended a rehearsal. They knew what they had seen in performance and
read in Stanislavski's manuscript. Their contribution was to clean up and
clarify the expression of ideas. Moreover the book was not completed by
the time Stanislavski left France. Further work was done in Moscow with
the help, for a time, of Mrs Gurevich.

The fact remains, however, that legally the Hapgoods' claims stand. The
consequences of that all-embracing agreement of April 1930 continue to
determine who shall read what and where and in which form. All translations of texts for which Mrs Hapgood or her heirs hold the copyright must
be based on her English version. Access to the results of the careful and
patient scholarship which had been applied and continues to be applied to

Stanislavski's manuscripts, both by his immediate colleagues and pupils and others in the Soviet Union, is denied both to working professionals and to interested readers since the Soviet edition may not be translated and made available in the west. The current view of the System in the West is still, therefore, dependent on the editorial decisions made by Mrs Hapgood. Such a notion of a fixed, once-for-all text is entirely alien to Stanislavski's spirit of enquiry and research.

That Stanislavski granted Mrs Hapgood a free hand in these matters is true. That he also and repeatedly offered a free hand to anyone willing to undertake the task of sub-editing – Mrs Gurevich, Grigori Kristi, responsible for the Soviet version of *Building a Character* – is also true. The fact is that the increasingly serious, scholarly criticisms of the accuracy and of Mrs Hapgood's translation have not been met and there is a permanent and damaging divergence between the English-language and Russian editions. This will be perpetuated when the new 12 volume Soviet edition of the complete works appears. Those fortunate enough to read German or Spanish, however, can turn to the Soviet-based East German or Argentinian editions.

Stanislavski could not foresee the consequences of his decisions. His concerns were more immediate. He was happy to have reached what seemed a promising agreement. He was, as he had told Ripsi, up to his ears in debt, although he did receive 13,000 roubles, he never quite knew from where. Igor's health was still precarious and the need for foreign currency was as pressing as it had been when he wrote *My Life in Art*. Unlike the despised first edition of *My Life in Art,* however, he treasured his copy of *An Actor Prepares* when it was finally brought out, in English, in 1936.

In July, Stanislavski, Lilina and the Hapgoods returned to Badenweiler where work on the book continued. At the same time he was preparing a production of Rimski's *Golden Cockerel*. In August he was joined by Leonidov to whom he read the largely-completed book. Leonidov responded. 'This is not a System, it is a complete culture'. In late October Stanislavski said goodbye to Mrs Hapgood whom he was not to see again for seven years and began the journey back to Moscow, arriving there on November 3.

CHAPTER TWENTY-SEVEN

STALIN

When Stanislavski returned to Russia after the American tour he had found a society in a state of effervescence, exploring the possibilities of a limited degree of free enterprise. Now, in 1930, he returned to a country concerned with centralization. The first steps had been taken towards the enforced collectivization of agriculture; heavy industry was being developed with little regard to human cost. The era of false accusations and show-trials was not far distant. Lunacharski had been sacked by Stalin and Maiakovski had committed suicide. The world was being turned over to middle-ranking mediocrities.

Immediately after his arrival he fell ill. He nonetheless continued to plan the production of *The Golden Cockerel* and to work on his book. The four books had now become seven. After *Work on a Role* he would discuss the creative state and problems of performance in greater detail, then go on to the role of the director and after to the specific problems of directing and performing opera. He set out his ideas in a letter to Mrs Gurevich, written on December 23 and 24, providing a rough diagram demonstrating how the elements of the System interconnected. He needed very much to engage her help.

She, however, had her own work to do and it was evident that what Stanislavski was offering was a full-time job. She was, in any case, not entirely comfortable with the semi-fictional form he had decided on. Her doubts were not without justification. The books gain to an extent in immediacy. The fictional form conveys the sense of a working method, of something learned through practice; the System is not presented as an abstract theory to be learnt and then consciously applied. On the other hand, for someone who claimed not to be a writer to take on the difficulties of creating fiction was perhaps unwise. The lectures given at the Opera Studio are much easier to follow while the existing sections of *Various Trends* display a certain mordant humour. The fictionalized classes in *An Actor's Work on Himself*, based on stenographic records, are not as convincing as the records themselves.

Mrs Gurevich was also worried about Stanislavski's terminology which in the prevailing climate of crude materialism could be vulnerable to attack as 'idealist'. She did as much as she could to bring the book into line with contemporary thinking. Stanislavski had no objection to this. If she wanted to replace the *Magic* If by the Creative If he could see no problem. In a letter written on April 9, 1931 he claimed that he had no knowledge of psychology. Yet his library contains a large number of works annotated in his own hand. But he insisted that the System was based in nature and not speculative or created concepts; what was important were the phenomena themselves not the descriptive terms attached to them.

Mrs Gurevich had read the signs aright. Early in 1931 the Association of Proletarian Writers, RAPP, held a ten-day conference, from January 25 to February 4 at which an attack was launched on the System. It was declared to be idealistic and inimical to proletarian art. Meierhold was given an opportunity to defend his system of Bio-mechanics as a viable alternative. Apart from an article written for the 1926 edition of the *Encyclopaedia Britannica* Stanislavski had published nothing. The attack, founded on half-knowledge and hearsay, was renewed when a second conference was held in December. The System was accused of being 'an-historical', dealing in 'abstract timelessness' of reducing 'multiform social qualities into a few basic laws of the biological behaviour of man in general' and of translating 'socio-political problems into the language of ethico-moral concepts' and transforming the 'complex processes of the actor's perception of reality into primitive, childlike credulity, naiveté and the Creative If' – the word 'magic' was not allowed to pass their lips. At the December conference Meierhold also got his come-uppance. Bio-mechanics were declared to be no more than the obverse side of the Stanislavski coin. Yet if the Stanislavski system was 'idealist' why was Pavlov, the determined behaviourist, interested in it? The attack in January had been led by the dramatist Aleksandr Afinogenov. He was intellectually more subtle than many of his associates. What he objected to in the System was its 'biological psychologism', the suggestion of fixed qualities in nature. He saw personality as a product of the complex interplay of social forces. If the System could be redefined in those terms it could be useful.

As chance would have it, even as Afinogenov was delivering his paper Stanislavski was reading his play, *Fear*. He recommended it to Nemirovich who agreed to direct. In the event, it was Stanislavski who staged the play as Nemirovich had other commitments. The production gave Stanislavski the opportunity to discuss with Afinogenov the problems which had been raised at the RAPP conference. On September 12 he made it clear that while he could not find alternative ways of expressing the System himself, if anyone else could find new terms he would accept them. He again declared his ignorance of psychology. Nothing came of it but Stanislavski was careful to write an introduction to the 1938 Russian edition of *An Actor's Work on Himself: Part One* (*An Actor Prepares*) in which he denied all scientific or philosophical status or pretension to the vocabulary used. He also denied, quite misleadingly, having invented the terms at all, claiming that they had arisen naturally in the process of rehearsal. All the evidence indicates how very much the terminology was Stanislavski's own and what a difficult time colleagues had keeping up with the constant changes.

The attack on the Art Theatre's working method was, however, only one aspect of a much larger crisis. Stanislavski spent most of the summer of that year drafting an appeal to the government in order to protect the Art Theatre against the imbecilities of the bureaucrats. He worked hard on it and it was probably, in political terms, one of the most important documents he produced. The fears that he had expressed to Leonidov in September 1929 were fully confirmed. Heitz and the artistic-political advisory group that came with him were undermining the very foundations of the theatre's creative life. They were bringing to the stage the same concern with output and mass production that characterized Stalin's first Five-Year Plan. The theatre was being pushed to put on more productions and give more performances. In 1929/30 it had played 795 times and, in 1930/31, 751 times. Given that the season lasted some 260 days this meant three performances a day. It was an old battle refought. The Proletkult had been succeeded by a number of groups, not least the Blue Blouses who specialized in topical Living-Newspaper productions. Their presentations soon fell into a predictable format of song, slogans and sketches. Audiences became bored. New groups, known as Agit-Brigades, had been set up as part of the first Five-Year Plan. They were putting together as many as twelve productions a year. While quantity was the prime consideration all seemed well. It was only a year later, in 1932, when an 'Olympiad' of these groups was held that the government realized how deplorable the actual quality of the performances was.

Stanislavski grasped the dangers of the situation. In January he wrote to Heitz politely pointing out that in the seasons prior to his illness, with the exception of *The Armoured Train*, all productions had taken a year to prepare. Hence their quality. Heitz failed to take the point. By the summer Stanislavski had lost all patience. His contempt for the artistic-political advisory committee was boundless. There were four drafts of his appeal and in one he wrote:

'If the artistic-political advisory body has as its educational objectives the furtherance of the artistic enlightenment of those members of the proletariat who are interested in such things, to keep them up-to-date with developments in the world of the arts and to enable theatres to make contact with them, thus improving mutual relations and understanding, then it cannot but be welcomed in its present form and the theatres themselves and those serving on the artistic-political advisory boards should be given new directives consistent with those aims.

If, however, these advisory boards are to continue issuing orders, even of the most general kind, concerning the artistic life of the theatre which they do not and indeed cannot understand without lengthy, specialized study, then in logical and practical terms it must be understood that these committees will not only fail to produce results but will cause damage to institutions, impeding the work the theatres are doing and encouraging superficial attitudes in those who know absolutely nothing of what we do.' (SS, VI, p. 435.)

In what was probably the final draft he first defended the System. It was not a philosophical treatise but a practical method for working actors. Its goal was truth and quality. Second, the demands being made on the Art Theatre and its members were totally unreasonable. He had seen the pitiful standards of the three-a-day theatres in the United States. To expect the Art Theatre to go on providing the equivalent number of shows, as it had in the 1930/31 season, was to impose a burden that could only lead to nervous exhaustion.

Stanislavski had to make his position plain. He was no more interested in plays on topical subjects, in primitive agit-prop, in pot-boilers to attract new audiences than he and his mentor Fedotov had been forty years earlier:

'They are trying to make us offer the audience pot-boilers and imagine that in that way we can educate new audiences. No, that's false. Audiences can't be educated through pot-boilers any more than actors can be educated by them and be responsible towards an audience . . . .

. . . I am sounding the alarm because I see terrible dangers. I am an old hand in the theatre and I know where danger comes from. I would be happy if the government were to heed the warnings I utter and having taken the rudder from my hands would allow me, perhaps, on the eve of my death to steer my vessel in the hope and quiet of the harbour of socialism.' (SS, VI, pp. 289–99.)

He saw one way to avert the catastrophe that threatened the Art Theatre:

'1. the establishment of precise governmental and party directives concerning its place in the contemporary situation as a theatre of classical drama and of the best artistically significant plays in the contemporary repertoire;
2. the removal from it of tasks demanding above all hasty work or an inordinate dissipation of its energies in guest appearances;
3. the recognition of its right to compete with other theatres not in the quantity of contemporary plays produced but in the quality of its presentations.' (Ibid, p. 300.)

The protest had its effect. By the end of the year Heitz had been removed and the committee with him. The Art Theatre was freed from the control of the Central Executive Committee and made directly accountable to the government with the title Moscow Art Theatre of the USSR. It is inconceivable that such a decision could have been made without Stalin's consent. Perhaps those fifteen visits to *The Days of the Turbins* had produced their results.

Somehow time was found for staging plays and operas. Only one production was actually premiered, Afinogenov's *Fear*, which opened on December 24 and was acclaimed by the President of the Academy of the Science of Art with the words, 'I place this play among the outstanding victories of Soviet theatre'. The production was also remarkable for the fact that Stanislavski took Knipper out of the cast three weeks before the opening. She was too light-weight and refined for the role of Clara. The role was given to Sokolovskaia. For the rest Rimski-Korsakov's *The Golden Cockerel* and Rossini's *Barbiere Di Seviglia* were in rehearsal at the Opera Theatre while preliminary work began on Bulgakov's adapation of *Dead Souls*.

Stanislavski's opera productions, destined for his own theatre, went comparatively smoothly. He retained total control so that the work done in the Onegin Room at Leontievski Lane eventually found its way onto the stage. He was sufficiently confident to ignore Nemirovich's proposal in February 1931 to merge his Music Theatre and the Stanislavski Opera Theatre. The dramatic productions for the Art Theatre were considerably more problematic. Stanislavski's new working method, the Method of Physical Action, was still a mystery to those who did not regularly attend rehearsals at Leontievski Lane and even then it was difficult to grasp. Leonidov, the first to be initiated into the new method, regularly summarized the System in his notebook, and complained that Stanislavski made life difficult. He was also not a little disconcerted when, after he had struggled his way through the unsuccessful *Othello*, he was told that it was probably not possible to experience an entire tragic role truthfully but that there had to be moments when representation took over. But the real problem was that the work rehearsed by Stanislavski in the intimacy of his flat failed to transfer to the main stage. The problem had been inherent in *Othello*. The disparity between Stanislavski's concept and the final staging might be explained by the sheer distance between Moscow and Nice but the fact was that working away from the main building, not confronting the day-to-day practical problems, Stanislavski could not ensure that his ideas were adequately realized. They were too subtle, too finely nuanced, too small-scale, and, there was no director capable of expanding them into a larger space. Thus neither *Dead Souls*, which opened on December 9, 1932 after two years' work, or Ostrovski's *Artists and Admirers* which opened on September 23, 1933, corresponded entirely to his wishes. The tense relationship with the theatre was exacerbated when on October 16, 1931 he payed one of his rare visits to the theatre to see a run of Acts Three and Four of *Dead Souls*. He took immediate exception to the sets. The furniture and props were distorted, exaggerated, 'hyperbolical'. They conveyed nothing of the claustrophobic atmosphere of a back-woods province. Everything was too grand. It was the now familiar battle over the grotesque, the problem of directors attempting to make statements through design rather than through acting. Stanislavski demanded that the design be simplified. He was still arguing with Simov, one of the designers, in June of the following year.

The production was a success. Stanislavski attended the first night seeing extracts from the beginning and the whole of Act Four. When he appeared in his box after the final curtain he was given a huge ovation.

Enthusiastic as the public had been the critics were less generous, making unfavourable comparisons with Meierhold's production of *The Inspector General*. Meierhold himself looked appalled, bored and angry by turns, standing in the foyer between acts dispensing curt comments. He admired Bulgakov's adaptation but the rest merely served to point up the differences between himself and Stanislavski, between a director who imposes a style and and an idea and uses actors and a director who draws out their latent possibilities. But Meierhold still represented the artistic and intellectual élite. The German and Russian avant-garde were coming together to form a powerful movement. In 1932 Brecht was in Moscow for a showing of his film *Kuhle Wampe* which did not enjoy any great success. The next year, however, Taïrov staged *The Threepenny Opera* and Tretiakov began to bring out Russian translations of his plays. Piscator was also resident in the Soviet Union. What none of them could foresee was Zhdanov's speech to the Moscow Writers' Congress in 1934, proclaiming the doctrine of Socialist Realism condemning everything they stood for as Bourgeois Formalism, soon putting a brutal stop to experiment. The Art Theatre suddenly found itself the embodiment of the party line.

Stanislavski as usual, pushed his own line, continuing his search for new Soviet plays that described the revolutionary experience. In September 1931 Gorki drew Stanislavski's attention to Nikolai Erdman's play *The Suicide* already in rehearsal at the Meierhold Theatre. Gorki was convinced that Meierhold was turning it into a farce. In October Erdman read the play to Stanislavski who laughed uproariously. There was however the problem of getting the play past the Repertkom. Stanislavski, characteristically, went to the top and sent the script direct to Stalin. Stalin's reply, dated November 9, 1931 and accompanied by Repertkom reports, was a polite indication that it would be wise not to go any further. He referred the actual decision about permission to a stage lower down the line since he was, he declared, an amateur in artistic matters. Everyone was aware that the 1925 production of Erdman's *The Mandate* had provoked anti-Stalin demonstrations.

Stanislavski let the matter drop. Meierhold, for reasons best known to himself, took Stalin's letter as a sign of encouragement and spent the next eighteen months working on a production that never got to a first night. He misjudged the times and was ultimately to pay for it. Gorki was also instrumental in persuading Nemirovich to include Bulgakov's *Molière* among the theatre's future plans. This was to prove as controversial as *The Suicide*.

Stanislavski continued to receive foreign visitors. In February 1931 the young Joshua Logan attended rehearsals for *The Golden Cockerel* where he saw Stanislavski applying the 'sitting on hands' technique, not allowing the singers to move until they had discovered the truth of their behaviour. Later he saw *Boris Godunov* which he considered superior to the production at the Paris Opera notwithstanding Chaliapin's performance in the title role. When he informed Stanislavski of his ambitions to create a theatre on the Moscow Art model, he received the same reply Max Reinhardt had received many years before: don't copy, find your own answers. In July, Bernard Shaw visited Stanislavski at the sanatorium outside Moscow where he was resting.

Despite these marks of respect Stanislavski felt lonely and lonely where it counted most, in his own city, in his own theatre. His last years are filled with recurring complaints that he is isolated. There were obvious reasons for this. He had to be protected on medical grounds but there was also, in the background, consciously or unconsciously, the battle for the succession. It was not in the interest of those within his immediate circle to let anyone else in. The mantle had to fall on someone; someone had to be seen as the true recipient of the master's wisdom. Stanislavski was becoming a cult figure. Young actors who turned up for rehearsal found themselves having their boots inspected to see whether the degree of shine was commensurate with the honour of being admitted to the Presence. Stanislavski, always immaculate himself, with gleaming boots and impeccable linen, probably never knew this.

He saw no one as his successor. His collaborators at the Art Theatre seemed to him no more than adequate and their failure to put his production ideas into practice did not increase his respect for their talents.

'I am alone, all alone, I have no one who understands me through and through. In my whole life I have had one and a half pupils, you know. Only Sulerzhitski understood me completely and Vakhtangov half understood me.' (From the Diary of O. S. Sobolevska, K. S. Archive.)

Kachalov remarked, not unkindly, in 1936 that Stanislavski's problem was that he only ever saw the artist in people, he was never greatly concerned with the person. He did not bother to keep up with them outside work.

When in 1938, his beloved Chaliapin died his main concern was that the singer had died taking the secret of his technique with him. 'He found it! he found it!', he repeated. When asked what, he pointed to his throat and said, 'Here, here'.

In the summer of 1932 both Stanislavski and Nemirovich were in Berlin. They decided that a 'troika' – Moskvin, Kachalov and Leonidov – would assist them at senior management level. None of the three was, however, in his first youth. Moskvin was 58, Kachalov 57 and Leonidov 59.

In January 1933 Stanislavski reached the age of 70. Among the many messages of congratulation was one from Harold Clurman on behalf of the Group Theatre in New York. Work continued on *Artists and Admirers* and *Barbiere* and preliminary work began on *Carmen*. In April Ernest Ansermet, who had founded the Suisse Romande orchestra, attended a rehearsal of *Barbiere* and noted how the central character, Figaro, departed from the accepted interpretation. On April 23 he attended a rehearsal of *Carmen* and afterwards thanked Stanislavski for having made his visit to Moscow a memorable one.

By July 1933 *Barbiere* and *Artists and Admirers* were substantially ready but Stanislavski was already too ill to complete the work. He did not attend a private performance of *Artists* given on the 14th. The emphysema was worse and the attacks of breathlessness, diagnosed as asthma, more frequent. It was imperative to go abroad. In August he left for Nice. He sent his final notes for the play from Berlin where, as usual, he broke his journey. He arrived in Nice on September 22. The play opened in Moscow the following day to no great enthusiasm. *Barbiere* which opened a month later enjoyed a considerable success.

In Nice he was able to resume work on the second half of *An Actor's Work on Himself*. During November and December he worked on the chapter on Diction. Mrs Hapgood had written him a desperate letter in August of the previous year asking him to send her anything he had ready. There was nothing. Left to himself he had reverted to his habitual pattern of indecision. So much so that Mrs Gurevich, for all her affection and devotion, gave up the unequal task of trying to keep abreast of the endless revisions and withdrew as his collaborator.

In January 1934 the French edition of *My Life in Art* appeared with a preface, as planned, by Jacques Copeau. Stanislavski continued to work on *Carmen* which he saw more and more as a popular drama. Chaliapin, who was performing in Monte Carlo, came over to see him, the first time the two men had met since the American tour. Nemirovich kept in touch. He felt the need for reconciliation. The two men had had so little genuine contact in recent years. In March he wrote to Stanislavski giving an enthusiastic account of Shostakovich's *Lady Macbeth of Mtsenk* which he had just directed at his Music Theatre. Stanislavski replied that if Shostakovich was a genius that was a comfort. In May Nemirovich proposed that to celebrate the 75th anniversary of Chekhov's birth, Stanislavski should direct a new production of *The Seagull* while he himself staged *Ivanov*. Stanislavski replied that he was not interested in the past, although in the autumn, after his return from France, he did start rehearsing a new production of *Three Sisters* which, he insisted, had nothing to do with the original production but constituted a completely new approach.

In June Stanislavski went up to Paris where he stayed for some seven weeks. Stella Adler was in Paris with her then husband, Harold Clurman. She decided to call on Stanislavski and enlist his help. For some time all the pleasure had gone out of her acting, she had lost the creative urge. Stanislavski found himself confronted with a woman whom he described as being in a state of panic, clutching at him and begging him for help. In response to her suggestion that she might have misunderstood the System he gave her what was his normal reply: if the System doesn't help you, forget it. However, he agreed to help her and to work on the role she had played in an unsuccessful production of *Gentlewoman*. Every afternoon for five weeks she and Stanislavski worked together, using French. Adler employed a secretary who took down Stanislavski's statements verbatim. What struck Stella Adler most was Stanislavski's insistence on physical action as the basis for building a performance, his rejection of any direct approach to feelings and his abandonment, except as a last resort, of Emotion Memory, which, under the influence of Boleslavski, had become a fundamental feature of Stanislavskian acting in America. It has been suggested that Stanislavski deliberately played down the emotional aspects of acting because the woman in front of him was already over-emotional. The evidence is against this. What Stanislavski told Stella Adler was exactly what he had been telling his actors at home, what indeed he had advocated in his notes for Leonidov in the production plan for *Othello*. He could not foresee the furore this change of emphasis would cause when reported back to the Group Theatre in New York. Adler told Lee Strasberg he had misunderstood the function of Emotion Memory. He angrily rejected the new Method of Physical Action, declaring that either Adler had misunderstood what had been said to her, or that Stanislavski had gone back on himself. At all events he had no intention of modifying the version of the System he had developed. Passions ran high and the conflict persisted for many years. Strasberg was in Moscow in 1934, although he appears to have been more interested in Vakhtangov's productions than in Stanislavski's. Adler's version of the System was confirmed by Harold Clurman who visited Russia at the end of 1935 and discussed the Method of Physical Action with Stanislavski. Everyone could claim to be right. The battle for the succession, for recognition as the sole true heir to the master and his thought had spread beyond the confines of Russia.

Stanislavski would have found such concerns with doctrinal purity, based on mistaken notions of consistency, curious. He was never afraid to change his mind. Stella Adler assumed, mistakenly, that Stanislavski's position as he outlined it to her was the position he had always occupied. She was no more than the fortunate recipient of his latest thinking. Lee Strasberg had not necessarily misunderstood the exercises on Emotion Memory. He was using material passed on by Boleslavski and Ouspenskaia neither of whom had any knowledge of the Method of Physical Action. Account must also be taken of Stanislavski's tendency to deny all knowledge of previous practice. Faced with one of his own long-abandoned exercises he asked, 'What idiot thought that one up?' The unfortunate actress who, during the rehearsals for *Tartuffe* in 1938, referred to 'emotional states' was sharply told that he had no idea what she was talking about.

He acknowledged, too, cultural and geographical differences. He had always been clear, for example, about the temperamental gulf which separated the French from the Russian actor, of the radically different role which the intellect played in the creative process as conceived within the French and Russian traditions. When he told Joshua Logan in 1931 to find his own way he acknowledged by implication that the needs of the American actor might differ quite specifically from those of his own compatriots. All the elements of the System were valid and essential but the balances among those elements and the emphasis given to them changed with time and place.

He was equally aware that individual actors found the various aspects of the System difficult or easy in varying degrees, according to their own natural gifts. It was impossible to legislate absolutely for all actors at all times. What was important was the end result. The System he repeated again and again only existed to provide access to truthful performances. It was not a moral obligation.

As always when he was away, Stanislavski's anxieties concerning the future of the Art Theatre increased. It was difficult to see where new ideas were coming from. Nemirovich had directed a number of new plays, most of them quickly forgotten. People were still looking to him for a lead. His black mood was not helped by a depressed letter from his brother, Vladimir. In his reply he repeated a complaint he had made to Nemirovich thirty years earlier: he had been forced into roles he did not like. How much happier he would have been just to go on being an actor, an actor and no more. But who among his colleagues could take over?

'People often say to me, why don't you tell us what's to be done? Tell us what's to be done and it will be. I said do *Rigoletto* five years ago and no one took any notice but said "Fine", "It'll be done". Is it the fault of my weakness and incompetence on the management side? All right, yes.

That's my tragedy. All my life I have been someone else, not my real self. All my life I've played the part of the "Manager", the "Boss", the "tough-guy", the "hard-liner". Now I am old I'm not up to these roles any more and more often misfire and give up. These roles are hard for me and there's no one I can pass them on to. If you've worked on nothing this year then the fault is partly mine and partly because the whole of our staff are turgid and talentless. This turgidity and lack of talent drives me mad.' (SS, VIII, p. 377.)

On July 28 he left for Berlin and by August 4 was back in Moscow, already concerned by what he had learned of Hitler's Germany and the fate of colleagues like Reinhardt who had been forced into exile. Like others of his generation he had seen the Great War as the war to end all wars. Now it seemed that hostilities might break out once again.

On his return home, Stanislavski supervised rehearsals for *Artists and Admirers*, *Fear* and *The Tsar's Bride* prior to the opening of the season. He began work on *Three Sisters*, surprising his cast by dispensing with the usual long preparatory period 'at the table', and resumed work on *Carmen*, the last opera he was to see right through.

He had not lost his ability to shock – not through an outrageous production style but through adherence to his own realist principles. *Carmen* opened on April 4, 1935 to mixed notices. Stanislavski's crime in the eyes of more conservative critics was to have insisted on a real social setting, on a chorus of women who looked as though they might actually have worked in a cigarette factory and on gypsies who did not look as though they had strayed in from a second-rate *zarzuela*. He had carried through his intention to turn the opera into a popular drama, that is, a drama where ordinary people were faithfully represented. But conventional views of so well-known an opera as *Carmen* were not so easily dislodged. Having read the reviews Meierhold went somewhat reluctantly to a performance. He found a production full of insight and invention, infinitely superior to Nemirovich's ten-year-old production *Carmencita and the Soldier* which had been so universally acclaimed. All he found there was a few women turning about the stage, waving fans. There was still much, he concluded, to learn from the old master.

Stanislavski's production might have raised even more eyebrows had he been able to cast the title role as he wanted. In 1935 the black American singer, Marian Anderson was in the Soviet Union. Her sensational New York début was still a year away. On January 21 she sang for the Opera Studio. Afterwards Stanislavski asked her to work with him on *Carmen*. She replied that she would be happy to do so some time in the future. She was, however, never to return to Russia, a missed opportunity she regretted.

Stanislavski's major project in the straight theatre in the 1934/5 season was Bulgakov's *Molière*, which Gorchakov had been rehearsing for about a year. Of all the plays with which Stanislavski was connected in the last years of his life none was more problematic than this, famous now as a theatrical *cause célèbre*. Two versions of the history of its ill-fated production have come down to us, neither, as it turns out, accurate.

Four years after the play's seven-night run in 1936 Bulgakov wrote his *Theatrical Novel* better known to English readers as *Black Snow*. Ostensibly it is an account in disguised form of the production of *The Days of the Turbins*. Its real subject is the internal life of the Art Theatre during the production of *Molière* and it offers a witheringly satirical portrait of Stanislavski at his most wilful and autocratic. It is almost as though Bulgakov was aware of all the private criticisms of Stanislavski's character which Nemirovich had made in earlier years. The portrait is one-sided and grossly unfair. True, Stanislavski did recline on a sofa in what looked like a lordly manner. What else could a man with his heart condition do? There was also a measure of ingratitude since the Art Theatre and Stanislavski had done all that was possible to protect and help Bulgakov during the difficult period that had followed the première of *The Days of the Turbins* and the banning of *Flight*. They had after all given him a permanent job as assistant director and writer-in-residence. Part of his anger was undoubtedly directed against the growing atmosphere of sycophancy that surrounded Leontievski Lane.

The other account is provided by Nikolai Gorchakov, who directed the play under Stanislavski's supervision, in his book *Rezhissiorski Uroki Stanislavskovo*, available in English in truncated form as *Stanislavski Directs*. Gorchakov's chapter was intended as a response to Bulgakov's novel and as a justification of Stanislavski's misgivings about the play. Unfortunately, according to the Soviet experts Vladimir Prokoviev and Anatoli Smelianski, he reports rehearsals he did not attend, incidents which did not occur, and even concocts a letter Stanislavski is supposed to have sent him after the play was taken off. This casts doubt on the rest of Gorchakov's book particularly the expressions of ideological conformity attributed to Stanislavski. At all events Gorchakov's act of political and artistic piety was rewarded with a Stalin Prize.

Molière appears to have been written after the banning of *Flight* and at the same time as the adaptation of *Dead Souls*. Bulgakov read an early draft to the repertoire committee of the Art Theatre on January 19, 1930 while Stanislavski was still in Nice. There was uncertainty as to what kind of play was being offered. Bulgakov was quite clear that he had written a 'romantic drama' – in the sense presumably that Schiller had written romantic drama. He knew perfectly well that Molière did not actually die on stage at the end of *Le Malade Imaginaire*. The play was intended to show how Molière's shining genius had been crushed by a cabal of bigots with the connivance of an absolute monarch. In March he was informed that the play had not been accepted. Gorki then intervened. Bulgakov was given a full-time appointment in September and in October the play was accepted as suitable for production although Nemirovich made the firm stipulation that it could not go on before May 1933 when Stanislavski and Moskvin, who was to play the title role, would be available. *Dead Souls* must come first.

Bulgakov read the play to the company on November 17, 1931. Stanislavski, who still went out rarely, did not attend. Gorchakov began rehearsals the following year.

Stanislavski's illness in 1932 and his two-year absence abroad caused a further hiatus so that work did not resume in earnest until the autumn of 1934. In the meantime Moskvin had pulled out of the cast, ostensibly for personal reasons, and had been replaced by Sanitsin, while Bulgakov had reworked the text. The new version was ready by March 1933. On March 5, 1935 Stanislavski saw a run-through, with the exception of the final scene, at Leontievski Lane. The run was followed by a discussion with Bulgakov, the director and the cast which was, as usual, taken down verbatim. A basic disagreement between Stanislavski and Bulgakov began to emerge. Stanislavski who was always awe-struck in the presence of literary genius was looking for a Great Man and could not find him. The thrust of all his questions and comments called Bulgakov's entire view of his subject into question. The tone of the conversation is polite but there is evident tension beneath the surface. Stanislavski asked for additional scenes showing Molière at work. He could not believe that Molière was unaware of his own genius. Bulgakov tried to push all these suggestions away. Now he did not feel he had the energy to start yet again after five years. Stanislavski was sympathetic but pointed to his own *Notebook* with all his jottings of thirty years for his book. Nonetheless he felt that they should look at certain scenes in rehearsal and judge what rewriting needed to be done. Bulgakov reluctantly agreed.

Bulgakov was being evasive. The clatter of his typewriter could be heard back-stage as he constantly made changes on his own initiative. In fact he went on rewriting up to the opening in February 1936. What he did not want was someone to take over his play lock, stock and barrel.

In the ensuing tug-of-war Stanislavski tried to pull the play in the direction he thought it should go. Pursuing his idea of giving greater emphasis to Molière the artist he proposed introducing scenes from Molière's plays into the rehearsal scene between Armande and Moirron. Gorchakov could not see how Molière's text could be married with Bulgakov's. The idea was tried out with some excitement, albeit in Bulgakov's absence. Rehearsals were more and more becoming an acting class as Stanislavski applied his new Method of Physical Action. The plan for a rôle was created out of logical sequences of physical objectives and actions. Thinking itself, he insisted, was a physical action. The physical plan would trigger the unconscious and allow for minor variations and discoveries within the overall scheme. A play was ready, as it were, when the scheme was ready.

The real crisis came in the second and third weeks of April. On the 13th Bulgakov did not appear at rehearsal. He was suffering, it seems, from neuralgia. Perhaps, Stanislavski commented wryly, his neuralgia was brought on by the rewrites. Act Three, scene one, The Cabal of Hypocrites, was scheduled for the 17th. Stanislavski now decided to take a completely new line on the scene. It was too quiet. He saw it as the climax of the play and he wanted noise and conflict. He also started moving chunks of dialogue around from one scene to another. When Bulgakov read the daily account of this rehearsal he sent, as he had done in 1926, an ultimatum: do my play as it is or not at all. He stopped attending rehearsals.

In 1926 he had had to bow to the demands of the censors. This time the censors were not – or so it seemed – involved. Stanislavski treated the matter as a purely artistic dispute. He told the cast they must respect the author's wishes and use all their skill to overcome any difficulties.

It seems surprising that no one in the Art Theatre realized they were sitting on a political time-bomb. After the first reading of the play in 1930 Markov had stated that he saw no ideological problems. Many members of the company recognized that there were autobiographical elements in the script but most interest centred on identifying members of the Art Theatre company with members of Molière's troupe. The stark equations Louis XIV = Stalin, Molière = Bulgakov, Hypocrites = State officials, or the fact that the entire subject of the play was Bulgakov's public protest against the treatment he had received, did not appear to have struck anybody. Perhaps it was simply unthinkable that anyone should go that far. The play had become politically more dangerous with each year it was delayed. In 1930 it might just have passed but 1936 was the year of the new Stalin Constitution, the judges, and the great show-trials.

The play opened on February 11, 1936 after 286 rehearsals. It lasted seven performances before it was taken off. The official criticism in *Pravda* was fortuitously reminiscent of Stanislavski's own reservations: the play had failed to show the greatness of Molière and had concentrated on sordid domestic detail. The party line on the classics had changed. They were now being rehabilitated. For Bulgakov it was the end of any hope of a career as an accepted writer.

CHAPTER TWENTY-EIGHT

THE METHOD OF PHYSICAL ACTION

Stanislavski continued working on *An Actor's Work on Himself* throughout 1935 and the first half of 1936. In March and May of 1935 and January 1936 he sent a total of 15 chapters to Mrs Hapgood in New York. On June 7, 1936 he had finished work on the sixteenth and final chapter of *An Actor Prepares*. His perspective on the System had altered since he began writing. Originally he had set out to summarize and tabulate his earlier experience. Part One of *An Actor's Work on Himself* was based on his work between 1908 and 1914. Part Two was based on his greater concern with the actor's technical means following the problems raised by *Mozart and Salieri* and *Cain* and his work on opera. The shape of the book was largely determined but he was caught between the necessity to honour his contract and his desire to incorporate his new ideas on the Method of Physical Action. Part One remained largely unaltered, although some sections were revised. As with *My Life in Art*, no sooner had the first American edition of *An Actor Prepares* appeared in New York in November 1936 than he was revising it and drafting new material for inclusion. *An Actor Prepares* had also undergone further cuts and changes which Stanislavski had to sanction at a distance. Yale University Press had rejected it on the grounds that it was overlong and uncommercial. Mrs Hapgood, using her power of attorney, then turned to Theatre Arts Books, who agreed to publish provided she made further cuts. This she did with Stanislavski's full accord. *An Actor Prepares* and *An Actor's Work on Himself: Part One* are substantially the same but differences between Mrs Hapgood's cut version and Stanislavski's revisions cause concern.

Despite categorical instructions from his doctors that he was to stop work, Stanislavski embarked on his last important venture as a teacher. In January 1933, the government had finally responded to his request, made in the summer of 1931, for a definition of the functions and status of the Art Theatre. Among the tasks assigned to it was the creation of an Academy for the training of young artists. With this in mind in July 1935 Stanislavski created a new Opera-Dramatic Studio.

He gathered round him a small group of young directors and actors, making it quite plain that what he intended setting up was essentially a laboratory, a place for creative experiment. There would be no question of gearing the work to a performance; it would be done for its own sake. The task was the development of a methodology and an exploration of the Method of Physical Action. True to this spirit he was happy for a young actress to work on the role of Hamlet as an exercise in character creation. The mode of teaching was essentially that of the master-class, where Stanislavski would comment on prepared work and elucidate aspects of the System. After discussion it was agreed that they would concentrate on *Hamlet* and *Romeo and Juliet*, although some work was done on *The Cherry Orchard*.

Work at the new Studio was irregular, depending on Stanislavski's slowly deteriorating health. Teaching was flexible and various approaches were tried out but the principle of establishing a logical line of physical actions remained. Stanislavski was still preoccupied with the problem that had concerned him in 1906: where was the actor's point of entry into the character? It seemed to him more and more that the actor had to be engaged, in his own person, with the problems the character had to solve, he had to experience the Given Circumstances in his own right. A great deal of time was therefore devoted to exercises on Here, Today, Now: what would *I* do if *I* were in this situation? Thus in preparing the opening scene of *The Cherry Orchard* the students were invited to determine in precise terms what they would do if they went to the station to meet someone and found the train was late. By engaging with the situation, the Given Circumstances, they experienced the characters' situations as real, not as textual. Many hours were spent in establishing the facts of the action, the basic situations, the characters' objectives, actions and through-line so that the total structure of the play became clear.

From time to time Stanislavski would summarize his teaching. On June 13, 1938, a few weeks before his death, he kept his assistant directors back after the session and provided them with an outline scheme for working on a play, conceived in three stages. The first stage: preliminary work by the director to establish a provisional superobjective, breaking down the play first into broad episodes and then into smaller incidents, establishing basic actions for every character in each incident. The director and the actors would then establish through discussion, 'sitting on their hands', the organic progression of the plot. Then, still 'sitting on their hands', the individual actors would establish, and write down, their line of physical actions, individually and in relation to the actor opposite, bearing in mind the purpose behind each episode, until they experienced the absolute necessity to move. Stage two: an analysis of the text into a logical sequence of ideas and the images they provoke. The sequence of objectives is defined. The text is then approached using random words and phrases or approximations to the text. Stage three: bring together the logically established lines of physical actions and thoughts, the author's and actors ideas and images and the inner monologue which each actor has created for himself. In parallel with this the actors perform exercises and improvisations to fill out the gaps in the script so as to give the rôle solidity and depth.

Once this preliminary work has been done there are five further processes to be gone through: first, a more detailed consideration of the episodes and incidents in the play; second, a deeper investigation of the given circumstances in terms of historical and social background, period manners and behaviour; third, the cast are to establish the inner and outer characteristics of the person they are playing as they are revealed in the script. Once the inner characteristics have been established the actor can use his knowledge and observation of other people to find the outward forms. Fourth comes the establishment of the perspective of the role, the distribution of energy, where to give out and where to hold back. Finally comes the question of fixing the specific rhythm and tempo for each incident, for each episode, for each character and for the through-line of the play as a whole.

Although this was the last summary he ever gave of his working method it should not, for all that, be considered as definitive. He would certainly have changed it had he lived.

Ill as he was, Stanislavski only stopped work when he had no choice and resisted all well-meaning attempts to slow him down. The brain, still as active as ever, impelled an increasingly inadequate body. Pathetic and futile attempts were made to insulate him from the world. He had always been an avid reader of newspapers. The deteriorating situation in Europe concerned him and his immediate entourage would have prevented him learning about it if they could. When, however, Gorki died in July 1936 they decided this would be too much and tried to hide the newspapers. It took him a few brief moments to see through his nurse's lame excuses for the missing papers and guess what they contained. The crude subterfuge was not repeated.

Stanislavski had to die the way he had lived - working. Apart from his work with students he still had two major projects of long standing, with trained professionals, which he wished to complete: *Tartuffe* and *Rigoletto*. His original intention had been to produce *Molière* and *Tartuffe* in tandem. Perhaps if he had been able to work on both plays at the same time he would have made fewer changes to Bulgakov's script. The *Molière* he wanted, the genius, would have been part of his working life. In March 1936, no sooner had *Molière* been taken off than he cast *Tartuffe*, engaging as his assistant director the 43-year-old Mikhail Kedrov who also played the title role. Kedrov had joined the Art Theatre in 1924. Vassili Toporkov has left an account of rehearsals. Stanislavski was still worried that his System was identified with a kind of restricted 'naturalism' and wanted to prove by working on a verse classic that it was universal. He made it quite clear at the outset that he was not interested in the finished product but in the rehearsal process. It was important for actors to reexamine and renew their technique. The methods he used were precisely those he summarized two years later for his students at the new Opera-Dramatic Studio: precise physical actions, leading to precise emotions, precise rhythms for section, precise expression in voice and body.

Even after almost two years' work the play was not ready. At the time of Stanislavski's death the actors had not even run a single act complete and no work had been done on Act Five. Kedrov and his colleagues nonetheless decided to ask the Art Theatre management to allow them to continue rehearsing to see whether it would be possible to mount a performance in homage to Stanislavski. A demonstration performance was arranged in the Art Theatre foyer. Kedrov gave the actors a single instruction before they went on: no concern for feelings, no displays of personality and emotion, only concentration on action. The months of painstaking work paid off. The management and the other members of the company acknowledged the advance in acting technique. What they had seen had been truthful in terms of human behaviour and viable in terms of theatre. The production received its first public presentation in December 1939.

Rigoletto, too, was left incomplete. As a project it preceeded *Tartuffe* by two years. Stanislavski worked on the production from 1929 onwards. In the autumn of 1935 he saw the first costume sketches and started serious work with Kristi as his assistant. However, apart from any intrinsic artistic merit, the production is remarkable for having finally brought Stanislavski and Meierhold together, two luminaries in a world of increasing shadows.

Towards the end of 1936 friends became aware that Stanislavski and Meierhold were meeting regularly. Neither was forthcoming about the content of their talks. Stanislavski would say no more than that they had discussed 'various matters connected with the theatre'. Meierhold was equally reticent. It would appear, however, that they mainly talked of the problem of repertoire both for the theatre and for opera. In the summer of 1937 Meierhold visited Stanislavski at the sanatorium in Barvikha near Moscow when they talked of wide-ranging reforms both in the theatre and in training. They were trying to find answers to what Meierhold described as 'agonising questions'. Stanislavski had already given an indication of his growing closeness to Meierhold in April when in response to a disparaging comment thrown out in a discussion with a group of young directors he stated that he was by no means against Meierhold. It was quite possible that Meierhold might direct something at the Opera Theatre providing, of course, 'he did not get up to his tricks'. In 1937, Stanislavski was looking for all possible opportunities to involve Meierhold in his work – outside the Art Theatre, of course, as Meierhold would never be allowed to set foot there while Nemirovich was alive.

Meierhold had become a more sober director. In 1936 he had written a paper *Meierhold Against Meierholdism* in which, quoting Lenin, he had called for a move towards simplicity of form and presentation. He had taken Gorchakov to task for over-dressing *Molière*. In that production he had seen the mirror of all his own faults. He had also surprised those who saw him as the unremitting advocate of 'theatricality' by praising Stanislavski's *Carmen* for stripping away all clichés and theatricality and for having its feet firmly planted not on the stage floor but on the ground.

It should not be imagined that all differences between Stanislavski and Meierhold had disappeared. Each was too individual an artist for that. But both men had worked and experimented and reflected on the essential problems of the theatre for forty or more years, and with an intensity and depth that no one else could match. Their differences, the interaction of their varied and often opposing experience, could now be a source of further progress. They had, moreover, finally found common ground, a concern for opera. Meierhold was now convinced that the outstanding problem of contemporary Soviet theatre was the creation of new opera.

Meierhold was now under serious attack. His kind of formal experiment was condemned by party 'experts' who were busy enforcing the doctrine of Socialist Realism. He could not, or would not, the press proclaimed, come to terms with the realities of Soviet life. On January 8, 1938, after a matinée of *The Inspector General* the Meierhold Theatre was dissolved. The Second Moscow Art Theatre had gone the same way two years earlier.

Stanislavski seized his opportunity. At the end of his comments on Meierhold in April 1937 he had told his young colleagues that Meierhold could not, of course, take on full responsibility for a production as he had his own theatre. That barrier had now been removed. Meierhold for his part had heard fragmentary accounts of the methods Stanislavski was using in the preparation of *Tartuffe*. Meeting Nikolai Chushkin at the Post Office in Gorki Street soon after his theatre had been shut down, he asked for further details. Accompanying Meierhold back to his flat, Chushkin did his best to describe both what he had seen at Leontievski Lane and the work which Kedrov was doing back-stage at the Art Theatre itself. Meierhold then let drop that he would soon be working with Stanislavski and that indeed they had met several times.

Stanislavski, in fact, kept his intentions regarding Meierhold as secret as he had kept their earlier conversations. He suspected, rightly, that most people saw the two of them in crude oppositional terms and would not easily accept Meierhold into the fold. His mind, however, was made up. There would be no discussion. He had tried to point colleagues in Meierhold's direction, suggesting that his expertise in physical staging could be useful and also, as far as *Rigoletto* was concerned, that he had a deep knowledge of the Renaissance, but to no avail. On March 7, 1938,

Rumiantsev telephoned Stanislavski to tell him that there would be a full run of *Rigoletto* the following day. Would he be present? He can hardly have expected the response: 'No I shall not be at the rehearsal but Vsevolod Emilievich Meierhold will see it in my place.' Stanislavski then gave strict instructions that his decision was only to be announced just before the rehearsal. It was greeted with stunned silence. Meierhold entered quickly and was shown to the chair specially reserved for Stanislavski. It was a symbolic enthronement. It did not, as could be expected, go down well with everybody. Meierhold was Meierhold. The leopard cannot change his spots. Stanislavski countered all objections with the curt reply, 'The theatre needs him'.

Grigori Kristi, to whom Stanislavski had now entrusted the task of ordering and collating his manuscripts, was quite clear that Meierhold was seen as the solution to the problem of the gap between rehearsals at Leontievski Lane and the theatre. Stanislavski took the view that none of his assistants was capable of translating his ideas into action. Meierhold was another matter. In 1926 Stanislavski had described him as the only director of flair and imagination in the whole of Russia. *Rigoletto* was not going well. It needed a firm hand. That hand was to be Meierhold's. What Stanislavski envisaged was a division of function: he would take care of the inner - content, Meierhold would find the outer form. In conversation with Rumiantsev during rehearsals Meierhold insisted that he was a realist, but a stripped-down realist, a realist of sharply-defined form. Having engaged him Stanislavski gave him absolute authority and made it plain that he was to be obeyed.

There were, however, personal as well as professional reasons why Stanislavski should turn to Meierhold. He had always relied on a close associate, a kind of artistic and spiritual son. No such person existed in his entourage after the death of Vakhtangov and the departure of Michael Chekhov for America. From the bright band that had set out in Pushkino to create a new theatre only one true theatrical genius had emerged, the critical, lucid, rebellious but infinitely affectionate Meierhold. Now, with Gorki dead and Chaliapin dead, there was no one with whom to plan the next phase in the development of Russian theatre.

Meierhold was no mere passive recipient of favours. Like Stanislavski he possessed energy. His determination to create new opera was undiminished by the lack of imagination and understanding displayed by the authorities. On May 25 Stanislavski came to the Onegin Room to see students' work on *The Merry Wives of Windsor*. He was not alone. Behind him were Meierhold and Shostakovich who had been friends for many years, once sharing a flat in Leningrad in the late Twenties. Shostakovich was just emerging from a period of disgrace. *Lady Macbeth of Mtsensk* which Nemirovich had produced with such outstanding success in 1934 had suddenly been banned after more than two hundred performances. In January 1936 Stalin had finally attended a performance and had taken violent exception to the work. On January 28 a scathing attack appeared in *Pravda* under the title 'Muddle Not Music' and the work was taken off. Shostakovich withdrew his Fourth Symphony, one of his most advanced works and set to work on the Fifth, 'An Artist's Response to Just Criticism', which, when performed in 1937, did something to restore him to favour. But he was still tainted with his reputation for 'Bourgeois Formalism'. Meierhold, disgraced himself, and with nothing to lose, felt it important to bring Shostakovich and Stanislavski together. A further meeting was arranged on June 12 when the two men found many points of agreement on the problems of staging opera, particularly crowd scenes. Meierhold also tried to arrange a meeting with Prokoviev but this did not come off.

Relations between Meierhold and Stanislavski had not been so close since the beginning of the century. In the last months of Stanislavski's life they met and discussed frequently, particularly Meierhold's plan to stage Mozart's *Don Giovanni*. Both were concerned with the problem of how to break the work down. How many scenes, or episodes, would there be? Fifteen to 18 Meierhold suggested. No, 20 to 25 Stanislavski responded. There was a creative excitement in their talk which Stanislavski had not experienced for many years. He was now fully convinced that all differences apart Meierhold was the only person who could take his place. One of his last instructions was, 'Look after Meierhold, he is my sole heir not only in our own theatre but in general'. Stalin's police did indeed look after Meierhold. Having allowed him to succeed Stanislavski and complete the staging of *Rigoletto*, they arrested him on June 20, 1939 as a German spy just as he was planning the production of *Don Giovanni* he had discussed a year before with Stanislavski. He was tortured and later shot at a prison near Moscow. Had Stanislavski lived the story might perhaps have been different. Time was however running out.

The summer was approaching. At the end of June Meierhold went on tour with the Opera Theatre but kept in constant touch by telephone. Nemirovich was abroad. On the evening of August 2 preparations were almost complete for the annual departure to the sanatorium in Barvikha. Everything was packed, including the precious manuscripts which Stanislavski took everywhere with him. He was still working on Part Two of *An Actor's Work*, dictating it in the hot summer days, but it was far from complete. In March 1937 Mrs Hapgood had spent some ten days working with him, trying to push the book forward but she did not leave with anything in publishable form.

Stanislavski seemed to be in good form. Lilina had written a quick postcard earlier that day, full of confidence, saying how cheerful he had been recently. When the moment came to leave, however, things went badly wrong. His doctor and his nurse have both left slightly different but not irreconcilable accounts of the events of that evening. Dr Shelagurov went into his room and found him, in his pyjamas, sitting in an armchair with his eyes closed. When he asked him how he felt his reply was slow and muted but he still expressed a desire to go. His pulse was arrhythmic and his temperature had gone up to 39.2. There could be no question of making the 30 kilometre journey to Barvikha. The stretcher men who were ready to take him downstairs and the two waiting cars were sent away. According to the nurse at the moment they were due to depart he had a sudden attack of nausea and collapsed onto the pillows. This would be consistent with a further heart attack. Later that evening further examination revealed:

'In the lungs at the back particularly on the left hand side moist crepitations could be heard. In the area of the heart the usual factors – dull sounds and a fluttering arrhythmia. No pain in the abdominal cavity.' (Dr Shelagurov in *O Stanislavskom*, p. 523, Moscow, 1948.)

It proved impossible to bring his temperature down. Camphor injections were prescribed to assist the functioning of the heart. Stanislavski's mind often drifted away but suddenly on the 7th he spoke of Nemirovich, quoting one of Lermontov's most famous poems:

'Who's looking after Nemirovich? You see now he's "a lonely white sail". Perhaps he's ill. Is he short of money?' (Dukhovska in *O Stanislavskom* pp. 550–51, Moscow, 1948.)

It was a touching impulse towards a man for whom, in spite of everything, he still felt some loyalty and affection. Lermontov's verses seemed to sum up their early quest together:

'White now the one lone sail is gleaming
There in the azure mist of the foam.
Of what in far-flung lands is it dreaming?
What has it lost in the land of home?'

But the end suggested their darker days:

'But it, like a rebel, begs for the storm,
As though in storms it might find peace.'

Nemirovich had made one last attempt at reconciliation at the beginning of 1936 when he once again wrote a long letter setting out their differences trying nonetheless to find points of contact. It was too late for them to work together again and Stanislavski's growing relationship with Meierhold made it finally impossible.

Nurse Dukhovska then asked if he would like to dictate something to his sister, Zinaïda. He looked at her and said, rather severely: 'Not something but a whole world of things. But I can't now, I get things muddled up so.' These were his last words. At 3.45 in the afternoon when Nurse Dukhovska came to take his temperature his whole body suddenly quivered, as if with fright. His face was convulsed, he turned deathly pale, his head dropped forward. He had already stopped breathing.

It had never occurred to Lilina during the preceding two months that he might die. His first books since *My Life in Art* were appearing. On June 15 his production plan for *The Seagull* had been published. At the end of July he had signed a rough proof copy of the Russian edition of *An Actor's Work on Himself: Part One* believing that what he held in his hands was the final copy. The book was not actually ready until the autumn. On September 2, Lilina wrote:

'At three in the afternoon they sent an advanced copy of his book; the labour of his life, three weeks after his death. Why is fate so cruel? Who knows, if he had seen this book in his lifetime what a boost it might have been, what a stimulus to go on living.' (K.S. Arch.)

Such optimism was not justified. After being pushed and driven for fifty years or more the body had finally given out.

CONCLUSION

Tributes flowed in from all over the world. The body was buried in the cemetery of the New Maiden Monastery where Russia's great are laid to rest. Nearby is Chekhov's grave with its symbolic cherry tree. That corner of the graveyard has since been reserved for the members of the original Moscow Art company.

Stanislavski left behind a mass of unrevised manuscripts. *An Actor's Work on Himself II* and *An Actor's Work on a Role* remained unfinished. Reconstructed versions of them did not appear until the fifties and sixties and even there serious differences between the Russian and English language editions subsist. Stanislavski has been used, rejigged and modified with varying degrees of intelligence and seriousness. That is perhaps healthier than any attempt to codify his thinking into a rigid set of rules. As one of his colleagues in late life, Maria Knebbel, remarked, the System is not a cookery book with a recipe for every problem. What is important is the spirit of honest enquiry, the asking of simple questions, why? what for? and the acknowledgement that with every play, every role, the process begins again.

SELECT BIBLIOGRAPHY

Works in Russian

STANISLAVSKI

Works, Documents by:

Sobranie Sochinenii, 8 vols, Moscow, 1951–64.
Rezhissiorskie Eksempliari K. S. Stanislavskovo, 4 vols (of 6), Moscow, 1980–1986.
Iz Zapisnikh Knizhek, 2 vols, Moscow, 1986.
'Chaika' v Postanovke, Leningrad/Moscow, 1938.
Rezhissiorskii Plan *Otello*, Moscow/Leningrad, 1945.
Stanislavski Repetiruiet (Ed., I. Vinogradskaia), Moscow, 1987.
Besedi K. S. Stanislavskovo v Studii Bolshovo Teatra v 1918–22gg.
Noted down by K. E. Antarova, Ed., L. Gurevich, Moscow, 1952.
Stanislavski, Reformator Opernovo Iskusstva, Materiali, Dokumenti, Moscow, 1983.
Iz Perepiski K. S. Stanislavskovo i V.I. Nemirovich-Danchenko, (1902–17gg), in Istoricheskii Arkhiv, No. 2, 1962.

Works on:

ABALINKA, N.
Sistema Stanislavskovo i Sovietski Teatr, Moscow, 1950.
(Ed.) Nasledie Stanislavskovo i Praktika Spovietskovo Teatra, Moscow 1953.
GORCHAKOV, N. G.
Rezhissiorskie Uroki K. S. Stanislavskovo, Moscow, 1951.
K. S. Stanislavski o Rabote s Aktiorom, Moscow, 1958.
KLIMOVA L. P.
K. S. Stanislavski v Russkoi i Sovietskoi Kritike, Moscow, 1986.
KRISTI, I.
Rabota Stanislavskovo v Opernom Teatre, Moscow, 1952.
NOVITSKAIA, L. P.
Uroki Vdokhnoveniia, Moscow, 1984.
POLIAKOVA, E.
Stanislavski-Aktior, Moscow, 1972.
Stanislavski, Moscow, 1977.
STANISLAVSKI, 1863–1963, Moscow, 1963.
STROEVA, M. N.
Rezhissiorskie Iskaniia Stanislavskovo, 2 vols, Moscow, 1973, 1977.
TOPORKOV, V.
Stanislavski na Repetitsii, Moscow, 1950.
VINOGRADSKAIA, I.
Zhizn i Tvorchestvo K. S. Stanislavskovo, Letopis, 4 vols, Moscow, 1971–76.

VOLKENSTEIN, V.
  Stanislavski, Moscow, 1922.

Individual Productions:
CHUSHKIN, N., Gamlet-Kachalov, Moscow 1966.
NEKRASOV, V., 'Bezumnii Den ili Zhenitba Figaro', Moscow, 1984.

Magazine Articles:
TEATR,
  January 1983, Misli o Teatre, Iz Zapisnikh Knizhek, 1898–1936.
  October 1983, Stanislavski Repetiruiet 'Molière'.
VOPROSI TEATRALNOVO ISKUSSTVA, 1978,
  Maria Knebbel, K Voprosu o Metode Deistvennovo Analiza.

NEMIROVICH-DANCHENKO

Works by:

  Iz Proshlovo, Moscow, 1936.
  Rezentsii, Ocherkii, Stati, Interviu, Zametki (1877–1942), Moscow, 1980.
  O Tvorchestve Aktiora, Moscow, 1984.

Works on:

PROKOVIEV, V. N.
  Dni i Godi VI. I. Nemirovicha-Danchenko, Moscow, 1962.
SOLOVIEVA, I.
  Nemirovich-Danchenko, Moscow, 1962.

MOSCOW ART THEATRE: LETTERS, ARTICLES, MEMOIRS

CHEKHOV Anton
  Pisma, 13 vols, Moscow, 1974–83.
  Perepiska, 2 vols, Moscow, 1984.
CHEKHOVA, Maria
  Pisma k Bratu, Moscow, 1954.
CHEKHOV, Mikhaïl
  Literaturnoe Naslednie, 2 vols, Moscow, 1986.
KNIPPER-CHEKHOVA, Olga
  Perepiska, 2 vols, Moscow, 1972.
FILIPPOV, Boris
  Aktiori bez Grima, Moscow, 1977.
GORKI, M.
  Perepiska, 2 vols, Moscow, 1986.
KACHALOV, V. I.
  Sbornik Statei, Vospominanii, Pisem, Moscow, 1954.
KEDROV, M.
  Stati, Rechi, Besedi, Perepiska, Moscow, 1978.
LEONIDOV, L. M.
  Vospominaniia, Stati, Besedi, Perepiska, Zapisnie Knizhki, Moscow, 1960.
LILINA, M. P.
  Maria Petrovna Lilina, Ocherk Zhizni i Tvorchestva, Moscow, 1960.

MARKOV, P. A.
  Dvenik Teatralnovo Kritika, 4 vols, Moscow, 1974–7.
  V. Khudozhestovonom Teatre, Moscow, 1976.
  Kniga Vospominanii, Moscow, 1983.
MOSKVIN, I. M.
Stati i materiali, Moscow, 1948.
MAIAKOVSKI, Vladimir
Sobranie Sochinenii, 12 vols, Vols IX and XI, Moscow, 1978.
MEIERHOLD, V. E.
  Stati, Pisma, Rechi, Besedi, 1891–1939, Moscow, 1968.
PIZHOVA, Olga
  Fragmenti Teatralnoi Sudobi, Moscow, 1986.
POPOV, A. D.
Tvorcheskoe Nasledie, Moscow, 1979.
PROFFER, E., (Ed.)
Neizdannie Bulgakov, Teksti i Materiali, Ardis, Ann Arbor, 1977.
SULERZHITSKI, L. A.
  Povesti i Rasskazi, Stati i Zametki o Teatre, Perepiska, Vospominaniia o L. A. Sulerzhit-
    skom, Moscow, 1970.
VAKHTANGOV, Ye.
  Materiali i Stati, Moscow, 1959.
  Evgeny Vakhtangov (Eds., Vendrovskaia, Kaptereva), Moscow, 1984.

INDIVIDUAL BIOGRAPHIES

BEREZKIN, V. I.
  V. V. Dmitriev, Leningrad, 1981.
DURILIN, S. H.
  Maria Nikolaevna Ermolova, Moscow, 1953.
GIANITSOVA, S.
  S. Pamiatiu Naedinie, Moscow, 1985.
KOONEN, A.
  Stranitsi Zhizni, Moscow, 1985.
LIVANOV, B.
  Stati, Pisma, Vospominaniia, Moscow, 1983.
NEKHOROSHEV, Yu., I.
  Dekorator Khudozhvenostovo Teatra Viktor Andreievich Simov, Moscow, 1984.
POLIAKOVA, E.
  Sadovskie, Moscow, 1986.
RUDNITSKI, K.
  Meierhold, Moscow, 1981.
SHCHEPKIN, M. S.
  Letopis Zhizni i Tvorchestvo (compiled T. S. Grits), Moscow, 1966.
  Mikhail Semeonovich Shchepkin, Zhizn i Tvorchestvo, 2 vols, Moscow, 1984.
SHCHEPKINA-KUPERNIK, T.
  Ermolova, Moscow, 1983.
SIMIRNOV-NESVITSKI, Yu.
  Vakhtangov, Moscow, 1987.
VULF, V.
  A. I. Stepanova – Aktrisa Khudozhestvenovo Teatra, Moscow, 1985.
ZOGRAF, N.
  Aleksandr Pavlovich Lenski, Moscow, 1955.
ZORKAIA, N.
  Aleksei Popov, Moscow, 1983.

THEATRE HISTORY

ALPERS, B.
Teatr Mochalova i Shchepkina, Moscow, 1979.
Iskaniia Novoi Stseni, Moscow, 1985.
EFROS, N.
MXAT 1898–1923, Moscow, 1924.
Ezhegodniki MXAT, 1943, 1944 (2 vols), 1945 (2 vols), 1946, 1947, 1948 (2 vols), 1949–50, 1951–52, 1953–58.
Istoriia Russkovo Dramaticheskovo Teatra, 6 vols (of 7), Moscow, 1977–82.
Istoria Sovietskovo Dramaticheskovo Teatra, Kniga 1, 1917–45, Moscow, 1984.
KHAICHENKO, G. A.
Stranitsi Istorii Sovietskovo Teatra, Moscow, 1983.
Malii Teatr, 2 vols, Moscow, 1978, 1983.
MOROV, A.
Tri Veki Russkoi Stseni, 2 vols, Moscow, 1978–84.
MIKHAILSKI, F. H. (Ed.)
Moskovskii Khudozhestvenii Teatr v Sovietskuiu Epokhu, Materiali i Dokumenti, Moscow, 1974.
SMELIANSKI, A.
Mikhail Bulgakov v Khudozhestvenom Teatre, Moscow, 1986.
Sovietskii Teatr 1926–32, Part One, Leningrad, 1982.
STROEVA, M. N.
Chekhov i Khudozhestvenii Teatr, Moscow, 1955.
ZOLOTNITSKII, D.
Akademicheskie Teatri na Putiakh Oktiabr, Leningrad, 1982.

DRAMATIC THEORY AND CRITICISM

BELINSKI, V.
Sobranie Sochinenii, 9 vols., Vols I and VIII, Moscow, 1976, 1982.
O Drame i Teatre, 2 vols, Moscow, 1983.
CHERNICHEVSKI, H. I.
Izbrannie Stati, Moscow, 1978.
DOBROLIUBOV, N. A.
Literaturnaia Kritika, Moscow, 1979.
FELDMAN, O. M., (Ed.)
GORE OT UMA na Russkoi i Sovietskoi Stsene, Moscow, 1987.
GOGOL, N.
Izbrannie Stati, Moscow, 1980.
GRIGORIEV, A. A.
Teatralnaia Kritika, Moscow, 1985.
LUNACHARSKI, A.
Sobranie Sochinenii, 8 vols, Moscow, 1966–69.
NINOVA, A. A. (Ed.)
Dostoievski i Teatr, Sbornik Statei, Moscow, 1983.
OSTROVSKI, Aleksandr
Sobranie Sochinenii, 12 vols, Vol X, Moscow, 1978.
O Literature i Teatre, Moscow, 1986.
PUSHKIN, Aleksandr
Sobranie Sochinenii, 8 vols, Vols VI, IX, Moscow, 1976, 1977.
TOLSTOI, L. N.
Literatura, Iskusstvo, Moscow, 1978.

WORKS IN OTHER LANGUAGES

AMIARD-CHEVREL, Claudine
Le Théâtre Artistique de Moscou (1898–1917), CNRS, 1979.
BLAIR, Frederika
ISADORA, Equation, 1986.
CRAIG, E. G.
On the Art of the Theatre, Heinemann, 1980.
Craig on Theatre, (Ed., J. Michael Walton), Methuen, 1983.
DIDEROT, Denis
Oeuvres Esthétiques, Garnier, 1968.
GARFIELD, David
A Player's Place, Macmillan Publishing Co., 1980.
HIRSCH, Foster
A Method to their Madness, W. W. Norton & Co., 1984.
HOUGHTON, Norris
Moscow Rehearsals, Harcourt, Brace & Co., 1936.
PAECH, Joachim
Das Theater der Russischen Revolution, Scriptor Verlag, 1974.
RICCOBONI, Louis
Réflexions Historiques sur les Différens Théâtres de l'Europe, (Facsimile Edition), Forni
    Editore, Bologna, 1969.
Observations sur la Comédie et sur le Génie de Molière (Facsimile Edition), Forni Editore,
    Bologna, 1978.
ROBERTS, J. W.
Richard Boleslavsky, His Life and Work, UMI Research Press, Ann Arbor, 1981.
SENELICK, Laurence
Gordon Craig's Moscow Hamlet, Greenwood Press, 1982.
Serf Actor, The Life and Art of Mikhail Shchepkin, Greenwood Press, 1984.
SANDER, Hans-Dietrich
Marxistische Ideologie und Allgemeine Kunsttheorie, Kylos-Verlag, Tübingen, 1975.
SAYLER, Oliver
The Russian Theatre under the Revolution, Little, Brown & Co., 1920.
Inside the Moscow Art Theatre, Brentano's, 1925.
STRASBERG, Lee
A Dream of Passion, Bloomsbury, London, 1988.

APPENDIX

PRODUCTIONS DIRECTED OR SUPERVISED AND ROLES PLAYED AT THE
SOCIETY OF ART AND LITERATURE, THE MOSCOW ART THEATRE, THE OPERA
STUDIOS & THE STANISLAVSKI OPERA THEATRE: 1888–1938.

Year & Date	Productions Directed or Supervised	Rôle
	THE SOCIETY OF ART AND LITERATURE	
1888		
December 8		Baron, *The Miserly Knight* (Pushkin)
December 11		Yakovlev, *Bitter Fate* (Pisemski)
1889		
January 15		Don Carlos, *The Stone Guest* (Pushkin)
January 19		Don Juan (ibid.)
February 6		Baron Oberheim, *A Cup of Tea*
February 9		Obnovlenski, *The Rouble* (Fedotov)
March 11	*Burning Letters* (Pisemski)	Krasnokutski
April 20		Baron von Aldringen, *A Debt of Honour* (Paul Heyse)
April 23		Ferdinand, *Kabale Und Liebe* (Schiller)
November 26		Imshin, *A Law Unto Themselves* (Ostrovski)
1890		
January 3		Piotr, *Don't Live as You Wish* (Ostrovski)
January 6	(For the Mamontov Circle)	Samuel, *King Saul* (Mamontov)
March 18		Laviraque, *Honour and Revenge* (Sollogub)
April 5		Paratov, *Girl Without a Dowry* (Ostrovski)
1891		
January 3		Taliski, *Why There was Strife* (Krilov)
February 8	*The Fruits of Enlightenment* (L. Tolstoi)	Svesdinstsev
November 14	*Foma* (Dostoievski/Stanislavski)	Rostanev

1892
January 23   Moréaque, *Anna de Quervilliere*
                                                             (Legouvé)
March 22   (With artists of the Mali)   Bogusharov, *The Lucky Man*
                                                             (Nemirovich–Danchenko)

1893
October 31   (Mali Artists and the Society)   Dulchin, *The Last Sacrifice*
                                                             (Ostrovski)
December 10   (With junior members of the Mali)   De Santos, *Uriel Acosta* (Gutskov)

1894
February 7   *The Governor* (Diachenko)   George Darci
April 20   Ashmetiov, *The Barbarian* (Ostrovski)
April 25   (Lyric Scenes)   Agesander, *Aphrodite* (Krotkov/
                                                             Mamontov)
December 15   *Light Without Heat* (Ostrovski &   Rabachev
                  Soloviov)

1895
January 9   *Uriel Acosta* (Gutskov)   Acosta
April 10   Smirnov, *The Bear* (Chekhov)
November 2   Police Officer, *Let's Keep it in the
                                                             Family* (Ostrovski)
December 6   *A Law Unto Themselves* (Pisemski)

1896
January 19   *Othello* (Shakespeare)   Othello
April 2   *The Assumption of Hannele*
                  (Hauptmann)
November 19   *The Polish Jew* (Erckmann–   Matthias
                  Chatrian)
December 19   *Girl Without a Dowry* (Ostrovski)

1897
February 6   *Much Ado about Nothing*   Benedick
                  (Shakespeare)
October 12   Morozov, *The Appointment*
November 17   Man with a Big Moustache, *A Burning
                                                             Heat* (Ostrovski)
December 17   *Twelfth Night* (Shakespeare)   Malvolio

1898
January 27   *The Sunken Bell* (Hauptmann)   Heinrich

THE MOSCOW ART THEATRE

October 14   *Tsar Fiodor Ioannovich* (A.
                  Tolstoi)
October 19   *The Sunken Bell* (Hauptmann)   Heinrich
October 21   *The Merchant of Venice*
                  (Shakespeare)
November 4   *A Law Unto Themselves*   Imshin
                  (Pisemski)
December 2   *La Locandiera* (Goldoni)   Ripafratta
December 17   *The Seagull* (Chekhov)   Trigorin

1899
February 19   *Hedda Gabler* (Ibsen)   Lövborg
September 29   *Death of Ivan the Terrible* (A.   Tsar Ivan
        Tolstoi)
October 3   *Twelfth Night* (Shakespeare)
October 5   *Drayman Henschel* (Hauptmann)
October 26   *Uncle Vania* (Chekhov)   Astrov
December 16   *Lonely People* (Hauptmann)

1900
September 24   *Snow Maiden* (Ostrovski)
October 24   *An Enemy of the People* (Ibsen)   Dr Stockman

1901
January 26   (100th Performance)   Psaltery Player, *Tsar Fiodor*
January 31   *Three Sisters* (Chekhov)   Vershinin
September 19   *The Wild Duck* (Ibsen)
October 27   *Michael Kramer* (Hauptmann)   Kramer
December 21   *In Dreams* (Nemirovich–   Kostromskoi
        Danchenko)

1902
March 26   *Small People* (Gorki)
November 5   *The Power of Darkness* (L. Tolstoi)   Mitrish
December 18   *The Lower Depths* (Gorki)   Satin

1903
February 24   Consul Bernick, *Pillars of Society*
        (Ibsen)
October 2   Brutus, *Julius Caesar* (Shakespeare)

1904
January 17   *The Cherry Orchard* (Chekhov)   Gaev
October 2   Maeterlinck Triple Bill
October 19   Shabelski, *Ivanov* (Chekhov)
December 21   Chekhov Triple Bill

1905
March 31   *Ghosts* (Ibsen)
October 24   *Children of the Sun* (Gorki)

1906
September 26   *Woe From Wit* (Griboiedov)   Famusov

1907
February 8   *The Drama of Life* (Hamsun)   Kareno
December 12   *The Life of Man* (Andreiev)

1908
September 30   *The Blue Bird* (Maeterlinck)
December 18   *The Inspector General* (Gogol)

1909
December 9   *A Month in the Country*   Rakitin
        (Turgenev)

1910
March 11   *Enough Stupidity in Every Wise*   Krutitski
        Man (Ostrovski)

1911
September 23   *The Living Corpse* (Tolstoi)
December 23   *Hamlet*

1912
March 5   *A Provincial Lady* (Turgenev)   Liubin

1913
March 23   *Le Malade Imaginaire* (Molière)   Argan

1914
February 3   *La Locandiera* (Goldoni)   Ripafratta

1915
March 26   *The Siege During the Plague* and   Salieri
                Mozart & Salieri (Pushkin)

1917
                                                      Rostanev, *The Village of
                                                        Stepanchikovo* (Adapted from
                                                        Dostoievski) – Rehearsal only
December 25   *Twelfth Night* (Shakespeare) (First
                Studio)

1920
April 4   *Cain* (Byron)

1921
June 9   *Rimski-Korsakov Evening*
July 14   *Pushkin Musical Evening*
August 2   *Werther* (Massenet)
October 2   *The Inspector General* (Gogol)

1922
June 15   *Evgeni Onegin* (Tchaikovski)
November 17   On tour in Zagreb   Shuiski, *Tsar Fiodor Ioannovich*
                                                        (A. Tolstoi)

1924
January 7   (On tour in USA)   Metropolitan. *Tsar Fiodor*

1925
April 5   *Il Matrimonio Segreto* (Cimarosa)

1926
January 23   *A Burning Heart* (Ostrovski)
May 18   *Nicholas I and the Decembrists* (A.
                Kugel)
June 15   *Les Marchands de Gloire*
                (Pagnol/Nivoix)
October 5   *The Days of the Turbins*
                (Bulgakov)
November 28   *The Tsar's Bride* (Rimski-
                Korsakov)

1927
April 12   *La Bohème* (Puccini)
April 28   *Le Mariage De Figaro*
                  (Beaumarchais)
October 29   *Les Soeurs Gérard* (Ennery &
                  Cormon)
November 8   *Armoured Train 14–69* (Ivanov)

1928
January 19   *May Night* (Rimski-Korsakov)
February 17   *Untilovsk* (Leonov)
March 5   *Boris Godunov* (Moussorgski)
April 20   *The Embezzlers* (Kataiev)

(ACTING CAREER ENDS
OCTOBER 1928)

1930
February 26   *Queen of Spades* (Tchaikovski) –
                  Production Plan
March 14   *Othello* (Shakespeare) –
                  Production Plan abandoned

1932
May 4   *The Golden Cockerel* (Rimski-
                  Korsakov)
November 28   *Dead Souls* (Gogol/Bulgakov)

1933
June 14   *Artists & Admirers* (Ostrovski)
October 26   *Il Barbiere Di Seviglia* (Rossini)

1935
April 4   *Carmen* (Bizet)

1936
February 11   *Molière* (Bulgakov)
May 22   *Don Pasquale* (Donizetti)

POSTHUMOUS PRESENTATIONS

1939
March 10   *Rigoletto* (Verdi) – completed
                  Meierhold
December 4   *Tartuffe* (Molière) – completed
                  Kedrov

INDEX